ENGRAVED ON STEEL

To our grandchildren

Amber, Giles, George, Barney and Harriet

Engraved on steel

The history of picture production using steel plates

Basil Hunnisett

ASHGATE

© Basil Hunnisett, 1998

All rights reserved. No part of this publication may be reproduced, stored in a retrieval system, or transmitted in any form or by any means, electronic, mechanical, photocopying, recording, or otherwise without the prior permission of the publisher.

The author has asserted his moral rights.

Published by
Ashgate Publishing Limited
Gower House
Croft Road
Aldershot
Hants GU11 3HR
England

Ashgate Publishing Company
Old Post Road
Brookfield
Vermont 05036–9704
USA

British Library Cataloguing-in-Publication data.

Hunnisett, Basil
　Engraved on steel: the history of picture production
　using steel plates
　1. Engraving – History
　I. Title
　765′.09

Library of Congress Cataloging-in-Publication data.

Hunnisett, Basil.
　Engraved on steel: the history of picture production using steel
　plates / Basil Hunnisett.
　Includes index.
　ISBN 0-85967-971-3 (cloth)
　　1. Engraving—19th century.　2. Engraving—20th century
　3. Engravers—Biography.　I. Title.
　NE485.H86　1997
　765′.09′034—dc20　　96-20433
　　　　　　　　　　　　　CIP

ISBN 0 85967 971 3

Printed on acid-free paper

Typeset in Baskerville by Raven Typesetters, Chester
and printed in Great Britain at the
University Press, Cambridge

Contents

Glossary	vii
Preface	viii
Acknowledgements	ix
List of illustrations	xi

PART ONE

1	The prehistory of steel engraving	3
2	The quest for the unforgeable document	30
3	Mezzotints on steel	63
4	British steel line engraving: books	110
5	British steel line engraving: prints, maps, book plates	144
6	Other intaglio prints on steel; paper, equipment	187

PART TWO

Introduction		233
7	German steel engraving	237
8	French steel engraving	265
9	Steel engraving in other European countries	305
10	American steel engraving	329

11 Twentieth-century steel engraving   344

List of sources   355
Index   367

Glossary

Acero grabado, Grabado en acero	Spanish
Gravure sur acier	French
Incisioni in acciaio	Italian
Stålgravyr	Swedish
Staalstich	German
Staalgravure	Dutch
Staalstik	Danish, Norwegian

Preface

The art of engraving has ancient origins and the aim of the present work is to explore the study of steel engraving further in the wider context of its beginnings and its use outside the British Isles.

Although engraving on steel had antecedents in Germany, France and America, it is generally accepted that when it surfaced in Britain, it was more fully exploited there, and most Continental writers on the subject generally ascribe the 19th-century development to Charles Heath and the many engravers then working in London. The new expertise spread quickly to Germany via Henry Winkles, to France taken by English engravers working in Paris, to the Netherlands about 1830 and, later on, to Switzerland and other places in Europe. The close links with America through Jacob Perkins were cemented by the arrival of British engravers during the first half of the century.

Publishers also had an important part to play here, where, for example, Fisher and Virtue had agents in France and Germany and, in due course, Virtue set up a branch office in America. The export of books with translated texts and titles to plates tended to stultify local publishing enterprise, and there was a thriving export of plates to illustrate texts produced locally, especially in France. British engravers were employed for specific projects in Germany, although, unlike America, there is little indication of engravers actually emigrating to work there permanently.

Slowly the part played by steel engraving in 19th-century culture is becoming more appreciated, and interest in its history and present-day uses is gradually growing.

Acknowledgements

This study could not have been undertaken without the co-operation of a number of people, whose help is gratefully acknowledged: Dr Ernst Andres of Bern whose profound knowledge of topographical prints has been invaluable; Dr Edith Fischer of Vienna whose help on Austrian affairs has been much appreciated; Ad Stijnman of Oudewater, Netherlands for his great help on Dutch and German steel engraving, stemming from his own interest in aquatint on steel; Dr W.S. Rogers of Toronto on his family history; Mr Adrian Stocks, London, for his most generous and invaluable access to family information; Dr Eugene C. Worman of Amherst, Massachusetts, for access to his work on Bartlett and Virtue; Colin Narberth and Son Ltd St Albans for their help in identifying banknote vignettes. Others whose help and encouragement is gratefully appreciated are Mr L. Worms of Ash Rare Books, Mr John Heath, CBE, of Bath, Mr John Buchanan-Brown of London, Mr Jeremy M. Potter of Brighton, John Kinnane, formerly editor of the *Antiquarian Book Monthly Review*, Professor Paola Pallottino of Bologna and Miss F.B. Pomeroy of London.

Inevitably, the resources of libraries and museums have been drawn upon, and many thanks are due to the patient and helpful staff who have made life much easier for the author. These include: Bibliothèque Nationale and Bibliothèque Forney, Paris; British Library and Department of Prints and Drawings, British Museum, London; Bavarian State Library, Munich; Swiss National Library, Bern; Art Library of the Swedish National Art Museums, Stockholm; Deutscher Bucherei, Leipzig; Yale Center for British Art, New Haven, Connecticut; Victoria and Albert Museum Library, London; Public Library, Brighton; Public Library, Worthing; Public Library, Birmingham; Faculty of Art and Design Library, Brighton University; the National Library of Spain, Madrid; the American Antiquarian Society, Worcester, Massachusetts; the Museum and Art

Gallery, Brighton; the Bodleian Library, Oxford; and the Tower of London Armoury.

Illustrations are mainly from the author's own collection. Mrs Rose Tisdal of Alhambra permitted the use of a plate from her rare copy of Beattie's *Switzerland*. The original for Plate 122 was supplied by the Chalcographie du Louvre, Paris and Plates 124–8 and 130–3 are reproduced by permission of the British Library (1401.h.30; 651b & c; MF607). Mr A. Peters also assisted with some photography.

The debt to the patience of my wife is incalculable, and is very much appreciated.

BH

List of illustrations

Sizes refer to page, mount or, in a few items, casings.

Colour plates (between pages 78 and 79)

C1 Engraved title page vignette of W. Beattie's *Switzerland*, engraved by R. Wallis and hand coloured

C2 Mosaics of Olivetree and flowers from J. Ruskin's *The Stones of Venice*, engraved by J.C. Armytage (289 × 200 mm)

C3 The Dryad's Waywardness, from J. Ruskin's *Modern painters*, engraved by R.P. Cuff (286 × 200 mm)

C4 Canaan . . . , engraved by W. and A.K. Johnston, from *Bible*, 1846

C5 Cryptonix coronatus, from W. Jardine's *The Natural history of game birds*, etched by W.H. Lizars and hand coloured (168 × 108 mm)

C6 Public promenade dress and Morning visiting dress from *The Ladies cabinet . . .* , vol. IX, 1843 (163 × 100 mm)

C7 Watercolour of Lumb Stocks at work, probably done by his son Arthur (150 × 126 mm)

C8 Watermeadow, etched by M.M. Ralph, printed from three separate steel plates (400 × 220 mm)

Black and white plates

1 Flemish 11th-century book cover (226 × 158 mm)   p.8

2 Guard of a 16th-century two-handed sword and engraved design and maker's name on a 17th-century basket-hilted sword   p.17

3 Milanese steel shield, mid-16th century   p.18

4 'Arraignment of St George' on the 'Engraved' suit of armour 1509 (278 × 224 mm)   p.19

5 Armour engraving in the style of Daniel Hopfer   p.21

xii LIST OF ILLUSTRATIONS

6   Engraving on a child's matchlock gun, late 16th century   p.23
7   A Flintlock Boxlock pistol, c.1810   p.25
8   Basket-hilted sword of the late 17th century   p.26
9   Jacob Perkins (222 × 140 mm)   p.33
10 Head of Minerva on steel saw blade engraved by C. Warren, May 1818 (89 × 63 mm)   p.38
11 German banknote dated 1st February 1923 (189 × 115 mm)   p.43
12 Stamps of Great Britain, Canada and the United States of America (reduced to 89 per cent of actual size)   p.46
13 Stamps illustrating the stamp engraving process from France, Switzerland, Denmark, Norway and Sweden (reduced to 64 per cent of actual size)   p.49
14 New Zealand stamps (reproduced in actual size)   p.52
15 Stamps from Holland and France (reproduced in actual size)   p.54
16 Stamps from Holland, Portugal, Belgium, Denmark, Switzerland, Spain (reproduced in actual size)   p.58
17 Revd W. Richardson, mezzotinted by W. Ward (425 × 352 mm)   p.65
18 Infant Samuel, mezzotinted by T.G. Lupton (162 × 119 mm)   p.67
19 Warkworth Castle on the River Coquet, mezzotinted by T.G. Lupton (148 × 210 mm)   p.69
20 Prince Arthur and Hubert, mezzotinted by T.G. Lupton (186 × 136 mm)   p.71
21 Christ in the garden, mezzotinted by W. Ward (186 × 203 mm)   p.72
22 Sadak in search of the Waters of Oblivion, line engraved by E.J. Roberts   p.73
23 The Deluge, mezzotinted by John Martin (150 × 217 mm)   p.75
24 The milk girl, mezzotinted by H.E. Dawe (159 × 126 mm)   p.77
25 The Fortune teller, mezzotinted by S.W. Reynolds   p.81
26 Four portraits of the Kildares and Cathcarts, mezzotinted by S.W. Reynolds   p.82
27 Charles Warren's bust after Behnes, mezzotinted by S.W. Reynolds (337 × 239 mm)   p.83
28 George Granville, mezzotinted by S.W. Reynolds, jun. (351 × 280 mm)   p.84
29 Felix Harbour, colour mezzotint by W. Say (101 × 155 mm)   p.85
30 Midsummer night's dream, mezzotinted by S. Cousins (103 × 164 mm)   p.89
31 New laid eggs, mezzotinted by S. Cousins (158 × 113 mm)   p.90
32 Inscription on a proof impression of a mezzotint plate (156 × 240 mm)   p.91
33 Noble and ignoble grotesque, from Ruskin's *The Stones of Venice* (288 × 105 mm)   p.97
34 The Revd John Harris, DD, mezzotinted by R.E. Sly (587 × 400 mm)   p.99
35 Truth and untruth of stones, from Ruskin's *Modern painters*, mezzotinted by C.A. Tomkins, printed in brown (288 × 185 mm)   p.101
36 St George of the seaweed, from Ruskin's *Modern painters*, mezzotinted by G. Allen (288 × 185 mm)   p.104

LIST OF ILLUSTRATIONS   xiii

37 William Sinclair, printed in photogravure (238 × 188 mm)   p.108

38 Cieling [sic] of the Star Chamber, engraved by J.T. Smith (282 × 203 mm)   p.111

39 From T. Campbell's *The pleasures of hope*, 1820, engraved by C. Heath (165 × 90 mm)   p.112

40 Lucy from *The Keepsake*, 1829, engraved by C. Heath (185 × 118 mm)   p.113

41 Zella from *The Keepsake*, 1830, engraved by C. Heath (185 × 118 mm)   p.114

42 From E. Cook's *The poetical works*, [1869], engraved by H. Adlard (198 × 135 mm)   p.115

43 The sailor's children, from *The Casquet of literature*, 1874, engraved by Robert Scott (219 × 146 mm)   p.117

44 Frontispiece and engraved title page of *Goldsmith's History of Greece*, 1821, engraved by Perkins, Fairman and Heath (175 × 97 mm)   pp.118–19

45 From T. Campbell's *Gertrude of Wyoming*, engraved by C. Heath (157 × 90 mm)   p.120

46 From T. Campbell's *The Loves of the angels*, engraved by E.J. Portbury (195 × 125 mm)   p.122

47 Two versions of the frontispiece and engraved title page of *The Literary Souvenir*, 1826 (133 × 80 mm)   pp.124–5

48 Ehrenbreitstein from Byron's *Childe Harold's pilgrimage*, engraved by W. Finden (220 × 140 mm)   p.126

49 Rameswur – Caves of Ellora from R. Elliot's *Views in India . . .*, engraved by W. Woolnoth (270 × 185 mm)   p.127

50 Constantinople from above Scutari . . . from J. Pardoe's *The Beauties of the Bosphorus*, engraved by R. Brandard (270 × 185 mm)   p.129

51 Cemetery and mosque of Ayoub from J. Pardoe's *The Beauties of the Bosphorus*, engraved by C. Richardson (270 × 185 mm)   p.130

52 Gen. Sir W.F. Williams from H. Tyrrell's *The History of the War with Russia*, engraved by D.J. Pound (277 × 183 mm)   p.132

53 Removal of wounded soldiers . . . from H. Tyrrell's *The History of the War with Russia*, engraved by G. Greatbach (277 × 183 mm)   p.133

54 Frontispiece and title page to *The Wars of the Jews* by Josephus (176 × 108 mm)   pp.134–5

55 Engraved title page to W. Jardine's *The Naturalists' Library*, engraved by W.H. Lizars and hand coloured (165 × 108 mm)   p.136

56 George Virtue (254 × 202 mm)   p.138

57 Edinburgh Castle from the Grassmarket (73 × 120 mm)   p.139

58 Method of sewing steel engraved books   p.139

59 Front board of Finden's *The ports, harbours* . . . (280 × 190 mm)   p.140

60 Front board of Tomlinson's *Cyclopaedia of useful arts* . . . (264 × 172 mm)   p.142

61 Front board of Tyrrell's *The History of the War with Russia* . . . (287 × 190 mm)   p.143

62 *Art Union* advertisement for Graves and Warmsley (275 × 202 mm)   p.148

63 The Shepherd's Bible, engraved by J.C. Webb (200 × 210 mm)   p.149
64 Cherry ripe, engraved by P. Lightfoot   p.153
65 Title page of J. Thomson's *Castle of Indolence*, drawn by W. Rimer (286 × 427 mm)   p.154
66 The last embrace, engraved by C. Rolls   p.155
67 The convalescent from Waterloo, (detail) engraved by G.T. Doo   p.156
68 Whittington, engraved by T.A. Prior   p.157
69 The meeting of Wellington and Blucher at Waterloo, engraved by L. Stocks (303 × 1332 mm)   p.162
70 Progressive proof of The meeting of Wellington and Blucher . . . (303 × 1332 mm)   p.162
71 Detail of The meeting of Wellington and Blucher at Waterloo (120 × 186 mm)   p.163
72 'Secret' message in The meeting of Wellington and Blucher . . . (126 × 186 mm)   p.164
73 Mrs Ellen Stocks (90 × 130 mm)   p.164
74 Duncan Gray, engraved by F. Engleheart (530 × 400 mm)   p.165
75 The Gypsy Queen, engraved by F. Holl (430 × 337 mm)   p.166
76 The Lady of the lake from *Six engravings . . . of the Lady of the Lake*, engraved by T. Brown   p.167
77 Cambridge University Almanack 1837, engraved by E. Challis (210 × 295 mm)   p.168
78 Map of The roads from Cork to Killarney, engraved by F.P. Becker (263 × 196 mm)   pp.174–5

79 Map of Turkey in Europe, vignettes engraved by J. Rogers, map engraved by J. Rapkin (detail)   pp.178–9
80 Sketch to illustrate the battle of Dunbar 1650, engraved by W. Hughes (276 × 182 mm)   p.181
81 Caledonian Railway (detail) . . . engraved by J. Bartholomew (189 × 295 mm)   p.183
82 Book plate for Harry A. Keyser (95 × 67 mm)   p.185
83 Book plate for Francis Scott (110 × 90 mm)   p.185
84 Book plate for Sir Henry Hope Edwardes (52 × 50 mm)   p.186
85 Book plate for Edward V. Bullen (85 × 64 mm)   p.186
86 Captain Cook, engraved by H.T. Ryall, finished proof   p.188
87 Captain Cook, engraved by H.T. Ryall, etched state (417 × 275 mm)   p.189
88 Mr Watkins Tottle and Miss Lillerton, etched by G. Cruikshank (186 × 117 mm)   p.191
89 Oliver's reception by Fagin and the boys, etched by G. Cruikshank (205 × 127 mm)   p.193
90 The name on the beam, etched by G. Cruikshank (195 × 135 mm)   p.194
91 The Escape No. 1, etched by G. Cruikshank (195 × 135 mm)   p.195
92 The breaking up at Dotheboy's Hall, etched by H.K. Browne (195 × 135 mm)   p.197
93 Title page of *Old St. Pauls*, by W.H. Ainsworth, etched by H.K. Browne (205 × 135 mm)   p.198

94 My first fall in life, etched by H.K. Browne (213 × 132 mm) p.199

95 I am married, etched by H.K. Browne (214 × 135 mm) p.200

96 Consecrated ground, etched by H.K. Browne (214 × 135 mm) p.201

97 The morning, etched by H.K. Browne (214 × 135 mm) p.202

98 The story of the princess, etched by H.K. Browne (214 × 135 mm) p.203

99 The ferry, etched by H.K. Browne (214 × 135 mm) p.204

100 Lion and lioness, etched by H.S. Beckwith (276 × 222 mm) p.205

101 El Toro, etched by W.B. Scott (276 × 222 mm) p.206

102 Ruffs and plover, etched by Elizabeth Scott (276 × 222 mm) p.207

103 Rodolph at the Porter's-lodge, etched by T. Onwhyn (172 × 103 mm) p.208

104 *The Castle of Indolence*, plate VIII, etched by H.W. Collard (286 × 427 mm) p.209

105 Page of *L'Allegro*, etched by M.B. Foster (247 × 171 mm) p.211

106 Frontispiece and title page to *The Virginians*, etched by W.M. Thackeray (197 × 125 mm) pp.212–13

107 The ruling passion, etched by W.M. Thackeray (197 × 125 mm) p.214

108 The three dogs, engraved by C. Mottram (212 × 252 mm) p.216

109 Music, page 32 of *The Drawing Room Table Book*, engraved by T.A. Dean (265 × 175 mm) p.219

110 Water stain on Rebekah and Eliezer, engraved by C.H. Jeens (313 × 240 mm) p.220

111 Foxing on Mosque of Omar, engraved by R. Dawson (233 × 320 mm) p.223

112 London Bridge from Surry [*sic*] side of River Thames, engraved by J.T. Wood (131 × 173 mm) p.225

113 Print of Liège, engraved by A. Cruse, steel plate from which it was printed, and a 19th-century burin (145 × 220 mm) pp.226–7

114 Autolycus (*The Winter's Tale*), engraved by L. Stocks (280 × 380 mm) p.229

115 Portion of view of Hudson City and the Catskill Mountains, with four language titles, engraved by R. Brandard (122 × 184 mm) p.234

116 Figures in military costume, etched by Daniel Hopfer (149 × 236 mm) p.238

117 London, engraved by P. Ahrens (107 × 156 mm) p.246

118 Kloster Maulbronn, engraved by L. Hoffmeister (96 × 150 mm) p.250

119 Hong Kong, engraved by A.H. Payne (108 × 165 mm) p.255

120 The Spinner, engraved by A.H. Payne (171 × 132 mm) p.257

121 Goetz von Berlichingen, engraved by X. Steifensand (245 × 163 mm) p.263

122 Vue de la Baie de Naples, etched and slightly engraved p.268

123 Frontispiece and engraved title page from *Le Keepsake français*, 1831 (187 × 117 mm per page) p.274

124 Title page of Gavard's *Galeries historiques de Versailles* (431 × 292 mm) p.278

125 Louis Philippe d'Orléans, etching (431 × 292 mm) p.279
126 Chateaux des Tuileries, engraved by J. Skelton (292 × 431 mm) p.281
127 Versailles vers 1688..., engraved by G. Chavanne (292 × 431 mm) p.282
128 Plafond du Salon de la Roi, engraved by J. Huguenet (431 × 292 mm) p.284
129 Vignette from Chateaubriand's *Poésies*, engraved by C.L.V. Mauduit (226 × 137 mm) p.286
130 *Chants et chansons populaires...*, etched title page by J.D. Nargeot (278 × 177 mm) p.288
131 From Combien j'ai douce souvenances, etched by C.F. Daubigny (278 × 177 mm) p.289
132 From Clémence Isaure, etched by Mlle E. Goujon (278 × 177 mm) p.291
133 From Clémence Isaure, etched by Mlle E. Goujon [2] (278 × 177 mm) p.292
134 Esther et Assuérus, engraved by A. Revel (280 × 167 mm) p.295
135 From *Blanche de Castile*, engraved by Mégard et Cie (227 × 135 mm) p.298
136 Le duc d'Orléans part du Palais-Royal, engraved by Laderer and J.F. Pourvoyeur (275 × 202 mm) p.301
137 Fraternal love, engraved by G. Bertinot (275 × 202 mm) p.302
138 The Kiss of Judas, engraved by B.J. Chevron (275 × 202 mm) p.303
139 Forrach im Murgthale, engraved by J. Axmann (151 × 97 mm) p.306
140 Heidelberg, engraved by F. Eissner (152 × 98 mm) p.307
141 Imogen in the cave, engraved by D.I. Desvachez (280 × 380 mm) p.309
142 Mr Hieronymous van Alphen, engraved by J.B. Tetar van Elven (130 × 90 mm) p.310
143 Portrait after Ary Scheffer, engraved by W.F. Wehmeyer (190 × 120 mm) p.312
144 Engraved title page of *Nederlandsche Muzen-Almank voor 1839*, engraved by H.W. Couwenberg (201 × 135 mm) p.313
145 Visser en visservrouw, engraved by J.H.M.H. Rennefeld (195 × 133 mm) p.315
146 Dutch children, engraved by D.J. Sluyter (219 × 146 mm) p.316
147 Murillo, engraved by L. Calametta (275 × 202 mm) p.318
148 Engraved title page of *Album St Moritz...*, engraved by C.U. Huber (235 × 352 mm) p.322
149 Samaden, engraved by C.U. Huber (235 × 352 mm) p.323
150 Wüdensweil, engraved by R. Ringger (235 × 350 mm) p.324
151 *Album vom Zürich-See*, engraved by R. Ringger (235 × 350 mm) p.325
152 Engraved title page of J. Frey's *La Suisse illustrée...* (310 × 220 mm) p.326
153 Souvenir von Zug, engraved by C. Rorich (230 × 320 mm) p.327
154 Last page of *Perkins & Fairman's Running Hand...* (155 × 245 mm) p.329

155 Third page of *Perkins & Fairman's Running Hand* ... (155 × 245 mm) p.330

156 John G. Whittier, engraved by A.C. Warren (227 × 128 mm) p.337

157 Engraved title page of *Poems by John G. Whittier*, engraved by J. Andrews and J. Duthie (227 × 128 mm) p.338

158 [The Bridal of Pennacook], engraved by A.C. Warren (227 × 128 mm) p.339

159 Part cover with wood engraved illustration for part 4 of Tomes's *The War with the South* (234 × 175 mm) p.340

160 United Grand Lodge Masonic certificate, engraved by the Brothers Warrington p.345

161 Table-mat, *c.*1970, reproducing The Walls of Southampton, engraved by J.C. Armytage (190 × 220 mm) p.346

162 Table-mat, *c.*1980, reproducing View of the Railway Terminus, Brighton, engraved by T. Jeavons (194 × 220 mm) p.347

163 Fine British print Calendar, 1988 (400 × 296 mm) p.348

164 Stubble plain, etched by M.M. Ralph p.349

165 Jasper, engraved by R.D. Swartley p.350

166 Elk, engraved by R.D. Swartley (157 × 200 mm) p.351

167 Exhibition at Ditchling Museum, 1991 p.353

Part One

1

The prehistory of steel engraving

The art of engraving on metal is of considerable antiquity, but because of the nature and use to which steel was put, its use as a surface upon which to engrave made it one of the later manifestations of the engraver's art. Steel's qualities resulted in its prime use as a tool, and as a cutting instrument, which could not have existed much before the 11th century BC, when the technology of steel was sufficiently advanced. The working of metal has a much longer history, however.

Copper was thought to be the first metal, discovered *circa* 5000 BC in Anatolia, western Turkey. By 4000 BC, gold was being used for jewellery in Sumeria, and *circa* 2000 BC, iron was found near the Turkish-Armenian border.

The working of iron appears to have been first accomplished by the Chalybes, an ancient people living on the south-eastern shore of the Black Sea. They were said by Strabo to inhabit the mountains above modern Trebizond (Trabzon), where traces of early iron workings have been found.

These inventions were of prime importance in the history of civilization, and man was able to move out of the Stone Ages into the Bronze and Iron Ages as working methods improved. The Chalybes, subjects of the Hittite kings, also discovered steel, and archaeological evidence indicates that by 1400 BC they had mastered the techniques of carburizing, quenching and tempering iron to make the harder metal. Between 1400 and 1200 BC they held the monopoly of its manufacture, but when this civilization collapsed due to the rise of the Urartians, Babylon and Nineveh, their workers were dispersed over the ancient world, taking their craft with them. By 1200 BC, iron production was known in southern Italy and Egypt, but in the latter country, the earlier objects were only carburized. Quenching was not known there until 900–700 BC, and tempering was only fully understood in Roman times.

The properties of iron vary with the carbon content. Wrought iron, with little or no carbon is soft and malleable, steel, with 0.15 to 1.5 per cent of carbon, has a wide variety of properties, and cast iron, with 1.5 to 5 per cent of carbon, is hard, brittle and has a low melting point. Steel can be tempered to many degrees of hardness, and had been formed by heating and hammering, changing the surface of wrought iron by the diffusion of carbon, a process called carburization or cementation. This discovery was made when charcoal furnaces were used to provide the higher temperatures required to work iron, as opposed to those for copper, etc. Charcoal is obtained by the slow burning of wood, until recent times a plentiful fuel, and also a rich form of carbon. Wrought iron placed upon the bed of such an effective furnace, combined with the carbon and became carburized steel.

The advantages of steel for tools and weapons was quickly realized, and by 800 BC the making of much harder and stronger objects through quenching was widespread. Quenching involved preserving the red-heat structure of the steel by sudden cooling, plunging the heated metal into cold water or similar liquid. In order to make a tougher, less brittle metal, the art of tempering was used, achieved by extended heating at a moderate temperature, followed by a long period of cooling.

From the 11th century BC there was a noticeable increase in the use of iron and steel for agricultural implements and weapons in Syria, due to the use of better furnaces and more experience in their working. The Urartu (inhabitants of Ararat) and the Assyrians were the first people known to use iron weapons. This enabled the Assyrian Empire in particular to expand rapidly, and those who possessed iron were able to conquer other groups, so that at this point iron and steel became man's principal utilitarian metal, displacing copper. The Romans, who probably made the most effective and extensive use of their properties were able to set up and hold a great Empire for a considerable period.

Engraving

Engraving was used by most of the great cultures, primarily as a means of decoration. The technique of engraving on metal was preceded by the method of chasing, where blunt tools comprising a tracer, shaped like a chisel, and a punch are employed to impress a design into the metal, merely displacing, not removing parts of it. A hammer is used to propel the tools. Although it is quite a different method from burin work, the results are not easy to distinguish, and in a number of cases, authorities have stated that the same piece of metal has been engraved or chased, for example, the Alfred jewel.

Engraving involved the use of the burin, a sharp steel cutting tool of lozenge section, which removes small slivers or strips of metal from the surface of the plate. The modern burin or graver has a wooden handle shaped to fit closely into the engraver's hand, and over which he or she has complete control. A sharper, cleaner edge is given to the lines, resulting in its characteristic crisp appearance which chasing lacks. The displaced metal can be recovered, melted down and re-used.

The earliest attempts at engraving came in Palaeolithic times, when patterns were cut by sharp pieces of flint on materials such as soft stone, bone or ivory. Because stone can be worked directly from its natural state, it was probably one of the earliest materials to be engraved. Flint tools were unsuitable for use on metal, except perhaps to scratch marks on the surface. Obsidian, a volcanic rock similar in appearance to bottle glass, could also have provided a sharp edge for working soft materials, although the full artistic excellence of engraving could never have been achieved by such rudimentary tools.

It is an open question, therefore, how the delicate engraving of individual hairs in fine lines on the gold helmet found at Ur was executed. The piece dates from *circa* 2700 BC, and belonged to Prince Meskalamdug of the First Dynasty of Ur. It is now housed in the Iraq Museum at Baghdad. The same consideration applies to a gold ornament, shaped like a vulture, found in Egypt and dated to Dynasty XII (*c.*1950 BC). The feathers are outlined with a graver, and the small nick at the end of each cut is clearly visible. Yet another example is the lunulae or crescent-shaped plates of gold, fashioned in Ireland, dating from *circa* 1800 BC, found at Shannon, and now in the National Museum of Ireland in Dublin. It is thought that they were some kind of necklace, but their actual use is uncertain. The decorative patterns have several repeated elements, executed in straight lines (including cross-hatching in the end compartments) except where the outer lines follow the curve of the crescent shape.

It seems very unlikely that iron or steel tools were available in prehistoric times, and although in theory, copper or bronze tools could have been hardened and tempered, modern experiments with bronze tools has shown that their edges splintered very quickly, and were useless for ordinary work on copper, gold or bronze. True engraving on metal had to wait until steel tools were available. It is possible that they could have been manufactured from *circa* 1400 BC, but because the need for them was not of paramount importance, it is not surprising that the earliest use of steel tools is probably for the inscriptions on bronze gates, made for the Assyrian king Shalmaneser III (859–825 BC). Some time later further evidence for their use appears on an Egyptian bronze figure of a goddess (*c.*750 BC), where recesses for inlays seem to have been made by steel tools, indicated by the extreme sharpness of the angles in some of the rectilinear patterns. In Cairo there exists a set of steel engraving tools which were left at El-Amarna by an Assyrian smith *circa* 600 BC, showing signs of wear. One of the first craftsmen known to us by name is Mentor, a Greek silver engraver and chaser, who worked sometime before 356 BC. Engraving reached great heights in classical times, and in Rome was expertly done, mainly by goldsmiths, who, as befitted their status, were free men, not slaves. Pytheas, for instance, in the 1st century BC, engraved cups with scenes of domestic life so delicately worked that in later times, casts could not be taken from them, nor in Pliny's day (1st century AD) were there artists competent to copy them.

The excellence of the artistry and craftsmanship of early Iron Age engraving of the same period is exemplified by the Bugthorpe (Yorkshire) scabbard plate of the early 1st century BC, and the Desborough (Northamptonshire) mirror, early 1st century AD. The engraving is executed in bronze, and features the sinuous line of the La Tène culture, in direct contrast to the straight-line engraving of the Irish lunulae. The Desborough mirror is regarded by some authorities as the finest example in Britain of Iron Age art.

Although many skills laid dormant during the Dark Ages after the disintegration of Roman civilization in the 5th century AD, that of the metalworker was able to survive. In Britain, examples such as the Tara brooch, made in Ireland in the early 8th century, employed designs akin to those in the *Book of Kells*, a celebrated 8th–9th century Celtic Irish Gospel book. This source of design inspiration was also used for the engraving (or chasing – authorities disagree) of the floral ornament on the flat gold back plate of the Alfred jewel (late 9th century). The jewel is thought to have been a terminal for an *aestel*, a pointer used by readers and copyists instead of a finger, following the text of a manuscript to avoid soiling the membrane. The engraving still shows some of the characteristics of the lunulae, but the craftsmanship is little better. Superior artistry and workmanship is shown on the Fuller brooch, engraved on silver, a piece of 9th-century Anglo-Saxon jewellery. In contrast, straight lines are virtually absent from this design, and the engraving is of outstanding quality.

Further evidence of the Irish Celtic manuscript influence is shown on the engravings which decorate the metal book-cover of a manuscript copy of the Gospels of SS Matthew and Mark, written at Liège between 1050 and 1075. The cover was designed for this book and was not a later addition, the evidence for this coming from the angel depicted at the lower border of the cover. The source of this design is clearly the painted miniature at the top of folio 6, verso. A close examination of the engraved area shows evidence of both chasing (with a slight swelling of metal at the edges of the lines) and engraving (with sharp edges and pointed ends to the lines). The metal is copper, characterized by typical green staining and the dark oxidized brown patina visible on the edges of the cover and on the clasps, where the metal has been exposed due to wear from under the gilding which covers most of the surface. Although the design shows up in black, there is no evidence of the application of niello (Plate 1). As late as the 12th century, contemporary manuscript influence is reflected in engraved plates, such as those on the Emperor Barbarossa's chandelier at Aix-la-Chapelle. When it was taken down for cleaning *circa* 1828, prints were made from some of the plates which decorated it, showing that if the technique of printing and a suitable material on which to print had been readily available, a thriving print trade would have been perfectly possible. In theory this always had been so from any engraved surface.

The development of European civilization into the Middle Ages brought about many changes in thought, ideas and ideals, many of which influenced whole areas of achievement, especially in the realms of architecture and art. Engraving played an important part in this activity, manifested chiefly in the production of monumental brasses.

Monumental brasses came into being because the earlier stone effigies and memorials were very expensive and easily damaged. They first appear at the beginning of the 13th century, possibly as a result of a brass worker being asked to provide a metal inlay for a stone tomb. He realized that the effigy and inscription could both be worked on a single sheet of brass (more accurately, latten, which was an alloy of 64 parts of copper, 29.5 parts of zinc, 3.5 parts of lead and 3 parts of tin). Cologne was the largest centre manufacturing plates, and exported to most parts of Europe. Brass was used at the time for the making of book covers, shrines and reliquaries, and in the second half of the 15th century, latten was also used to make the panel stamps for decorating bookbindings which originated in Holland. The artists producing the designs were inspired by murals, stained glass windows, manuscripts and sculptures, and there is thought to have been an international pool of designs from which all could draw.

Engravers of brasses were not an entirely separate craft, since some were thought to have been bell-founders, masons or goldsmiths. This may account for differing treatments of brass designs since bell-founders and masons were used to working on a larger scale than that of goldsmiths. These craftsmen, however, were probably united in a guild, possibly the little known Mystery of Latoners. They earned on average less than a shilling a day, it is thought. Only one engraver from the early period left his name on a 13th-century brass to Bishop Philip, formerly in the Church of the Jacobins at Evreux in Normandy, the inscription on which ran 'Guillaume de Plalli me fecit', according to a drawing which is the only surviving representation of it.

1 Flemish 11th-century book cover

Brasses were prepared by copying or tracing the design from a drawn original, using paint to outline it on the metal. A burin with a lozenge section engraved the first fine lines, and a triangular section scorper, together with a flat chisel, removed larger areas of unwanted metal. From the 13th century to *circa* 1410 a conventional and bold style of design used wide and deeply engraved lines on the brass. Between *circa* 1410 and 1450 shading was introduced, so the engraved lines were cut less deeply, and designs became finer and more intricate. Brasses averaged 3 feet in length, but the largest existing specimen is 12 ft 7 in. long and 6 ft 4 in. wide depicting two bishops from Schwerin, 14th century. H. Trivick in his *The Craft and Design of Monumental Brasses* (1969, page 32) writes that it is 'full of craft but empty of art'.

Thus engraving had reached an advanced state by the end of the 14th century when the first effects of the Renaissance were seen. A sense of exploration, back to antiquity and forwards into unknown parts of the world, an enhanced interest in learning in an atmosphere of intellectual independence, a desire to shake off the strictures of the Gothic Middle Ages, allied to increased wealth derived mainly from commerce, shaped this new era. Fresh influences were at work in the arts, and in order to accommodate and record these developments, an improved means of communication was a matter of some urgency. The need to replicate images and words on a scale hitherto undemanded made itself felt.

Goldsmiths held the key to much of the development which ensued. Gold, because of its attractive colour, uniformity, shine and malleability became a symbol of wealth and luxury early in the world's history, and the smiths who worked it were given a respect and rank above all others in the same field. They became influential members of society, many as bankers, and because of the high standards of workmanship demanded by patrons, a rigorous training was given to apprentices, producing very skilled workers, adept at many aspects. The artistic training in interpreting other people's designs, or the creation of their own, gave them a dual role of craftsman and artist. This gradually changed in Renaissance times as greater account was taken of artistic achievement on its own, and many who had trained as goldsmiths went on to become eminent artists. One such was Lorenzo Ghiberti (1378–1455), sculptor, painter and goldsmith, and by this time, the artist was expected to be an educated person, a man of taste, and fully able to enunciate and practice the principles of his art.

The goldsmith's art became more refined, his creations more elaborate and expensive, and the orders of patrons more exacting, so that the craft found it increasingly difficult to meet the demands made on it. A piece which survived this period is the Founder's Cup at Oriel College, Oxford, dated *circa* 1325–50. This was engraved by French secular goldsmiths, who used engraving extensively, employing a variety of motifs such as flowers, trees, leaves and coats of arms. Later in the 15th century, patrons' attitudes changed, becoming more mercenary, so that much artistic work was destroyed when objects were melted down to provide the metal needed for currency. The goldsmiths reacted strongly to what they saw as vandalism, and the artists among them turned to the use of intrinsically valueless materials such as canvas and paint as media, more likely to be preserved for their artistic worth alone. In Italy, another factor was a financial depression which prevented some young goldsmiths buying the raw materials for their work. By the late 14th century, engraving seems to have become a specialized occupation among the goldsmiths, resulting in a much higher standard of work. This excellence is reflected in the early prints taken on paper, possibly produced originally by goldsmiths wishing to take a copy of the designs they had created for specific works of art. This could be achieved in the manner of a brass rubbing, giving a positive image, but a more direct method would be to take an impression from the engraved lines filled with ink, where the design and any lettering would be reversed. A print industry had been a possibility from earliest times, but two major factors mitigated against it until the 15th century. The first was the lack of a suitable medium upon which to print, since most writing was done on animal membrane, and the second was the absence of a market for more than a small number of copies.

A viable alternative to membrane was paper, a cheaper and more suitable material which became the prime vehicle of the printed word when it arrived in the 15th century. Paper was known and used in Europe in the first decade of the 12th century, having been before that a jealously guarded monopoly of the Chinese and the Moors. At first it was imported from the East into Europe, where by the middle of the 12th century it was common enough to be used as wrapping paper, but *circa* 1150 the Moors set up a paper-mill at Jativa, in Valencia, Spain, which was soon doing a great trade, even exporting back to the East. Paper first appeared in Sicily in 1102, but by 1221 Frederick II, king of Naples and Sicily ordered that no public documents were to be written on paper, possibly due to fears about its poor quality when compared with membrane.

The first mill in Christendom was set up at Fabriano, Italy in 1276. The Church now accepted paper made by Christians, since they had previously regarded the works of the infidel Moors with great hostility, and it had to overcome prejudice due to its untried durability right up to the end of the 15th century. Further mills appeared at Bologna (1293), Genoa, Padua, etc., and by the 14th century Italy held a virtual monopoly in its manufacture. This was broken when France set up its own mill near Troyes in 1348, and Ulman Stromer imported Italian workmen to operate a mill at Nuremberg in 1390.

For some time the market for paper was small, and was not sufficiently common to be available for the proofing of engravings until early in the 15th century. The earliest dated engraving is 1446, but it is generally accepted that other known undated prints may precede this by at least ten years (i.e. 1436). In this year, Johann Gutenberg was well on the way to solving many of the problems associated with relief printing from movable types, if the evidence of Hans Dunne is to be believed, and the goldsmiths, with one eye on the profits made by the monks on their religious prints, must have had some idea of how to bring paper and engraved plates together some time before this. The earliest hint of this activity comes in a reference of 1398 to several 'stamps' being cut in a block of lead to make pictures for the Eglise des Chartreux at Dijon by the painter Jehan Malouel. A soft metal, engraved by the same means as that used for monumental brasses, combined with paper, perhaps from the mill at Troyes, could have provided some successful prints, although the definition of the image and number of copies produced would not have been great. Ink, derived from the oil paint used for house and decorative painting since antiquity was readily available, and if the print was to be taken from lines incised in the metal, it would have been a simple matter to substitute ink for the niello used by goldsmiths to fill those lines in their work.

The earliest line engravers to produce prints on paper are thought to have come from the Upper Rhine, the area around Basle, Colmar and Strasburg. By the mid-15th century, paper supplies were close to hand at Troyes, Metz and Epinal in France, and at Nuremberg in Germany, with a centre in Basle itself. The first engravers tended to copy existing works, using their skills to produce multiple copies of devotional subjects, similar to those done on wood, but as the influence of the Church on art declined, so more secular artists came along to supply designs. In Italy, where a near contemporary school of engraving emerged, probably in Florence, the printing of copies was poor until about 1470. This, coupled with an unfavourable view of engraving held by artists of the first rank, combined to reduce the art to a lower status than that accorded it in Germany, where for a long time, first rank artists continued to treat engraving as a prime art form.

It was Martin Schongauer (c.1445–91), more of an artist than a craftsman, who made print-making into an independent art, extending it from merely a means of reproducing existing designs. He lived most of his life at Colmar, not far from Strasburg, in which latter city he is thought to have learned the art of engraving from the Master, an engraver known only by his initials, E.S. His imagination, observation and sense of fun show through his works and he used the engraved line to capture action as well as delineate objects, such as in a spirited drawing. His work had a lasting influence in Germany and Italy until the coming of Durer. One of the very few engraved portraits of the 15th century is of Israhel van Meckenem and his wife Ida. Meckenem (d. 1503), who lived at Bocholt, was one of the first professional engravers, and is best remembered for his copies of Schongauer, Durer and Holbein, whose work he did not hesitate to correct and amend. A total of 570 prints is ascribed to him, and he contrasts with Schongauer in that he was more of a craftsman than an artist, due to his training as a goldsmith. As a result he excelled in the engraving of ornament, which played a great part in the dissemination of cheaply produced motifs, thus assisting in the international spread of Renaissance art. Books of ornament were common in the 16th century for many arts and crafts, forming a rich pool of design from which all workers could benefit. Meckenem introduced the practice of re-cutting his plates when they had been worn by the printing process.

The art of engraving was therefore well established by the end of the 15th century, but in order to replicate designs, an efficient form of printing was needed to make it artistically acceptable. The earliest attempts to print from an intaglio surface were primitive in the extreme. After inking and wiping the excess from the surface of the plate, dampened paper was placed upon it, followed by one or more sheets of paper to act as blankets, which surface was then rubbed over with a rounded tool or burnisher. In order to draw ink out of the incised lines, considerable pressure was required, which inevitably was exerted unevenly across the surface, especially if the printer was tired. Patchy and generally poor impressions often resulted. The early relief printing press, where a platen covered the whole of the printing surface in one pull, was also unsatisfactory, exerting insufficient pressure unevenly.

The solution came with the invention of the rolling press some time before 1500. It worked on the principle of a mangle, where two rollers, placed one above another, were set into a frame similar to that of the relief press, which had stout wooden 'cheeks' with a capping beam over the top. Since there was only a small portion of the roller in contact with the plate at any one time, the pressure exerted was greater, and the practice of damping the paper, inherited from the relief printers, improved contact with the plate, creating something of a vacuum which assisted the removal of ink from the incisions on the printing surface. A mangle, used for flattening cloth after washing could have originated in Italy, from whence it appeared in Paris in 1292 and in Augsburg in 1320. Another use for the mangle was as a calender to smooth and polish cloth and paper, a 'mystery' which reached England from France in the second half of the 15th century. The first existing representation of a rolling press appeared *circa* 1515 in the sketch-books of Leonardo da Vinci, but the object of this one was to stretch and roll copper strips. He also illustrated another press with a design engraved on the rollers which was then transferred to metal passed between them. Although Esban Hesse mentions the use of the former machine in connection with iron working in 1532, the first recorded use of it was in France in 1552, when cast plates or bars were reduced to the correct thickness for coining. The second machine was used in the mint at Hall, near Innsbruck in 1566. These metal-working presses were of much heavier construction than the presses used for printing, and the design of the latter changed very little until the 19th century. The replacement of wood by iron occurred then for spokes, necks and roller bearings. Such presses are still in use today by many intaglio printers.

The artistic use of steel

The development of iron and steel as man's primary useful metal tended to obscure its possibilities for decorative purposes. When polished, it could outshine silver and even gold, but it lacked the intrinsic value and rarity of precious metals. The shine was rather bright and hard, which lacked popular appeal, and rust proved a problem, although there is no evidence of serious deterioration in some polished steels which must be over 200 years old.

The infinite degrees of hardness with which steel could be invested gave it the edge over other metals from the end of the 14th century. The production of iron and steel had undergone some important changes in medieval times. From about 1135, water-mills were introduced, and as the demand for steel rose, the use of water-driven bellows increased the temperatures of the shaft furnaces in 14th-century use. As newer furnaces were built (at Namur, 1340, Liège, 1400 and Nassau, 1474), it was possible to make steel in them, rather than in the old hearth fires, provided a proper degree of carburization was available. Before this, steel production was a 'hit or miss' affair and the making of a bar of steel was a lengthy and costly business. Steel relies on a fairly precise carbon content, which fact was not fully understood until the 18th century, so it is not surprising that in the early days only the relevant portions of an iron object were converted into steel, e.g. cutting edges. This was effected by case carburization, where only the outside of the iron came into contact with carbon, and converted it into steel, the core remaining iron. The process was known in the ancient world, was imperfectly understood in the Middle Ages, but was familiar to Theophilus, writing *circa* AD 1100. When more efficient methods of production appeared in the 15th century, the technical problems were gradually surmounted, and due to the growth of trade, the need for a longer-lasting material to stand the strain of faster production (e.g. of coins) was necessary. England imported most of its steel from the Continent during the Middle Ages, using it mainly for the production of armour, weapons and the finer types of tools and instruments.

The decoration and artistic working of steel began with the preparation of tools, many of which were design achievements in themselves. Early iron tools were sufficiently hard to work softer metals such as gold, silver, copper and brass. As iron and steel themselves became the materials worked, the need for harder, tougher tools made good steel more necessary, combining its lasting qualities with the ability to take and retain a cutting edge, as well as the stamina to withstand repeated blows. The manner of use was also important, since graving tools were subjected only to hand pressure, whereas punches and chasing tools were driven by hammers. Graving tools are only cutting instruments, but punches can be used to impart a fairly complex design at one blow. Decorated punches are among the earliest artistic uses of steel, needing a great deal of expertise to engrave a faultless original, each duplicate of which was expected to be as unblemished as its producer. Any faults in the original would be repeated in the copies.

The earliest recorded use of decorated iron punches is in the arts of minting and bookbinding. In the 14th century the goldsmiths used them for decoration and hallmarking. During the 15th century they were used by printers and possibly gunsmiths, although this last trade may not have used punches extensively until the 17th or 18th centuries.

The manufacture of punches and dies for striking coins and medals was one of the earliest mass production processes. Coins were originally cast, but the finish imparted by striking made them more attractive and difficult to counterfeit. Before the 6th century BC, coins in Asia Minor and Greece were struck on one face only, using a lower die (anvil) for the design. Four punches were clamped together for the upper impression, which produced an effect similar to the four sails of a windmill. The die and punches were made of hardened bronze or iron, and were fashioned from freehand designs, using burins to cut intaglio high reliefs by the method of die-*cutting*. This was similar to the work of the gem engravers and has led to speculation that the two activities were related. Many of the Imperial Roman coin dies were cut in soft iron, and although some may have cracked in the hardening process, this risk was reduced by the mass of metal used. In the Middle Ages dies were made by a different process where steel punches were hammered into a block of metal; a single punch could produce many exactly similar dies until it was worn out. This method of die-*sinking* resulted in uniformity of impression and faster die production, both very necessary in a time of expanding commerce and trade. Dies so produced lasted longer because the metal compressed by the punch was harder, but, because the strike could produce small fractures, the risk of damage during the annealing process tended to be greater. Punch sizes ranged from those used for single letters to those used to produce larger 'hubbed' dies for a complete design. It is recorded that the mint at Bruges used 2,000 dies in an

18-month period, 1468–69. Very few old dies exist, having been melted down for re-use. The first dies to be cut in steel were probably produced by the Venetian engraver Vittore Gambello (*c*.1460–1537), who was granted a patent for light steel armour of high temper from 1509 for five years by the Senate of Venice. This connection between the armourers and engravers on steel is further demonstrated by the production of an obverse die in 1499 by Urs Graf, to which a new reverse was engraved about 1520. This engraver made the first dated etching on iron.

The second use of punch type tools occurred in bookbinding. The roll made of papyrus or membrane had been replaced by the book form by the end of the 5th century AD, when the first known binding was found on an Egyptian copy of the Acts of the Apostles. The earliest known binder's tool was made of iron, dates from the 8th century AD and was found at Swanley in Kent. There exists a series of such tools dating from the 12th to mid-16th century, all made of iron, and since most bindings were executed in monasteries, which also operated mints, it has been suggested that binding tools were made by the moneyers. It is not clear when brass superseded iron for these tools, but it may be associated with the appearance of lettering on the spines of books, which began early in the 16th century in Italy, when chains were removed from libraries and volumes were stored spine outwards. Such lettering was not common until *circa* 1660 and since the tools were small and finely engraved, subjected only to hand pressure in use, an easily cut metal such as brass would have been more suitable. Panel stamps, which decorated bindings from the 13th to the mid-16th century, were engraved in intaglio in iron, brass, latten, bronze or copper, and the lettering may owe something to the influence of the monumental brass engravers.

Goldsmiths had used simple punches for chasing and repoussé work since time immemorial, but decorated punches came in during the 14th century for the hallmarking of gold and silver, a quick and efficient means of authentication. They were also useful for the production of repeat decorative designs, such as those used *circa* 1388 to form a row of fleur-de-lis shields by Guillaume Arrode, goldsmith to Charles VI of France. Punched work supplanted engraving to some extent, and was another step towards the mass production of objects. It is assumed that the engraving of such punches was done by the goldsmiths on iron or steel.

When Johann Gutenberg was experimenting with printing from movable types in Mainz, it is not difficult to believe that, as a former goldsmith, he would have been familiar with the cutting of steel punches for making matrices, a process exactly similar to that operated by Arrode and others. Tradition attributes the use of steel punches for letter production to Peter Schoeffer, a contemporary of Gutenberg, but in the account books of the Ripoli Press, operating near Florence *circa* 1480, appears an entry for a quantity of steel which, although it was also used for making casting moulds, could have been provided for punches. Steel punches, as opposed to sand moulds, would appear to have been the best method of obtaining matrices for the smaller types used in the early Indulgences, and in order to produce the great quantity of type required by printers around 1480, it is almost certain that steel punches would have been used to provide the matrices required. Vanoccio Biringuiccio, in his *Pirotechnia* (Venice, 1540), takes it for granted that hardened steel was used for punches, and during the 16th century punch cutting and type founding became specialist trades, since it was uneconomic for printers to cut their own. Once enough matrices had been made, punches lost their immediate value, and there is evidence that printers tended to trade their matrices rather than punches. Joseph Moxon, in his *Mechanick Exercises* (1683), also took it for granted that punches were made of steel in the printing trade. He enumerated the various kinds of steel available, such as English, Flemish, Spanish, Swedish and Venetian, selecting the Forest of Dean, Gloucestershire as the source of the best English steel. The smaller punches were made from lengths of square steel rod, cut to about $1\frac{3}{4}$ in. long, but the larger ones of Great Primer upwards were forged as required, and the centre of the shank was made thicker to prevent it bowing when struck by a hammer. By the mid-18th century, it was estimated that an expert punch cutter could make an average of 1 to $1\frac{1}{2}$ punches a day.

Weapons of varying kinds were among the earliest iron or steel objects to be decorated, but it is the sword which most frequently claims the engraver's attention. Bronze swords were known by 1500 BC, and soft iron swords were used by the Gauls when they sacked Rome *circa* 390 BC. The Romans used steel extensively for offensive weapons, but as the Empire crumbled, Gothic immigrants brought a new kind of sword into Europe. Because of the expense and difficulty in making bars of solid steel, most swords manufactured up to the 15th century (and sometimes beyond) contained soft iron cores covered in patches converted to steel, usually near the surface. As technology improved, it became possible to case carburize the whole external skin, especially the cutting edges where sharpness and durability were essential. A flourishing sword industry operated in the Middle and Lower Rhine from the 6th century AD, and by the 15th century, Milan had obtained a good reputation in the field. Early swords had a crosspiece welded on, designed to protect the user's hands and separating the hilt from the blade. Used by Christians, the sword, when set upright on its point, became a cross, and before battle, or on other solemn occasions it was the custom to kiss the centre of the cross as one would a crucifix, and because of this, some swords have representations of saints engraved on the blade adjacent to the centre. The fuller, or centre part of the blade was often incised

THE PREHISTORY OF STEEL ENGRAVING   17

2a Guard of a 16th-century two-handed sword

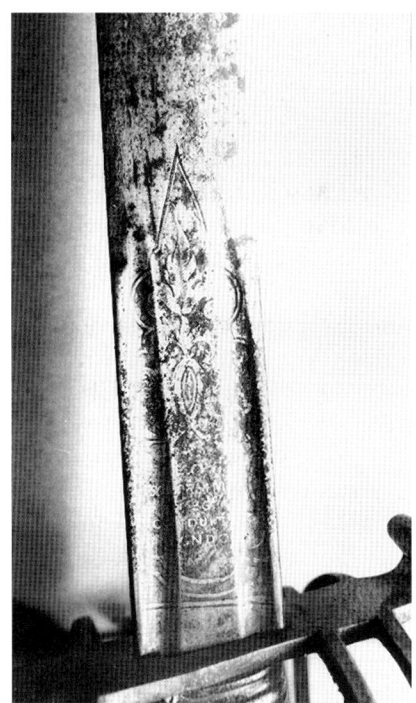

2b Engraved design and maker's name on a 17th-century basket-hilted sword

3 Milanese steel shield, mid-16th century

with pious mottoes, names and other decoration, such cuts being inlaid with pewter, tin, gold or silver. This decoration became more elaborate in the course of time, extending to the whole length and width of the blade (Plate 2). In these later examples the design is etched into the steel although the hilt decorations are engraved.

The work of the swordsmith is very often linked to that of the armourer. Early armour, made of iron, was very heavy to wear, so at the beginning of the 13th century the master armourers of southern Germany and northern Italy turned to steel, which, although it was harder to work than iron, was so much lighter in relation to the strength it gave. The suits of mail and other accoutrements, such as shields (Plate 3) produced in Milan followed a traditional pattern, while at Augsburg and Nuremberg, the Germans made plate

4 'Arraignment of St George' on the 'Engraved' suit of armour 1509

armour, first worn in the early 13th century, and which almost from the beginning was decorated. This was mainly achieved by shaping the plates, and it is not until the end of the 14th century that engraving appeared, when fingernail shapes were cut into gauntlets. A monumental brass was the source of this information, since no actual examples of armour can be dated earlier than *circa* 1430, and another brass at Laughton, Lincolnshire, dated 1400 shows a suit of armour apparently decorated by engraving. During the 15th and 16th centuries elaboration became increasingly common, culminating in the 'Engraved suit' of armour, made by Conrad Seusenhofer of Innsbruck, Court Armourer to Emperor Maximilian I for presentation to King Henry VIII in 1509. It comprised armour for both rider and horse. The engraving on the former is more flowing and curvaceous, having been executed on the Continent. By comparison, the work on the horse armour is more angular, and although intended to match, was probably done in England by German craftsmen. The motifs were taken from the acts of Saints Barbara and George (Plate 4). Later examples in the style of Daniel Hopfer are also illustrated (Plate 5).

Engraved work on armour, as opposed to the earlier relief ornament, was no detriment to its efficiency. Weapons would slide off the plates without catching, and plates would slide over each other without impediment, which may account for the popularity of engraving on field, tilting and parade armour. In a number of cases the engraved lines were filled with niello, a black shiny composition, used extensively by the goldsmiths, which further preserved the smooth, polished surface necessary for proper protection.

The hardness of steel made engraving with the burin alone very difficult, and although fine lines could be cut, deeper recesses needed further help. Etching was used as a practical method of effecting this, which was thought to have been known in antiquity, and well known to goldsmiths and metalworkers before the 15th century. Nitric and sulphuric acids were used as mordants in Europe by the 8th century AD, but weapons with etched decoration cannot be dated earlier than 1470.

In 1431, Jehan le Begue compiled a collection of recipes for artists, which appears to have been widely used. The first part was derived from another compilation by Jehan Alcherius, which included a method of etching iron, transcribed from a book lent by Fra Dionisio, of the Order of the Servants of St Mary, seen in Milan, March 1409. A solution of equal parts of vinegar (acetic acid) and water was the solvent for 1 oz. each of ammonium chloride, pure alum, sublimed silver and copper sulphate, which was boiled, and thus concentrated. The mixture would reinforce the mild etching action of the acetic acid with small amounts of hydrochloric and sulphuric acids, but the attack on the iron would be accelerated by the electrolytic action of the silver. A second recipe, used for corroding iron, removing spots on metals and cleansing wounds was made from Roman vitriol (copper sulphate), distilled with spurge (a plant containing acrid milky juice), which, when used to write on iron or any other metal, would bite the letters in very quickly.

THE PREHISTORY OF STEEL ENGRAVING 21

5 Armour engraving in the style of Daniel Hopfer

The etching procedure followed by the armourers included the use of nitric acid as a mordant, which is not mentioned in the earlier recipes. Their method employed a coating made of gum, resin and wax, which was carefully dabbed on to the lightly engraved metal, although it is difficult to see how this could have been accomplished without filling the incised lines. A second tracing with a point sufficient to pierce the ground was probably made to allow the mordant to bite, but the precise method is uncertain. Probably a low wall of wax was raised around the area to be etched, making a miniature bath into which the mordant was poured. The graver was only used to commence and finish the work.

Jehan le Begue's work also contained a number of recipes for quenches used in tempering iron and steel, as well as hints for preventing rust on them, referring especially to the care of arms and armour. By the early 15th century the etching of iron and steel was known in Milan, an important armour manufacturing centre, but their mordants were not as strong as those used at Nuremberg and Innsbruck, the main European centres of the craft.

The designers and engravers of armour were frequently engaged in its construction, and in this way, they came to regard iron and steel as the natural materials to be etched and engraved. Since copper was comparatively easy to cut with gravers, it was not necessary to etch it, and therefore some of the early German etchers used iron or steel plates from which paper prints were made. This idea was certainly about in 1460, when a book on the industrial arts by Paulus Paulirinus described a craftsman (*cirapagus*) as one 'who engraves skilfully on brass, iron or wood both pictures and text with the object of printing them on paper'.

The period from 1500 to 1536 produced a number of printing plates etched on iron. Evidence of surviving plates and the quality of impressions from them suggest that all the etched plates by the Hopfer family were on iron. Durer made six plates on the metal, Urs Graf etched the first dated plate on iron in 1513, and much of the work, especially landscapes by Hirschvogel and Lautensack are also thought to have been of the same kind. The link with the armourers is not very strong, but is sufficient to support the idea that etching derived from this craft.

Nuremberg, the site of the first paper-mill in Germany, opened in 1390, also hosted Anton Koberger's great publishing operation from 1470, and was the workplace of Durer, Hirschvogel and Lautensack. It was also one of the most important sites for armour manufacture and so the raw material for iron plates was readily to hand. Daniel Hopfer was only 50 miles away at Augsberg, while Altdorfer, influential master of landscape and the leader of the little Masters, lived only a few miles away at Regensberg. The etching process used by the artists followed closely that used by the armourers; even the composition of the etching ground was similar.

The use of iron as an etching material was a regional one, due almost entirely to the influence of the armourers, so it virtually disappeared as the arts of etching and engraving spread across the Continent to The Netherlands, France and England. Regional constraints of all kinds tended to disappear, and once more engraving on steel reverted to being an art in itself, instead of a means to another art. Engraving on armour and monumental brasses continued throughout the 16th and early 17th centuries, but both were in a gradual decline, so that after 1680 armour was no longer worn or manufactured, and by the early 18th century the vogue for brasses was over. Memorials inside a church were replaced by incised stones outdoors in churchyards and cemeteries.

Engraving on steel took a new lease of life in the decoration of guns. Although firearms were decorated from their earliest appearance *circa* 1325 in Germany, the urge to turn them into works of art began about 1560. The great gun manufacturing centres of Augsberg, Nuremberg and Munich were also the main producers of armour, so the attention of designers and engravers already employed there could be turned with little effort to the decoration of the steel locks at the heart of each weapon. Daniel Hopfer II was still busy engraving helmets for Maximilian II in 1566, and if the work on them is compared with the standard of decoration used on a wheel-lock pistol, *circa* 1565, it would seem that the problems of applying ornament to the awkward shape of guns was being mastered in a specialist approach. As an example, simple tendril designs appeared even on a child's gun of the same period (Plate 6).

Engraving on guns employed a slightly different set of techniques in that

6 Engraving on a child's matchlock gun, late 16th century

designs were etched, engraved or chiselled on the gun itself or on steel plates and mounts attached to it. Chiselling was a term applied to low relief carving on the cold steel, which usually was beautifully executed, but required a great deal of hard physical labour to achieve. On the same piece of decoration, therefore, some parts were chiselled, and the shallower lines engraved, while etching was used, as with armour, to start the process off. Etching by itself was a rare form of decoration, possibly due to the difficulty of confining acid to the decorated areas.

Decoration was applied after the working parts had been perfected on some types of gun, which were made entirely of one material, usually brass or steel, so some caution was necessary when applying the decoration since deep cutting or etching could weaken the weapon's structure. The first all steel pistol was made in Germany about 1575, and manufacture continued until the early 19th century, notably the series made at Doune in Scotland.

One way of avoiding structural damage during decoration was by the use of engraved plates or mounts, made of steel among other materials, which could be secured to the stock or barrel. The best of this work came from Brescia, already famous for its two 15th-century engravers, Giovanni Antonio and Giovanni Maria. It became the most important centre of Italian gun making between 1550 and 1575, and not, as might have been expected, the armour producing cities of Milan and Turin. From the end of the 16th to the 19th century, Brescian gun decorators were dominated by the Cominazzo family, whose especial form of decoration consisted of steel mounts with intricate foliage designs, pierced to show the underlying material as a contrast. They reached a peak during the 17th century, and their guns were exported all over Europe.

Engraving designs were disseminated by the general books of ornament then in vogue. At Nuremberg, those of Jost Amman and Virgil Solis were in use, and at Munich, those of the French engraver Etienne Delaune, published in Paris (1580) were employed by Daniel and Emanuel Sadler (or Sadeler). They were the most important German gun decorators of the time, using a great deal of chiselled ornament in the form of figures surrounded by sprays of foliage. They may have been connected with the European family of Sadelers, emanating from the Low Countries, whose main concern was the fine print trade.

Under Louis XIII's patronage and with Louis XIV's custom of presenting guns to visiting rulers, the designers and engravers of 17th-century France were kept busy producing new forms of firearm decoration. The gunsmiths produced their own pattern books to take account of the specific problems presented by the awkward shapes they were decorating, and of which Thomas Picquot's *Livres des diverses ornaments...* (1638) was one of the earliest, followed by Jean Berain's *Diverses pièces très utiles par les arquebuzieres...*

(1659). The most influential book was *Plusiers models* ... (*c*.1660), put together by a group of gunsmiths known as Thuraine et le Hollandois, since it illustrated a type of ornament (monsters recumbent in foliage, masks and grotesques) which required line engraving for its exploitation, and became the most prominent form of decoration in the late 17th century. The use of line was even more marked in the patterns of the engraver De Lacollombe, *circa* 1700, where martial designs were incorporated to match Louis XIV's war exploits. Continuous handling has smoothed away much of this period's decoration, so little remains in pristine condition.

Continental decoration was always flamboyant, and became even more so when sporting guns became popular in the 18th century, but the English engravers were far more restrained. An 18th-century sidelight on gun engraving is given by the work of William Caslon, best known as a punch cutter for printing types, and his master Edward Cookes for the Ordnance Office. Cookes was the official engraver of gun locks in London at different times, the first period running from 1707 to *circa* 1716. He was paid fourpence for engraving each lock, with a further fourpence for hardening them afterwards. From 1716 to 1719, Caslon was the official engraver at a reduced price of threepence a lock, and in a warrant of 18 January 1716/17, he was 'to engrave His Majesty's Cypher and Crown, wth the Broad Arrow and date of the year, on the 600 Repaired musqu^t Locks according to the contract'. Over the three years it is estimated that he engraved about 8,400 locks for a total of £105 – an average of £35 a year. This was not a princely sum, and in order to cut the price to gain the contract, Caslon may

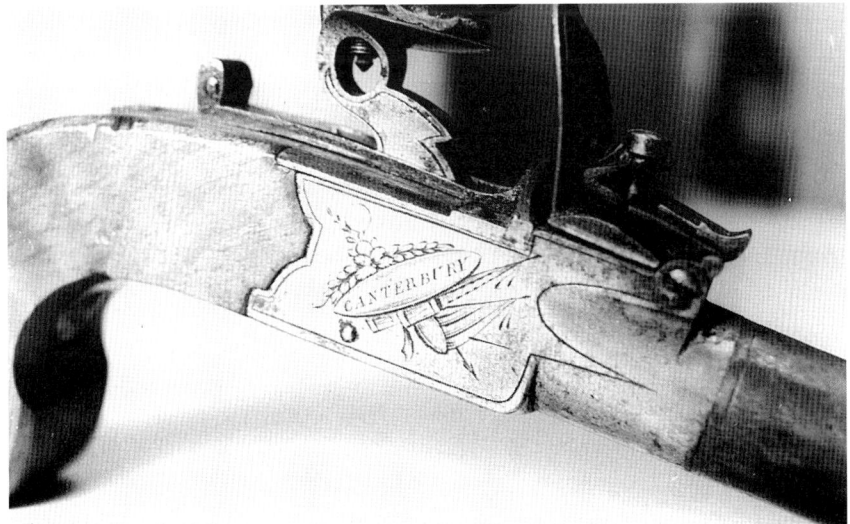

7   A Flintlock Boxlock pistol, c. 1810

8 Basket-hilted sword of the late 17th century

have used punches, similar to those employed by the inspectors of ordnance to mark tested guns. This would speed up the work, and an example from the Tower Armouries shows letters and figures more deeply indented than the Crown.

The peak of decoration was reached early in the 19th century with Nicholas-Noel Boutet, who produced his best work between 1800 and 1815, and although the technical achievement on contemporary English locks is high, the imaginative content falls far short of continental examples (Plate 7).

Steel reached its height as an artistic medium in the 18th century. Abraham Darby's improvements in the quality of iron produced by the coke-fired furnace from 1709 contributed to an extension of the range of steels available from 1710, which in turn enabled the production of a really hard steel for tools, so that ordinary steel could be worked more readily. Sword hilts became renowned for their hardness and resistance to rust, and although predominantly plain, were sometimes decorated with chiselling and piercing (Plate 8). Engraving was the basis of damascene work on hilts and blades where gold wire was hammered into fine engraved lines. Some sword cutlers who assembled the various parts of the sword were also gun makers, jewellers, goldsmiths and even hatters and haberdashers. The Bavarian family Sadeler produced sword hilts, purse mounts and buckles in addition to their gun work.

In 1735, John Barrow's *Dictionarium polygraphicum* (reprinted 1758) noted that 'Engraving on steel is chiefly employed in cutting seals, punches, matrices and dies proper for striking coins, medals and counters' (pp. 297–8).

J.B. Pictorius, in his *Den geheimen illumineerkunst*..., published in Leyden in 1747 gave a recipe (no. 133, pp. 206–7):

To make steel, iron, copper and other metals such that one can engrave and cut into it. Take equal parts of sal-ammoniac, common salt, and ground wine-stone, heat it up in a strong earthenware pot, lay the metal in the solution and let it cook for an hour; it will get soft, and then you can engrave upon it in any way you please. If you want to harden it again, heat the steel, take it out of the fire and put it into cold water; it will harden; the less you heat it, the less it will harden.

One popular and typically 18th-century use of steel was for an inexpensive form of jewellery and other household items, known as cut steel. It was mainly exploited in England, and one of the earliest references to 'Woodstock work' in the late 16th century is thought to have referred to cut steel, although glove making may be an alternative interpretation. Woodstock, 8 miles north-west of Oxford, was home to an important centre of cut steel work in the early 18th century, and its products were much admired at home and abroad, especially in France, where by 1740 *bijouterie d'acier* was well known. After 1759, when Louis XV encouraged the wealthy to donate their jewellery to a depleted national treasury, cut steel was an ideal substitute for diamonds and marcasite, but it has a character and beauty of its own which ensured its attractiveness well into the 19th century. Cut steel was also to be found in many other objects, such as furniture displaying pierced or engraved steel mounts, fire fenders and clothing accessories, e.g. buckles, chatelaines and scissors. Not much of this ware was engraved, but the expertise involved in its manufacture was of importance to early 19th-century steel engravers, notably Charles Warren.

After Woodstock, Birmingham was an important cut steel centre, having acquired a reputation for producing cheap steel from *circa* 1690, and in the second half of the 18th century, 50 per cent of its working population was estimated to have been engaged in the light steel trade, while at Wolverhampton there was an important buckle manufactory. Shoe buckles came into fashion about 1693, replacing shoe strings, and by 1737 entertainment tickets announced that 'Gentlemen cannot be admitted wearing shoe strings', so buckles were now obligatory items of wear. One 'toy' manufacturer (i.e. who made light steel articles) was Matthew Boulton senior, who moved from Lichfield to set up in Snow Hill, Birmingham about 1710. His son, Matthew (1728–1809), entered the firm about 1742, by which time it was specializing in the production of shoe buckles. Much of the output was exported, chiefly to France, from whence it was re-imported into England. The fact that the buckles came from France made them more attractive to the fashionable world! Matthew took over the firm on his father's death in 1759, and in 1762 had moved to new premises at Soho, Birmingham, where he set up a great manufactory to produce a wide range of goods in all sorts of metals, including buckles in silver and steel. The latter were decorated with studs made of decarbonated cast steel which were case hardened and then faceted by cutting against a pewter wheel, fed with fine emery and water. Polishing was effected by using finer emery and water applied with a hard brush, followed by ironstone and water, and finally with a special putty applied by hand. This was a long process and for the final polish there was 'no effectual substitute for the soft skin which is only to be found upon the delicate hands of women' (Gill, p. 279). These brilliant, rust resistant studs were then rivetted on to pierced base plates, usually made of brass, cut into appropriate shapes. The decoration of cut steel work depended largely on the shape and polish of individual pieces. Engraving was rarely used, but sometimes on a chatelaine, for example, there was simple engraved ornament, occasionally accompanied by the owner's device or initials.

Events in France leading up to the Revolution had virtually stopped the steel trade to the Continent by 1784, and had it not been for royal intervention, the steel trade at home might have collapsed completely. Boulton had made two fine steel chains for Queen Charlotte in 1767, and as trade declined she helped to revive it by wearing steel buckles, buttons and slides at Court. Buckle makers from Wolverhampton, Walsall and Birmingham later obtained an audience with the Prince of Wales at Carlton House in 1791, as a result of which, he, as arbiter of fashion, ordered the wearing of buckles at his court. This artificial revival did not last long, and consequently, some of the unemployed workers migrated to London, where it was said that if they could punch holes in brass plates, they could do a similar job on copper ones. Thus they became stipple engravers and found work with masters such as Bartolozzi, and publishers such as John Boydell on his monumental illustrations to Shakespeare. Cut steel work continued into the 19th and 20th century, when one of the leading exponents was Michael Blümelhuber (1865–1936), born at Unterhimmel near Steyr in Austria, in which latter town he established a workshop devoted to the art of 'Stahlschnittkunst'. He produced some exquisitely designed objects carved from steel, such as the twin knives in a sheath made for the List family in 1896, a Unika-plakette 'Evangelium' 1921, and an elaborate key with angels and the dove for Linz Cathedral in 1924. In 1926 he prepared a design for a head to a miner's stick, embellished with a carved face. A number of people came to Steyr to work on cut steel, chief among them Hans Gerstmayr whose pendant with a design of interlacing leaves was typical of other work by the group.

Further inventions and improvements changed and re-orientated the iron industry. The greater understanding *circa* 1750 of the part played by carbon in steel production by the Swede T.O. Bergmann and in Birmingham Joseph Priestley's experiment on nails, such as those used by carpenters, in 1786 led to a better understanding of the nature of steel, and with a greater ability to control its manufacture, a further extension of the range of steels was available for a variety of needs. Much of the English industry's output up to 1815 was devoted to materials for the Napoleonic wars, but a depression set in until a resurgence in output *circa* 1830. Steel for engraving plates, therefore, was readily obtainable at a time when copper was in comparatively short supply. In the 18th century, copper production processes took anything up to 18 months to complete, which did not improve until the mid-19th century. The manufacturers thus could not respond quickly to extra demands made upon them, so that when large orders for copper were placed in the second half of the 18th century, it became scarce and expensive. Large quantities of copper were already used by the brass makers, and from about 1742, Bolsover, Hancock and Boulton used a great deal in the manufacture of Sheffield plate. But the greatest demand came from the Royal and merchant navies. Copper was used to sheathe the keels of war and trade ships to prevent the growth of marine organisms from 1761, and it was common practice by 1780.

A.G. Thomas, quoting W.H. Pyne, who, writing under his pseudonym 'Ephraim Hardcastle' in *Wine and Walnuts; or, After Dinner Chit-Chat*, (Longman, 1823–24, 2 vols), wrote of Thomas Rowlandson that he 'etched as much copper as would sheathe the British Navy'. Corrosion necessitated frequent replacement, so for many years the price of copper rose and was in short supply. This had its effect on the engravers, some of whom tried all sorts of alternatives before settling on steel.

The quest for the unforgeable document

Documents which represent sums of money are all subject to forgery, since they are one of the forms most vulnerable to misuse. Banknotes, stamps, bonds and certificates all come into this category, especially when the individual signing of such documents was largely abandoned in the mid-19th century. Certificates and cheques are two of the exceptions, even if, with the advent of modern cash registers, the whole of the cheque is not filled out by hand.

Ever since the emergence of paper currency in Europe in 1661, banks received the attentions of forgers, who, if undetected, could become wealthy on the proceeds. The problem is still with us. Early notes were of simple design printed either letterpress or, more commonly, intaglio, the latter being relatively more difficult to imitate. The heavy penalties imposed by law, including death, did not deter forgers, and so the banks had a constant struggle to keep ahead by elaborating their designs, and, until the middle of the 19th century, validating each note with a personal handwritten signature and date. Eventually the printed image alone was insufficient deterrent, so watermarks, threads and security strips were introduced into the paper-making process.

The quest for the unforgeable note was intensified in the last decade of the 18th century, when most of the technology was available and only required technical expertise to bring it together. The main source of expertise was supplied by the engravers employed by the various mints, producing coins and medals, usually for a government. The engraving of steel punches and dies and their hardening to withstand the constant striking of metal blanks was a skill perfected during the technical advances made since the 15th century. The acquisition of skills took a long time, and since work was always available, the mint engravers tended to be an exclusive body. Individuals were little known outside their profession, but it was one branch of steel engraving which continued unbroken to this day, and was joined in the 19th century by the small group of banknote engravers, of whom today it is estimated that there are less than 20 of the first rank in Europe. There are, of course, an additional number in America where much banknote engraving is carried on.

The use of steel in the printing of paper currency dates from 1792, and seems to have come simultaneously from France and the USA. As the demand for notes increased through the expansion of trade and commerce so more care was necessary to ensure that each note was an exact printed copy of another. The main requirement was for a master from which any number of printing plates could be made without resorting to engraving duplicate plates each time, which, even if done by the same engraver, were bound to exhibit minor differences. In theory it mattered very little how many copies a copper plate could produce because as soon as it was worn out, it could be replaced by a similar one taken from the original master.

This was behind the attempt made by the Parisian mint engravers to produce a master for the printing of 'assignats' for revolutionary France. This currency, based on that used by the financier John Law for his bank in the early 18th century, was backed by the hypothetical value of land owned by the Government, notably that confiscated from the Church and aristocracy. The earlier notes were printed in relief, with, for the 50 sols note, two portraits of the king and other decoration engraved on a single steel punch. Line engraving was used from December 1791, and a new process was authorized by a decree of 21 November 1792. A 400-livre note employed an engraving of an eagle carrying a serpent in its beak, a symbol of immortality, as its main feature. It was designed by Nicolas-Marie Gatteaux (1751–1832) and engraved on steel by [Pierre] Alexandre Tardieu (1756–1844), renowned for portrait engraving, who was later recognized by the award of the Légion d'honneur in 1822 and admission to the Institut de France. This engraving was case hardened and there are two proofs in the Cabinet d'Estampes, Bibliothèque Nationale, one of which is marked 'Après le Trempe' (after tempering [or hardening]). It was then to be a master for 'le laminage' a process operated by Louise-Étienne Herhan, who borrowed the idea from his brother-in-law, Gengembre. It worked by covering the intaglio steel matrix with a copper plate, which together were passed through a rolling press, transferring the design in relief, thus making a patrix. The process was repeated with the second plate and a softer copper plate thus producing another intaglio plate to be used for the actual printing. Inimitability was not achieved, however, since both copper plates tended to stretch variably, and so the printed results would differ in size and not be precisely similar. As a result, the notes were counterfeited on a grand scale. Because of the imperfect results and his poor workmanship, Herhan had an argument with his former master, Jean-Pierre Droz (1746–1823). Droz, an excellent workman, was, according to accounts of his stay in Birmingham (1788–90) with Matthew Boulton, a vain boaster, and left Boulton in difficulties which ended in litigation. On his return to France, Droz engraved for the assignats and for the 25 livres he successfully multiplied by laminage in June 1792, two medallions engraved on steel by Antoine Nicollet and J.G. Fiesinger. The design of the left-hand medallion was a figure representing the genius of the Constitution, and on the right hand was a portrait of the king. Le laminage was also used for the 50-livre note under the decree dated 14 December 1792. The design by Gatteaux was engraved by Tardieu, and represented the figure of France seated, holding a trident and three symbolic crowns, beside her a cock and map of the world in two hemispheres, with the legend 'Liberté, Égalité' below.

In 1793, the revolutionaries decided to destroy all vestiges of royalty in the currency, and five sessions took place in November and December 1793 with a sixth and last in December 1794, each followed by a bonfire. The final act came on 19 February 1796 when some remaining material, including the original steel matrices for the 400- and 50-livre assignats were broken and burnt on the Place de Vendôme, within a short distance of the former Capucin monastery where they had been created. This was a curious situation where Gatteaux, who had designed and engraved much of the work, assisted in its deliberate destruction.

Massachusetts was the first American state to issue paper currency in 1690, and it was here that Jacob Perkins (1766–1849) (Plate 9) turned his attention to the urgent problem of fraudulent notes. In 1786 he had engraved steel dies for striking the copper state coinage, so it was but a short step to producing dies carrying an individual design which could be combined with others to produce a larger one. Sixty-four separate dies cut in hard steel were clamped together to form a 'check-plate' in 1792, which became the master for producing an intaglio plate in copper, soft iron or soft steel using a screw press which applied direct vertical pressure, thus largely eliminating the stretch problems encountered in the French process. The amount of pressure required was excessive and a good impression difficult to obtain, so that it was only *circa* 1804 when Perkins has mastered the appropriate techniques of annealing and case hardening steel that he was able to take the next step of producing a roller die. This obtained a better impression by applying pressure on a comparatively small part of the plate at a time, so that the application of the steel cylinder die, engraved with a suitable design or part thereof could produce a better result with the same or less pressure than before. For this, the hard steel dies combined in a suitable manner had a soft steel cylinder rolled across them to take the impression in relief, which was then case hardened and rolled

Engraved by permission, for the Mechanics Magazine, from an Original Painting by Harding.

9   Jacob Perkins

over a soft steel plate, which, when hardened, became the printing plate. Case hardening at this date was an uncertain process and there was a fair proportion of spoilt plates. The loss of expensive engraving was unacceptable, so thick blocks of steel were used to help overcome the problems of warping, cracking, etc. The normal rolling press had to be adapted to print these blocks. Perkins explained his method in an eight-page pamphlet entitled *The Permanent Stereotype Steel Plate, with Observations on its Importance, and an Explanation of its Construction and Uses, C. Stebbing, Printer, 1806*. In it, Perkins noted that 26 banks had been using the system for three years with no case of counterfeiting, and in his terms for supplying dies, he indicated that there would be no charge for his services if his notes were forged. After 1 July 1809 all Massachusetts banks were legally obliged to adopt Perkins's steel plates, as did many other banks across the United States of America. Meanwhile, *circa* 1803, Perkins had met Gideon Fairman (1774–1827) when the latter arrived in Newburyport to help William Hooker engrave a series of maps and charts. Fairman was born at Newtown, Connecticut, and was sent to Albany in 1792 to Isaac and George Hutton, who were jewellers and engravers. During his four years' apprenticeship he patented (with Isaac) an 'improvement in the art of engraving' no details of which survive, but it indicates an inventive turn of mind which probably appealed to Perkins. In 1810 Fairman moved to Philadelphia at Perkins's suggestion, and soon afterwards he joined the established firm of George Murray and John Draper as a partner. They bought Abel Brewster's banknote printing plant in 1811, which became the most lucrative part of their business. Murray and Perkins registered two joint patents in June 1813, one of which was for a rolling press with a portion cut away on the upper roller (the so-called D roller) which enabled the plate to be returned quickly for re-inking. The partnership was dissolved in July 1818, and the participants went their separate ways.

A number of alliances were formed and re-formed among this early group of engravers until the middle of the 19th century, all doubtless seeing a lucrative market to be tapped, and it would seem that most of the American line engravers of the period worked for banks at one time or another. In addition to Perkins, several engravers were credited with inventions and improvements to the engraving process. James Bogardus (1800–74) was, like Perkins, a man of many parts. Apprenticed to a watchmaker, he specialized in engraving and die-sinking, patenting a machine for engraving watch dials. William Rollinson (1762–1842) emigrated from Dudley, Worcestershire in 1789 and after working in New York, went on to banknote engraving, and is credited with several improvements in the technique of banknote manufacture. James David Smillie (1833–1909) showed a different kind of ingenuity when he attached to his ruling machine the mechanism of an old town clock, so that it covered appropriate areas of the plate while he slept! Cyrus Durand (1787–1868) invented several machines for ruling geometric patterns to execute banknote designs by his younger brother, A.B. Durand. An eminent practitioner, James Smillie (1807–85) was born in Edinburgh, learned his skills in that city, and arrived in New York *circa* 1829. His first commissions were for banknote engraving, and although he is best known as a landscape engraver, he became a partner in a banknote printing firm, Rawdon, Wright, Hatch and Smillie. After 1861 he returned to banknote engraving to offset the reduction in demand for his other work, probably due to a change in public taste. James's younger brother William Cumming Smillie (b.1813) worked on security engraving for the Canadian government. Freeman Rawdon (b.1804) worked in New York from 1828, mainly with his brother Ralph, and appeared to be the senior partner of the firm. Charles Cushing Wright (1796–1857) was a self-taught engraver of coins and medals, notably those carrying a likeness of George Washington, while George W. Hatch (*c.*1805–67), a pupil of A.B. Durand, completed the list of partners.

One of the earliest banknote engraving partnerships ran for five years between 1817 and 1822 in Philadelphia. The eldest partner Benjamin Tanner (1775–1848) worked as an engraver from 1799 and was the brother of Henry Tanner, the cartographer. The second was Cornelius Tiebout (1775–*c.*1832), apprenticed to a goldsmith and trained in London for three years, he worked in Philadelphia from 1799 until *circa* 1825, and the youngest was Francis Kearny (1785–1837) a line and aquatint engraver who was brother to an eminent naval officer and nephew to another.

Asher Brown Durand (1796–1886), apprenticed in 1812 at the age of 16 to the engraver Peter Maverick (1780–1831) was for about 15 years, ending in 1836, one of the outstanding engravers of his day. He was trained in portraiture by Samuel Lovett Waldo (1783–1861) which resulted not only in some excellent portraits, but in some banknote designs which established a tradition still observable in American banknotes. He turned professional painter in 1836, but may have retained connections with the firm run by his elder brother Cyrus, known variously as Durand and Co., Durand, Perkins and Co., and Casilear, Durand, Burton and Edmunds. John William Casilear (1811–93) was also a pupil of Peter Maverick and worked on banknotes until about 1854, when he took up landscape painting.

Among later Philadelphia firms was Spencer, Huffy and Danforth established in 1844. Asa Spencer (d.1847), the inventor of the rose engine lathe for engraving intricate ornamental designs, had accompanied Perkins to London in 1819, returning home *circa* 1822. The firm only lasted three years until Spencer's death, when Moseley Isaac Danforth (1800–62) moved to New York to set up Danforth, Underwood and Co. He had worked in London for the Annuals between 1827 and 1837, gaining a good reputation there.

Another New York banknote engraver Waterman Lilly Ormsby (1809–83) wrote a *Description of the Present System of Bank Note Engraving . . . ; added, a New Method to Prevent Forgery* (New York, 1852), showing that despite all efforts to frustrate counterfeiters, there was still a need to seek new methods of fighting the crime.

By mid-century, American engravers had found markets overseas and had enlisted the aid of some eminent artists to design for them. Felix Octavius Carr Darley (1822–88) was primarily a book illustrator from 1843, but later did a number of banknote designs for the Japanese government.

William Shirlaw (1838–1909) was born in Paisley, Scotland, and emigrated to the USA when a child. *Circa* 1858 his first job was as a banknote engraver, and his bolder approach to design put him in a class with Alfred Jones (1819–1900) whose vignettes showed a great deal of originality in their boldness, delicacy and incisiveness. Shirlaw had turned to painting by 1870, including 'The Sciences' on the ceiling of the Library of Congress, Washington, and eventually became the first President of the Society of American Artists.

The first of May 1858 saw the amalgamation of seven independent firms then operating, led by Rawdon, Wright, Hatch and Edson into the American Bank Note Company. From this time most banknote engravers became employees, and so their names are rarely known, the imprint on the notes being that of the company and, as in Britain, attempts to introduce initials or signatures of artists and engravers into the design, however subtly, were discouraged. They therefore rarely achieved a reputation outside this field, especially in view of the length of time it took to train through the various stages, based on practice and experience. An early president of the new company was Charles Toppan (1796–1874), a nephew by marriage of Jacob Perkins. He joined the firm of Murray, Draper and Fairman in 1814, and went to London in 1819 as chief engraver to Perkins. On his return to America, he joined up with John Draper who had left the partnership in July 1818, and together the firm survived until its merger into the new company. M.I. Danforth was also a vice-president.

Even after this great merger some further companies were set up, such as the Columbia Bank Note Co. in 1871 by John Geikie Wellstood (1813–*c.*1889), of Scottish origin and who spent many years as a banknote engraver. Other banknote engravers who were best known for their other work included William Edgar Marshall (1837–1906) whose engraved portrait of Abraham Lincoln achieved an enormous circulation and Stephen Alonzo Schoff (1818–1904), whose larger plates were well known to a wider public.

In Britain, flat copper plates were first used for banknote printing by Francis Nixon of Dublin *circa* 1755, and Thomas Bell produced a press with engraved copper cylinders in 1785 for use in Preston, Lancashire. These developments spread throughout the industry by 1816 at which time John Oldham was using a new process involving steel plates in the Bank of Ireland, said to resemble that of Perkins.

Joseph Chesswood Dyer arrived in England as Perkins's agent in 1810, and took out two patents which he drew to the attention of the Bank of England. Steel plates and a press were provided, Dyer supervised the work, but by 1813 the Bank engravers had given up, saying that steel took four times longer to engrave than copper and half the plates were ruined in the hardening process.

One of the devices thought to be a deterrent to forgery was the employment of vignettes, small pictures which would be difficult to copy, and which would introduce a 'fine art' aspect to the banknote. Charles Warren (1767–1823) claimed a successful deterrent in his engravings for the Plymouth Stock Bank, and an extension of this idea was to provide frames and backgrounds which were so intricate as to preclude imitation. It is interesting to note that Edmund Turrell, a London engraver, in his evidence to the Society of Arts Committee in 1818, expressed his opinion that most banknote forgers probably came from the ranks of those employed in engraving for the calico printers in Birmingham, Manchester, etc., and not from the writing engravers who were usually blamed. The English calico industry was using steel roller dies to reduce time and costs in preparing the copper cylinders which printed the intaglio designs, introduced by Joseph Lockett in 1808.

After Wilson Lowry's invention of the ruling machine *circa* 1790, many mechanics produced modifications, the most significant of which was the rose engine, a variety of ornamental lathe, produced by Asa Spencer (d.1847), a watch and clockmaker from New London, Connecticut. He patented his first machine in 1812 and by 1815 had met Perkins to whom he sold the rights in August of that year. This lathe could engrave flat, convex and concave surfaces, and was different from the machine invented by Cyrus Durand which could rule both straight and wavy lines. The geometrical decoration, together with vignettes, has formed the basis of many designs on printed notes, certificates, etc. up to the present day.

For years, the Bank of England had received suggestions from a number of people on the subject of forgery, notably that from J.B. Barber Beaumont in 1817, suggesting the use of steel instead of copper plates. This idea was developed in *The Report of the Committee of the Society of Arts Relative to the Mode of Preventing the Forgery of Banknotes* (Society of Arts 1819). The committee's deliberations commenced in April 1818; by May, Charles Warren had

10   Head of Minerva on steel saw blade engraved by C. Warren, May 1818

engraved a head of Minerva on a steel saw blade (Plate 10), and by June five different engravers had produced a composite plate by their own particular methods. A similar plate actually named the engravers below their piece of work. This use of more than one engraver on a plate was thought to be another device to make it more difficult for a single engraver to imitate. Richard Williamson, who had etched on steel in 1807, produced a design which was printed in the *Report*. The published impressions had been taken after the printer had done 12,000 in 16 hours. The subject was the back of a Monmouth Bank note, featuring the cypher 'B.S & Co'. He further estimated that the plate could produce 100,000 impressions and made the point that the closeness and fineness of the steel enabled ink to be wiped off more easily than with copper, and gave more brilliant impressions. These points were endorsed when the Bank of England's method of printing two impressions from only one inking of the plate was explained. The first was a normal one, but for the second a piece of pasteboard was inserted beneath the plate, making passage through the press more difficult, and the impression lighter in colour than the first. Williamson also produced a plate inscribed 'Twenty shillings' from which 200,000 impressions had been taken, printed in blue and dated 25 March 1825.

After years of trying to interest the Bank of England in siderography, as Perkins's process was called, Dyer judged it the right time for Perkins to come in person to press its advantages. A further development since 1809 was the making of a press which carried a 4 ft diameter cast iron cylinder, with 36 curved intaglio steel plates $\frac{5}{8}$ in. thick in two rows of 18, which were screwed on, presenting a curved printing surface which was inked by rollers, and excess ink being scraped off by a 'doctor' blade, as with the calico printing machines. A web of paper was passed between the cylinder, and an impression cylinder beneath it ensured good contact with the plates. The preparation of the curved plates needed more engineering skill than that possessed by most engravers and printers, so it is here that siderographic printing became a separate process from the normal engraving and printing industry. This was the press brought from America in June 1819, and by December, Dyer had written *Specimens and Description of Perkins and Fairman's Patent Sideographic Plan, to Prevent Forgery. Being the Reports as Made to the Commissioners for Preventing the Forgery of Banknotes*. This included a testimonial signed by 81 influential people, 27 of whom were engravers and some of whom, like Charles Warren, had contributed to the Society of Arts' *Report*. The pamphlet was biased towards persuading the Commissioners that their system, having been tested in America for 11 years, and constantly updated, had all that they were looking for, especially as rival schemes appeared to be more theoretical than practical.

Although siderography could provide copper plates, Perkins argued in favour of steel, and gave figures to back his claims. Again, these are probably the best he obtained in order to prove his point, but he reckoned that his master steel plates could produce up to 20 satisfactory roller dies. Each die could give 100 good steel plates (or 500 copper ones) and from a single plate could be printed half a million good copies. He also stated that a machine similar to that brought to London had been in operation in Philadelphia for a long time, and before leaving home, he had himself printed upwards of 400,000 impressions from one steel plate (equivalent to 14,400,000 impressions from 36 plates). Seven steel engravings accompanied the 48-page pamphlet. One has a vignette designed by Robert Smirke (1752–1845) an eminent book illustrator, and engraved by William Finden (1787?–1852) who became one of the 19th century's foremost steel engravers. The background of the two blocks 'I Promise ...' and 'For the Governor ...' is done in 'stump' engraving, where either the name of the bank or the denomination is printed in very small letters, in this case, the words 'One pound'.

For all his experience and ingenuity, Perkins failed to impress the Bank of England directors, who perhaps saw him as a dangerous competitor, and he was left to his own resources. Since 1806 J.C. Dyer had represented Perkins's interests in England, where patents were taken out for the latter's process. Charles Heath (1784–1848) and his father James (1757–1854) who was at that time Historical Engraver to the King, were seen as valuable friends, and in 1818 Charles presented examples of the American's work to the Society of Arts. Charles was thus closely involved with Perkins's attempts and became a partner in 1819 of the English business of Perkins, Fairman and Heath. In 1820 George Heath (1779–1852), Charles's half-brother, also became a financial backer. Among their new enterprises, the firm went into the lucrative country banknote market with the help of Henry Corbould (1787–1844) as designer and Charles Heath as engraver. Banbury, Derby, Dewsbury, Glamorgan, Halifax, Hemel Hempstead, Huddersfield, Ludlow, Poole, Rochdale, Saffron Walden, Swansea, Wrexham and York all used steel-engraved notes. In February 1822, Charles Heath, in correspondence with the Ipswich banker Dawson Turner, was writing that 'our Steel engraving is flourishing beyond all our hopes'. The Portuguese government had ordered 8 million notes to replace all that were then in circulation, and they hoped that the Prussians would follow suit. The Manchester calico trade was likely to produce great business, presumably by ordering dies to engrave their printing plates. The Commercial Bank of Calcutta was also a customer, and the British Linen Company Bank paid 500 guineas for separate dies, 100 gns for each steel plate, 15 gns for each back plate, each plate to print 150,000 perfect impressions and the dies were to be the exclusive property of the Bank (who probably held them). By April 1825, Charles Heath was reporting that they had obtained an order from the Provincial Bank of Ireland, expecting to print millions of notes in a few years, the National Scotch Bank wanted 500,000 and a Bank for Aberdeen, 100,000. He was rather upset that three forgers had imitated Perkins's notes printed for the Leeds Bank, but at least the miscreants were in custody! One of their most attractive private banknotes was that done for Cyfarthfa and Hirwain Iron Works 1825, printed from a 'Patent hardened steel plate' with the central vignette of the Iron Works designed by Penry Williams.

They went on to prepare dies for embossing duty stamps on banknotes, and to construct steel plates for use in the Stamp Office to print the Duty Ace of Spades for playing cards when the duty was reduced in 1828. This latter contract lasted until 1883, and steel was particularly useful here since the engraving had to be shallow and fine so that card sharpers could not detect the Ace by the thickness of ink on the card.

Siderography had very little relevance outside the field of security printing, but the use of steel made great strides throughout the industry. In Edinburgh, for instance, William Home Lizars (1788–1859) was well known in the engraving of notes for local banks. His father Daniel worked in the same field, and when he died in 1812, William had to take over the business at the age of 24 to support the family. In the early 1820s, Lizars spread his influence outside Scotland: a note 'eng^d on steel' with three vignettes was done for the Sunderland Bank. In 1826 he took over engraving plates for the Bank of Scotland from the London engravers. As a result he was seen as an important competitor by Perkins, according to an exchange that was started in *The Scotsman* in 1827/28. An article commending Lizar's banknotes appeared on 28 April 1827, to which the Editor, for some reason, would not permit a reply, so Perkins separately published a three-page reply, headed by a short letter explaining the facts. Lizars was claiming an improvement on Perkins's work and the letter ends with a challenge to the Scotsman to produce a design which the American undertook to imitate in a quarter of the time and money spent. The result, if it ever took place, is not recorded.

The economic advantages of long runs from steel plates was keenly appreciated by security printers especially in the first decade of steel (1820–30), where quotes gave alternative prices for copper and steel plates, always in the latter's favour for very long runs.

By the middle of the 19th century the individual signing of banknotes was discontinued mainly because of the number of notes involved and the multiplicity of signatures. The spectre of forgery had receded. The vignettes were no longer signed by artist or engraver, and the only credit which remained was that of the printer. There are exceptions to this, as, for example, the Belgian National Bank notes of 1929 which were designed by C. Montald and engraved by G. Minguet on the front and by M. Poortman on the reverse.

The employment of well-known engravers to provide vignettes is illustrated by the proofs found in the print collection of Lumb Stocks (1812–92) where the wildlife cartouches have a pencilled note 'Bank note Plate'. A larger design, taken from a partially inked plate, appeared on notes issued by the City Bank of Sydney from 1864 to 1918. Similar designs from the same source are that for the Uruguay 50 pesos 1872 and probably the Banco Italo-Germanica 500-lira note, 1874. Despite the appearance of

'Bradbury, Wilkinson & Co. engravers' on one plate it is likely that they were just the printers, and there is strong evidence that they subcontracted the engraving to Lumb Stocks who is almost certainly the engraver of all these plates.

After the Bank Charter Act of 1844, the country banks declined in importance, and with them the need for specialist notes. The last such bank went out of business in the 1920s, so the many 19th-century security printing businesses gradually lost their home markets. Increasing business from overseas customers kept a number of firms, such as Waterlow and De la Rue, afloat into the 20th century. More recently, the field has become dominated by Bradbury, Wilkinson and Co. in England and the American Bank Note Co. in America, which produces the largest share of the world's banknotes. The Department of Engraving at the US Mint permits the public to watch the production of dollar bills from behind tinted windows; a veil of secrecy covers most security printing operations. Security printers employ their own engravers who are occupied on no other work. Their training became much more specialized after the usual seven-year apprenticeship, at the end of which the engraver cut writing and minor details on a plate. After 15 years he was allowed to work on the vignettes, and after about 20 years he could tackle portraits, the most difficult part of the work. This meant that a single note could be the work of several engravers, each at a different stage of their career. It took Alan Dow of Bradbury, Wilkinson and Co. 18 months to engrave the Queen's portrait on the 1990 £5 note.

The design influence of steel engraving has been felt long after its decline as an intaglio process. The much faster method of transferring a steel-engraved impression on to a lithographic plate also permitted the use of harder (and more durable) paper. The German inflationary note of 1923 (Plate 11) shows the design of a vignette portrait (of Merchant Gisze after Hans Holbein) and geometric line work which owed much to engraving techniques. The use of relief, intaglio and lithographic printing on one note was yet another security device.

The problems of forgery with which this chapter began are always with us. A newspaper dated 12 December 1992 reported that the Republic of Ireland's £20 note had been imitated in Dublin just a month after its issue as a measure to combat forgers!

Bonds and share certificates

Although bonds and share certificates possessed a monetary value, they did not have the same purchasing power as currency, and there was not quite the same need to provide forger-proof documents. None the less, security printers were employed to make them, using special paper, ink and

11   German banknote dated 1st February 1923

engraving techniques. The early certificates were of a simple nature, stating the essentials of the transaction in varying designs of lettering, ranging from the copperplate running hand to decorated capital letters, accompanied by the usual flourishes and embellishments for the important words. From an inspection of a number of examples it is very possible that they were designed to be engraved on steel, even if, in the end, they were not printed from steel plates. The certificates issued by the Herne Bay Pier Company in 1833 were produced by E. Colyer, engraver and printer to the company, 27 Fenchurch St., London. Examples of this kind are found up to *circa* 1870, when vignettes and extra geometric line work became universal design features. Perkins's designs using the rose engine lathe reached their peak in the 1840s and continued to be used until World War II. Vignettes appeared *circa* 1830 when, for instance, the share certificate of the Manchester Exchange carried a view of the building, drawn by William Thomas. A Wear Valley Railway share certificate of 1848 features a central vignette of a train passing through a deep cutting, which subject was used for many other railway shares, e.g. The Blue Ridge Railroad Company in South Carolina, 1869. In this case, four small vignettes of allegorical subjects were introduced into the corners of the document. In 1859, a closely printed certificate in Russian was issued for the Grand Russian Railway Company, where a border, giving the impression of a design in relief of various figures and scenes was designed by H. Catenacci and engraved by E. Morice. The engravers, Nissen and Parker of London, produced a certificate for the Ottoman Railway Company in three languages and two scripts in 1862. All these examples were printed in monochrome, normally black and white.

By *circa* 1885 a design change came about when a pattern of central vignette, heading and text were printed in black. Around it was placed an elaborate geometric border, printed in colour. The pattern was so well established that a house style could be detected, e.g. that by Waterlow and Sons. One of the earliest certificates in this format was produced by the American Bank Note Company for the Missouri, Kansas and Texas Railway Company in 1887, where the central vignette is of a group of cows beside a pond in black and a border printed in bright green. A Loan Bond for the Chinese government in 1913 had a certificate produced by Roberts and Leete, engravers and printers, London, and in the same year, Bradbury, Wilkinson and Co. excelled in a vignette of Genoa Harbour with a carmine frame for the Genoa District Water Works Company Limited. Charles Skipper and East printed a French share certificate in 1927 with a pictorial frame of palm trees and village scenes of Madagascar, which was different from the usual run of designs.

The visual appeal of later certificates has gradually declined, especially after World War II, and although there have been exceptions, modern share certificates are very stark in design and more suited to computer operations. The design influence of steel engraving in this field has now entirely disappeared.

Postage stamps

Following the steel-engraved work done in connection with banknotes and share certificates, many of the same considerations applied to the production of postage stamps, and some of the security backgrounds first steel engraved for banknotes were used again for postage stamps. It was desirable that the printed images should be exactly similar, and should not be easily imitated, although the revenue accruing at the time of issue on a sheet of 240 1$d.$ stamps was only £1 at face value – hardly worth the forger's attention.

The size of the stamp was small compared with banknotes, etc., so that it took up little room on the letter envelope, many of which were smaller than those used today. The fine lines of steel engraving were ideal for such designs, and this, combined with the use of siderography for their replication pointed to the use of a firm already expert and experienced in this work. Perkins, Bacon and Petch had for a long time produced master dies and printing plates in steel, and were the obvious choice for postage stamp production in Britain. Stamps had been in use for tax purposes since 1783, and the Stamp Office had experimented with all sorts of devices, mainly involving embossing the documents affected. The principle of the stamp and the means of producing them were already to hand and well known when, in July 1839, Rowland Hill, the progenitor of the adhesive postage stamp, visited Perkins, Bacon and Petch to review their process, explained to him by John Butters Bacon. The use of gum was the one new factor in all this and provided an extra item of cost in the production.

The first postage stamps were issued in Britain in May 1840 and were produced as a family effort by the Heaths and Corboulds. Charles Heath, the eminent steel engraver was asked to engrave the die for the Penny Black, but in the event, his son Frederick Augustus Heath (1810–78) did the work from designs by Henry Corbould (1787–1844), whose family was related by marriage to that of Charles Heath. This first die was in use from 1840 to 1855, when it was retouched by William Humphrys (1794–1865) to become Die II. Forgery was made more difficult by the hand punching of letter combinations, at first in the lower corners, and from 1858 in all four corners of the stamp (Plate 12). The one difficult production factor was the printing process. Intaglio printing requires great pressure to transfer ink from the incisions to the paper and, to that end, close contact is obtained by damping the sheets before printing. When dry the paper shrinks which ordinarily would not matter or be noticed. This was so with the early stamps where each was cut from a sheet with a pair of scissors, but when, in 1854, perforations were introduced to facilitate separation by hand, shrinkage sometimes meant that the perforations fell in the design and not in the

12   Stamps of Great Britain, Canada and the United States of America (reduced to 89 percent of actual size)

margins (Plate 12). In extreme circumstances, the shrinkage showed a millimetre difference in the size of the image, as shown most dramatically in the Canadian January 1855 Jacques Cartier issue, where three varieties of wove paper were tried to obviate the problem. The damping of paper in the early British stamps produced a blue effect on some paper, probably due to the presence of prussiate of potash in the paper, or its incidence in the printing ink.

Intaglio printing was always a slow process by its very nature, and until the technical problems were solved in the 20th century, mainly by the use of fast rotary presses, there was no improvement in the speed of printing in the 19th century. This, together with the stranglehold held by the Perkins patent on siderography, led to rivals looking for alternative suggestions. One such was proposed by a steel engraver of French origin, Jean Ferdinand Joubert de la Ferté (1810–83). He had come to England in the 1840s and had taken an immediate interest in stamp engraving, resulting, in due course, with his appointment as chief engraver to De la Rue and Co. To them he proposed the use of a French economical method, *en épargne*, whereby a steel die was engraved, cutting away the background and enabling the resulting plate to be printed in relief at a much faster rate, and avoiding the complications of the Perkins patent. He also introduced De la Rue to acierage or steel-facing, in the development of which he was a collaborator, enabling metal plates to withstand the wear of printing almost indefinitely.

The engraving of steel dies for relief printing became an accepted method by the majority of stamp printers, and explains the unusual inclusion of an engraver's name for works printed in relief. The method was very detrimental to Perkins, Bacon and Co., and enabled De la Rue to obtain the contract for printing British stamps from 1855 to 1911. Joubert remained as chief engraver until 1865, and among his earliest work for them were the British fiscal stamps of 1853–54, and the October 1855 issue of East Indian stamps for which he engraved the Queen's head, a great improvement on the earlier locally produced efforts in Calcutta. In 1911 the British stamp-printing contract went to Harrison and Co., who used J.A.C. Harrison (fl. 1911–39) as their engraver. Intaglio printing returned in 1913 for high value stamps and has continued up to the present, where the current issue with photographs by Prince Andrew are engraved on steel and printed intaglio. It is more remunerative to forge higher values, and this is the reason why a number of countries follow the same practice. From 1934, steel engraving's nearest rival from the 19th century, photogravure, dominated British stamp printing.

Philately developed its own vocabulary for printing processes, using 'recess' for intaglio and 'surface printed' or 'typographed' for relief printing. By placing a price on stamps unrelated to their face value, it also enabled the forger to find another market for his wares, especially in the early days of the hobby. Many of the rewards went to imperfect stamps with parts omitted, inverted designs etc. and there has been a tendency to produce copies of these as well as forgeries of scarce, sought after issues. In recent years collectors have chosen engraving as a subject for their thematic collections, especially as several countries have produced relevant issues. In 1966 France produced a stamp showing the engraving of a die as part of their annual series of Stamp Day issues which started in 1944. It was designed and engraved by P. Biquet. Switzerland in 1980 marked 50 years of their use of the transfer roller die. Denmark celebrated the 50th anniversary of stamps printed by steel engraving, which showed the detail of the original die for the 1 ore 1933 issue in reverse, and a burin. It was engraved by C. Slania. The subject of the 1991 Norwegian Stamp Day design was engraving, and of four stamps, one was devoted to preparation of making a steel die, two stamps to the actual engraving and the fourth to printing the proof. They also came in a miniature sheet where engraving tools were displayed in the margins. Ironically, the stamps were produced by offset litho (Plate 13). Paul Gaimard's *Voyage en Island et en Groënland pendant les années 1835 et 1836* ... (Paris, 8 vols, 1838–52), with illustrations after Auguste E.F. Mayer (1805–90), marine painter from Brest, was the source for Iceland's Stamp Day miniature sheets for 1986, 1987 and 1988, all etched on steel by Slania, and it would seem that the originals were also steel engravings.

Czeslaw Slania (b.1921) occupies a special place in the history of stamp engraving. Originally from Poland, he started work in Sweden on 1 October 1959, and has stayed there, engraving stamps for many countries, including Great Britain. Up to 1986 he was credited with over 700 designs and is still working at the age of 75. He was honoured by Denmark and Monaco, and in 1972 was made Engraver to the Swedish Court. When he was 70 in 1991, he was unusually honoured by the production of a miniature sheet for his anniversary (Plate 13).

Some countries, such as Germany, took the view that low value stamps were not a security risk, and relief printed them, most of the early dies being engraved by H.G. Schilling. In 1900, intaglio printing was first used for the high values (1–5 marks) and were engraved by Professor W. Roese. This pattern continued until the Air stamps of 1926/27, when the three high values were relief printed again. In 1927 photogravure was introduced, but the Charity stamps of 1930–35 were all engraved, despite being low values, and commemorative issues up to 1939 alternated intaglio and photogravure processes. In 1938–39 the stamps for Hitler's Culture Fund and his 49/50th birthday were engraved by R. Klein, who went on to design other issues. The Winter Relief Fund issue of seven values, in November 1938, was engraved by Axster-Hendtlass. All these issues were printed at the Imperial Printing Office, established in 1879, but from 1939, the State Printing works in Vienna was used to print some issues, e.g. the 1940 issue, engraved by F. Lorber, the 1941 Mozart Anniversary, engraved by H. Fanzoni, and the 1942 European Postal Congress issue 6+14 Pf. engraved by A. Schuricht. The 12+38 Pf. of the same issue was engraved by R. Zenziger and printed at the Government Printing Works, Berlin. F. Lorber (fl. 1941–57) regularly

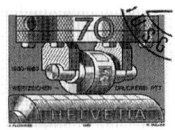

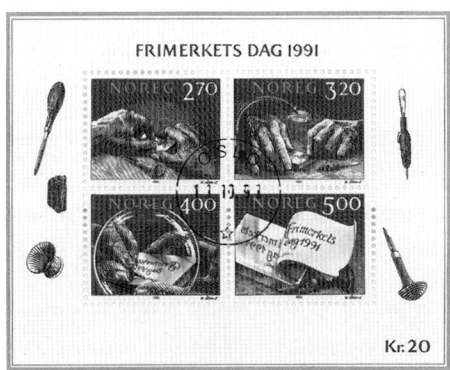

13 Stamps illustrating the stamp engraving process from France, Switzerland, Denmark, Norway and Sweden (reduced to 64 percent of actual size)

designed and engraved German stamps for a number of years, and from 1948 to 1955 worked on Austrian stamps. In 1957 he did the Portuguese Almeida Garrett commemorative issue. Most of his work was printed by the Viennese State Printing Works: it is probable that he worked in that city. The 12 values of the 1943 Armed Forces and Heroes Day issue employed a number of new engravers: W. Hartz, J. Piwczyk, L. Schnell, W. Goritz and B. Chibada. Nearly all these engravers worked regularly on intaglio issues until 1945. In West Germany and West Berlin after the war, L. Schnell began engraving again in 1950 and did the majority of the work, joined by J. Piwczyk in 1951, and G. Schulz in 1952, where once more intaglio was the main process. P. Winkler, E. Falz and H.J. Fuchs arrived in 1955, joined in 1956 by H. Thorweger and H. Braband in 1960 and P. Nowraty in 1962.

In contrast to the selective use of steel engraving, some countries such as the USA, Canada, New Zealand and France used it extensively for their stamps. In the USA, local issues for places such as New York, Providence, Rhode Island, etc. were printed in intaglio, during 1845–46, but the first general issue, on 1 July 1847, was printed by the firm of banknote engravers, Rawdon, Wright, Hatch and Edson of New York. The stamps carried the initials RWH and E at their foot. By 1851, the firm Toppan, Carpenter, Casilear and Co. of Philadelphia was employed, but the National Bank Note Co. printed the so-called *premières gravures* in 1861. In 1869–70 the National Bank Note Co. was used, followed in 1875 by the Continental Bank Note Co. and in 1879 The American Bank Note Co. (formerly Rawdon, Wright, Hatch and Edson). The situation was regularized in 1895 when the Bureau of Engraving and Printing was given a government contract, and they printed all subsequent issues, with only a few exceptions, in intaglio.

From 1914, rotary presses were introduced, and until 1954 the same stamps were produced by either flat or curved plates. This resulted in stamps of differing dimensions, depending on whether the curved plate impressions were made sideways or vertically on to the paper; those so produced were wider or taller than the stamps from flat plates.

Engravings were used as the subject for two issues. In 1928 the design of the 50th anniversary of Valley Forge was after an engraving by J.C. M'Rae, and in 1931 an etching by Henry Bryan Hall (1808–84) provided the design for the 150th anniversary of the death of General Casimir Pulaski issue. A feature of later US issues was the use of lithography with intaglio, which started in 1943–44 with the Flags of Oppressed nations issue. The flag in the centre of the design was lithographed and the frame engraved, where multi-coloured flags and their flat, solid colours would have been very difficult to render by engraving. The stamp issued on 5 October 1963 to honour Cordell Hull shows how little portrait line engraving on steel had changed since the 19th century (Plate 12).

Canada engraved all its issues, with very few exceptions, from 1851 to 1963. Thereafter several methods joined intaglio. Rawdon, Wright, Hatch and Edson, New York, engraved all the early issues, and when they changed their name on 1 May 1858 to American Bank Note Co., they used the new name on the 1859 issue and others until 1867. On 1 July 1867, the Dominion of Canada came into being and the first of the new stamps were engraved and printed by the British American Bank Note Co., which had two branches, one in Ottawa, where the main work was done, and the other in Montreal. The 12½ cents (6d.) yellow green belongs to this series, the last in which was the 150th anniversary of New Brunswick, 16 August 1934 (Plate 12). The American Bank Note Co. also had a branch in Ottawa, which, in 1923, became the Canadian Bank Note Co.; one of their printings was the Royal Canadian Mounted Policeman in the June–November 1935 issue (Plate 12). As was the practice with most firms of security engravers, the names of individual engravers are rarely known.

New Zealand's first stamps were engraved in 1855 by William Humphrys (1794–1865), who had re-engraved the original Penny Black die in Great Britain. Perkins, Bacon and Co. provided the plates and worked them, but later printings were done locally in Auckland. This pattern was followed for later issues, so no one firm had a monopoly. Humphrys had already engraved the triangular Cape of Good Hope stamps in 1852, and had executed a design for South Australia in 1855 (Plate 14). By 1862, the original plates showed some signs of wear, and by January 1874 a new set of designs was commissioned to be relief printed, the lower values by De la Rue in London and the two higher values (2s. and 5s.) were designed, dies engraved and plates made by the Wellington firm of Bock and Cousins. They also did the third series during 1882–97, and the dies of the New Zealand Exhibition issue of 1906 were engraved by W.R. Bock for relief printing.

William Bock (c.1840–c.1906) was the third son of the well-known Tasmanian engraver Thomas Bock (1790–1855) who had been apprenticed to Thomas Brandard of Birmingham (d. 1830) (father of Robert and Edward Paxman Brandard). At the age of 33, Thomas had been sentenced to 14 years deportation for administering drugs to a young woman. William was the third of his seven colonial born sons, and had achieved some fame by writing illuminated addresses for the New Zealand government. The 1898 pictorial issue was intaglio, engraved and printed by Waterlow and Sons, but after this, most of the stamps were relief printed, some being done entirely in New Zealand, but most split between London and New Zealand. Plates were made in London and printed mainly at the Government Printing Office in Wellington. During World War I Perkins, Bacon supplied steel plates for surface printing the definitive issues which ran from 1915 to 1919

14   New Zealand stamps (reproduced in actual size)

(Plate 14). This was unusual in that their normal practice was to print from intaglio plates made by their patented method of siderography. Intaglio printing revived with the fourth Health issue, in 1932, where the Hygea design was engraved by H.J. Plat, who also did the 1933 Pathway to Health stamp. The Air stamps of 1935 were engraved by the Stamp Printing Office of Melbourne. A mixture of printers was used for subsequent issues, including John Ash of Melbourne, De la Rue and Co., Waterlow and Sons, Note Printing branch of the Commonwealth Bank of Australia, Melbourne and, more recently, Bradbury, Wilkinson and Co. In 1946, photogravure was introduced into the Peace issue for two values, and from 1950 it became as popular a method as intaglio. By 1960, intaglio was in decline and was rarely used. The last use was in the 1963 Health issue (Plate 14).

In France, the first stamps of 1849 were relief printed by M. Hulot until 1875, from then until 1880 by the Bank of France and afterwards by the Government Printing Works, but engravers were employed to make the dies, the earliest being Jean Jacques Barre (*c.*1790–*c.*1856). He was general engraver at the Hôtel des Monnaies until he was succeeded in 1855 by his son Albert Desiré Barre (1818–78), who continued to engrave dies from 1862 to 1875. The plates of the 1849 issue were used again in 1870 during the siege of Paris. [Louis] Eugène Mouchon (1843–1914) engraved in 1876 the dies for several long-running series including the sower, which ran from 1903 to 1936 (Plate 15). He was a sculptor and medal engraver, taught by his father, and had commenced his stamp die career by engraving the portrait of King Luiz of Portugal for the issues of 1882–86. He designed and engraved the dies for the head of Queen Wilhelmina of The Netherlands for an issue which ran from 1898 to 1923 (Plate 15), and early in 1903 a Serbian series depicting King Alexander I was followed in September 1904 by two more stamps commemorating the coronation of Peter I and the centenary of the Karageorgevich dynasty, the latter being relief printed at the French Government Printing Works in Paris. Mouchon was made a Chevalier of the Légion d'honneur in 1895, led a succession of eminent engravers, many of whom were similarly honoured, and had a distinguished career outside stamp engraving, notably in book illustration.

The first French issue to carry pictures was the 1917 War Orphans set, five values of which had dies engraved by Léon Henri Ruffé (1864–*c.*1928), an engraver and painter. A pupil of Baudé, he was an exhibitor at the Paris Salon from 1884 and gained a medal of honour in 1928. He was made an Officer of the Légion d'honneur in 1927.

The first French intaglio stamp was issued on 15 May 1928 for the Sinking Fund and was engraved by Abel Justin Mignon (1861–*c.*1932). He did five or six more designs until 1931, including the view of Mont St Michel in 1929 (Plate 15). An unusual feature appeared on French intaglio stamps

15 Stamps from Holland and France (reproduced in actual size)

from this date, which consisted of the names of the designer at left and engraver at right below the main design, as with ordinary engravings. Sometimes the names were reversed. Where only one name occurs, the same person designed and engraved the die. This obtained until *circa* 1946, when some designs carried no names (Plate 15, Palais du Luxembourg, July 1946) and others had the names incorporated into the design (Plate 15, Abbaye Saint-Mondrille, 1949). Mignon was joined and succeeded by Antonin-Jean Delzers (1873–1956) who began with the 1929 Arc de Triomphe design, went on to the 1930 Sinking Fund stamp, the die for the relief printed Peace design 1932–39, the 150th anniversary of the US Constitution with the figure of France congratulating the USA (17 September 1937) (Plate 15), and his last commission was for the 3 francs with the arms of Havre, in 1942.

A contemporary was Achillé Ouvré (1872–1951), whose first engraved design was in March 1934 for the centenary of the death of Jacquard. He was an engraver specializing in portraits, notably of writers, and an illustrator, becoming President of the engraving section of the Salon. The 1935 stamp for the Tercentenary of the French Academy's founding by Cardinal Richelieu and portrait of Paul Cezanne, 1939 are typical of his work (Plate 15), and he also did the 1936 Air stamps. He worked right up to the end of his life; his last design at the age of 79 was for the National Relief Fund, 1951, which carried three portraits. He contributed nearly 40 engravings for French stamps in his time.

Henri Lucien Cheffer (b.1880) also had between 40 and 50 French stamps designs to his credit from 1929, one of which was the 300th anniversary of the publication of René Descartes's *Discours de la méthode* (1937). At the age of 22, he received an honourable mention at the Société des Artistes Français in 1902.

Jules Piel (1882–*c.*1966) also belonged to this age group, although his connection with French stamps did not commence until 1936 with his engraving of Alphonse Daudet's mill at Fontvielle (Plate 15). Up to 1954 he had done 58 engravings for French stamps. His last design was for the December 1966 Red Cross Fund issue. He gained the Prix de Rome in 1910 and was a gold medallist at the Société des Artistes Français in 1922.

A slightly younger group of men came to the fore with Georges-Léo Degorce (1894–*c.*1943) who began stamp engraving in 1937 and had done 11 designs by 1943. Gabriel-Antoine Barlangue (fl. 1900–52) was a pupil of Delzers (q.v.), who probably introduced him to stamp work, where between 1937 and 1952 he had engraved 25 designs.

Albert Decaris (b. 1901) gained his Prix de Rome in 1929, and from 1935 he engraved French stamps on a regular basis. According to one authority he is credited with about 500 stamps and he was still going strong in the 1980s. He became a member of the Institut de France in 1943, and was elected 'peintre titulaire de la Marine' in 1973.

Pierre Gandon (b. 1899) specialized in stamp design from 1941 in France, the colonies and overseas, and continued for about 40 years, taking over the engraving of the annual Red Cross Fund stamps in 1967 from Jules Piel. From 1941 to 1961 Raoul Jean Serres (fl. 1898–1961) engraved 49 designs for French stamps, his last being the 1961 Stamp Day issue. The final engraver worthy of mention is Charles Firmin Mazelin (1882–c.1964) who between 1942 and 1964 was involved in 59 French issues. Over 50 different engravers have been employed on French intaglio stamps, many of them having achieved a high rank in the art world.

The situation in Australia until federation in 1913 was that each state produced its own stamps. Victoria was remarkable in that only three dies were engraved outside the state, and stamp production was in the hands of private contractors from 1850 to 1859, when the last contractor was taken over by the Government Stamp Printing Branch from 1 January 1860.

The first contractor was Ham, Campbell and Co., of which the leading figure was Thomas Ham (1821–70). The eldest son of a Baptist minister, by the time he was 16 he was living in Birmingham, where he probably trained as an engraver, and by the time the family had emigrated to Melbourne in 1842, he was 22 and out of his indentures. He set up in Collins St, East Melbourne (where his father's church was), engraved the corporation seal for the town of Melbourne, and became the sole contractor to the Government for engraving and lithography. From 1847 he published a series of maps, and eventually became lithographer and chief engraver to the Survey Office. In 1849, Thomas prepared a steel plate engraved with 30 designs of the 'Half-length' variety, from which he printed stamps lithographically. This process was faster, and Alois Senefelder, the inventor of lithography, regarded this transfer from an engraved plate as the most significant part of his invention. The steel plate was used not only by Ham, whose contract was completed in May 1850, but by his successors until 1860, and in 1891, after the lithographic plates had been destroyed, the surviving dies were used to produce copies of early stamps for other members of the Universal Postal Union, a requirement of Victoria's request to join that body. The twopenny die had been injured about 1852 as these later printings showed, and had been replaced by another showing the Queen on her throne ('full-length'). Ham engraved a steel plate by hand of 50 stamps, each with a different letter combination (as in contemporary British stamps), and they inevitably showed minor variations between the impressions, which were printed in intaglio direct from the plate. This lasted for two years, at the end of which, Campbell and Co. took lithographic transfers and printed from them. This was probably done to circumvent the Perkins siderography patent, but it is significant that the 1*d*. (1856) and 6*d*. (1858) issues were intaglio printed by Perkins, Bacon and Co. This was another issue reprinted in 1891 from the original steel plates.

In New South Wales, the first 1*d*. issue of 1 January 1850 was engraved by Robert Clayton of Sydney, but was not very successful and was re-engraved in August by H.C. Jervis. The 2*d*. value, issued on the same day was engraved by John Carmichael, and by April was entirely re-engraved by Jervis, who engraved four more dies up to April 1851. A new design for the 2*d*. in July 1851 was engraved on steel by Carmichael, as was the 1*d*. issued in December 1851. In April 1856, Perkins, Bacon and Co. had produced plates which were printed in New South Wales, some of which were designed by Edward Henry Corbould.

The distinctive triangular Cape of Good Hope stamps were from 1853–63 intaglio printed by Perkins, Bacon and Co., the original die being engraved by William Humphrys, but from February to April 1861, a provisional issue was required, where C.J. Roberts steel engraved the so-called 'wood block' issues, which were printed in Cape Town from stereotyped plates. Early in 1863 Perkins, Bacon and Co. handed over the printing plates to De la Rue, who made all subsequent impressions of the triangular stamps, which were eventually withdrawn on 1 October 1900.

William Ridgway (fl. 1840–95) engraved the die for the first issues of Sarawak in 1869, which were lithographed in Glasgow. He also engraved the dies for the 1895 issue, intaglio printed by Perkins, Bacon and Co.

Charles Henry Jeens (1827–79) worked for Perkins, Bacon and Co. and probably engraved the Antigua 1*d*. design by E. H. Corbould in August 1862, intaglio printed by Perkins, Bacon and Co., and, after 1872 by De la Rue from the same plates. He also engraved the Queen's portrait for a number of other issues of St Lucia, St Vincent, etc.

In many other European countries, intaglio printing followed a similar pattern and, when technology had improved in the post-World War I period, for commemorative and serial issues. Cost of production and speed of printing played their part and, since relief printing was well established and practised in all European countries, the use of steel engraved relief dies was almost universal. Most countries also tried to use indigenous engravers and printers (usually the State Printing Office), but on occasions they turned to London, Vienna and Haarlem for assistance, especially if a foreign engraver had been employed.

Belgium was virtually alone in Europe using a British engraver for its early issues. On 1 July 1849 the Stamp Works at Brussels intaglio printed a portrait of King Leopold I, the die engraved by John Henry Robinson (1796–1871), which survived sufficiently well to produce reprints for special occasions in 1929 and 1945. By October 1849, Robinson had engraved

16   Stamps from Holland, Portugal, Belgium, Denmark, Switzerland, Spain (reproduced in actual size)

a re-designed stamp which was printed in sheets of 200, but the capability of the press had improved so much by 1861 that the sheet size had increased to 300 stamps.

Between 1884 and 1896 [Louis] Eugène Mouchon (1843–1914) engraved some dies for relief-printed stamps, and he also designed the 1 June 1893 definitives, together with [François Joseph] Henri Hendrickx (1817–94). Hendrickx was an eminent Belgian painter, illustrator and engraver, who probably designed the frame of the stamp, as he had engraved one very similar for the preceding (1884–91) issue (Plate 16).

The first engraved stamps of The Netherlands were done by Johan Wilhelm Kaiser (1813–1900) in 1852 depicting the head of King William IV. Kaiser was born and worked in Amsterdam and became Director of the School of Engraving there in 1859. For the 1898 definitive series depicting the head of Queen Wilhelmina, the high values only were intaglio engravings. The head was designed and engraved by Rudolf Stang (d.1927), a German engraver from Dusseldorf. The frame was engraved by William Steelink (1826–1913) who worked in Amsterdam and was an eminent engraver of book illustrations (Plate 16). After this, intaglio prints continued to be reserved for high values and were also used for commemorative issues such as the Cultural and Social Relief Fund 1935–41, using engravers such as S.L. Hartz, Mrs. Reitsma-Valença and Kuno Brinks.

In Sweden, intaglio printing was not originally a popular process, and was first used for the high values of the 1891–1904 issue, printed by the Jacob Bagge Bank Note Co. The Royal Swedish Postal Administration set up a Stamp Printing Office, which installed rotary presses for intaglio printing in 1920, and renewed them in 1938. Hasse W. Tullberg engraved from 1920–36. Sven Ewert was a major engraver from 1931 to 1959 and from 1953 A. Wallhorn came in to assist him, together with H. Gutschmidt from 1954. In 1959 C. Slania succeeded Ewert as head engraver, and his work was featured on well over 700 stamps for a number of countries, probably constituting a world record.

Portugal issued its first intaglio stamps with the high value definitives of 1894, engraved and printed in Leipzig by Giesecke and Devrient. Waterlow produced the Vasco da Gama stamps of 1898, and in 1924, the Camoens anniversary stamps had the low values engraved by J.A.C. Harrison and the high values by G. Fairweather. George Harrison did the three Independence issues of 1926–28, all printed by De la Rue, and in 1940, the Portuguese centenaries issues were printed by the Bank of Portugal and engraved by Pedroso (Plate 16) and Renato Araiyo (fl. 1940–50), who became a regular engraver up to 1950. In 1949, Bradbury, Wilkinson and Co. engraved and printed a number of issues.

Denmark first produced stamps in April 1851 with relief plates engraved on steel and printed by M.W. Ferslew (fl. 1851) of Copenhagen. The 1904–05 issue portraying King Christian IX (Plate 16) was engraved on steel by Benjamin-Louis-Auguste Damman (b. 1835), a Parisian painter and engraver, who had three times been a medallist as an engraver at important exhibitions (1879–1900). For some unexplained reason, the stamps were printed from copper plates. In 1907 the definitive values were intaglio engraved and printed at the Imperial Printing Works, Berlin as was the 1912 stamp of the GPO Copenhagen; the same printer did the 1913 definitives, with the two high values in intaglio, engraved by Chr. Danielson (fl. 1905–13). From 1933 all Danish stamps were intaglio printed at the Post and Telegraph Office in Copenhagen and from 1933 to 1943 most of the engraving was done by J. Britze (fl. 1933–43) (Plate 16 – a portrait of King Christian X), who also engraved a single Swedish design in 1942. Sven Ewert (fl. 1932–59), the Swedish engraver, commenced his Danish work in 1945 with a design for the King's birthday, followed by definitives for King Frederick IX (Plate 16) which was among the first series to carry the names of the designer and engraver at the foot of the stamp. In some cases, only initials are given, as in the 1961 issue, where the designer was V[iggio] B[ang] and the engraver B. E[kholm] (Plate 16). C. Slania appeared in 1962, doing most of the work on Danish stamps for a considerable period (Plate 16).

The State Printing Works in Vienna printed all Austrian stamps from 1850 and the first printed in intaglio were the high values of the 1908 definitive issue. The engraver was Ferdinand Schirnböck (1859–1939), who engraved dies both for surface and intaglio plates until 1929. Schirnböck had been trained at the Engraving School of the Viennese Academy from 1880 to 1886, and later specialized in the engraving of banknotes as well as stamps. Hans Ranzoni (presumably the younger 1896–1945), a Viennese engraver, worked from 1934, and although he died in 1945, a Hans Ranzoni (perhaps a son?) was engraving until 1963. The elder Hans (1868–after 1930) may possibly have been involved. Photogravure was used from 1936 to 1949, when intaglio reappeared as a main process, and among the new set of engravers was F. Lorber (fl. 1948–57), who engraved some issues during 1948–55, as well as his work on Portuguese and German issues already noted. Friedrich Teubel (b. 1884) did some issues during 1952–53; he was known as a city view engraver and of book plates.

The Government Printing Works in Madrid printed the majority of Spanish stamps, but produced no intaglio issues until the definitives depicting the king were produced in 1909, engraved by B. Maura (fl. 1900–09), who also engraved a number of dies for relief-printed issues. On the other hand, Bradbury, Wilkinson and Co., engraved and printed an issue in 1876, which illustrated well the difference in quality between the London and local productions. In 1926, Waterlow's first production was the Red Cross issue and a succession of well-executed stamps followed, such as those for the Catacombs Restoration Fund, 23 December 1928, bearing the portraits of Pope Pius X and King Alfonso XIII. There were two issues distinguished by the colours used; one set was issued from Santiago, the other from Toledo. They were well produced, of a larger size than usual, and were issued in millions of copies hoping to raise a great deal of money. Philatelically, they are common and worth very little, but Waterlow thought it a good idea to place their name prominently below the design (Plate 16). In 1930 two local engravers, Camilio Delhorn (fl. 1930–49) and J.L. Sanchez Toda (fl. 1930–55) began working for the London printers. They dominated stamp engraving until *circa* 1947, from when it appears that the State Printing Office used their own engravers. An example from 1963 illustrates in the aerial view of the Poblet monastery issue the fine work then being done (Plate 16).

Switzerland began its printing operations in Berne, with Stampfli and Co., for whom, in 1882, Johannes Burger (b. 1829) engraved a die for relief printing. He began engraving at Zopflingen and went to a school of engraving in 1851, but in 1859 took up permanent residence in Munich. From 1886 to *circa* 1905 Max Girardet (b. 1857) printed Swiss stamps at his engraving printing house in Berne. He learnt engraving with his father, Edward, and worked in Paris for Goupil, later returning to Berne. Some French engravers were employed such as Frédéric Florian (b. 1858) and Jean Sprenger (b. 1869), who engraved several issues 1914–31, including the die for the famous William Tell stamps, first issued in 1914 (Plate 16). He also engraved the 3- and 10-franc values of the 1914 mountain scenery issue. The 5-franc value of 'The Rütli' was engraved by A.A. Burkhard, whose name appears on the stamp, and in 1928 it was re-drawn by the same designer, but engraved by Jean Sprenger, whose name was substituted on the stamp. From 1906, The Mint shared the printing of stamps with the Survey Office, both in Berne, but from 1923 the Federal Printing works appeared in the same city. Photogravure came into use in 1932 alongside intaglio printing and from 1938 engraving for the latter was carried on mainly by Karl Bickel (fl. 1938–50), and from 1941 by A. Yersin (fl. 1941–58). In 1959 K.A. Bickel, Jun., appeared as an engraver.

Finally, intaglio printing came very late to Russian stamps, in 1913. Relief printing was used from 1858 at the State Printing Works, St Petersburg, which appeared to employ its own engravers. On 1 January 1913 intaglio was used for the 1–5 rouble high values of the definitive series. It was used sporadically e.g. for the tenth anniversary of Lenin's death in 1934, engraved by A. Troitsky, the first to second, fourth sixth and seventh series depicting War Orders and medals, between 1943 and 1952, followed by views of the Republican capitals, 1958–62, and some other important anniversary issues.

This review is intended to highlight the various ways in which steel-engraved printing has been applied to stamps, including some of the engravers, and is by no means exhaustive of the subject.

3

Mezzotints on steel

Mezzotint was the earliest form of intaglio engraving to benefit from the introduction of steel plates. Only about 130 satisfactory prints can be obtained from a copper plate before it becomes worn in the printing process, but it did exhibit a wide range of tones from the characteristic deep velvety blacks to white highlights. It was aptly named the *manière noire*. There was a direct relationship between the size of a plate and the number of impressions available, since the return on the work invested in the engraving depended on these factors. Many mezzotint plates were published by the engraver, who usually employed an assistant to 'rock' the plates and, possibly, a printer whose work he was expected to closely supervise if, indeed, he did not perform the process himself.

Steel plates brought a fresh set of factors into play, because the harder metal could not be rocked to the same depth as copper. The deep, velvety blacks were less intense, so that etching was used to provide the deeper recesses for the dark passages, and it became usual to etch the main design before the rest of the ground was rocked. Strength of tone was added using stipple, line and even aquatint, so that the majority of mezzotints were described as 'mixed method' or 'mixed mezzotints'. Even in the early days of steel mezzotints, an edition of 1,200 good impressions was possible, and as techniques improved, larger plates could be engraved, many of which decorated the walls of middle-class Victorian houses. The time taken to mezzotint a plate was considerably less than that for a comparable line engraving, so by the middle of the 19th century when work was scarce, line engravers were glad enough to co-operate with mezzotinters, and it is perhaps significant that the number of engravers who worked solely in mezzotint was comparatively small.

From *circa* 1820 to 1900 in Britain, statistics compiled from currently available studies indicate that a maximum of 220 engravers worked in the medium, of whom about 95 worked either solely or as a major part of their print work in mezzotint. Approximately 80 used it as a second process, and the remainder used it occasionally, down to the production of a single plate in some cases. This compares with about 600 line engravers in steel so far identified. There were three distinct groups working, the first being those who completed their work before 1850, e.g. John C. Bromley, George Clint, Henry E. Dawe, J. Egan, Thomas Hodgetts, John Martin, G.H. Phillips, S.W. Reynolds sen., William Say, Charles Turner and William Ward. They were very much influenced by 18th-century traditions (Plate 17 of Revd W. Richardson, painted by James Ward, engraved by William Ward, 1821). The second group's work extended over the middle of the century, and included Thomas L. Atkinson, Samuel Bellin, Samuel Cousins, W.T. Davey, W.O. Geller, C.G. Lewis, D. Lucas, T.G. Lupton, H.T. Ryall, W.H. Simmons, Frederick Stacpoole, C.A. Tomkins and William Walker. The third group worked mainly in the second half of the century and beyond, being largely responsible for a revival of mezzotint after a period in the doldrums. Thomas Gooch Appleton and Henry T. Greenhead spearheaded this movement with help from Sir Frank Short and Sir Hubert Herkomer. Others in this group were G. Allen, T.O. Barlow, R.S. Clouston, G.H. Every, James Faed, G.S. Hunt, R.B. Parkes, J.B. Pratt and S.E. Wilson.

Of nearly 200 prints judged to be great from the Victorian era, 105 were mezzotints and 69 were done in line, testifying to the print publishers' interest in mezzotint as being the faster process, and therefore more economic.

In 1812, James Watt, partner of Matthew Boulton, the Birmingham steel manufacturer, suggested the use of steel to Charles Turner (1774–1857), who had been searching for an alternative to copper as a means of increasing the number of impressions obtainable from a plate. Turner had just been appointed Engraver in Ordinary to the King, and had been working with J.M.W. Turner on the latter's *Liber Studiorum* when he tried steel, but his experience with what must have been a hard plate (possibly a saw blade) did not advance beyond an attempt to rock it.

The arrival of Jacob Perkins with his soft steel plates in 1819 revolutionized the process. While he waited for the result of his bid in connection with the use of siderography for printing banknotes, he sold steel blocks, mainly to the mezzotinters, who were not deterred by their thickness of around one inch. By September 1820 he had sold nearly a thousand blocks, one of the earliest purchasers being William Say (1768–1834) who engraved a small pure mezzotint portrait of Queen Caroline after Arthur William Devis, from which hardened block 1,200 impressions were taken, several of which are in the complete collection of his work, presented by his son to the British Museum. It is perhaps fortunate that Say did not know of the view taken by a 20th-century author, when Malcolm Salaman wrote in his *Old English*

17   Revd W. Richardson, mezzotinted by W. Ward

Mezzotints (1910, p. 42) that 'I cannot forgive Say for having been the first to encourage by his own practice the introduction of steel plates'.

In February 1821, Wilson Lowry gave Charles Turner a Perkins steel plate on which the latter was able to engrave a mezzotint portrait which obtained Sir Thomas Lawrence's approval. Softer than his earlier plate, Turner went on to adopt steel for many of his later engravings.

The earliest book illustrations to be mezzotinted on steel were done by George Maile (1800–42), a young engraver barely out of his articles, for James Smith's edition of the *Compleat Angler* (1822). They were portraits of Izaak Walton after Housman and Charles Cotton after Lely, which showed a certain proficiency in flesh tones, but stipple mars the facial outlines. Thomas Zouch's *Life of Izaak Walton* (1823) used the plates again, and the advertisement to the volume noted that they were 'engraved on steel plates', although erroneously ascribing them to Mr Mitan (whether James or Samuel is not known). A. Whitman's monograph on *Samuel William Reynolds* (1903, pp. 1–16) indicates that Reynolds went to Paris in 1825 for four years, and during that time had taught George Maile to mezzotint. George, who lived in Paris from 1824 until his death in 1842, probably brushed up his technique with Reynolds – he clearly had the rudiments before he left England. J.L. Hodson, writing in the *Art Journal* (1887, p. 210) expressed the opinion that mezzotint was unsuited to book illustration because the peculiar effects it produced required a larger area for their development.

The foremost exponent of steel mezzotint was Thomas Goff Lupton (1791–1873), who found that he could not make a living from the number of copies he produced from his portraits mezzotinted on copper. He tried nickel and a Chinese alloy, tutenag, before settling on steel, and in 1822 mezzotinted a portrait of Munden the comedian, painted by Lupton's master, George Clint. For this, Lupton was awarded the Society of Arts' Gold Isis medal, presented on 30 May 1822, but only a few copies were printed from this plate. In order to discover how many copies could be obtained from a soft steel plate the same subject was engraved again and 1,500 impressions had not worn the plate out. Grounding (or rocking) the plate was a longer and more laborious job, but the results offset this expenditure of time and energy. 'Infant Samuel' after Sir Joshua Reynolds, published 1 August 1822 (Plate 18) at 3*s*. 6*d*. for prints and 5*s*. for proofs is a good example of Lupton's artistry, as, in a different vein, are 'The Passage boat' and 'A group of cattle', both after Cuyp, published by Cooke in 1824 at 10*s*. the pair.

The early development of steel mezzotint owed much to the entrepreneurial activities of William Bernard Cooke (1778–1855), who, with his brother George (1781–1834) had produced a number of volumes, mainly of views on the Thames, southern coast of England and the Rhône. They

18 Infant Samuel, mezzotinted by T.G. Lupton

projected a series of 36 English river views, and it appears that J.M.W. Turner, who was to draw most of them, suggested that steel mezzotint should be used. This was done, and *River Scenery* (or *Rivers of England*) came out between 1823 and 1827, designed to be uniform with, and a companion to *Southern Coast of England*. The first three plates engraved by Lupton and Charles Turner, gave trouble at the printing stage and had to be replaced. 'Totnes on the Dart', engraved by C. Turner, due to be published in 1825, was cancelled. The reason in both cases could have been the unsatisfactory quality of the steel plates used, so in the end, only 15 of the J.M.W. Turner plates were issued, with further plates after Thomas Girtin and William Collins, a total of 20. 'Arundel Castle with rainbow' and 'The Medway – thunderstorm with rainbow' were unfinished. The views have achieved a place in the history of landscape, and claims have been laid to their being the first landscapes engraved in mezzotint on steel. It is more likely that Charles Turner's 'Rembrandt's Mill', engraved in 1822 has pre-eminence. Thomas Lupton engraved five of the Turner views of which Plate XI 'Warkworth Castle on the River Coquet', published 1 September 1826, was one (Plate 19), Charles Turner did four, William Say did 'Brougham Castle ...' in 1825, and 'Kirkstall Lock ...' in 1827, G.H. Phillips did two, 'Dartmouth on the River Dart' in 1825 by S.W. Reynolds and 'Kirkstall Abbey...' in 1826 by John Bromley. These plates probably initiated the engravers into the use of steel, and Thomas Lupton went on to engrave six plates after J.M.W. Turner as a sequel (two in each of the years 1826, 1827, 1828) which were published as *Ports of England*, but this was an unsuccessful venture, and even though Lupton had started on a seventh plate in 1828, it had to wait until 1856 to be published, along with the original six, with five more mezzotints. By 1856 Ernest Gambart, the Belgian printseller, had acquired the plates, and with a text by John Ruskin, *Harbours of England* achieved a success denied its predecessor. Lupton also started a series of marine views after J.M.W. Turner, but only two were published, namely, 'The Eddystone light-house, represented in a storm at night' in 1824, and 'A sun-rise – whiting fishing at Margate' was a companion print in 1825.

    The Cookes also saw an opportunity to tap a new clientele, willing and able to spend money on decorating their homes. The traditional market for engraving was into the libraries of the affluent, cabinets of the collector, and private studies of the artist. The brothers therefore hit upon the idea of making their patrons and the public at large more familiar with engraved work by exhibiting it at their London home. Only a very few engravings were exhibited at the Royal Academy and other galleries, so in April 1821 they held their first exhibition, consisting of over 420 engravings by 91 engravers at 9 Soho Square, organized by a committee of 16 engravers, with

19   Warkworth Castle on the River Coquet, mezzotinted by T.G. Lupton

W.B. Cooke as Honorary Secretary. The 1822 exhibition was confined to drawings, but in January 1823, another, described as the second in the series, contained a group of about 240 engravings in the two first-floor rooms. The catalogue listed six steel mezzotints, and this was probably the first time that the public had been able to see them. Number 283 was 'Rembrandt's Mill' after Rembrandt, engraved by Charles Turner. A note appended in the catalogue reads 'This beautiful subject (being the first landscape engraved on steel) is just published'. This print is Plate 1 in *Gems of Art* (q.v.). Number 300 was 'Four landscapes from Claude, forming No. 1 of a new work. Engraved on steel and entitled "The Beauties of Claude Lorraine" to comprise in the whole, fifty of the most choice subjects selected from the "Liber Veritas" engraved by Thomas Lupton'. In a list of Cooke's publications issued in 1824 there was announced 'Twenty-four landscapes by Claude Lorraine, engraved on steel by eminent engravers. Selected from Claude's "Liber Veritas" (containing 300 designs), the prints being engraved on steel, insure [*sic*] to the purchasers such impressions as possess peculiar depth and brilliancy, the lighter tones retaining all their purity and clearness'. Four parts had then been issued with six plates in each; the price was one guinea a part. Number 309 was the 'Infant Samuel' after Reynolds, engraved by Lupton.

The *European Magazine* (1823, p. 57) review of the exhibition observed that 'the mezzotint engravings on steel by T. Lupton and C. Turner are singularly interesting on account both of their intrinsic merit and of their being the earliest specimens of an invention of incalculable importance'. Incidentally, George Cooke never seems to have liked steel, borne out by George Hollis's remark in his obituary of George in *Arnold's Magazine of the Fine Arts* (1834) to the 'hated metal'.

Another of Cooke's ventures was *Gems of Art, Forming a Choice Collection Engraved from Pictures of Acknowledged Excellence, Beauty and Variety Painted by Esteemed Masters of All Ages and All Countries* (London, published by W.B. Cooke, 9 Soho Square 1823[–27] in six parts of five plates each). Bromley, Lupton, Reynolds, Turner and Ward were the engravers of 30 plates, most of which carried the legend 'Engraved on steel'. Plate 1 was 'Rembrandt's Mill' engraved by C. Turner, published 1 January 1823; he also contributed Plates 4, 5 and 17. Samuel William Reynolds (1773–1835) engraved three plates in Part 2, including Plate 9 'Distant view of Rome from Tivoli' after Poussin, published 1 December 1823. He engraved four plates in Part 3, No. 15 being taken from the picture exhibited at 9, Soho Square in 1824 'by artificial light'. In the 1824 advertisement for the work, Plate 13 was listed as 'A Magdalene' after Correggio engraved by Reynolds, but in the contents list of the published parts, Plate 13 is 'Jael and Sisera' after James Northcote. It seems likely that this plate was substituted at the last moment, but in the V. & A. (Victoria and Albert Museum) copy J.7.d the 'Magdalene' is inserted between Plates 12 and 13, increasing the total to 31 engravings. Lupton contributed Plate 18 'Prince Arthur and Hubert' after James Northcote, published 1 August 1824 (Plate 20) and William Ward, ARA (Associate of the Royal Academy) (1766–1826) engraved Plate 26 'Christ in the Garden' after Correggio, published 1 September 1825, which was probably one of his last commissions (Plate 21). W.B. Cooke retired from his print shop and gallery in 1830, and two large sales of his stock took place.

J.M.W. Turner's interest in steel mezzotint ceased about 1826, and he reverted to line engraving to interpret his works. John Martin (1789–1854) on the other hand, found the process ideal for reproducing his rather dark and dismal biblical and literary subjects. Often compared with Blake as a visionary artist, Martin was prolific as a painter and engraver. He first attracted attention as an artist in 1812 when 'Sadak in search of the Waters of Oblivion' was exhibited at the Royal Academy. E.J. Roberts engraved a version in line for *The Keepsake*, 1828 (Plate 22). Martin's own career as a mezzotinter on steel began with a commission from the publisher Septimus Prowett to engrave 24 designs accompanying an edition of Milton's *Paradise*

20 Prince Arthur and Hubert, mezzotinted by T.G. Lupton

21 Christ in the garden, mezzotinted by W. Ward

Lost, each plate being done in a large and small format.

The work began part publication in 1825 and in order to keep up with production targets, two printers were employed. C. Lahee and Chatfield and Co. had been established commercial printers for some time, but most printers would have found it difficult to take on his very large plates, so he 'poached' Lahee's chief printer, a Mr Wood, to work in a print shop Martin built himself. It was built under his studio with the latest equipment, including large presses necessary to take the size of plates he was then engraving. Moreover, it gave him greater control over the printing process which he rightly considered to be as important a part of the production process as the actual engraving.

Martin also wanted to experiment in producing various artistic effects by using different strengths of ink, and used the 18th-century art of selective

Painted by J. Martin.   Engraved by E.J. Roberts

SADAK.
IN SEARCH OF THE WATERS OF OBLIVION.

22   Sadak in search of the Waters of Oblivion, line engraved by E.J. Roberts

inking (or 'painting the plate') with materials he blended himself. A very thick mixture was applied to the darkest areas, a slightly thinner one to the medium tones, a thin mixture of oil and ink to the lighter tints, and finally a mixture consisting of whiting and oil, with a dash of burnt umber, which gave some warmth to the pure white. This meant that he did not rely entirely on paper colour for the white contrasts as was normal practice, and there is no doubt that this kind of treatment was best done by the engraver, who knew what kind of effect he was aiming at. He printed the plate first with ordinary ink to assess his subsequent processes, a luxury afforded by a steel plate, since with the rapid deterioration of a copper plate, early impressions needed to be near perfect in order to obtain the maximum of good prints. A steel plate allowed some experimentation to obtain the desired effect. He also used different mordants in the preliminary etching, experimenting, as did many other engravers of the time, to find those which best suited the engraver. Damage to a large plate (average size 21 in. × 30 in.) for whatever reason was more serious than to a smaller one, due to the greater loss of time and work involved.

The first four large plates, 'Belshazzar's Feast' in 1826, 'Joshua commanding the sun to stand still' in 1827, 'The Deluge' in 1828 and 'The Fall of Ninevah' in 1830 were produced in editions of around 600, at a rate of 8–10 perfect impressions a day, some of which (anything up to 50 per plate) were given to interested people, including magazine and newspaper editors. Such production would have been impossible without the use of steel plates and his own press – commercial charges would have been extortionate. There were six more plates of similar size, the last being the largest, i.e. 'The Destroying angel' in 1836.

The practice of producing illustrations to go with any unillustrated edition of a work, usually literature, resulted in a series of *Illustrations of the Bible*, issued in parts between 1831 and 1835, where the pictures were taken entirely from Old Testament stories, the drama and excitement of which best suited Martin's talent. Therefore, they are to be found in all sorts of editions, sometimes with the addition of maps and wood engravings in the text. 'The Deluge' (Plate 23) is taken from the *Illustrated Family Bible*, with notes by John Kitto, published by James Sangster, undated but probably about 1871. There are no plate marks on the prints and the paper is smoother than the usual plate paper, so it is likely that they were printed lithographically. At the front of the book there appears a 'List of steel engravings'. The lithographic reproduction of Martin's work was alluded to in evidence given to the Committee of Fine Arts in 1835, when he said that 'Various shops in Windsor have got my works lithographed, and selling at very low prices, to my complete ruin; and if I am not protected by some new law, I shall be compelled entirely to leave that branch of the profession by which I live'.

Martin was among popular artists working for the annuals, and is reckoned to have done 27 designs between 1826 and 1837, three of which he engraved himself. His plate of 'Marcus Curtius' engraved by Henry Le Keux for the *Forget-Me-Not* of 1829 had sold 10,000 copies, both in the annual and as separate plates. The publisher Rudolf Ackermann showed Martin a proof

23 The Deluge, mezzotinted by John Martin

from a further printing to show that the steel plate had worn but little.

His print workshop closed down in the 1840s and in February 1848 he 'determined upon retiring entirely from that branch of my profession that relates to engraving, printing and publishing', and offered some of his stock of plates at 500 guineas each for the large ones to McQueen the printers, and probably to other interested persons. Not all the plates were disposed of in this manner; the steel plates of the large 'Joshua...' and 'The Destroying angel' appeared for auction on the first day of the sale of his effects on 4/5 July 1854. Martin Campbell illustrated all 165 of Martin's known engraved works in his catalogue *raisonné* in 1993.

John Charles Bromley (1795–1839), son and brother of eminent mezzotinters, gained a reputation in his comparatively short life of achieving a high degree of finish in his engravings, the majority of which were engraved on steel. He was awarded a medal by the Society of Arts for an etching when he was 12 years old, and produced 'Kirkstall Abbey...' in 1826 for *Gems of Art*. His 'Trial of Lord William Russell' in 1830 and 'Trial of Queen Caroline' were both after Sir George Hayter; his last plate 'The Reform Banquet 1832' after Haydon in 1837 was of imposing size and character. His later productions were not as good, no doubt due to the fact that 'premature decay had materially enfeebled his frame' (*Art Journal*, 1839, p. 90). He died, aged 44, leaving a widow and seven children.

George Clint (1770–1854) worked for Turner's *Liber Studiorum* for which he received 6 guineas a plate, and went on to engrave portraits such as 'A portrait of John Poole' after Pickersgill, in 1827, another of John Bannister in 1829, George Cooke, the engraver and John Bell the publisher. He was also T.G. Lupton's master. In later years he abandoned engraving and turned to painting, especially of miniatures.

Henry Edward Dawe (1790–1848) was taught by his father Philip, an eminent mezzotinter, and became one of 'Turner's engravers'. His repertoire of subjects was wider than most, ranging from the usual portraits (including some of Russian officers and those painted by his brother George) to landscapes and representations of old and modern classics. He published 'The Milk Girl' after Gainsborough on 2 January 1832 (Plate 24) which carries the imprint of Ackermann and Tilt who were the real vendors. He engraved mezzotints on steel for *Gems of the Old Masters and Choice Selections for the Scrap Book*, published 1833–34, and altogether produced a considerable body of work in that medium.

James Egan (*c*.1799–1842) also died at a young age of consumption, which he fought for about eight years until he succumbed, leaving a widow and three children. The advertisement in the *Art Journal* (1842, p. 267) summarizes the sad facts of a life which had not been very pleasant:

MEZZOTINTS ON STEEL 77

24   The milk girl, mezzotinted by H.E. Dawe

CASE OF URGENT DISTRESS. — The attention of the generous and benevolent is earnestly entreated to the following case:— MR JAMES EGAN, the eminent mezzotinto engraver, died in the month of October, leaving three children, of the ages of 13, 11, and 7, utterly unprovided for. He had long struggled with difficulties in his profession, which he had just been enabled to overcome, having received the public approval, and that of the publishers, for his recent works, more especially for his engraving after Cattermole's 'English Hospitality in the Olden Time,' when death deprived his family of a protector, the Arts of a valuable assistant, and his friends of an associate, for whose amiable qualities and considerable talents they entertained the highest esteem and respect. Under these circumstances, public sympathy and assistance are earnestly applied for; and it is confidently hoped that aid will be supplied by the charitable, who appreciate British Art, in order that his young and interesting children may be rescued from present want and future misery.

Subscriptions for this truly benevolent purpose will be received by Mr. F. G. Moon, Threadneedle-street, publisher; Mr. A. W. Bailey, Cornhill, publisher; Messrs. Graves and Warmsly, 6, Pall-Mall, publishers; S. C. Hall, Esq., F.S.A., Barrister-at-Law, Rosery, Old Brompton; John Lucas, Esq., painter, 3, St. John's Wood-road, Regent's-park; Mr. C. E. Wagstaff, engraver, 14, Hastings-street, Burton-crescent; Mr. R. Lloyd, printer, Pear Tree Cottage, Holloway.

Born at Roscommon of humble parents, he came to England in 1825 and worked as a servant to S.W. Reynolds, for whom he was occasionally permitted to lay a ground, and gradually he learnt the whole art of mezzotint. He was not happy with Reynolds and left to set up a business of laying grounds for other engravers, but it provided only a meagre existence and through long hours and severe privation by 1834 he had developed consumption. He had married *circa* 1828, but his first successful plate 'Guilt and innocence' after John Herbert did not appear until 1835. Four plates after S.J.E. Jones, 'The young husband', 'The young wife', 'The Citation of Wycliffe', and 'The Tribunal inquisition' form a core to his work, taken largely from genre subjects, although he also did one or two portraits. His last, and probably his best, mezzotint was 'English hospitality in the olden time' after George Cattermole, and in a review published in the *Art Union* (1842, p. 17) 'the result of his labours cannot fail to be satisfactory to the publisher [Moon], who will be justified in consigning any picture to his hands, and this is no small advantage when, although we have so many mezzotint engravers, the number of artists of real power is very limited'. He was also described as 'undoubtedly the best artist in his particular department of the arts which that country [Ireland] had produced' (*Art Journal*, 1842, pp. 256–7).

Thomas Hodgetts (fl. 1801–46) was another of 'Turner's engravers', but is best known for his many mezzotint portraits; he was also a landscape painter. Examples of his work on steel are his very large plate of 'George IV' standing in Garter robes, after Sir Thomas Lawrence, published by

C1 Engraved title page vignette of W. Beattie's *Switzerland*, engraved by R. Wallis and hand coloured

C2   Mosaics of Olivetree and flowers from J. Ruskin's *The Stones of Venice*, engraved by J. C. Armytage

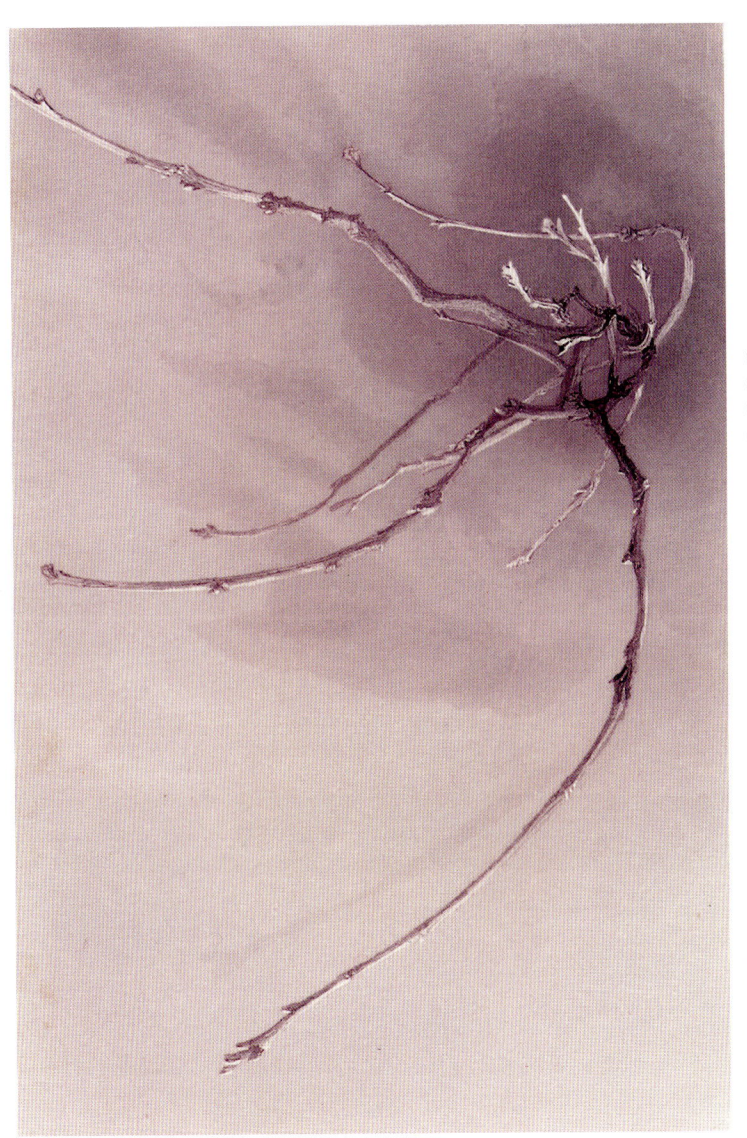

C3 The Dryad's Waywardness, from J. Ruskin's *Modern painters*, engraved by R. P. Cuff

C4   Canaan..., engraved by W. and A. K. Johnston, from *Bible* 1846

C5 Cryptonix coronatus, from W. Jardine's *The Natural history of game birds*, etched by W. H. Lizars and hand coloured

C6   Public promenade dress and Morning visiting dress from *The Ladies cabinet...*, Vol. IX, 1843
     Hand coloured

C7   Watercolour of Lumb Stocks at work, probably done by his son Arthur

C8　Watermeadow, etched by M. M. Ralph, printed from three separate steel plates

Colnaghi in June 1829, followed by 'Mrs. Waylett ...' after F. Meyer, published by William Sams in January 1830, which by contrast was a small oval engraving. 'The Right Hon. William Huskisson, MP.' after Richard Rothenwell was published by Colnaghi in 1832, and among his later prints, published in 1839, were portraits of 'Anne, Countess of Mornington' after her granddaughter Lady Burghersh, and 'The Duke of Cleveland' after A.W. Devis. His son assisted him in some of his plates, believed to be Robert M. Hodgetts (fl. 1820–40) who worked for a time from 1837 in Edinburgh. Thomas also worked on some plates with H.E. Dawe.

George Henry Phillips (*c.*1800–*c.*1852) is little known by his personal life, but he must have been acquainted with J.M.W. Turner by 1825 to have been asked to engrave 'Mouth of the river Humber' in 1826 and 'Arundel Castle on the river Arun' in 1827 for *Rivers of England*. Up to 1825 he exhibited landscapes and worked on miniatures, but had concentrated on mezzotint after that date. He was working for Moon, Boys and Graves by 1827, when he engraved a large plate of M.W. Sharp's 'The spoilt child', and two portraits after Sir Thomas Lawrence, 'Countess Gower and child' in 1830 and 'Lady Dover' in 1838 were typical of his work. He also did 'Lover's leap, Hastings' after Thomas Creswick for W.B. Cooke in 1832, which was almost Martinesque in appearance; Phillips in fact engraved some designs after Martin during the latter's lifetime. In 1844 he engraved Francis Danby's 'The opening of the sixth seal' which was used to provide a print to 2,250 subscribers in Bristol 'on the plan of the Art-Union'. Other prizes included the original painting and the engraved steel plate, which cost 650 gns, but '[the plate's] value after 2250 impressions are taken from it is not explained' (*Art Union*, January 1844, p. 20). Among his later plates was another with a Sussex setting, 'The Cricket match between Sussex and Kent at Brighton', after W. Drummond and C. Basébe, in 1849, and a pair of plates after Joseph J. Jenkins 'Baptism (the ministration of the Holy)' and 'The solemnization of matrimony (Church of England)', in 1852.

The four remaining engravers were eminent in their field, and had taken to steel for some of their work, although copper was perhaps their most familiar metal. Samuel William Reynolds (1773–1835) was a very experienced engraver at the top of his profession aged about 47 when steel was introduced, and might have been expected to continue in his use of copper. This seems not to have been the case since his pupil and assistant Samuel Cousins did all but one or two of his plates on steel, and Reynolds's second apprentice David Lucas also used steel, so the master could not have been unaffected. Cousins is reported to have remarked that the increase of commissions received by mezzotinters as a result of the introduction of steel led to Reynolds taking 'another pupil on the strength of it'. David Lucas was apprenticed in 1823.

Reynolds's earliest plate to be inscribed 'Engraved on steel' was 'Distant view of Rome from Tivoli' in 1823 for *Gems of Art*. Only one other plate was so inscribed, namely a portrait of Lady Georgina Agar-Ellis after J. Jackson, which shows mezzotint tones at their best, about a third being light tones and a quarter very dark ones typical of the method. He is described as 'Engraver to the King', a title he held from 1820. He also engraved ten more plates for *Gems of Art*, one-third of the total number, but probably much of the work was done by Cousins, who, after about nine years with the master, was still unable to put his name to more than a few plates each year. Reynolds, a rapid worker, was reputed to have engraved a full-length portrait in a day and a night, with not the best result. There must have been a hitch with the thirteenth plate for *Gems of Art*, advertised as 'A Magdalene' after Correggio, since a substitute was inserted.

Reynolds worked with William Say on a portrait of Napoleon, probably on steel. He was engaged on a series of 357 plates after the works of Sir Joshua Reynolds (with whom no relationship was clearly established) for which he travelled the country with Cousins, preparing copies and outlines from 1820 to 1826. Mezzotints were subsequently issued by Hodgson and Graves, such as 'The Fortune Teller' in 1836 (Plate 25) and the small portraits of the Kildares and Cathcarts in 1837 (Plate 26). One hundred and sixty-six plates may have been engraved on steel, mostly portraits, and at the sale of his effects on 18–20 April 1836, there were copper and steel plates, some plain, some grounded for mezzotint and others fully engraved. In June 1824 he published his plate of Charles Warren, the engraver who solved the problems of engraving on steel plates as opposed to blocks (Plate 27). The engraving was taken from a sculpted bust by William Behnes, an unusual use of mezzotint to reproduce a three-dimensional work of art. It is interesting to note that Malcolm Salaman in *Old English Mezzotints* (1910, p. 43) wrote that 'Fortunately ... Reynolds had done his best work before the fatal steel came near to killing the delicate and beautiful art', a pessimism not supported by the subsequent upsurge in mezzotint.

His son Samuel William Reynolds (1794–1872), was originally a portrait painter, some of whose works his father mezzotinted, but as Samuel the elder's health deteriorated, Samuel junior finished the outstanding plates, and in due course became so proficient that he took up mezzotinting on his own. Approximately 90 plates can be attributed to him, possibly on steel, issued between *circa* 1836 and 1846. 'George Granville, Duke and Earl of Sutherland' was a private plate of his, published in 1839 by William Walker, who also assisted in its engraving (Plate 28).

William Walker (1791–1867) was a Scottish line engraver, who was taught mezzotinting by Thomas Lupton, and married Reynolds's daughter Elizabeth in 1829. This was an example of how line engravers came to

25   The Fortune teller, mezzotinted by S.W. Reynolds

terms with competition from mezzotinters, and of collaboration between two branches of the profession. Later in the century, Walker set up his own photographic business, with an eye to the future of illustration processes. Elizabeth was a mezzotinter of some ability, helping her husband with some of his plates.

William Say (1768–1834) had been trained in mezzotint by James Ward (1765–1859), and in 1807 had been appointed engraver to the Duke of Gloucester. He had been practising for about 35 years when he was among the first to use steel and he went on to engrave more portraits and landscape plates. Examples of his work are 'Belinda at her toilet' after Henry Fradella, published by Colnaghi, 'Lamentations over the dead Christ' after Caracci, published by W.B. Cooke and 'Sir William Curtis, Bart.' after Sir Thomas

26 Four portraits of the Kildares and Cathcarts, mezzotinted by S.W. Reynolds

Lawrence, published 1 June 1831 by the engraver. Among his last work were three mezzotints printed in colour by James Lahee, probably by the painted plate method, using red, blue and black. These were illustrations to Sir John Ross's *Narrative of a Second Voyage in Search of a North-West Passage ...* (1835) (Plate 29).

Charles Turner (1774–1857) was finally encouraged to try steel again in

27   Charles Warren's bust after Behnes, mezzotinted by S.W. Reynolds

1821, and his first published plate in the metal was 'John Jervis, Earl of St. Vincent' after C. Carbonnier, the frontispiece to Volume 1 of Edward Brenton's *The Naval History of Great Britain* (1823–25). It was dated 6 December 1822 and was the first of 61 known steel engravings, some, like this, stated on the print to be such, with a possible 183 which also could be on steel. This is out of a total of 921 known engravings, not all of which are

28   George Granville, mezzotinted by S.W. Reynolds, jun.

mezzotints. His *Gems of Art* and *Rivers of England* plates took up some of his time in 1823, but he also engraved 'Pierce Egan' after George Sharples, 1 February 1823, and on 19 June 1823 the pair of prints after Sir Joshua Reynolds were published, namely 'The Mask' [Ladies Charlotte and Anne Spencer] and 'The Fortune Teller' [Lord Henry and Lady Charlotte

29   Felix Harbour, colour mezzotint by W. Say

Spencer]. The later states of these plates had the words 'on steel' suppressed, perhaps because the public had become familiar with its use, but Whitman, in *Charles Turner* (1907) observes that 'it was thought prudent to conceal from the public that the subjects were engraved on the harder metal' (p. 16). The increased number of impressions had destroyed the rarity value of the prints, and thus appealed less to collectors. Mezzotint steel engraving was introduced to a different audience when Turner engraved on steel a portrait he had engraved on copper on 8 September 1817, that of Jane Bowles after Sir Joshua Reynolds, and painted in 1775. The steel engraving was presented by R.H. Solly, Chairman of the Committee of Polite Arts of the Society of Arts to the members through Volume 42 of their *Transactions* (May 1824).

Turner published his own plates from 50 Warren St, Fitzroy Square, although Colnaghi is named as co-publisher on occasions. Regarded as one of the most prolific mezzotint engravers of his time, Turner's plates were truly mixed method, including the use of etching and aquatint to finish the plate, knitting the work together and improving the final result. His was a nervous personality, liable to be short-tempered, exacerbated perhaps by his infirmity of a club foot. His 19-year-old feud with J.M.W. Turner (no relation) over payment for *Liber Studiorum* plates is indicative of his relationships with other people. Ironically, one of his last steel plates was a portrait of the great painter dated 31 July 1856. His impressions and plates were sold at Sothebys in a sale which commenced on 8 February 1857 and lasted for a week. He had prepared a rather inaccurate list of his own plates up to 1845.

William Ward (1766–1826) was in his mid-fifties when steel was introduced, and had a high reputation as a mezzotint engraver, exemplified by two royal appointments and an ARA, conferred in 1814. Two of his mezzotint portraits had appeared in Cooke's first exhibition of engravings in 1821, and he used steel for five plates, which were to be some of his last work in *Gems of Art*. The plates were 'Angels', 'Meditation', and 'The Gipsey fortune teller', all after Sir Joshua Reynolds, 'Laughing boy' after Murillo, and 'Christ in the garden' after Correggio, which is inscribed 'Engraved on steel by W. Ward ARA' (Plate 21).

His mantle descended upon his son William James Ward (1800?–40), whose ability as a mezzotinter equalled, if not surpassed that of his father. He came from a family steeped in artistic tradition. His mother Marie was George Morland's sister (George had married Anne, William Ward's sister), and his cousin married John Jackson RA. He obtained Society of Arts medals as a teenager, and in his early twenties he joined his father in the 1821 Cooke exhibition where by his one plate he was known as W. Ward jun. His second name was rarely used, which has led to some confusion in the attribution of plates. He also seems to have taken to steel early on. His portrait of 'HRH the Duke of Sussex, Grand Master of the United … Masons' after G.H. Harlowe, published on 10 February 1825 was 'Engraved on steel' and published by William Sams. Other portraits and genre subjects followed, and in 1830 he was made Engraver to HRH the Duke of Clarence, who extended the appointment in 1836 to Engraver to HM King William IV. Ward's life was prematurely ended by the effects of insanity which overtook him some time before his death, due, it was said, to his odd and dangerous custom of rising from a warm bed and immediately plunging into a cold bath every day throughout the year (*Art Union*, March 1840, p. 39).

Another member of the family was George Raphael Ward (1797–1849), son and pupil of James Ward (1769–1859), the younger brother of William Ward. Although a miniaturist, he was best known as a portrait engraver, and examples of his work include 'Sir William Follett' after F.H. Say, published by McLean in 1843, and a private plate of William Mackenzie after T.H. Illidge in 1847. In a review of the portrait of the 'Marquis of Granby' after Francis Grant it was said that 'as an engraver of portraits, there are none who surpass him' (*Art Union*, 1847, p. 392).

The second group of engravers started their careers during the time steel was being used, and many were line engravers who changed over to mezzotint, largely because more money was to be made with the publishers of prints, where a mezzotint plate could be finished more rapidly than one in line.

Thomas Lewis Atkinson (1817–*c*1890) was the only pupil taken by Samuel Cousins, and after seven years' apprenticeship, he worked first for Graves, although many of the leading publishers appeared in his large list of prints. The first plate to attract attention was 'Feeding the horses' after J.F. Herring in 1848, of which the *Art Union* said 'Mr. Atkinson's name is new to us; if this be his first appearance as an engraver, it is a highly successful one' (*Art Union*, 1848, p. 260). He helped with 'Peace' after Landseer in 1848, engraved by Frederick Stacpoole, whose first plate it was. His daughter Alma married the painter Valentine W. Bromley on 17 December 1873; the latter's 'Goddess Flora' was engraved by his father-in-law and published by McLean in 1877. He was well thought of to the extent that his name was put forward for election to the Royal Academy in 1873, but was not appointed. When W.H. Simmons died in June 1882 he left Rosa Bonheur's 'The lion at home' in an etched state. Atkinson was asked to finish it and it was published by Lefèvre in 1884. He engraved a number of plates after Landseer. For two of his plates after Millais, published by Thomas MacLean, he was assisted by Samuel Cousins. They were 'Little Miss Muffet', in 1885 and 'Perfect bliss' in 1866.

Samuel Bellin (1799–1894) started his career as a line engraver, having been trained by James Basire II. During the 1830s he turned over to mixed mezzotint and in 1843 produced 'Charles V in the studio of Titian' after Fiske for the Royal Birmingham and Midland Counties Art Union. Three mezzotint plates in 1845 brought favourable notices. 'Bellin bids fair to succeed Cousins, the best mezzotinter of the age' (*Art Union*, 1845, p. 136). One of these plates was 'HRH Prince Albert' after Lucas, published by Boys, which was jointly engraved by Bellin and Cousins, and again 'Confidence' and 'Diffidence', after R. Hannah, published by William Spooner were said to be '2 prints which will go far to establish the high reputation which Mr. Bellin has already acquired and confirm his position as one of the best artists of our English school' (*Art Union*, 1845, p. 324). Several plates after Frank Stone included 'Cross purposes' and 'Children playing with flowers' after E. Magnus which were both published by Boys in 1846. Bellin retired in 1889.

Samuel Cousins (1801–87) was by far the greatest and most influential of steel mezzotinters in this group. Born into an Exeter family of nine children, he showed great promise in drawing portraits from the age of seven, some of which were exhibited in a shop window. At the age of 11, his work was seen by Captain T.M. Bagnold who bought some, and sent them to the Society of Arts which awarded him a Silver Palette for one of them, and a drawing of Magdalen brought him the Silver Isis medal in 1814. S.W. Reynolds saw these drawings and offered to take Cousins on as an apprentice without a premium, which he did in October 1814, and at the end of seven years, in 1821, Cousins was employed as an assistant for another four years, during which time his name appeared on all the plates he had worked on. Of 61 eligible plates, his name is on only 11.

Cousins's first independent plate was one of his few on copper and was after Sir Thomas Lawrence, then President of the Royal Academy, who was so impressed by his work that he offered Cousins an exclusive contract to work for him. Cousins refused, but did engrave 33 plates after Lawrence before the painter's death in 1830. One of these plates was the famous portrait of Mrs Peel, of which Lawrence wrote on 7 November 1828:

> The print is far from doing justice to her beauty, nor does it to its attempted resemblance in my picture. The engraver makes excuses from the difficulty of the task, and the exceeding hardness of the steel plate, over which, he says, he had no control. He is, however, the first engraver in this delicate style of engraving, and has produced, I think, an admirable print, though the essence of the work be lost. I have been vexed and irritated by its having been exhibited in the print shops before proofs being sent to me ... (Williams)

and he must have been further so when J.M.W. Turner wrote to him: 'When I got off the coach at Hastings the other day, a woman came up with a basket of your "Mrs. Peel" and wanted to sell me one for sixpence' (Rawlinson, Vol. 1 p. xl). Cousins's view of steel came in a letter dated 19 February 1824:

> The increase of employment which has lately been thrown into the hands of the mezzotint engravers by the introduction of steel plates, has not only given us work which before went to the line engravers, but has encouraged men to speculate and publish extensive works in mezzotint, which have been successful from their good execution, and the cheap rate at which they can be produced. In consequence of this revolution in our art, more engravers in our line are wanted. (Whitman, A. *Samuel Cousins*, p. 34)

The majority of his work was portraits, but he did 11 after Sir Edwin Landseer's paintings, dating from 1837 to 1862, one of the best known of which was 'Bolton Abbey in the olden time', published 9 May 1837 by Thomas Boys. The picture was at Chatsworth, owned by the Duke of Devonshire, who would not let Cousins get near it, so he had to stand some distance away to do a reducing of a picture hung approximately 8 feet from the floor. There was some trouble in working the plate, and the engraver had to re-work it in 1840 in order to meet demand. It was repaired by Charles Tomkins (*c*.1812–*c*.1903) in 1858. His 'Queen receiving sacrament at her coronation' after C.R. Leslie was published by Moon, who intended to make it one of the largest prints ever engraved, and its eventual size was 43⅝ in. × 22¾ in. 'Beauty's bath' after Landseer, published by Graves was the first print to be stamped by the Printseller's Association. As the stamp had not arrived by 17 March 1847, and impressions were needed urgently, the first few were signed in pencil by the secretary, W. Walter and later impressions were stamped normally. Another of Landseer's plates was 'Midsummer night's dream' which was issued in 1857 (Plate 30). A later plate was perhaps more typical of his subjects. 'New laid eggs' after John Millais was published by Agnew on 1 March 1875 (Plate 31). A proof copy of this is in the collection of the engraver Lumb Stocks and was inscribed 'To Lumb Stocks Esqre, R.A. from S. Cousins' (Plate 32). This illustrates the exchange of proof copies between engravers, and other prints in the collection indicate some kind of relationship between them. 'With A. Willmore [*sic*] best wishes, 1869', J.B. Allen's 'Kind respects', 'J.T. Willmore's regards' and 'S. Fisher's compliments' are typical.

The fate of Cousins's original plates varied, for example that of his portrait of Shakespeare for the Shakespeare Society, in November 1848, was doomed to destruction by the council after the required numbers had been

30   Midsummer night's dream, mezzotinted by S. Cousins

31 New laid eggs, mezzotinted by S. Cousins

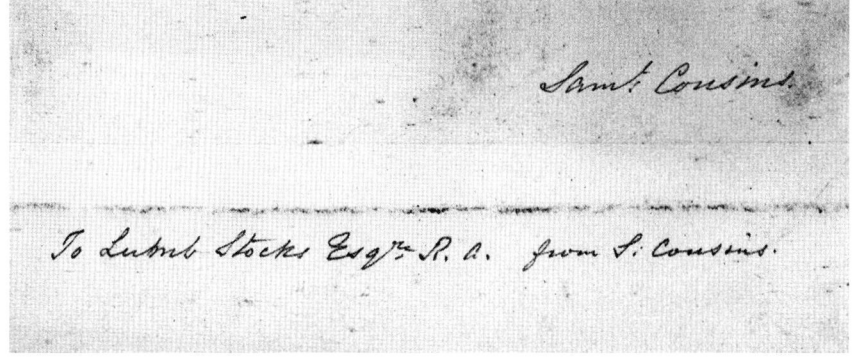

32   Inscription on a proof impression of a mezzotint plate

taken off. At least two plates had been acquired by Leggatt Bros, who were still printing from them in the 1890s, and in another case, the steel plate was in the possession of the original owner of the picture. Other plates were in existence in the 20th century, from which prints could still be taken. 'Mrs. Bradyll' after Reynolds was originally published in 1848, printed by Dixon and Ross and the plate sold to Graves in the 1860s, who ordered more copies which were badly printed by an assistant. Graves sent for Dixon and requested that he print them personally, and about 100 impressions were taken. In all, approximately 230 steel engravings can be attributed to him. Cousins, said usually to be kind and gentle, had his difficult moment with the printers. A curt letter dated 13 October 1862 announced to William McQueen that Henry Graves had insisted that the plate of 'The Maid and magpie' be given to Dixon. Graves complained 'and *with reason*, I think, of the manner in which you printed the plate of Lord Clyde' (McQueen letter file No. 18).

Many of Cousins's plates were etched by Benjamin Phelps Gibbon (1802–51), and he worked with his younger brother, Henry Cousins (c.1809–64), on several plates from 1826, including 'Thomas Campbell' after Lawrence, 1834. William Walker (his master's son-in-law) etched and published 'Daniel Sandford, D.D.' after J.W. Gordon, on 11 March 1829, and etched 'Robert Burns' after Nasmyth in 1830. Samuel Cousins was the first 19th-century engraver to be admitted to full honours of Royal Academician in 1855. This was a year after he had received a commission from the French Emperor to engrave Franz Winterhalter's portrait of Napoleon III, for which he was awarded the Légion d'honneur and a special gold medal as 'Graveur étranger'. By 1874 he was a member of the Royal Academy Council and their Hanging Committee, and he retired from the

RA in 1880. He died on Saturday 7 May 1887, and left his engraved plates, proofs and prints to his sister Susan, with whom he lived. He bequeathed £115,000 to the Royal Academy to be invested to provide annuities of not more than £80 each to needy artists of merit. His last work was a portrait of himself after Edwin Long, published on 9 May 1884 by the Fine Art Society. This is the second plate published on his birthday, because 'Bolton Abbey ...' was delayed, so that apart from about eight impressions, they were all dated on his birthday.

Henry Cousins (c.1809–64) lived under the shadow of his elder brother. He worked largely on portraits, e.g. 'Isambard Kingdom Brunel' after J.C. Horsley, 'Henry Hallam' after Thomas Phillips and 'Henry Liverseege' after W. Bradley. He also engraved after Landseer, 'La Sieste' after Winterhalter, and 'Vittoria d'Albano' after H. Vernet.

William Turner Davey (1818–c.1890) was taught by the line engraver Charles Rolls but, after experiments with lithography and other engraving techniques, finally settled on mixed mezzotint from *circa* 1847, when he engraved a pair of plates after John Herring, 'Labour' and 'Rest'. 'Eastward Ho, August 1857' and 'Home again, 1858' after Henry O'Neil were published by Moore, McQueen and Co. in 1864, and he combined with William Giller (1805–c.1868) to produce four plates of 'The Seasons' after William Hopkins in 1866.

William Overend Geller (1804–81) was the son of a house painter in Bradford, and is recorded as having taught himself steel and wood engraving when he was very young, and in turn, taught his brother James. In 1823 he spent some time with a relation in London and practised his painting there, but he had to return to help his father in Bradford. In 1827 with J.C. Bentley and three others, he started an art exhibition which lasted only five months. His first finished plate was a portrait of Revd Henry Heap, Vicar of Bradford, in 1832, but sales were poor. He employed a man to hawk prints round the streets, but met with comments such as 'he could see the original everyday' and 'he would not give three halfpence for it!' By this time he was married with a family and had engraved two more religious portraits, but Bradford could not support the arts, and in May 1833 Geller moved to London. There he met John Martin, J.C. Bentley and John Cousen (the latter two also from Bradford), and soon he was accepted as a mezzotinter of some merit.

Most of the works Geller published by himself did not do very well, such as the portrait of Thomas Campbell after Thompson in 1847, despite critical acclaim. He found the print publishers better able to provide him a living, among those so issued were 'Hon. Mrs. Norton' after John Hayter, in 1835, 'The Chief's companions' in 1841 and 'Favourites' in 1844, both after Landseer, published by Moon, 'Slave market, Constantinople' after

William Allen, etched by Charles Lewis in 1843 and 'Poor teacher' after R. Redgrave, published by Boys in 1845. 'Cymon and Iphigenia' after Reynolds was etched by F. Howard and printed in colours, but his best plate was considered to be 'The deathbed of Calvin' after Hornung, a Swiss artist. Of this plate, his daughter Angelina recalled that his anxiety and close application brought on a very serious illness. His doctor observed 'take care it is not *your* death bed' (*Bradford Antiquary*, 1895, vol. 2, p. 201). 'Benjamin Franklin at the court of France in 1786, receiving the homage of his genius and the recognition of his country's advent amongst the nations' after Baron Jolly of Brussels took him two years to engrave. It was done for Jay, Heidenberg and Emmerson of Philadelphia, and Geller afterwards sent six artists to colour impressions, among whom was his son William Henry, who sailed from Liverpool on the *City of Glasgow* in March 1854, never to be seen again. One of Geller's last plates was 'Burns at the plough' after Charles Hancock in 1857. He moved to Scarborough in 1867 to work for several years for Mr Sarony, an eminent photographer, but turned to painting for the rest of his life, exhibiting a few works from 1871 to 1875. He died 4 August 1881 in his seventy-eighth year, and was buried in Scarborough cemetery (*Bradford Antiquary*, 1895, vol. 2, pp. 200–3; *Yorkshireman*, August 1895, pp. 74–6).

The Art Unions in their early days employed mezzotinters until the number of subscribers exceeded the number of good copies a steel plate could produce. The first ever mezzotint plate prepared for a British Art Union was 'The taking down from the Cross' after David Scott in 1835, engraved by Robert M. Hodgetts (fl. 1820–40) for the second year of the [Royal] Association for the Promotion of the Fine Arts in Scotland. This supplied 1,300 members, but in the fourth year there were 2,800 members, for whom a line engraving was substituted. Geller engraved 'A Camaldolese monk showing the relics in the Sacristy of his convent at Rome' after William Simson for the Art Union of London's second year 1837–38, for which the Union set aside 150 gns. Mezzotint had the advantage of being engraved quite quickly where half of the engraver's work in grounding the plates was done by assistants, and thus deadlines could be met more easily. Line engravers could spend several years in the production of a single plate. The first print for the Royal Irish Art Union was 'Blind girl at the Holy Well' after T.W. Burton, engraved by Henry Thomas Ryall (1811–67) in a mixed method with the sky being mezzotinted. When just over 1,300 copies had been taken the plate was to be destroyed so that poor copies could not be printed, in order to keep faith with the subscribers.

Charles George Lewis (1808–80), member of a well-known artistic family, is equally renowned for his line engravings as for his mezzotints. He achieved a reputation among two publics, one by a series of 24 line engravings for the *Art Journal* from 1867 to 1882, of which 18 were after Landseer, and the other which patronized the printsellers. Prints included 'Grace Darling' after Parker, published by Ackermann in 1839, 'The first introduction of Christianity into Great Britain' after J.R. Herbert, published by Gambart in 1847, 'Shoeing the horse' after Landseer, published by Moon in 1848, 'The Allied generals with the officers of their respective regiments before Sebastopol' after T.J. Barker, published by Agnew in 1859 and 'Otters and Salmon' after Landseer, published by McQueen in 1871. These examples spread over the period of his work, illustrate his devotion to Landseer, and the variety of publishers from whom he obtained commissions. His relationships with artists and publishers were not always harmonious as, for example, his disagreements with Landseer and Graves, which may have been due, among other things, to his dilatory approach to his work, since 'Waterloo heroes' after J.P. Knight was three years in his hands before publication by Graves in 1845. He retired to Felpham near Bognor in 1877, and died of apoplexy while throwing money to a street band in June 1880.

David Lucas (1802–81) is considered by some to be among the most eminent of steel mezzotint engravers, and he is usually called 'Constable's engraver'. The son of a farmer at Brigstock, Northamptonshire, at the age of 19 his drawings were being hung in the local inn where they were seen by Samuel William Reynolds on one of his many journeys about the country. Since steel in 1823 was increasing the work available to mezzotint engravers, Reynolds was looking for another pupil, and offered the post to Lucas on payment of a ten shilling premium, which was very low, although Cousins had been taken on without a premium. Lucas was only two years into his seven-year indenture when Reynolds went off to Paris, and it was during the five years between 1825 and 1830 that he met John Constable, with whom he formed a partnership in 1829 to produce the celebrated series of 22 mezzotints under the title of *Various Subjects of Landscape, Characteristic of English Scenery* (published in five parts, 1830–32). The first four parts each contained four prints and the fifth contained six prints. Despite the masterly interpretation of Constable's work, due in no small measure to the close co-operation between artist and engraver, it was not a successful publication, although a second edition came out in May 1833.

Another series was planned when Constable died in 1837, and although F.G. Moon published six of the plates destined for this 'Appendix' in 1838, Lucas did not publish *A New Series of Engravings of English Landscape*, comprising 14 engravings, until 1845. This, too, was unsuccessful. One plate went rusty and had to be abandoned. So few copies of the original publication had been sold by 1843 that the artist's daughter Maria was able to supply the publisher James Carpenter with 186 sets (4,092 prints) to illustrate

Charles R. Leslie's *Memoirs of John Constable*. Lucas employed his brother Alfred to help with the printing, and used both black and brown inks, the latter lightening the dark tones closer to the original intention of the artist. Plates were published either by Samuel Hollyer or Constable himself, but in 1855, Henry G. Bohn had come into possession of the plates and issued *English Landscape Scenery. A Series of Forty Mezzotint Engravings on Steel . . . from Pictures Painted by John Constable R.A.* Of his larger single plates after Constable, the best are probably 'The Cornfield' of 1834, 'Salisbury Cathedral' of 1837 and 'Vale of Dedham' of 1839. 'Heroic action of Grace Darling' after Parker and Carmichael was published by Moon in 1839. For the Art Union of London, he engraved 'River scene, Devonshire' after Lee in 1839. He also did some portraits, and paintings after Gainsborough and W.P. Williams, as well as landscapes after J.D. Harding and other artists. By about 1850 he had virtually abandoned engraving, and took to drink, which eventually brought him to Felpham Workhouse, where he died. His great achievement was to form a unique collaboration with a great artist to produce prints of individual character.

Thomas Goff Lupton's (1791–1873) work as an early exponent of steel mezzotints has already been mentioned earlier in this chapter, but he went on to produce a considerable body of work of all kinds. His father, working as a goldsmith in Clerkenwell, no doubt influenced his son's decision to be apprenticed in 1805 at the age of 14 to George Clint, a mezzotint engraver. As a boy Thomas showed an interest in drawing, was at the heart of the mezzotint movement when it 'discovered' steel and continued to produce a number of plates which were primarily for local publication, for example: 'King William the Fourth' after Clint, published in Brighton by William Sams, Royal Library, 1 St James's Street, in May 1834; a portrait of the Marquess of Westminster, after William Jones of Chester, published by Seacome, Chester, and Ackermann, London, in 1839; 'Northumberland Hunt' after Snow, published by Currie and Bowman, Newcastle, in 1840. In 1833 he mezzotinted six plates after the Revd Edward Bury to illustrate a poem by Lady Charlotte Bury, entitled *The Three Great Sanctuaries of Tuscany, Valombrosa, Camaldoli, Laverna; a Poem with Historical and Legendary Notices . . .* published by John Murray in an oblong quarto format. He became President of the Artists' Annuity Fund in 1836, and during this time, took on a pupil, William Oakley Burgess (1818–44). 'The widow, or adieu to the weeds' after H. Richter was published by Moon, Boys, in 1833, 'Melancthon's first misgiving' after G. Lance was published by Leggatt in 1840, 'Bandits disputing' after George Cattermole, was published by Ackermann in 1840, and 'His Grace the Duke of Wellington' after H.P. Briggs was published by Colnaghi in 1840. The advertisement from the *Art Journal* (July 1840, p. 120) is as follows:

> Messrs. C. and P. have the honour likewise to announce, that in the course of the present Month they will have ready for Publication, a
>
> HIGHLY-FINISHED FULL-LENGTH PRINT OF
>
> ## HIS GRACE THE DUKE OF WELLINGTON,
>
> Engraved in Mezzotinto on Steel, by Mr. LUPTON, from the admirable Portrait, painted in March last for the Town of Sheffield, by H. P. BRIGGS, Esq., R.A.
>
> In announcing the Engraving from this very fine Picture, the Publishers feel justified in stating that, as a Likeness of his Grace, it is equalled only by Sir Thomas Lawrence's celebrated Picture in the Collection of the Right Honourable Charles Arbuthnot, painted in 1823
>
> Prints. £1 1s.   Proofs, £2 2s.   First Proofs, £3 3s.
>
> Names of Subscribers received by
> MESSRS. COLNAGHI AND PUCKLE, 23, COCKSPUR-STREET.

London:– Printed by PALMER and CLAYTON, 9, Crane-court, Fleet-street; and Published by WILLIAM WEST, at the Art-Union Office, No. 1, Catherine-street, Strand,–Wednesday, July 15 1840.

He became acquainted with John Ruskin in the 1850s, and mezzotinted some plates for his books, notably *The Stones of Venice* (1851–53), which in turn introduced him to George Allen (1832–1907). Allen had attended Ruskin's drawing lessons at the Working Men's College in 1854, became his assistant, and was recommended to learn mezzotint engraving from Lupton. The original plates of *The Stones* ... were still being used for the third edition, in 1874, 'of which I sign each with my own hand, certifying it as containing the best states of the old plates now procurable' and he explained that 'The state of the old plates, which the death of my very dear friend Thomas Lupton prevents me from retouching, compels me in justice to the purchasers, to limit the present edition to 1500 copies ...' (Preface to the 1874 edition). The mezzotints in the fourth edition, in 1886, published by George Allen were re-engraved by him and, with one exception, carried his name, together with that of the etcher T. Boys. Plate III of volume III still carried Lupton's name, however, so it was probably still the old plate, retouched by Allen (Plate 33). Although Lupton must have retouched earlier plates, it seems that his original work had ceased during the 1850s, because the *Art Journal* obituary (1873, p. 203) begins: 'It is a long time since the name of this distinguished mezzotint engraver appeared in association with any print, that it can scarcely be known by the present generation.' His work was characterized by the use of a lighter black ink, which

33 Noble and ignoble grotesque, from Ruskin's *The Stones of Venice*

offset the charge of hardness sometimes levelled at steel plate prints, but at the same time, he achieved a brightness which made his prints pleasant to look at. Lupton died 18 May 1873 in his eighty-third year.

William Henry Simmons (1811–82) was one of the more prolific engravers of his time, as well as having the good fortune to engrave what became some of the most popular works of the Victorian era. He averaged approximately three major plates a year in the 1870s and is likely to have produced nearly 150 in his working life. Apprenticed to William Finden in the late 1820s, he had taken mezzotint as his chief means of expression by about 1836, but returned to line for 'The Light of the World' after Holman Hunt in 1860 for example. He probably found that working for the print publishers was more congenial and lucrative than for the book publishers, but it took some time before his talent was recognized. By 1843, his engraving of Grant's 'The Shooting party', published by Graves, achieved a review in the *Art Journal*, in 1861 'The first lesson in navigation' after John C. Hook appeared and in 1863 J.D. Luard's 'The welcome arrival' and 'Nearing home', published by Moore, McQueen and Co. gained him the comment that 'Mr. Simmons ... now takes rank with the best of our mezzotint engravers'; (*Art Journal*, 1863, p. 32). It had taken 20 years to achieve this accolade, but after that, he became one of the most sought after engravers of the period. Two engravings after T.F. Faed, 'The milk maid' and 'The orange girl' started the publishing career of Messrs. Brooks in 1864, and in 1870 he finished engraving William P. Frith's 'Marriage of the Prince and Princess of Wales'. Graves the publisher inherited a problem by purchasing the picture, plate and subscription list from Mr Flatou, who had done a special deal with a picture dealer in the Strand to exchange two pictures (sold at Christies for £49) for 200 guineas worth of proofs, a claim he had to go to court to establish against Flatou's widow and the new owner. An example of Simmons's portrait engraving was that of 'Anne, Duchess of Cumberland' after Gainsborough, published by Graves in 1870. In 1877 he was elected to the Graphic Society, and had exhibited regularly at the Royal Academy from 1857 to 1882. In 1880 he received a second prize at the Sydney Exhibition. 'Old monarch' after Rosa Bonheur was published by L.H. Lefèvre in 1881, and he was engaged on the same artist's 'Lion at home' when he died, and it was finished by T.L. Atkinson.

By the 1840s, mixed mezzotint was employed by a number of artists whose works have achieved very little notice and yet who produced some good work. One such is Richard Evan Sly (fl. 1842), a London engraver who mezzotinted a painting by James M. Scrymgeour of the Rev. John Harris DD (author of *The Great Teacher, The Great Commission*, etc.), and dedicated it to the Trustees and Treasurer of Cheshunt College. This work was published by Thomas Ward in December 1842, and is a proof signed by the

34   The Rev. John Harris, DD, mezzotinted by R.E. Sly

subject. When found by the author in a 'junk' shop, it was folded several times, torn and with small pieces missing, hence its present appearance (Plate 34).

Although authorities disagree about some details of his life, it would seem that Charles Algernon Tomkins was born about 1821 and died about 1903. It is possible that he was related to the earlier generation of engravers represented by Peltro William Tomkins (1760–1840), so that his interest in mezzotint engraving could have its roots in the 18th century. His first important plate was published in 1849 and strictly he should be considered in the third group of engravers, but his work was largely unaffected by most of the factors which characterized that group, and he is much more at home in this second group, whose work he carried on to the end of the 19th century. His first significant plate was 'Taking the veil' after Thomas Uwins in 1849, and he went on to produce nearly 100 plates for the print publishers, such as 'H.R.H. the Duke of Gloucester' after Sir Joshua Reynolds, published by Graves in 1863, 'The little rake' after Eden U. Eddis published by McQueen in 1874, and his considerable work after Landseer is represented by the famous 'Dignity and impudence' of 1884. He also did a few plates for Ruskin such as 'Truth and Untruth of Stones' after Turner and Claude, printed in brown and used to illustrate John Ruskin's *Modern Painters*. In the 1888 edition the plate appears in Volume 4, p. 315 (Plate 35). He exhibited six plates at the Royal Academy between 1872 and 1897, and was elected ARA in 1899. Among his last plates was 'Maidens at the well' after Herman Philips in 1893.

Tomkins married in his mid-twenties and had a son Charles John (1847–*c.*1900), who was probably his pupil in mezzotint engraving. He followed his father in the production of portraits, genre subjects and works after Landseer, but was by no means as prolific, achieving only a third of his father's output. His earliest important plate was 'By appointment' in 1876, which was the first of 12 exhibited at the Royal Academy until 1892. His last work was an original mezzotint 'Queen Victoria' in 1897. Father and son's output ended almost at the same time, due probably to the eventual collapse of the market for reproductive mezzotints.

The third group of mezzotint engravers was a second generation to whom steel was a natural medium for the art, but they were not always convinced that the hard physical work in engraving the steel was necessary. Etching and the continental use of widely spaced lines were largely used by this new generation, but other factors made themselves felt. By *circa* 1850 there was not the shortage of copper which earlier had made steel more attractive, and from about 1860 electroplating considerably lengthened the life of plates, as well as the use of electrotypes which themselves could be steel-faced. This removed at a stroke the pre-eminence of steel, although

MEZZOTINTS ON STEEL 101

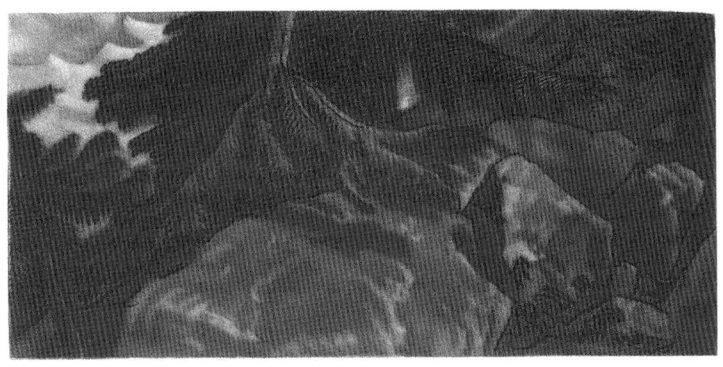

Turner and Claude. C.A.Tomkins.

49. Truth and Untruth of Stones.

35 Truth and untruth of stones, from Ruskin's *Modern painters*, mezzotinted by C.A. Tomkins, printed in brown

there were arguments as to the quality of prints, due partly to the granular nature of an electrostatic deposition. In this period, therefore, it is very difficult to establish, in the absence of the plate itself, which prints were done from steel or steel-faced plates. Moreover, as with etching, the artistic community had re-discovered mezzotint as an original process, and since artistic results were preferred to long runs, the need for steel plates was further eroded. This view took some time to spread, and it has been said that artists and engravers had lost the art of engraving on copper. The division between the artistic and reproductive engravers was emphasized in 1880 by the establishment of the Royal Society of Painter-Etchers and Engravers, followed by the foundation of the Society of Mezzotint Engravers sometime afterwards by Gerald Philip Robinson (1858–1942), who was Mezzotint Engraver to Queen Victoria from 1890, and to King Edward VII from 1901. He was the first President of the Society, and the Royal Society feared that the reproductive engravers might secede to the new body, but for a number of reasons they need not have worried. The Society of Mezzotinters appears to have had only a short life, and nobody among contemporary mezzotint engravers seems to have heard of it.

Most publishers issued mezzotints, but the firm taken over in 1785 by Paul Colnaghi (1751–1833) concentrated more on that form than any other. Paul left Milan to evade the consequences of his father's debt-ridden estate after the latter's death in 1783, and resided first in Paris, then in London. Anthony Torre took Paul into his printselling business in 1785 and by 1788 Paul was in sole command of it. The French Revolution and Napoleonic Wars hit the print trade badly, since none could be exported to France, but Colnaghi survived by issuing the very popular 'Cries of London' and stipple works by Francesco Bartolozzi. He became printseller to the Prince Regent and other members of the Royal Family, was naturalized, married and had two sons, Dominic (1790–1879) and Martin (d. 1851). By 1824 Martin had split the family by his unfortunate behaviour. His debts were paid by his father, but bankruptcy was no stranger to him in later days. Paul and Dominic moved into 14 Pall Mall East, and Martin stayed at 23 Cockspur Street not far away and continued on his own for some years. When Paul died, Dominic took over with his sister Caroline, and the firm was then known as P. and D. Colnaghi. Its most celebrated mezzotint publication on steel was a series of portraits of 'Royal and noble ladies'. They published the works of Samuel Cousins and David Lucas, and by the 1870s the firm was thought to be the chief publisher of mezzotints, with the possible exception of Mrs Jane Noseda in the Strand. Martin was not so heavily involved in print production, and a statement that the firm was dissolved and taken over by Hodgson and Graves in February 1839, was followed in October of the same year by another that a firm of Colnaghi and Puckle, 23

Cockspur Street, printseller to HM the Queen, the Queen Dowager, HRH the Duchess of Kent etc. announced 'an illuminated history of the Eglinton Tournament' (*Art Union*, 1839, pp. 13, 149, 175). Martin had evidently obtained enough capital by the sale of his old stock to Hodgson and Graves to attract a new partner and start again.

Henry Graves embarked on a notable mezzotint venture with his complete works of Gainsborough when the fire at his premises in 1867 found 20 pictures by the artist by good fortune in the hands of the engravers, and another eight, which had featured in a recent National Portrait Exhibition, were rescued at great risk to the staff and taken to the Senior United Services Club opposite for safe keeping. Publication of the undertaking was announced in 1873.

Modern studies credit Thomas Gooch Appleton (1854–1924) and Henry T. Greenhead (1849–1926) with the 'revival' of the art of mezzotint, inasmuch as they went back to the late 18th and early 19th century for their inspiration in connection with the portraits chiefly engraved for the print publishers. Samuel Cousins's 'The Strawberry girl' after Reynolds in 1873 was considered to be the first of the new trend. Appleton's earliest important plate was 'The Rosary' after Luke Fildes in 1876, and the following year he sent the first of 14 engravings to the Royal Academy. Typical of his portrait work is that of Mary Amelia, Countess of Salisbury, and among his last work was 'Kathleen Mavourneen' after Charles E. Marshall in 1903.

Greenhead worked mainly for Graves, and apart from portraits, engraved some contemporary paintings. He flourished from 1896 to 1910, when he exhibited plates at the Royal Academy, and among his later work was 'Barbara' after Henry Singleton in 1908.

Artists such as Sir Hubert Herkomer (1849–1914), known primarily as a painter, were also expert engravers, including mezzotint. He published his Oxford Slade lectures on etching and engraving in 1892, and was also associated with the photographic aspects of the work.

Sir Frank Short (1857–1945) made his reputation as an etcher, of which he was instructor at South Kensington from 1891, but he also used mezzotint to reproduce plates from Turner's *Liber Studiorum* which attracted Ruskin's attention, and resulted in Short working on plates after Turner throughout his career. He also made his mark with plates after G.F. Watts, notably 'Endymion and Selena', as well as those after Constable, 'Flatford Lock' in 1890 and Peter de Wint, 'A Road to Yorkshire' in 1889. His approach to mezzotint gave it yet another aspect to support its revival among the artistic community, and even if his plates were not all of steel, certainly most were steel-faced.

George Allen (1832–1907) worked for John Ruskin as assistant, publisher and engraver for many years. Having studied mezzotinting under

36 St George of the seaweed, from Ruskin's *Modern painters*, mezzotinted by G. Allen (288 × 185 mm)

Thomas Lupton, he did about 90 plates, many of which were after Ruskin and appeared in the latter's works, such as 'St. George of the Seaweed' (Plate 36), which appeared in *Modern Painters*, and located in Volume 3, p. 323 of the 1888 edition.

Thomas Oldham Barlow (1824–89) was the most prominent of this group and, with Cousins, was thought to be the most highly paid engraver of his time. Born at Oldham, the son of Henry Barlow, an ironmonger, Thomas was apprenticed at the age of 15 (in 1839) to the engraving firm of Stephenson and Royston in Manchester to learn line engraving, but soon after the opening of the local School of Design, he became one of its first pupils, achieving first prize for a drawing in 1846. In the same year he obtained a prize for muslin design at the Manchester Exposition for Industrial Art. At the end of his apprenticeship in 1847 he moved to London at the age of 23, where he made his living engraving for book illustration, especially for Fergusson's architectural works, on the one hand, and the print publishers on the other. His first important plate was after John Phillips and published by Gambart in 1849. He probably learnt mezzotinting at the School of Design, and at a time when line engravers found it more lucrative to work in mezzotint, he turned to this medium to produce works such as 'The Huguenot' in 1857, published by Graves, and one of a number done after John Everett Millais. After John Phillips's death in 1867, many of whose pictures Barlow engraved, he concentrated on portraits after Millais, 20 of which were published by Agnew, shared between Barlow and Cousins. From 1873 he rose through the ranks of the Royal Academy, becoming RA in succession to Cousins in 1881, and from 1886 directed the etching class at South Kensington after R.J. Lane's retirement. On Cousins's death, Thomas inherited his set of engraving tools which later went to J.B. Pratt. In 1880 Barlow obtained a first prize at the Sydney Exhibition. His last work was a mezzotint version of Turner's 'Vintage of Macon', begun in 1886 and finished just before his death at the age of 65.

Another engraver who maintained the Cousins tradition was George H. Every (1837–1910). His earliest important work was 'Suffer little children to come unto me' after A. Hennings in 1854, done at the age of 17. He joined the contemporary interest in 18th-century work with portraits after Romney, Gainsborough, such as 'King George the third' and 'Queen Charlotte' in the 1860s and 'Edward Augustus, Prince of Wales' after Reynolds in 1865. 'His only playmate' after Heywood Hardy, published by Arthur Lucas in 1872, exemplified his engraving of childhood subjects, and 'Sunshine and shadow' after Marcus Stone was published by Francis Lucas in 1879. In the 1880s he did a number of plates after John Millais, including the celebrated 'Bubbles' of 1887. He exhibited at the Royal Academy from 1864 to 1905, the earliest plate being 'Persuasion' after James Craig in

1862. His later work included plates after Lord Leighton such as 'Wedded' in 1900, and 'The Coquette' after M.W. Peters in 1906.

From Scotland came members of the Faed family. James Faed (1821–1911) was the elder brother of the painter Thomas Faed, both sons of James, a miller, farmer and engineer living at Barley (or Burley) Mill, near Gatehouse of Fleet, Kircudbrightshire. His father's cousin, Sir George Faed, was an eminent soldier, and yet another relation had been an engraver, whose productions were hung in their home. James, jun. joined his brothers John and Thomas in Edinburgh about 1839, just before their father died. He engraved a number of plates after Francis Grant, whose 'The Countess Seafield' was done about 1846, followed by 'Lady E. Wells' 1855, exhibited at the Royal Academy, and, after his brother John he engraved 'Shakespeare and his friends' in 1859–60, done for members of the Cosmopolitan Art Association. After Thomas Faed he did 'Evangeline' in 1863 with another version in 1885, 'The Man of sorrows' after Noel Paton in 1879, and he turned to portraits towards the end of his engraving career with 'The Earl of Home' after George Reid in 1899. ''Tween the gloamin' and the mirk when the Kye comes home' of 1888 was engraved after his own painting.

Frederick Stacpoole (1813–1907) is another of the old guard who worked for the print publishers with some success in the second half of the 19th century. The son of a naval officer, he was educated at Ghent, and later at the Royal Academy Schools, where he obtained silver medals in 1839 and 1841. He would liked to have been a portrait painter, but lacked the means to maintain himself, so looked to mezzotint engraving to provide him with a living. His first plates were joint efforts. 'Peace' after Landseer in 1848 with T.L. Atkinson, and 'Mountain torrent' after Landseer 1850 with the painter's brother Thomas Landseer. Many of Stacpoole's plates were executed after Briton Rivière in the 1870s and 1880s, and he achieved some success with plates after other contemporary painters. He did not follow the trend for 18th- and early 19th-century styles. Among his later work was 'Sweethearts' after Charles B. Barber in 1891, but his last exhibited plate was 'Baby's first voyage' at the Royal Academy in 1899. Elected ARA in 1880, he retired in 1892 and spent the last years of his life painting.

The last important engraver to be brought up with steel was Joseph Bishop Pratt (1854–1910), the son of a mezzotint printer, Anthony Pratt, which relationship gave the son a feel for the medium at an early age. He was apprenticed to David Lucas from the ages of 14 to 19, when he completed his first commission 'Maternal felicity' after Samuel Carter in 1873. Circa 1889 he bought the set of tools used by Samuel Cousins from T.O. Barlow's widow. He worked for the print publishers during most of his career using the mixed method, but in 1896 he turned to pure mezzotint for his series of 18th-century portraits published by Agnew, and in 1902 he engraved the state portrait of King Edward VII after Luke Fildes. A similar engraving of Queen Alexandra followed in 1906. His last important plate was 'The Countess of Warwick and her children' after Romney in 1909. His son Stanley Claude Pratt (b. 1882) was also an engraver, studying under his father.

Others who worked in similar veins were George Sidney Hunt (1856–*c.*1924) who worked for Henry Graves on a considerable number of plates after Edwin Landseer, Robert Bowyer Parkes (1830–*c.* 1891) who engraved portraits, e.g. 'Mrs. Fitzherbert' after Sir J. Reynolds, published by Graves 1863, and contemporary painting, and Robert S. Clouston (d. 1911) who also engraved 18th-century portraits, after contemporary painting, and for the *Art Journal, Burlington Magazine* and *The Connoisseur.* He wrote what was in effect an open letter to the Royal Academy about its relationship to the art of engraving in the *Art Journal.* Evidently the engravers (probably mostly members of the Royal Society of Painter-Etchers) met yearly for an engravers' dinner, and in 1894 Philip Hamerton, the chairman, was asked to take up with the Academy the fact that only the smallest wall of the smallest room at Burlington House was given over to English mezzotints. At the next exhibition, about six examples were shown, and Clouston obviously thought that they, together with the fact that there was at the time no engraver holding Associated or full honours, represented a failure on the Academy's part. Stacpoole, the last 19th-century Associate had retired in 1892 and no more appointments were made until 1906 when Frank Short and William Strang were elected.

Clouston accepted that the decline in all types of engraving had been severely affected by the coming of photography, which had lessened the need for portrait painters and engravers, and in particular, photogravure, which threatened to equal the range of tones achieved by mezzotint, one of its chief merits. The reproduction of Sir Henry Raeburn's 'William Sinclair' for the *Art Journal* (1903, p. 360) illustrates this very well (Plate 37). Even steel has a part to play here, since many photogravure plates were steel-faced to lengthen their lives. Clouston ends:

Nor do I take up cudgels for engravers, but for engraving; I claim adequate recognition for the art I love, and I would be neglecting what I owe to it if I did not say, and say plainly, that the Academy, in slighting the art which is more purely English than any other, is culpably neglecting its duty. (*Art Journal,* 1896, p. 218.)

Clouston emigrated to Australia in 1909 and died there after an accident in 1911.

That some engravers included photogravure in their repertoire of meth-

37 William Sinclair, printed in photogravure

ods is illustrated by the career of Walter Alfred Cox (1862–c.1910). He was the fourth son of Thomas Henry W. Cox, an art printer, and began his working career as a clerk in a City silk merchant's office. He took up drawing as a hobby, which won him a silver medal for a crayon copy of 'Great expectations' at the St Pancras Industrial Exhibition of 1880. In 1879 he was apprenticed to the Danish line engraver J. Ballin, with whom he stayed for three years, at the same time attending evening art classes at the West London School of Art. When Ballin returned to Copenhagen to become Engraver Royal to the King, and to work for the Danish government, Cox took up etching as a means of earning his living, and worked for the print publishers, turning later to mixed method plates. Engraving commissions fell off, so Cox attended special lessons in photogravure at the Regent Street Polytechnic during the 1890s, working then for Graves and Fores, but at the turn of the century there was a revival of etching and pure mezzotint, in which medium he worked for Graves. During the Boer War he engraved 'The Gentlemen in khaki' after Caton Woodville, the sales of which produced £5,000 for the Widows and Orphans South African War Fund, because publisher, printer, artist and engraver accepted no payment for their services.

By this time mezzotinters had almost entirely reverted to copper, which was steel-faced where necessary, but modern artists, when asked for their views on the use of steel were unanimous that present needs were met by copper. In a letter to the author, Lawrence Josset (b. 1910) the eminent mezzotinter and pupil of Sir Frank Short wrote:

The origin of the 'limited edition' came directly from the plate wearing out from the abrasive inks and the pressure of the printing press. This is understandable in the past, but today it has become somewhat 'precious'. Relating scarcity with artistic merit is deplorable. So much has been lost regarding techniques of printing and engraving by the fact that all craftsmen in the past kept their 'tricks of the trade' very much under their hat. Indeed, I know an old printer who destroyed all his notes when he retired.

It was also said that when Dominic Colnaghi died in 1879 a vast knowledge of engraving and engravers went with him.

There is a small group of mezzotinters today, however, some of whom work in Great Britain, who use whichever metal suits them for a particular commission. Mark Balakdjian, working in London, is thought to use steel plates at times, but Holly Downing, who moved from Sussex to California in the 1980s, has always used steel-faced copper.

4

British steel line engraving: books

This chapter is designed to elaborate on the early days of steel-engraved book illustration in works produced up to the end of 1825, to investigate some of the bibliographical peculiarities encountered, and to look more closely at the construction of the books themselves.

Steel engraving was eminently suited to the illustration of books, which was its most important use, and began with the publication in 1807 of John Thomas Smith's *The Antiquities of Westminster* ... . 'Rainy Day' Smith, engraver, author and sometime Keeper of Prints at the British Museum recalled at a meeting of the Society of Arts Committee on Polite Arts, held on 8 April 1823, how he had used an old steel saw blade in its unsoftened state to engrave a representation of the Star Chamber ceiling in 1802 (Plate 38). A number of burins were broken, and instead of spending only two days engraving on copper, it took him two months to complete it on steel. On page 29 of his book, he explains his thought that engraving on iron 'would admit of a greater degree of sharpness in the ornaments', but the labour was so great that it remained an isolated example for about 18 years. Smith received his soubriquet from his *A Book for a Rainy Day; or, Recollections of the Events of the Years 1766–1833,* in which he was very critical of the engravers who produced small book plates, instead of the larger and more impressive works previously in vogue.

The core of the 'incunabula' of steel-engraved book illustration consists of the 70 or so plates published in 20 works by Longman, who from the beginning, realized the commercial importance of the new metal, and used it to extend the editions of popular works in their repertoire. They had acquired the list of popular works previously issued by Sir Richard Phillips, who had, under a number of pseudonyms, published cheap educational books, such as *The Universal Preceptor* issued under the *nom de plume* of Revd David Blair. The twelfth edition (1820) carried a folding frontispiece of the

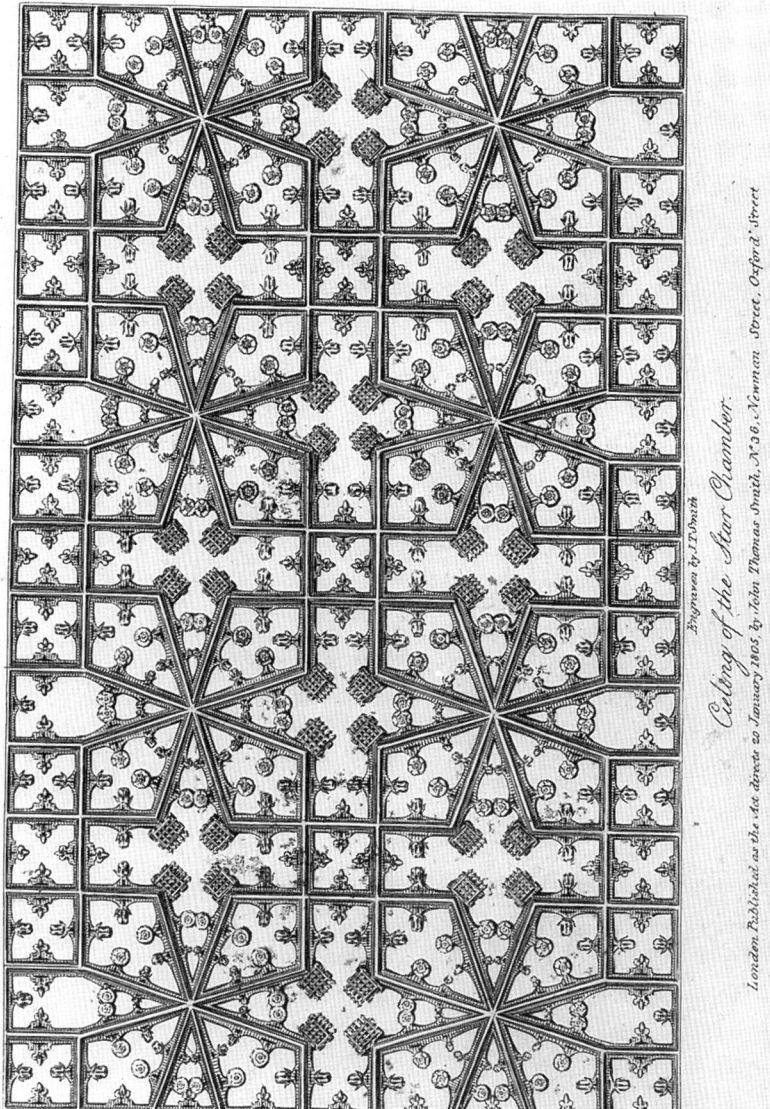

38 Cieling [sic] of the Star Chamber, engraved by J.T. Smith

solar system, engraved by Wilson Lowry, which was probably the second illustration to be engraved on steel. The Revd William Fordyce Mavor, Rector of Woodstock, became one of Phillips's authors, and one of his most famous contributions was *The English Spelling Book* ... which in 1821/22 acquired a steel-engraved frontispiece.

The first full set of four illustrations on steel was that commissioned in the summer of 1820, engraved by Charles Heath during the autumn and dated 1820, but published on 10 January 1821. This is why copies of this edition carry the date 1821 on their title page and the plates the date 1820. The volume was a reprint of Thomas Campbell's *The Pleasures of Hope*, his principal poem, first published in 1799 when the author was 21. Three thousand

39   From T. Campbell's *The pleasures of hope*, 1820, engraved by C. Heath

copies were printed, and in November 1824 a further 3,000 were taken from the same plates (Plate 39). There are copies with the title page dated 1822, but they are not accounted for in the Longman ledgers. Plate 39 referred to verses on page 32 (not 23 as engraved). A number of similarly composed pictures followed. In each example, figures stand to the right, looking left over angry waves, a ship may appear in the distance, and the atmosphere is sad and depressing. The stories, poems and pictures were very much to 19th-century taste, despite their heavily charged sentimentality. Plate 40 is from *The Keepsake* (1829), where Charles Heath engraved Richard Westall's 'Lucy' to illustrate the story of Lucy Hawkins, who met her first love again when he rescued their son from the sea. 'Zella' from *The Keepsake* (1830) was engraved by Charles Heath after Henry Corbould, and illustrated Mary Shelley's 'The evil eye' and shows the Greek mother watching ships go by, while she waits for her husband to return from his search for their kidnapped three year old son (Plate 41). Eliza Cook's *The Poetical*

40 Lucy from *The Keepsake*, 1829, engraved by C. Heath

41 Zella from *The Keepsake*, 1830, engraved by C. Heath

Works ... were published by Frederick Warne in 1869, and contained (p. 36) a poem 'The mother who hath a child at sea'. The vignette shows the mother imagining the terrors of a storm at sea, with the ship being tossed mercilessly upon the waves. Drawn by J. Marchant it was engraved by Henry Adlard (Plate 42). Alex Whitelaw's 'Ballad of the sailor's children' tells the

42   From E. Cook's *The poetical works*, [1869], engraved by H. Adlard

story of the father away at sea, not aware that his wife has died, leaving three children to fend for themselves. Here they gaze forlornly across the waves, hoping each sail is that of his ship (Plate 43). Painted by Beaume, engraved by Robert Scott, it was published in volume 3 of *The Casquet of Literature... Edited by Charles Gibbon ... in Six Volumes* (1874) by Blackie and Sons. Steel engraving was ideal for the long runs needed for such popular works as *Pinnock's Improved Edition of Dr. [Oliver] Goldsmith's History of Greece, Abridged for the Use of Schools* (1822), where the frontispiece is dated 1821 (Plate 44). It was published by G.B. Whittaker, who also issued William Pinnock's catechisms, e.g. *A Catechism of British Geography* (1823) with a steel-engraved frontispiece and title page, the former a portrait of William Camden, surrounded by decoration similar to that used on banknotes.

Charles Heath soon adapted his style to take advantage of the fine work obtainable from steel when he engraved the frontispiece, dated 1 December 1821 to the fifteenth edition, published 20 January 1823, of John Debrett's *The Peerage of the United Kingdom...*, publication of which was delayed due to the author's death in November 1822. Another of Campbell's poems *Gertrude of Wyoming*, first published in 1809, contained three engravings by Charles Heath after Richard Westall, dated 1822 (Plate 45).

Most of the steel engravings up to this time were done on the blocks provided by Jacob Perkins, which were quite thick and had to be printed on specially adapted rolling presses. The experiments conducted by Charles Warren and his plate maker Richard Hughes, resulting in steel plates soft enough to engrave, hard enough to give a large number of impressions and thin enough to print on ordinary rolling presses, represented an important breakthrough. This enabled engravers to adapt more readily to the new metal, and Warren first demonstrated this in May 1822 on the frontispiece and engraved title page of a new edition of Philip Doddridge's *The Rise and Progress of the Soul*.... Warren went on to engrave the frontispiece and title page, dated September 1822, for a reprint of *The Poetical Works of John Milton*, a volume in the series originally published by John Walker in 1818. In this earlier volume George James Corbould was paid 25 guineas for the engravings with a further 10 guineas for repairing the plates. The edition of 5,000 copies probably exhausted the plates, but for the 3 October 1822 edition, Warren received 50 guineas, twice Corbould's fee, and instead of being worn out after 5,000 impressions, the plates were printed from again in 1832, and were probably still in use for a 2,000 reprint in 1838. The engraving is inscribed 'C. Warren on steel plate'.

The 22nd of October 1822 saw publication of the twenty-second edition of Thomas Mawe's *Everyman his Own Gardener...*' actually written by John Abercrombie. The frontispiece was engraved on steel, possibly by Rest

LINE ENGRAVING: BOOKS   117

43   The sailor's children, from *The Casquet of literature*, 1874, engraved by Robert Scott

Fenner; Fenner worked the plate for 6,000 copies at a cost of 6 guineas. It was a very popular work since the twenty-first edition was issued in 1818, and the frontispiece was, in essence, the same design from at least the seventeenth edition in 1803.

The Poetical Works of James Beattie and William Collins was published in January 1823 in the British classics series. The frontispiece and title page had been engraved at the end of 1822 by 'C. Warren ... on his prep[are]d

44 Frontispiece and engraved title page of *Goldsmith's History of Greece*, 1821, engraved by Perkins, Fairman and Heath

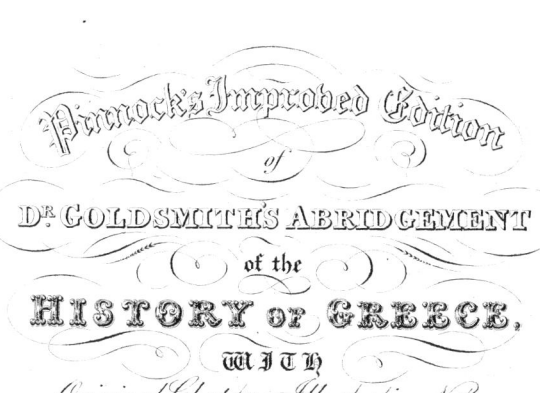

Pinnock's Improved Edition
of
DR GOLDSMITH'S ABRIDGEMENT
of the
HISTORY OF GREECE,
WITH
Original Chapters, Illustrative Notes,
Questions for Examination,
&c. &c.

LONDON.
Published by G. & W. B. Whittaker, 13, Ave Maria Lane
1823.
Perkins & Heath. Patent Hardened Steel Plate.

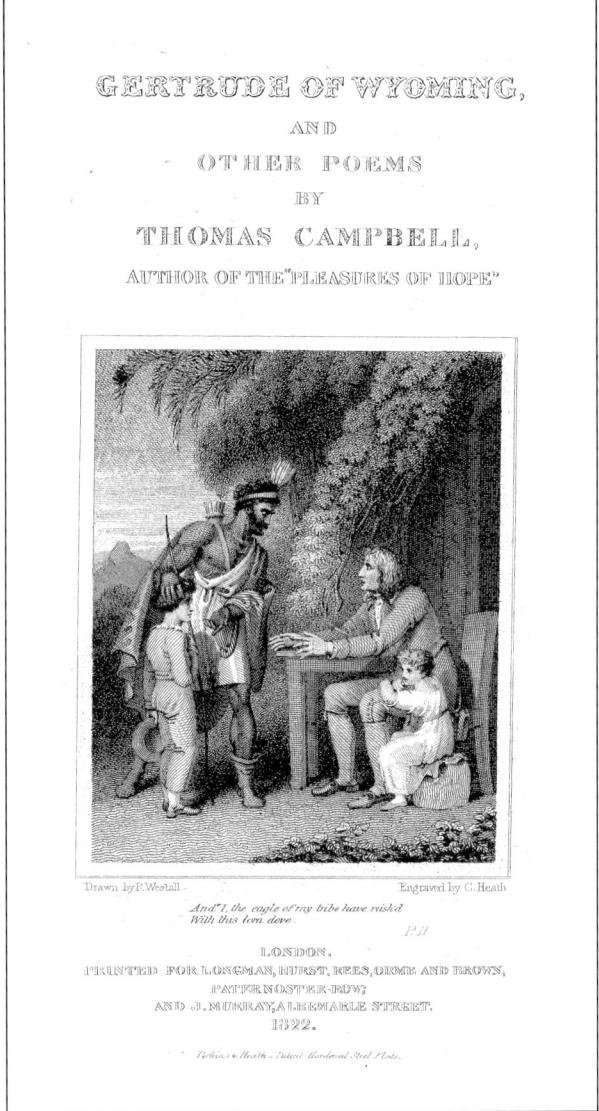

45   From T. Campbell's *Gertrude of Wyoming*, engraved by C. Heath

steel pl[ate]' and were the engravings submitted to the Committee of Polite Arts of the Society of Arts on 18 March 1823, which helped to secure the award of the Large Gold medal for the engraver.

In April 1823, Constable and Co. produced a ten-volume edition of *The Poetical Works of Sir Walter Scott* with the title page vignettes engraved by

Charles Heath. The portrait in volume 1 was engraved on copper, the combined cost of which (engraving, writing, repairing) was £32 with £12 10s. 0d. for printing 5,000 copies. The cost of the ten steel plates and working 10,000 copies was £625, and although the edition only ran to 5,000 copies, the remainder were probably kept for another edition, and in fact only 1,000 copies were issued in August 1825.

Longman also published an edition of Thomas Moore's poem *The Loves of the Angels* in 1823. Written in Paris, it went through several editions in quick succession, but as originally published, it contained no illustrations. In his entrepreneurial way, Charles Heath separately issued an engraved title page and three illustrations, three engraved by himself and one by Edward James Portbury (Plate 46).

The thirteenth edition of John Bonnycastle's *An Introduction to Mensuration and Practical Geometry* was published on 26 September 1823 in an edition of 8,000. The title page illustration was engraved by C.G. Cook.

In 1824, frontispiece portraits were engraved on steel for volumes 3 and 4 of *The Mirror of Literature, Amusement, and Instruction ...* published by J. Limbird. The frontispiece to volume 3 is a vignette of Lord Byron, engraved by Roffe, possibly Edwin, a member of a large family of artists and engravers.

Another popular book went into its fourth edition in August 1825 when Lt.-Col. Peter Hawker's *Instructions to Young Sportsmen* came out with a mixture of copper and steel plates. Henry Adlard engraved the frontispiece and three other plates on steel opposite pages 310, 320 and 370. The delicacy of steel engraving is beginning to show in these plates, especially in the delineation of bird plumage.

Finally, George Virtue, who was to dominate the field of steel-engraved books, published a very early attempt in [Catherine E.] *Oxberry's Dramatic Biography and Historic Anecdotes* in 80 weekly parts between 1 January 1825 and 12 August 1826. Volumes 1 and 2 have engravings on steel plates by John Rogers, who engraved a total of 86 plates for the work but it is not clear how many were on steel, apart from those so described.

The first type of book to benefit from steel engraving was the newly created annual, derived from the long-established German pocket-book. Large numbers were printed as the market strengthened, but among the early volumes was a casualty of the bank failures in November and December 1825. *The Literary Souvenir* (1826), edited by Alaric Watts, was published in November 1825 by Hurst, Robinson and Co., the junior partner of which, Joseph Ogle Robinson, was tempted to speculate in hops and house building with disastrous results. The firm's affairs were in bad shape, therefore, when they dishonoured a bill presented by Archibald Constable and Co. of Edinburgh, their co-publishers, and the publisher of Sir Walter Scott's works. The bankruptcy of both firms followed. It is not known how

46 From T. Campbell's *The Loves of the angels*, engraved by E.J. Portbury

many copies of the annual had been sold in the two months following publication, but it is likely that the remaining stock was impounded and brought nothing in after 14 January 1826, the date of the bankruptcy. Another version of the work then appeared, containing virtually the same text, printed by the same printer but with different illustrations, and whereas the original contained ten plates, including an engraved title page with G.S. Newton's 'Lover's quarrel', engraved by Charles Rolls and two pages of autographs, engraved by J.S. Messenger, the second version has no engraved title page or list of plates and only eight engravings. The new frontispiece was J. Boaden's 'The Village queen', engraved by Charles Marr, a plate used again in *The Amulet* (1831) (Plate 47) and the printed title page carries no date, but after page 410 the editor includes a postscript referring to this volume as the natural successor to that of 1825.

Topographical works also benefited by the introduction of steel engravings and most books of the period were so illustrated. A popular subject was the fortress of Ehrenbreitstein, the restoration of which, begun in 1817, was completed in 1828. Romantic interest was engendered by its inclusion in the third canto of Lord Byron's poem *Childe Harold's Pilgrimage*, first published in 1816 (Plate 48). The vignette was drawn by Thomas Creswick based on a sketch by Lieutenant Allen, and engraved by William Finden. Ehrenbreitstein (literally 'Broad stone of honour') is situated at the confluence of the Rhine and Moselle rivers, and its fortress was considered to be one of the most secure in Europe. Many views of it were published late into the 19th century.

Steel plates were renowned for their longevity, and it is not surprising that they were used several times in editions of popular books, and also in collected form as albums of previously published engravings. *Views in India, China and the Shores of the Red Sea* (1830–35) by Robert Elliot was published by Henry Fisher, in which the sketches were provided by Elliott, and worked up by other artists. The text was written by Emma Roberts who had lived in India for a time, and among the areas described were the Caves of Ellora, to which eight of the 62 plates were devoted. The caves contain some of the most striking works of ancient art still extant. A whole mountain near Darlutabad in the Deccan had been excavated about 6000 BC to provide 15 large and a number of smaller Buddhist temples and shrines, cut out in the hard granite. The instigator was said to be Beloo Rajah, who was cured of a disease on the site, and in gratitude commenced the building of the Kylas Temple Palace. In the plate of 'Rameswur – caves of Ellora', Elliot's sketch was worked up by George Cattermole and engraved by William Woolnoth (Plate 49).

The book had a companion volume when Lt. George Francis White published his 30 *Views in India, Chiefly among the Himalaya Mountains*... in 1838 with text by Emma Roberts, and the two books together formed the basis of Fisher's re-use of the plates in Emma Roberts's *Hindostan; its Landscapes, Palaces, Temples, Tombs*... undated but *circa* 1848. When Peter Jackson took over Fisher's firm from Henry's son Robert in 1849, many of its plates, including those from these works, came into the hands of a new publisher, set up by John Tallis, with the help of the printer Ephraim Tipton Brain in December 1853, called the London Printing and Publishing Company.

47 Two versions of the frontispiece and engraved title page of *The Literary Souvenir*, 1826

THE
LITERARY SOUVENIR;

OR,
CABINET OF POETRY AND ROMANCE.

EDITED BY

ALARIC A. WATTS.

> I have sung of war for knight;
> Lay of love for lady bright;
> Fairy tale to lull the heir;
> Goblin grim the maids to scare.
> *Sir Walter Scott.*

LONDON:
PRINTED FOR HURST, ROBINSON, AND CO.
5, WATERLOO-PLACE, PALL-MALL;
AND A. CONSTABLE AND CO. EDINBURGH.

THE VILLAGE QUEEN.

LVIII.

Here Ehrenbreitstein, with her shatter'd wall
Black with the miner's blast, upon her height
Yet shows of what she was, when shell and ball
Rebounding idly on her strength did light;
A tower of victory! from whence the flight
Of baffled foes was watch'd along the plain:
But Peace destroy'd what War could never blight,
And laid those proud roofs bare to Summer's rain—
On which the iron shower for years had pour'd in vain.

48   Ehrenbreitstein from Byron's *Childe Harold's pilgrimage*, engraved by W. Finden

49   Rameswur – Caves of Ellora from R. Elliot's *Views in India* . . ., engraved by W. Woolnoth

They in turn used the plates in Robert Montgomery Martin's *The Indian Empire* ... [1858–61]. Volume 3 contained 98 engravings, some of which had added subtitles referring directly to events in the Indian Mutiny. Thirteen plates from Roberts referring to China and the Red Sea were omitted and replaced by others, 12 of which were unsigned by artist or engraver. Although the 'letterpress descriptions by Miss Emily [*sic*] Roberts' formed the basis of the text, it was entirely re-written, presumably by Martin. Plates were also issued in annuals and albums, for example, William Miller's engraving of 'The British Residency at Hyderabad' also appeared in *Fisher's Drawing Room Scrap-Book for 1835* (p. 37), and in the Revd G.N. Wright's *The Gallery of Engravings* (1844, vol. 2, p. 74).

Thus, what started out as a travel book was turned into an opportunist publication to catch the public's eye when a suitable stirring event came along. George Virtue did the same for the Crimean war. He had published Julie Pardoe's *The Beauties of the Bosphorus* in parts up to 1840, a successful venture, with the pictures drawn by William Henry Bartlett. Virtue re-issued the volume in 1854, and in a new 12-page introduction, the author comments that

Never ... have the eyes of all civilised Europe been turned with such absorbing interest towards the 'Bosphorus' and the 'Danube' as at the present moment; a consideration which has induced the publisher of the two volumes, of which a reprint is here offered to the public, to form what were originally two distinct works, written by different hands, and produced at different periods, one continuous *tableau* of the theatre of impending war.

This must have been written in the autumn of 1853, since war was declared on 23 October. The other volume referred to was William Beattie's *The Danube; its History, Scenery and Topography*, published in 1844. So that the war could be followed pictorially, some engravings were modified, chiefly by adding the names of the principal places involved. 'The View from Mount Bulgurlhi' of 1840 becomes 'Constantinople from above Scutari ...' in 1854 (Plate 50), and a figure, possibly of Russian origin, was removed from a position at the base of the second large tree from the left. 'Eyoub' of 1840 became 'Cemetery and mosque of Ayub (Eyyub)' in 1854 (Plate 51), but with the addition of a strip down the left-hand side, the extent of which is indicated by the original position of the artist's name at the foot. Some extra islands appear between the first branch and trunk of the tree on the left of the picture, and the style of title lettering changed from voided capitals to a copperplate hand. The 1854 edition was issued again in 1874 as the first of a projected series of *Picturesque Europe. Containing more than four hundred engravings of views* ... with the addition of eight pages and six plates.

50 Constantinople from above Scutari... from J. Pardoe's *The Beauties of the Bosphorus*, engraved by R. Brandard

51   Cemetery and mosque of Ayoub from J. Pardoe's *The Beauties of the Bosphorus*, engraved by C. Richardson

Differences of another sort started to appear in volumes issued in the second half of the 19th century. An example of this comes in Henry Tyrrell's *The History of the War with Russia*, issued in parts between 1855 and 1858 by The London Printing and Publishing Company, in the three volumes of which were 66 steel engravings. A copy in the author's possession is bound up in six divisions in publisher's cloth, and therefore as issued by the publisher. It contains 66 engravings, but four of them are not as listed in the 'Directions to the binder', which call for portraits of The Duke of Cambridge and Lord John Russell, and two engravings of events in the war. There is only one portrait in the group supplied, engraved in the style of the other portraits, of General Sir W.F. Williams (Plate 52). Of the two views, one was of 'Sebastopol' and the other 'Constantinople from the heights above Eyoub' was first used in Robert Walsh's *Constantinople* ([1838–40] vol. 2, p. 43). The last one, 'Removal of wounded soldiers from the field of battle' (Plate 53) showed the contemporary trend for supplementary engravings in the frame around the main picture.

Books written for children were most frequently illustrated by wood engravings, which could be printed with the text and therefore more cheaply produced. It is true that the 'Juvenile' annuals were illustrated with steel engravings like their adult counterparts, but it is rare to find an 'ordinary' book prepared for 'Young persons' illustrated by steel, albeit small plates and not very well executed. The 24 in the edition of *Josephus*, published by Grant and Griffin *circa* 1850 are similar to those illustrated in Plate 54.

Colour was not really suited to the appearance of steel engravings, which depended so much on the wide range of tones it could produce and the maximum contrast between black and white. The practice of hand-colouring was well established from the 18th century, especially in the production of aquatints but, occasionally, publishers provided more expensive hand-coloured copies, and employed colourists for this purpose. Some works, however, depended on colour for their effectiveness such as Sir William Jardine's volumes of the *Naturalists' Library*, published and engraved in Edinburgh by his brother-in-law William Home Lizars. Plate 55 illustrates a steel engraving so coloured, but throughout the rest of Jardine's book etchings are used (as in chapter 6, and in colour plate 5). The application of colour by printing was in its infancy in the 18th century, but it was George Baxter (1804–67) who patented a method of applying colour to steel by means of wood blocks prepared by transfers from the master print. A steel engraving of the complete picture was printed in a neutral tint, e.g. grey or fawn to give a basis of the design, and oil colour was applied in subsequent operations, after which the print was hot-pressed to fuse the various colours. C.T. Courtney Lewis, writing in 1908, said that foundation plates were

52 Gen. Sir W.F. Williams from H. Tyrrell's *The History of the War with Russia*, engraved by D.J. Pound

53 Removal of wounded soldiers ... from H. Tyrrell's *The History of the war with Russia*, engraved by G. Greatbach

54 Frontispiece and title page to *The Wars of the Jews* by Josephus

THE

WARS OF THE JEWS,

AS RELATED BY

JOSEPHUS;

WITH

ADDITIONAL FACTS FROM JEWISH HISTORY.

ADAPTED TO

The Capacities of Young Persons.

SIXTH EDITION.

WITH TWENTY-FOUR STEEL ENGRAVINGS.

LONDON:
GRANT AND GRIFFITH,
SUCCESSORS TO
J. HARRIS, CORNER OF ST. PAUL'S CHURCHYARD.

55 Engraved title page to W. Jardine's *The naturalists' library*, engraved by W.H. Lizars and hand coloured

generally steel, and when Baxter retired in 1860, the sale of his effects contained 109 steel plates. He is known to have used mezzotint for 'Victoria, Queen of Great Britain, India [etc.]' after James Stewart in 1859, which is almost certain to have been a steel plate. Most of his plates were small to begin with and covered pictures of royalty, religious subjects, landscapes and the Great Exhibition of 1851, the catalogue of which he was chosen to illustrate. Some were book illustrations, one of his earliest being the frontispiece 'Hindoo and Mahomedan buildings' to Robert Elliot's *Views in India* ... (1830–35). The picture was 'engraved and printed in oil colours by G. Baxter, 3, Charterhouse Square'. Of his independent prints, 'The parting look' adapted from a painting by Edward Henry Corbould 1858 was very popular, and with a size of 25½ in × 18½ in. was one of his largest prints.

One other example of plates being printed in a colour to facilitate colouring has come to light in the United States of America, where William Beattie's *Switzerland* had the illustrations printed in brown ink and then hand coloured. *Switzerland* was the first important topographical work with steel engravings to be published in Britain and was issued in parts between 1833 and 1836. The vignette on the engraved title page, printed in brown ink and hand coloured, is illustrated (see colour plate 1). Only one or two such copies have been found, all in America, where they appear to have been done for special clients. The publisher was George Virtue (*c.*1793–1868) (see Plate 56).

John Henry Le Keux's patent of 1841 for using two or more plates did not gain wide acceptance due, no doubt, to the amount of work involved in preparing a separate plate for each colour, so printing steel engravings in a colour other than black was confined mainly to monochrome plates.

John Ruskin (1819–1900) was the important exponent of this method and from the beginning he regarded steel engraving as the principal means of illustrating his books. From his earliest illustrations in *Friendship's Offering* (1844), he employed a variety of engravers, and although he used aquatint, mezzotint and lithography, the majority of his plates were line engraved. Chief among his engravers was James Charles Armytage who engraved plate IV in volume 3 of *The Stones of Venice* (colour plate 2), first published in 1853, which Ruskin drew to illustrate a point about the use of olive trees as decoration in Byzantine mosaics, with special reference to those at St Mark's Cathedral, Venice. The mosaic was situated in a cupola of the building 150 feet above eye level and the author comments: 'I have printed the whole plate in blue, because that colour approaches more nearly than black to the distant effect of the mosaics, of which the darker portions are generally composed of blue, in greater quantity than any other colour (p. 179). Ruskin's first important work *Modern painters* began publication in 1843, but it was volume 4, published 1856 and volume 5 published 1860 which contained some remarkable engravings. Among them was 'The Dryad's Waywardness' (vol. 5, p, 73) engraved by R.P. Cuff, printed in mauve and which achieved a three-dimensional effect by very clever engraving, especially in the background, which must have been a physically hard task,

56 George Virtue

because the use of a ruling machine would have been limited at best (colour plate 3). The illustration accompanies Ruskin's discussion on the disposition of oak boughs.

Towards the end of steel engraving's heyday, many prints were copied on to lithographic stones, which were quicker to print and cheaper to produce. The 1871 centenary edition of Scott's *Works* is believed to contain litho-

LINE ENGRAVING: BOOKS   139

57   Edinburgh Castle from the Grassmarket

graphic impressions of steel plates, and the use of several colours occurs in a series of local views being issued in booklet form (Plate 57). The size was not unlike that adopted for present-day postcards.

The construction of books containing steel engravings changed considerably as publishers issued them in parts, divisions and complete volumes. The casing and sewing developed from the hand bindings used until *circa*

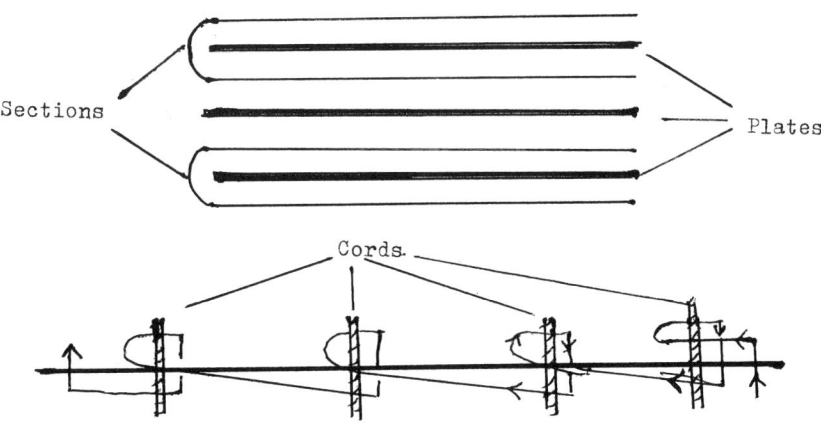

58   Method of sewing steel engraved books

the 1820s employing modern mechanisation techniques. Sewing underwent modifications so that plates and sections were sewn in and, instead of the thread being passed from outside to inside of the sections round tapes or cords, a kind of oversewing was used. Plate 58 illustrates the method used *circa* 1840 for copies of *American Scenery*, where sections of two leaves had plates inserted inside and between. Four thin cords were sawn in and the

59   Front board of Finden's *The ports, harbours . . .*

thread was passed through the section and plates via a hole near their folded edge, and followed the route shown from right to left, so that each plate was caught in six places. These perforations on the side of a plate usually indicate an engraving from a broken book. All the threads were taken up the outside of the spine, and glued down to it as the forwarding proceeded.

The decoration of the covers followed a conventional pattern, with some notable exceptions. The cloth was embossed blind by a pattern inside a rectangle consisting of tendrils and leaves, with a central vignette blocked in gold specially designed for the publication. The maritime motif was done on blue cloth for Finden's *The Ports, Harbours* ... of 1844 (Plate 59), the emblems of science, engineering, etc. on red cloth for Charles Tomlinson's *Cyclopaedia of Useful Arts* ... in 1854 (Plate 60) and the more descriptive design, again on red cloth, for Henry Tyrrell's *The History of the War with Russia* (1855–58) (Plate 61).

60 Front board of Tomlinson's *Cyclopaedia of useful arts* . . .

61   Front board of Tyrrell's *The History of the war with Russia* . . .

5

British steel line engraving: prints, maps, book plates

Prints

The print market in Britain in the first three decades of the 19th century was not as active as it had been previously, due mainly to the loss of the French market during the French Revolution and Napoleonic Wars (1789–1815). Rudolf Ackermann catered for the luxury end of the market with his hand-coloured aquatints, produced in both book and print form, in limited editions averaging 1,000 copies. The stipple productions of Bartolozzi and his followers provided slightly cheaper editions, but as always, the 'highest' form of the art – line engraving – was the most sought after, and in this the Boydell prints, especially those connected with Shakespeare, were the mainstay of the trade. The demand for prints had originally come from the collectors with their portfolios, but this had fallen off and there was 'a barren waste; the public had not been sufficiently educated to appreciate excellence in Art, and buyers of modern prints were few' (*Art Journal*, 1872, p. 18).

However, a new clientele arose that was more likely to buy prints to hang on their walls instead of filling portfolios, and thus keep up with fashions in art, buying prints of paintings hung in the Royal Academy and elsewhere, as well as buying the favourite artist of the day such as Wilkie, Landseer and their contemporaries.

The 1830s was a decade of social and political turmoil, and only a few long-established print publishers were able to exist in a limited market, but by 1840 conditions permitted a rapid expansion, and a number of new publishers appeared, both in London and the northern provinces. In 1839, a London directory listed 72 printsellers and publishers, but only a small percentage were in the latter category, able to approach the output of the few larger firms. There were three main publishers, Moon, Boys and Graves,

Thomas McLean and Thomas Agnew, who maintained a steady output from about 1817, the year in which Hurst, Robinson took over Boydell's stock, and Thomas Agnew was taken into partnership in Manchester.

John Boydell had died in 1804, and his stock of prints passed through various hands, coming, in 1817, into those of the Yorkshire bookselling firm of Joseph Ogle Robinson and Thomas Hurst (brother of a Longman partner) who were also in business as printsellers and publishers (Hurst, Robinson and Co.). In 1825 they moved to 6 Pall Mall in London, and published a few prints of their own, but when the firm failed disastrously in 1826, much of their immense print stock was bought by a partnership. This comprised Francis Graham Moon (1796–1871), Thomas Boys (fl. 1826–89) and Henry Graves (1806–92) the latter two being accountant and clerk respectively with Hurst, Robinson and Co.

Moon, at the age of 30, already had a thriving print and bookselling business in Threadneedle Street, left to him by his master Mr Tugwell, who died during Moon's apprenticeship, and although his knowledge of the art world was very sketchy, he and his partners had sufficient taste and business acumen to provide what the public wanted. This success was also helped by the benefits of steel engraving, namely highly finished plates, and long runs. Much of their business relied on the original stock, which included two sets of proofs for John Burnet's (1784–1868) engraving after Wilkie of the 'Blind fiddler', one set of which should have been destroyed, the second one representing the later, approved version of the print. They republished 'The Young bird' engraved by Burnet after his own painting, as a companion to his engraving after Wilkie of 'The Jew's harp'. The partnership's *Catalogue of Engravings* (1829) gives a good indication of their stock at the time. Other plates included the portrait of 'George the Fourth seated on a sofa' in 1829 after Sir Thomas Lawrence, engraved by William Finden, 'The Chelsea pensioners' after David Wilkie (who was paid £1,100 for the copyright) engraved by Burnet, and 'Nature' after Lawrence, engraved by George Thomas Doo, thought to be one of his best works.

In 1833 Moon left the partnership and went back to his original premises in Threadneedle Street. He was the youngest son of Christopher Moon, who had succeeded to a gold and silversmith's business of some standing, but when his father died at an early age, the children had to work hard to support themselves. The word 'liberality' is often applied to Moon and his dealings, for he seemed to reward both painters and engravers well, so that people liked working for him. G.T. Doo, J.H. Robinson, J.H. Watt, T. Landseer, J.T. Willmore and W. Greatbach are best known for reproducing the works of David Wilkie, Charles Eastlake, C.R. Leslie, Edwin Landseer and J.M.W. Turner. Many other contemporary British painters were also included, as well as royal family portraits by Winterhalter. In 1838 he published what was then described as 'the best known of English prints, and is certainly one of the most perfect examples of the English school' (*Art Journal*, 1872, p. 189, col. 2). This was Doo's engraving of 'John Knox preaching before the Lords of the Congregation', painted by Wilkie in 1832, which had taken 3½ years to engrave.

Moon was said to have issued over 200 publications, of which the majority were line engravings, and although his biographer in the *Art Journal* of 1872, Samuel Carter Hall, averred that most if not all of his plates were engraved on copper, the reverse is likely to have been the case. A number of plates are known to have been on steel, and since his son-in-law William Henry Bartlett drew extensively for the steel engravers, he must have been aware of the metal's advantages. His popularity was such that in 1830 he was elected a member of the Common Council of London, made a Sheriff in 1843 and in 1844 became Alderman of Portsoken Ward. In 1846 he was presented with a silver copy of the Warwick Vase with the inscription 'This tribute was offered by artists and amateurs in testimony of Mr. Moon's public spirit and love of Art, and of the liberality and taste which he has shown in his intercourse with painters and engravers'. He also received gifts from Emperor Nicholas of Russia, the Kings of Prussia and Hanover, and the French King Louis Philippe, who invited him to the Palace of St Cloud, a rare honour. In 1854 he became Lord Mayor of London, and as a result of the French Emperor's visit and entertainment at the Mansion House, he was knighted, although his services to art were thought to have been recognized at the same time. On a return visit to Paris in the following year, he was enrolled as a Chevalier in the Légion d'honneur.

He retired from business in 1853, and his stock was bought by his former partner Thomas Boys for 15,000 guineas, who promptly sold just the prints at auction for £20,000. The fate of about 12 steel plates caused some comment in the *Art Journal* (1855, pp. 314–15), when they were cut to pieces by Boys after a limited number of prints both plain and on India paper had been taken, to be sold at a trade dinner in the Albion Tavern. The majority of plates were mezzotints and of a large size, but one of the line engravings 'Crossing the bridge' after Edwin Landseer, engraved by J.T. Willmore was destroyed in the middle of its popularity. It had been engraved in 1847 and was still in demand in 1855, so Boys's action, despite the impressions he had taken from the plate, was not very sound financially. In the event, Willmore engraved a smaller plate for Ernest Gambart, which was published in 1859 and continued to sell well. Also destroyed was William Greatbach's principal plate 'The Waterloo banquet at Apsley House' after William Salter issued in 1839. Moon died at Western House, Brighton on 13 October 1871, and during the 28 years in which he traded, he had made a lasting impression on the 19th-century print trade which he took a leading part in founding.

G.T. Doo painted and engraved Moon's portrait in 1855.

Thomas Boys (fl. 1823–59), the second of the trio, left Graves in 1835 to set up on his own at 11 Golden Square, Regent Street, describing himself as prinsteller to the royal family. He concentrated on publishing first of all mezzotints, such as 'Cottage piety' after Thomas Webster, engraved by G.H. Phillips, in 1836, and 'The momentous question' after Sarah Setchel, engraved by Samuel Bellin, in 1843. A fine art distribution offered prizes totalling £6,582 by drawing lots to purchasers of a guinea's worth (or more) of his publications. These were originals, and engravings after them in many cases. The draw was due to take place on 5 October 1843. He then went on to lithographs, notably those of his cousin Thomas Shotter Boys, but after the purchase of Moon's stock in 1853, his business declined, and although the last of his plates was published in 1857, his financial problems caused his retirement in 1859.

Henry Graves (1806–92) was the youngest of the trio, and at the age of 26 was left at 6 Pall Mall with a new partner, Richard Hodgson, who possibly came from a contemporary publishing firm. The son of Robert Graves, a printseller, his elder brother was also Robert (1798–1863), the eminent engraver. Henry became an assistant to the art dealer Samuel Woodburn in 1822, after which he managed the print department of Hurst, Robinson, so had a very firm footing in the print business. When Boys left in 1835, Hodgson and Graves put out a *Catalogue of engravings, after the finest Pictures of the Schools of Europe*, on 2 May 1836, and later when the *Art Union* was established, the firm regularly advertised in it. In 1839 Hodgson put up the capital to start the *Art Union* periodical, but because he interfered with Samuel Carter Hall's editorship, the latter bought Hodgson out and became sole proprietor. By 1839, the firm had captured some prestigious royal commissions, and were 'Her Majesty's printsellers and publishers in Ordinary', but since the appeal of most prints was short-lived, a quick return was necessary. In 1841 Hodgson's place was taken by a Mr Warmsley for a short time and in June 1843, the firm offered 67 'recently published' works for sale with a full page advertisement in the *Art Union* (Plate 62). It is probable, however, that Wilkie's 'Blind fiddler' engraved by Burnet was the same stock which came to Moon, Boys and Graves in 1826, and not a recent publication at all. Even older was Thomas Stothard's 'Canterbury pilgrims' engraved by James Heath which was published on 1 October 1817.

Graves went alone by 1844 and traded as Henry Graves and Co. He had also taken office in professional associations, for instance, by December 1841 he had been elected Honorary Secretary, for the fourteenth time, of the Artist's and Amateur's Conversazione, that is, since he was 21. The firm became one of the major purveyors of prints, and used steel engraving for many of their productions, such as those after Landseer – 'Highland

180 THE ART-UNION. [June 1843.

SPLENDID ENGRAVINGS

RECENTLY PUBLISHED BY

GRAVES AND WARMSLEY,

PRINTSELLERS AND PUBLISHERS IN ORDINARY TO HER MAJESTY, 6, PALL MALL.

AFGHAUNISTAN, drawn on Stone by Louis and Charles Haghe, from the Original Drawings by Dr. James Atkinson. Twenty-six Plates, half-bound, 4*l.* 4s.; Coloured and Mounted, 10*l.* 10s.

AFGHAUNISTAN COSTUMES, by Capt. Hart, drawn on Stone by Charles Haghe, uniform with Atkinson's Sketches of Afghaunistan; containing Portraits of all the leading Chiefs engaged in the late war, the whole drawn from Life in their Picturesque Costumes. 26 Plates, imperial folio, half-bound morocco, 4*l.* 4s.; Coloured and Mounted, 10*l.* 10s.

ABBOTSFORD FAMILY, painted by Sir D. Wilkie, R.A.; engraved by R. Graves, A.R.A. 18 by 15 high. Prints, 1*l.* 1s.; Proofs, 2*l.* 2s.; India, 3*l.* 3s.; before Letters, 4*l.* 4s.

ABERCORN CHILDREN, painted by E. Landseer, R.A.; engraved by S. Cousins, A.R.A. 19 by 21 high. Prints, 1*l.* 11s. 6d.; Proofs, 3*l.* 3s.; before Letters, 7*l.* 7s.

ALFRED in the NEATHERD'S COTTAGE, painted by Sir D. Wilkie, R.A.; engraved by J. Mitchell. 23 by 17 high. Prints, 1*l.* 11s. 6d.; Proofs, 3*l.* 3s.; India, 4*l.* 4s.; before Letters, 6*l.* 6s.

BEDALE HUNT, YORKSHIRE, painted by Anson Martin; engraved by W. H. Simmons. 32 by 21 high. Prints, 3*l.* 3s.; First Proofs, 6*l.* 6s.

BLIND FIDDLER, painted by Sir D. Wilkie, R.A.; engraved by J. Burnet. 23 by 19 high. Prints, 2*l.* 2s.; Proofs (with white hat), 6*l.* 6s.

BOSWORTH, SALADIN, and STANDARD, painted by A. Cooper, R.A.; engraved by W. Giller. 18 by 15 high. Prints, 12s.; Proofs, 1*l.* 1s.; B. L. 1*l.* 11s. 6d.

DUKE of BUCKINGHAM and CHANDOS, painted by T. Jackson, R.A.; engraved by J. Porter. 14 by 20 high. Prints, 1*l.* 1s.; Proofs, 2*l.* 2s.

BURNS IN HIS STUDY, painted by Sir W. Allan, R.A.; engraved by J. Burnet, F.R.S. 15 by 21 high. Prints, 1*l.* 1s.; Proofs, 2*l.* 2s.; India, 3*l.* 3s.; before Letters, 4*l.* 4s.

BYRON (companion to Lawrence's Portrait of Sir Walter Scott), painted by T. Phillips, R.A.; engraved by R. Graves, A.R.A. 13 by 16 high. Prints, 1*l.* 1s.; Proofs, 2*l.* 2s.; before Letters, 4*l.* 4s.

CANTERBURY PILGRIMAGE, painted by T. Stothard, R.A.; engraved by James Heath. 38 by 14 high. Prints, 2*l.* 2s.; Proof, 5*l.* 5s.

CARD PLAYERS at a VILLAGE INN, painted by Sir David Wilkie, R.A.; engraved by C. G. Lewis. 25 by 20 high. Prints, 1*l.* 11s. 6d; Proofs, 3*l.* 3s.; before Letters, 5*l.* 5s.

CHELSEA PENSIONERS READING the GAZETTE of the BATTLE of WATERLOO, painted by Sir D. Wilkie, R.A.; engraved by John Burnet, F.R.S. 20 by 31 high. Prints, 3*l.* 3s.; Proofs, 6*l.* 6s.; India, 10*l.* 10s.; before Letters, 12*l.* 12s.

CHILDREN FEEDING RABBITS, painted by E. Landseer, R.A.; engraved by T. Landseer. Prints, 2*l.* 2s.; Proofs, 4*l.* 4s.; before Letters, 6*l.* 6s.

CHRIST RAISING the WIDOW'S SON, painted by Overbeck; engraved by Noel. 21 by 18 high. Prints, 10s. 6d.; Proofs, 1*l.* 1s.; B. L., 2*l.* 2s.

CORONATION of QUEEN VICTORIA, containing Original Portraits of the Royal Family, Great Officers of State, &c., painted by Sir George Hayter; engraved by H. T. Ryall, Historical and Portrait Engraver to her Majesty. 37 by 26 high. Prints, 4*l.* 4s.; Proofs, 8*l.* 8s.; before Letters, 12*l.* 12s.

COVENANTERS PREACHING, BAPTISM, and DRUMCLOG, painted by G. Harvey; engraved by Wagstaff. 26 by 22 high. Prints, 2*l.* 2s.; Proofs, 3*l.* 3s.; before Letters, 4*l.* 4s. each.

DUNCAN GRAY, painted by Sir D. Wilkie, R.A.; engraved by T. Engleheart. 14 by 19 high. Prints, 1*l.* 1s.; Proofs, 2*l.* 2s.; before Letters, 6*l.* 6s.

ENTHUSIAST, ABSTRACTION, &c., painted by T. Lane; engraved by Robert Graves, A.R.A. 12 by 10 high. Prints, 7s. 6d.; Proofs, 10s. 6d.

EXAMINATION of a VILLAGE SCHOOL, painted by G. Harvey, R.S.A.; engraved by F. Bromley. 29 by 23 high. Prints, 2*l.* 2s.; Proofs, 3*l.* 3s.

GAMEKEEPER'S RETURN HOME, painted by Sidney Cooper; engraved by G. H. Phillips. 24 by 20 high. Prints, 1*l.* 1s.; Proofs, 2*l.* 2s.

GEMS of STEWART NEWTON, consisting of Eleven highly-finished Plates, with Letter-press. 4to., full bound in morocco, and richly gilt, 1*l.* 11s. 6d.

GENTLE SHEPHERD and COTTAGE TOILET, painted by Sir D. Wilkie, R.A.; engraved by J. Stewart. 12 by 1[illegible] high. Prints, 12s.; Proofs, 1*l.* 1s.; India, 1*l.* 11s. 6d. before Letters, 2*l.* 2s.

GREENWICH PENSIONERS COMMEMORATING the BATTLE of TRAFALGAR, painted and engraved by John Burnet, F.R.S. 21 by 31 high. Prints, 3*l.* 3s.; Proofs, 6*l.* 6s.; before Letters, 12*l.* 12s.

HADDON HALL, DERBYSHIRE, drawn and lithographed by Douglas Morison. 26 Plates, half-bound, 4*l.* 4s.; Coloured and Mounted, 10*l.* 10s.

HAGHE'S BELGIUM and GERMANY, drawn on Stone and Tinted by Himself. 26 Plates, half-bound, 4*l.* 4s.; Coloured and Mounted, 10*l.* 10s.

HAWKING PARTY in the OLDEN TIME, painted by Edwin Landseer, R.A.; engraved by C. G. Lewis (the size of 'Bo[illegible]n Abbey'). Prints, 2*l.* 2s.; Proofs, 4*l.* 4s.; before Let[illegible]rs, 6*l.* 6s.

HAWK and the F[illegible]LCON, painted by E. Landseer, R.A., as Supp[illegible]ters to the preceding Plate; engraved by C. G. Lewis. [illegible]8 by 26 high. Prints, 1*l.* 1s.; Proofs, 2*l.* 2s.; before Letters, 3*l.* 3s. each.

HIGHLAND DROVERS DEPARTING for the SOUTH, painted by E. Landseer, R.A.; engraved by W. J. H. Watt. 82 by 24 high. Prints, 3*l.* 3s.; Proofs, 6*l.* 6s.; India, 10*l.* 10s.; before Letters, 12*l.* 12s.

HIGHLAND HOSPITALITY, painted by J. F. Lewis; engraved by W. Giller. 24 by 20 high. Prints, 1*l.* 1s.; Proofs, 2*l.* 2s.; before Letters, 3*l.* 3s.

HIGHLAND WHISKY STILL, painted by E. Landseer, R.A.: engraved by R. Graves, A.R.A. 23 by 19 high. Prints, 2*l.* 2s.; Proofs, 4*l.* 4s.; before Letters, 6*l.* 6s.; Artist's Proofs, 8*l.* 8s.

KEMBLE FAMILY, painted by G. H. Harlow; engraved by G. Clint, A.R.A. 82 by 25 high. Prints, 3*l.* 3s.; Proofs, 5*l.* 5s.; before Letters, 12*l.* 12s.

LASSIE HERDING SHEEP, painted by Edwin Landseer, R.A.; engraved by John Burnet. Prints, 2*l.* 2s.; Proofs, 4*l.* 4s.; B. L., 6*l.* 6s.

LIEUT.-GEN. SIR HUGH GOUGH, G.C.B., painted by a Chinese Artist, and engraved by J. R Jackson. 10 by 12 high. Prints, 12s; Proofs, 1*l.* 1s.; before Letters, with Autograph, 1*l.* 11s. 6d.

LORD JOHN RUSSELL, painted by Sir George Hayter; engraved by J. Bromley. 11 by 16 high. Prints, 1*l.* 1s.; Proofs, 2*l.* 2s.; B. L., 3*l.* 3s.

MELTON MOWBRAY HUNT, companion to 'The Royal Hunt,' painted by F. Grant, A.R.A.; and engraved by W. Humphreys. 32 by 21 high. Prints, 3*l.* 3s.; Proofs, 5*l.* 5s.; before Letters, 6*l.* 6s.

MELTON MOWBRAY BREAKFAST, painted by Francis Grant, A.R.A.; engraved by C. G. Lewis, the same size as 'The Royal Hunt.' Prints, 3*l.* 3s.; Proofs, 5*l.* 5s.; B. L., 6*l.* 6s.

PEDLAR SELLING HIS WARES, painted by Sir D. Wilkie, R.A.; engraved by J. Stewart. 14 by 19 high. Prints, 1*l.* 1s.; Proofs, 2*l.* 2s.; B. L., 4*l.* 4s.

PEEL, WELLINGTON, and STANLEY, engraved by Lewis, after Sir Thomas Lawrence, P.R.A. The size of Life, in imitation of the Original Drawings. Each 18 by 25 high. Prints, 1*l.* 1s.; Autograph Proofs, 2*l.* 2s.

PRINCE ALBERT, K.G., painted by G. Patten, A.R.A.; engraved by C. E. Wagstaff. 15 by 20 high. Prints, 1*l.* 1s.; Proofs, 2*l.* 2s.; India Proofs, 3*l.* 3s.; before Letters, 4*l.* 4s.

PRINCE ALBERT, K.G. (whole length), in the Robes and Jewels of the Order of the Garter, companion to Chalon's Portrait of 'The Queen,' painted by George Patten, A.R.A.; engraved by H. T. Ryall. 34 by 13 high. Prints, 3*l.* 3s.; Proofs, 5*l.* 5s.; Autograph Proofs, 8*l.* 8s.

PRINCESS AUGUSTA OF CAMBRIDGE, painted by E. Huess; engraved by C. W. Wass. 10 by 14 high. Prints, 10s. 6d.; Proofs, 1*l.* 1s.; Autograph Proofs, 1*l.* 11s. 6d.

QUEEN VICTORIA in the IMPERIAL DALMATIC ROBES, seated on the Throne of Homage in Westminster Abbey. Painted by Sir G. Hayter; engraved by H. T. Ryall. 22 by 31 high. Prints, 3*l.* 3s.; Proofs, 5*l.* 5s; before Letters, 8*l.* 8s.

QUEEN VICTORIA in the ROBES of STATE, painted by T. Sully, for the United States; engraved by C. E. Wagstaff. 15 by 20 high. Prints, 1*l.* 1s.; Proofs, 2*l.* 2s.; India, 3*l.* 3s.; B. L., 4*l.* 4s.

QUEEN VICTORIA'S FIRST STATE VISIT to DRURY-LANE THEATRE, painted by E. T. Parris; engraved by C. E. Wagstaff. 13 by 17 high. Prints, 1*l.* 1s.; Proofs, 2*l.* 2s.; India, 3s. 3s.; B. L., 4*l.* 4s.

ROBINSON CRUSOE and his MAN FRIDAY, painted by A. Fraser; engraved by C. Lewis. 25 by 20 high. Prints, 1*l.* 1s.; Proofs, 2*l.* 2s.

RAT HUNTERS, painted by Sir D. Wilkie; engraved by D. Mitchell. 10 by 14 high. Prints, 12s.; Proofs, 1*l.* 1s.; India, 1*l.* 11s. 6d.; B. L., 2*l.* 2s.

ROBERTS'S SPANISH SKETCHES. Twenty-six Plates, half-bound, 4*l.* 4s.; Coloured and Mounted, 10*l.* 10s., in portfolio.

ROYAL CORTEGE in WINDSOR PARK, painted by R. B. Davis; engraved by F. Bromley. The same size as 'The Melton Meet.' 32 by 21 high. Prints, 3*l.* 3s.; Proofs, 5*l.* 5s.; before Letters, 6*l.* 6s.

ROYAL HUNT on ASCOT HEATH. Painted by F. Grant, A.R.A.; engraved by F. Bromley. 32 by 21 high. Prints, 3*l.* 3s.; Proofs, 5*l.* 5s.; before Letters, 6*l.* 6s.

SIR JOSHUA REYNOLDS'S WORKS, Complete in 60 numbers. 10s. 6d. each, containing five Plates, forming three Volumes. 300 Plates.

SIR WALTER SCOTT in his STUDY, painted by Sir W. Allan, R.A.; engraved by J. Burnet, F.R.S. 15 by 21 high. Prints, 1*l.* 1s.; Proofs, 2*l.* 2s.; India, 3*l.* 3s.; before Letters, 4*l.* 4s.

SIR WALTER SCOTT, painted by Sir T. Lawrence; engraved by J. H. Robinson. 11 by 15 high. Prints, 1*l.* 1s.; Proofs, 2*l.* 2s.; India, 3*l.* 3s.; before Letters, 4*l.* 4s.

SNAP-APPLE NIGHT, painted by D. M'Clise, R.A.; engraved by J. Scott. 34 by 25 high. Prints, 2*l.* 2s.; Proofs, 4*l.* 4s.; before Letters, 5*l.* 5s.

SPANISH FLOWER-GIRL, painted by Murillo; engraved by J. H. Robinson. 9 by 13 high. Prints, 12s.; Proofs, 1*l.* 1s.; India, 1*l.* 11s. 6d.; B. L., 4gs.

STANFIELD'S SKETCHES on the MOSELLE, 26 Plates, half-bound, 4*l.* 4s.; Coloured and Mounted, in Portfolio, 10*l.* 10s.

SUTHERLAND CHILDREN, painted by E. Landseer, R.A.; engraved by S. Cousins, A.R.A. 26 by 20 high. Prints, 2*l.* 2s.; Proofs, 4*l.* 4s.; B. L., 6*l.* 6s.

TEMPLE of JUPITER, painted by J. M. W. Turner, R.A.; engraved by John Pye. 24 by 19 high. Prints, 1*l.* 11s. 6d.; Proofs, 3*l.* 3s.; India, 4*l.* 4s.; before Letters, 6*l.* 6s.

VENICE—THE GRAND CANAL, painted by J. M. W. Turner, R.A.; engraved by W. Miller. 27 by 21 high. Prints, 1*l.* 11s. 6d.; Proofs, 3*l.* 3s.; India, 4*l.* 4s.; before Letters, 6*l.* 6s.

VILLAGE POLITICIANS, painted by Sir D. Wilkie, R.A.; engraved by A. Raimbach. 23 by 19 high. Prints, £2 12s. 6d.; Proofs, 15*l.* 15s.

VILLAGE FESTIVAL, painted by Sir D. Wilkie, R.A.,; engraved by C. G. Lewis. 28 by 22 high. Prints, 2*l.* 2s.; Proofs, 4*l.* 4s.; B. L., 6*l.* 6s.

WELLINGTON, AS CHANCELLOR OF OXFORD, painted by H. P. Briggs, R.A.; engraved by Phillips. 19 by 29 high (whole length). Prints, 2*l.* 2s.; Proofs, 4*l.* 4s.; before Letters, 6*l.* 6s.

WELLINGTON AT WATERLOO, painted by A. Cooper, R.A.; engraved by F. Bromley. 24 by 20 high. Prints, 1*l.* 1s.; Proofs, 2*l.* 2s.; B. L., 3*l.* 3s.

WELLINGTON (Military Whole Length), painted by W. Simpson; engraved by G. H. Phillips. 20 by 30 high. Prints, 1*l.* 11s. 6d.; Proofs, 3*l.* 3s.; before Letters, 5*l.* 5s.

WIDOW'D DUCK, painted by E. Landseer, R.A.; engraved by John Burnet, F.R.S. 24 by 21 high. Prints, 1*l.* 1s.; Proofs, 2*l.* 2s.; B. L. 3*l.* 3s.

WILKIE'S ORIENTAL SKETCHES, made during his late Tour in the East. Lithographed in the finest style of Art by Joseph Nash. 26 Plates, folio, half-bound, 4*l.* 4s.; Coloured and Mounted, 10*l.* 10s.; Large paper, uniform with Roberts's Holy Land, 6*l.* 6s.

London:—Printed the Office of Palmer and Clayton, 10, Crane Court, Fleet Street, and Published by Jeremiah How, 132, Fleet Street.—June 1, 1843.

62 *Art Union* advertisement for Graves and Warmsley

drovers departing for the South' engraved by J.H. Watt in 1841, and 'Highland Whisky still' engraved by Robert Graves in 1842. It was said that Landseer received over £500,000 from Graves for the engraving of his pictures; in 1842, for instance, 500 guineas was paid for an 18 in. circular portrait of the Queen and her children. In 1869, the press reported that Graves had given £24,000 for W.P. Frith's 'Railway station' and its copyright. It was engraved by Francis Holl and was published in 1866. Later in his career, he produced a 'library' edition of Landseer's works, for part 18 of which 'The Shepherd's Bible' engraved by John Cother Webb (1855–1927) was published on 1 June 1885 (Plate 63). Webb was a pupil of Thomas Landseer, who had engraved the subject in 1858. A similar format was used for the works of Thomas Faed 1872 and other artists.

The firm suffered when a fire at Her Majesty's Theatre on 6 December 1867 spread to their premises, and completely gutted three of the four rear galleries behind the shop with the loss of many paintings, engravings etc. Fortunately Graves saved £30,000 worth of steel plates which were kept in

63 The Shepherd's Bible, engraved by J.C. Webb

iron safes, together with his trade books and subscription lists. Earlier in 1867 Dixon the printer had sent about 100 plates of portraits for safe keeping and to reduce the stock he held at 70 Hampstead Road but, as there had not been room for them in the safe, the plates were leant against the gallery wall. They were damaged by fire and water, so to complete their destruction, Algernon Graves defaced them with a penknife. Some eminent pictures were said to be in the hands of the engravers, notably Frith's 'Railway Station', even though the print had been issued a year earlier. The pictures in the gallery at the time of the fire were sold at Christie's on 7 March 1868, possibly to help finance the restoration work, since Graves had only partial insurance cover to the sum of about £30,000.

In 1873/74 Graves publicized Landseer by first, an exhibition of engravings after his work in Piccadilly, the catalogue of which was compiled by Algernon, Henry's son, and secondly by the preparation of 20 engravings of the artist's paintings of Queen Victoria's pet dogs, to be engraved by Thomas Landseer, Charles G. Lewis and Charles Mottram, among others. The firm declared 1,039 prints through the Printseller's Association between 1847 and 1894, to which can be added the numbers issued from 1835 to 1847. Henry died in 1892, and was succeeded by his son Algernon in 1896, by which time line engraving, and to some extent mezzotint, had been supplanted by photographic methods.

Thomas McLean (or M'Lean) (1788–1875) was the only other established firm to produce line and mezzotint engravings. He was at 26 Haymarket and spent nearly 50 years as a print publisher until his retirement, when he handed over to his son. Between 1840 and 1865 his principal plates were after Landseer, engraved by Thomas Landseer, Benjamin Phelps Gibbon, Charles Mottram and Peter Lightfoot. There were also engravings of royal personages, some in mezzotint, but his list was never as full as that of his rivals.

Outside the capital, there was a growing body of potential patrons with sufficient wealth and interest to purchase works of art, and especially prints. This was particularly so in the north-west of England where another firm of long standing was able to build a reputation to rival the metropolitan publishers.

From *circa* 1797 Vittore Zanetti had run his Repository of Art at 94 Market Street, Manchester. Thomas Agnew (1794–1871), born and raised in Liverpool, moved with his family to Manchester about 1810, and immediately entered into an apprenticeship with Zanetti, culminating in partnership in 1817. By 1835 he had become sole proprietor, the mainstay of the engraving business being portraits, especially those privately commissioned, of local worthies, and he employed S.W. Reynolds and Samuel Bellin as his principal engravers. The portrait of Dr Dalton after Allen engraved by

William Henry Worthington in 1839 exemplifies his work. By 1837 the firm had regular dealings with the London printsellers and publishers such as Colnaghi, Graves, Lloyd Bros, McLean and Gambart, with whom he had an account. In 1850 Agnew was granted a royal warrant, was becoming a major publisher in London through his agents, and had published engravings after Landseer and 20 after Millais. Between 1854 and 1856 Thomas's son William paid frequent visits to London, and in 1860 a branch was opened there in Waterloo Place. A Liverpool branch had opened in 1859. Thomas retired in 1861, by which time he had published over 1,000 prints. In 1887 the firm presented copies of 100 examples of their work to the Department of Prints and Drawings (presumably the British Museum), in which a wide range of engravers was represented, e.g. Atkinson, Barlow, Brandard, Cousen, Cousins, Goodall, Hollis, C.G. Lewis, W.H. Simmons, Smith and Stacpoole.

The Grundy brothers were sons of a cotton spinner and worked in Liverpool. The eldest was John Clowes Grundy (1806–67), who by 1839 was publishing prints such as 'Lancashire witch' after William Bradley, engraved by his brother Thomas Leeming Grundy (1808–41), and a portrait of Revd Hugh Stowell, engraved by H. Cousins (1809–64). He exhibited some framed prints at the Manchester Exposition 1845. His younger brother Robert Hindmarsh Grundy (1816–65) published prints such as Landseer's 'There's life in the old dog yet'. It was said *circa* 1840 that his taste and enterprise had contributed to the encouragement of art by the wealthy inhabitants of Liverpool and other large towns in Lancashire.

The social, political and cultural climate had settled down by *circa* 1840, so a number of new publishers appeared to increase competition with established firms. Welch and Gwynne, 'printsellers & publishers to the Royal Family' of 24 St James's Street, published a limited list which included William Fowles's portrait of Queen Victoria mezzotinted by B.P. Gibbon in 1839, Alexander Johnston's 'The gentle shepherd' engraved by Frederick Bromley in 1841, and a portrait of the Duke of Wellington after William Slater, line engraved by William Greatbach in 1844.

The supply of prints to Britain broadened its scope with the arrival in 1840 of the Belgian Ernest Gambart, who started in a poor way by trying to sell prints, including those published in France by Alphonse Goupil, but with little success, especially in the Midlands, so he returned to London to seek employment with Thomas McLean, possibly as a print colourist. He was dealing with Dixon and Ross late in 1842 and had established himself as a print publisher by 1843, importing foreign prints as well as exporting English prints to the Continent. His patronage introduced the use of foreign engravers to reproduce the works of English artists, as, for example, the commission to Auguste Thomas Marie Blanchard (1829–98) to engrave

Holman Hunt's 'Finding of the Saviour in the Temple' in 1868. The number of prospective buyers of this print was estimated in the *Art Journal* review (1868, p. 100) by its statement that 'the print … will be … destined to occupy the place of honour in tens of thousands of homes where Art is loved, and the Christian faith venerated'. Blanchard engraved several more plates for the firm. 'The Horse fair' after the French artist Rosa Bonheur was regarded by contemporaries to be Gambart's best plate, but as the original plate by Thomas Landseer 1856 was destroyed, C.G. Lewis re-engraved it in a smaller size in 1863 and W.H. Simmons did an even smaller one in 1871. Most of his later prints were line engravings and when, in 1871, he handed the firm over to his manager Pilgeram and his nephew Léon Henri Lefèvre, they continued the practice and a good number of prints were produced from the works of W.P. Frith, Holman Hunt, Phillips, Ward, Maclise, J.C. Hook, Frederick Goodall, Dubufe, Thomas Faed, Edouard Frère, Henry Lejeune, Alma Tadema and J. Tissot. The engravings were done by J. Ballin, A. Blanchard, W.T. Davey, W. Ridgway, H.T. Ryall, W.H. Simmons and F. Stacpoole. By this time the firm had been acknowledged as an 'English firm' by its use of mainly English artists and engravers. Lefèvre copyrights, engraved plates and prints were sold by auction in 1926.

In Newcastle upon Tyne, Currie and Bowman published Lupton's 'Northumberland House' in 1840 and Robert Turner also published there from 1852 to after 1870. Alexander Hill published in Edinburgh from about 1845 and in Leicester John Garle Browne worked from 1855 until the mid-1860s. The French house of Goupil acquired a London office in 1853, by when the public had a more favourable attitude to French prints than in the 1840s. Some printers also branched out into print publishing, such as Virtue and Co. whose *Art Journal* plates were printed for collectors in a large format in proof before letters, and taken before ordinary impressions were printed. The India paper print 'Cherry ripe' after Metzmacher, engraved by Peter Lightfoot for the *Art Journal* in 1872 had a mount measuring 26½ in. × 19 in. (Plate 64).

Lloyd Brothers published from 1847 to 1866. They were probably related to the plate printers Richard Lloyd 1831, which became Lloyd and Henning, 1832–35, then Lloyd & Co. 1836–43. Lloyd Brothers began with two plates engraved by William Holl and one by Henry Lemon in 1847. Dixon and Ross had published some plates between 1854 and 1862. McQueen operated under a number of names. Three brothers, J.H., F.C. and George Peter worked separately and together at various times, J.H. from 184 Tottenham Court Road, the address of the plate-printing business, and George Peter from 70 Berners Street. The firm of Moore, McQueen and Co. operated from 1861 to 1867, J.H. McQueen from 1868 to 1871 and George Peter from 1871 to 1883. After this, the firm went into

LINE ENGRAVING: PRINTS, MAPS, BOOK PLATES 153

64 Cherry ripe, engraved by P. Lightfoot

65 Title page of J. Thomson's *Castle of Indolence*, drawn by W. Rimer

66 The last embrace, engraved by C. Rolls

photographical means of reproduction and continued into the early part of the 20th century.

The art unions were probably the most influential publishers of all. From the mid-1830s, art unions sprang up everywhere, and although the lotteries with art objects as prizes were a great success, some subscribers, especially in the larger societies, were likely to get nothing for their subscription. To this end, the issue of an engraving of a modern picture to every member recompensed them for their outlay at minimal cost to the union. They were prized by many of their owners, and were given pride of place on their living-room walls. To prepare line engravings needed some forward planning, and so mezzotints, with a shorter execution time were tried in the early days when numbers were comparatively low. As thousands of members joined, mezzotints were unable to produce sufficient copies, and line engraving was employed, bringing with it the highest form of the engraving art and a 'high finish'. A wide variety of artists and engravers worked for the art unions, and in 1843 it was reckoned that line engraving was almost entirely confined to their publications. As time went by the plates became larger in size, and engravers of the first rank worked for them.

The Art Union of London was a major publisher, and the plate intended for 1845 was 'The convalescent from Waterloo' after William Mulready, which G.T. Doo was commissioned to engrave. It was said to be 'nearly completed' in January 1845, but illness appears to have supervened and delayed further work on it. The Union then had to think quickly and produce something to tide them over. As it happened, they had inaugurated a competition in 1842 for a series of designs, illustrating an epoch in British history, or the works of an English author. The winner of the 1844 competition was William Rimer, with illustrations to James Thomson's poem *Castle of Indolence* (Plate 65). They were etched in a hurry for publication in March 1845 by Jean Ferdinand Joubert de la Ferté (1810–83) who did four designs, Edward Webb (*c*.1805–54) also did four, Edward Richard Whitfield (b. 1817), pupil of Augustus Fox, who did two and H.W. Collard who also did two.

'The last embrace' after Thomas Uwins was engraved by Charles Rolls for the year 1847 (Plate 66), and this shows the small embossed stamp used to authenticate their prints, positioned in the centre of the bottom margin above the lettering. By mid-1848 'The convalescent from Waterloo' had been completed and distributed to 30,000 subscribers, but the *Art Journal* (1848, p. 132) review was scathing: 'The engraver was paid an ample sum, but the picture was not calculated to engrave well. The combination of great

67   The convalescent from Waterloo (detail), engraved by G.T. Doo

LINE ENGRAVING: PRINTS, MAPS, BOOK PLATES   157

68   Whittington, engraved by T.A. Prior

painter and great engraver has failed to produce a satisfactory print.' Despite that, it was very popular, but it is a sad commentary on the fate of such things that the copy from which Plate 67 was taken, shows the tears and marks it had received before it was consigned to a bric-à-brac shop from which it was rescued.

The Art Union of Glasgow presented its subscribers with T.A. Prior's engraving of F. Newenham's 'Whittington' in 1849 (Plate 68) which was 16 in. × 11⅜ in., and the Art Union of London used William Ridgway's engraving after George Smith of 'Light and darkness' for their 1871 plate which measured 21 in. × 30 in. The copy in the author's possession was mounted on a stretcher and placed within a narrow gold frame, and had obviously done duty in some Victorian home.

As commissions decreased, the art unions could command the services of the most eminent and fashionable engravers. One such was Lumb Stocks RA (1812–92) who, in February 1866, was given six years until April 1872 to complete what is now considered to be his best print. 'The meeting of Wellington and Blucher at Waterloo' after Daniel Maclise (Plate 69) was to be 44 in. × 12 in., a most unusual size, to represent an original mural 45 feet long, which adorns, with a copy of the print, the Royal Gallery of the House of Lords. As was usual in most important commissions, a signed and sealed agreement was drawn up (the beginning and end of which are show on pages 160 and 161).

He was required to report progress once a year, and one of the most important stages was the engraving of foreground figures before the background was filled in (Plate 70). He was to produce 3,000 copies and keep only eight proofs for himself. He had been married on 10 October 1839 and his Pearl wedding anniversary was commemorated in this print by a 'secret' message written into the engraving. On a stone located in the centre of Plate 71 he engraved 'To Ellen my affectionate wife for 30 years, December 10th 1869' (Plate 72). Mrs Ellen Stocks (Plate 73) was the mother of a girl and eight boys, the last of which, Bernard Octavius (1859–1915), was an eminent mezzotint engraver.

Not all the art unions could afford to commission their own engravings, so bought old and worn out plates from the publishers. The London Fine Art Association in 1876 used a plate size 14½ in. × 12 in. 'by kind permission of Messrs. Henry Graves & Co. [Copyright]' of Sir David Wilkie's 'Duncan Gray' (Plate 74). It had been engraved by Francis Engleheart (1775–1849) and had originally been published by F.G. Moon, presumably some time before he left the partnership with Boys and Graves in 1835. The print shows signs of plate wear, and was probably printed lithographically, since there is no sign of a plate mark. A similar example occurs where the National Fine Art Union published 'The Gipsy Queen' after E. Pingret and engraved by Francis Holl (1815–84) size 14½ in. × 11½ in. (Plate 75). Some of Holl's engravings after this artist had been published earlier by Lloyd Brothers. There were smaller unions which issued no engraving, such as the Brighton Art Union which in December 1864 only drew for ten paintings and 17 Parian statues.

The Royal Association for the Promotion of the Fine Arts in Scotland also issued a series of steel engravings for their subscribers, many of which were published in book form, although having the appearance of separate prints. The volume for 1868 was *Six Engravings in Illustration of the Lady of the Lake* and contained plates averaging 9⅝ in. × 7 in., as that in Plate 76, after a painting by Robert Herdman RSA in 1867, engraved by Thomas Brown (fl. 1868–87) and printed in London by McQueen.

Almanacks or calendars were popular from the late 17th century. They were printed on a broadside sheet with a pictorial heading at the top, and the calendar with miscellaneous information below, engraved on a single plate. The monopoly for them was held for many years by the Stationers' Company, who produced their own almanack, with the sole exception of those printed by Oxford University. The *Stationers' Almanack* during the 19th century employed only a few engravers for its pictures. Thomas Higham drew and engraved the plates from *circa* 1826 to 1839, and although he continued to engrave until 1844, the pictures from 1839 to 1844 were drawn by G. Moore. London monuments, gardens, buildings and bridges were all featured, e.g. in 1832 'New London Bridge', in 1837 'Proposed new Houses of Parliament' and in 1839 'Hyde Park Gardens'. From 1845 J. Marchant drew the pictures, engraved by Henry Adlard, who worked until 1876 with different artists from 1851 until 1854, when P. Phillips took over from 1855 to 1865, to be followed by John O'Connor until 1884. Views moved away from London in 1856 to places such as Chatham, Llangollen, Liverpool, Hastings and Worcester. B. Lasbury became engraver from 1876 to 1879, and from 1880 to 1889, John Saddler took over. Louis Godfrey engraved for the 1890 edition and was succeeded from 1891 by Herbert E. Sedcole (1854–c.1920).

The *Oxford Almanack* was illustrated by steel engravings from 1832, when the printing press had completed its move from the Sheldonian Theatre to Walton Street. The calendar was printed with ordinary type, not engraved as hitherto. The whole sheet was smaller than earlier ones and the set of 36 steel-engraved almanacks have a distinctive look of their own. Only three engravers were employed over the period 1832–70, and a change of engraver was precipitated by the emigration of Joseph Skelton to Paris, who had engraved many plates until his last of 1831. In 1829 Henry Le Keux, an architectural engraver, was consulted about changing to steel engraving for the 1832 Almanack, and was commissioned to engrave the five issues until

An Agreement made this thirteenth day of February, One Thousand Eight Hundred and forty-six, between the ART-UNION OF LONDON of the one part and Lumb Stocks, A.R.A. of 6, Richmond Villas, Seven Sisters Road in the County of Middlesex of the other part.

Whereas the ART-UNION OF LONDON, being desirous of having an Engraving made of a certain Picture, called the Picture (Wellington visiting a Veteran at Waterloo) painted by Daniel Maclise R.A., and now the property of the nation, the said Lumb Stocks hath tendered and offered to engrave the same upon a steel plate, and to superintend the taking the Impressions from the said Plate in manner and upon the terms hereinafter contained, which offer the said ART-UNION OF LONDON have accepted. Now therefore the said Lumb Stocks, in consideration of the sum of One Thousand One hundred pounds, to be paid to him in manner hereinafter mentioned, doth hereby agree with the said ART-UNION OF LONDON that he will provide a steel plate, and will engrave thereon a Line Engraving of the said Picture called the picture of Wellington visiting Veteran at Waterloo in his best style of Line Engraving; the said size plate Engraving being of the dimensions of four, four 1/2 inches by twelve inches, and the same to be completed within the period hereinafter mentioned in every respect fit for printing therefrom the first finished Impressions at the least. And also that he will, during the progress of the said Engraving, and at six distinct and successive stages of the Plate, deliver to the Council for the time being of the said ART-UNION OF LONDON Duplicate Proof Impressions, to be taken from the said Plate engraved Plate, for their examination. And also that he will during the progress of the said Engraving, whenever required by the said Council for the time being, produce to them at their Council-room the said Plate, in order that the Council may examine and ascertain the progress of the said Engraving. And the said Lumb Stocks doth further agree with the said ART-UNION OF LONDON, that he will, on or before the thirtieth day of April One Thousand Eight Hundred and seventy-two, complete and finish the said engraved Plate in every respect according to the provisions of this Agreement, and to the entire satisfaction of the said Council for the time being, and will deliver the same so complete and finished to the said Council for the time being of the ART-UNION OF LONDON. And that he will superintend the printing of three thousand Impressions from the said engraved Plate; and will from time to time retouch and keep the said Plate in such good order during the said printing as may be necessary for the due printing the said Impressions.

161

the said Plate by him as hereinbefore mentioned. And it is agreed that the said Samuel Stocks is to be at liberty to take Eight Proof Impressions and no more from the said Plate for his own use, but not to be at liberty to sell the same. Provided always, and it is hereby expressly agreed by and between the said Art-Union of London and the said Samuel Stocks, that in the event of any dispute or difference arising between them touching or concerning the manner in which the said Samuel Stocks is proceeding with the said Engraving, or as to the manner in which the same may be finished, or touching or concerning any matter or thing in any manner arising out of this Agreement, all and every such disputes and dispute, differences and difference, shall be referred to the Arbitration of John Frederic Robinson Esk^re. And the Award of the said John Frederic Robinson, whom made in writing under his hand, shall from time to time be binding and conclusive on the said parties. And that, for further and better enforcing the performance and observance of such Award, the reference or arbitration for or in respect of the same shall be made a rule of Her Majesty's Court of Queen's Bench at Westminster, according to the Statute in such case made and provided. Provided further, and it is hereby further mutually agreed, that in the event of the decease of the said Samuel Stocks before the said Thirtieth day of April One Thousand Eight Hundred and forty two and before the due completion of the said engraved Plate, or of his being prevented by illness for the space of Three calendar months from proceeding with the said Engraving, it shall be lawful to and for the said Art-Union of London to employ some other Engraver to complete the said Plate, and to superintend the taking of the said Impressions, and to retouch the said Plate as aforesaid, and out of the balance then unpaid to the said Samuel Stocks to deduct, retain, and pay the costs and charges relating thereto. And the said Samuel Stocks hereby covenants and agrees with the said Art-Union of London to take the utmost care of the said Picture, and not to do or suffer to be done any injury thereto. And also to deliver up the said Picture to the said Art-Union of London when the said Engraving is complete, or at any time after the date hereof upon being required by the said Council for the time being so to do. Provided always, that if the said Samuel Stocks shall be prevented by delivering up the said Picture before the said Thirtieth day of April One Thousand Eight Hundred and twenty two for a longer period than seven days without a sufficient cause, he is to be allowed an equal length of time beyond the said Thirtieth day of April for the completion of the said Engraving. And it is lastly agreed that the said Art-Union if required shall provide the said Samuel Stocks with a copy of the aforesaid printed particulars in his possession. In witness whereof the said Art-Union of London have hereunto set their Common Seal, and the said Samuel Stocks hath hereunto set his Hand and Seal the day and year first above written.

162

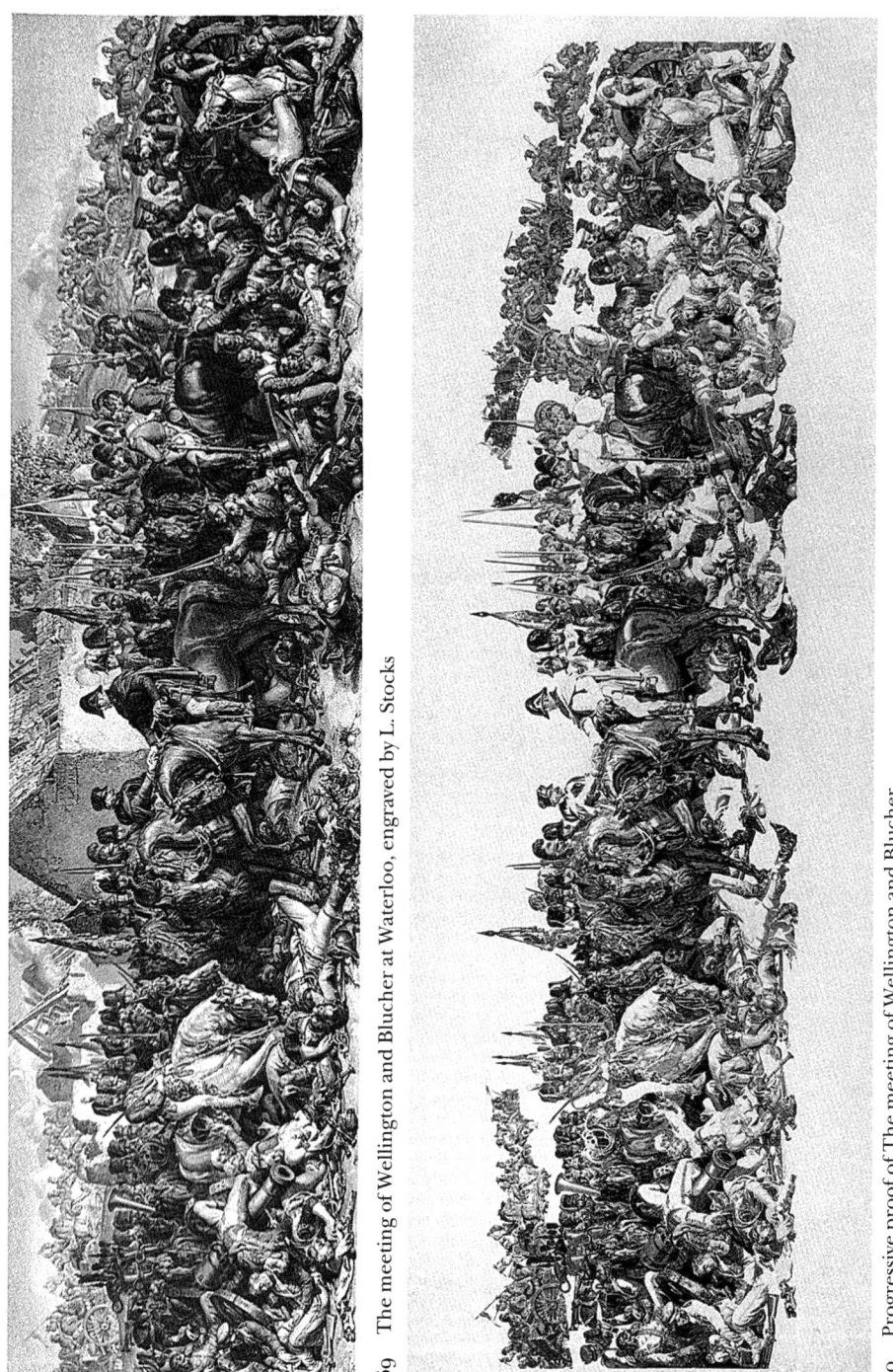

69 The meeting of Wellington and Blucher at Waterloo, engraved by L. Stocks

70 Progressive proof of The meeting of Wellington and Blucher

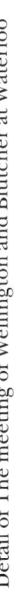

71 Detail of The meeting of Wellington and Blutcher at Waterloo

72 'Secret' message in The meeting of Wellington and Blucher...

73 Mrs Ellen Stocks

74 Duncan Gray, engraved by F. Engleheart

1836 at 225 guineas a plate which the Delegates thought was quite expensive, but after all, Henry was a top engraver. In an effort to reduce costs the engraver offered plates for 1837–39 'in his less elaborate stile [*sic*]' at £100 each on copper, but since in the past two copper plates had been worn out in producing the numbers required, it was not much of a saving. Another engraver was sought whose services would be less expensive. The Birmingham engraver William Radclyffe charged 82 guineas for his first plate in 1840, raising it to a more realistic £100 from 1841. He engraved a total of 15 plates, ending only with his death in 1855, in which year the last of Peter

75   The Gipsy Queen, engraved by F. Holl

76   The Lady of the lake from *Six engravings . . . of the Lady of the Lake*, engraved by T. Brown

77 Cambridge University Almanack 1837, engraved by E. Challis

de Wint's eight designs appeared. The last period from 1856 to 1870 was dominated by the work of Henry's nephew John Henry Le Keux, another architectural engraver, who both drew and engraved the designs, thus saving more money for the Delegates. The third artist was Frederick Mackenzie (1787–1854) who provided 12 pictures until the year before his death in 1854.

Thirty-five of the 36 steel plates still exist in the Oxford University Press. That of 1847 is the missing plate which had been used again for the Almanack of 1887. The plate for 1852 was used again in 1880 and that of 1845 in 1891. The designs were a mixture of landscapes and views of buildings, with one interior, that of St Mary's Church showing the arrival of the Vice-Chancellor for the university sermon (1834). The first steel engraving of 1832 showed the new University Printing House, completed in 1830.

At Cambridge the Almanack used a similar format with an average print size of 14 in. × 9 in. A series of plates from 1832 to 1847 was engraved by Ebenezer Challis, who drew the designs for at least four, among which was 'St. John's College, new buildings, &c.' in 1837 (Plate 77). The other main artist was G. Dodgson, who drew the six designs for 1840–43 and 1846–47, and for 1839 C.R. Cockerell drew 'The new University Library'. The plates for 1832–34 were printed by R. Backhouse; from 1836 the printer was Robert Lloyd.

Maps

Steel engraving from its inception subtly altered the face of maps. It increased the amount of detail which could safely be engraved on a plate, and resulted in some very fine work, especially in shading and hachuring, where lines could be laid together more closely than on copper. The durability of the plate enabled maps to be used through many editions over a period of time, and additions such as the railways which appeared during the 1830s could be inserted with little disturbance of existing features. The correction of the plate was more difficult, although the method of knocking up from the back was still possible, but more difficult than with copper, especially on a hardened plate. It is significant, however, that from the 1830s steel plates were engraved solely for the purpose of creating a lithographic transfer which speeded up the printing process and made it possible to add or correct details on the stone or zinc plate. Thus the steels were kept in pristine condition to create further lithographic plates or electrotypes. This accounts for the appearance of a steel engraver's name on a lithographic print.

One of the most striking examples of this practice occurs in the series of maps produced by, and issued with, the *Weekly Dispatch* newspaper

(1856–62) and bound into *The Dispatch Atlas* of 234 maps in 1863, so that readers could follow events all over the world. Engravers included Benjamin Rees Davies, John Crane Dower (*c*.1790–1847), Joseph Wilson Lowry (1803–79) and Edward Weller, and the plates were still in use until just before World War II. G.W. Bacon was the first publisher, but in 1863 the atlas was taken over by Cassell, Petter and Galpin. The use of lithography from steel plates was known from about 1835, and James Pigot produced *A Pocket Topography and Gazetteer of England circa* 1841 with 38 maps engraved by Pigot and Slater, Pigot and Son, or Pigot and Co., and from *circa* 1858 George Philip published maps engraved by J. Bartholomew and Edward Weller. The same process was used for *The National Gazetteer*, edited by N.E.S. Hamilton and published from 1863 to 1868 by Virtue and Co. to include 60 maps engraved by W. Hughes who earlier had worked for Virtue. These maps brought the geography of the world to a much wider public, and ordinary homes could now own an atlas, thus widening their horizons and enabling them to understand newspaper reports from all over the world.

One of the first uses of steel engraved maps was in the field of education, where folded maps appeared in small format schoolbooks such as those which had been issued by Sir Richard Phillips before his retirement in 1823, having sold out to Longman a year or two earlier. *A Grammar of General Geography* was re-issued in February 1821, for which Sidney Hall, of 18 Bury Street, Bloomsbury (d. 1831) had engraved seven maps on Perkins's hardened steel plate and printed by him. In November 1822 Hall was paid £2 for 'corrections and additions to steel plates' and by 1824 the plates were used in a further edition, as well as for Goldsmith's *Geography, Illustrated on a Popular Plan; for the Use of Schools and Young Persons* . . . .

Hall did a great deal of work for Longman, and from the publisher's ledgers comes information about his remuneration. For maps in Keith's *Geography* in February 1826 he was paid £29 8s. 0d.; plates and new drawings for *Keith on the Globes*, £42 in August 1826, map for *Brook's Gazetteer*, eighteenth edition, 23 November 1826 £26 5s. 0d. and map of the world for *Geography and History*, fifteenth edition, 26 February 1828 for £21. His largest assignment was for 21 plates engraved on steel for which he was paid £18 each, in December 1824 for Butler's *Atlases*, probably Samuel Butler's *A general atlas of ancient and modern geography* (1826) with 43 maps by Sidney Hall. Five hundred impressions were taken from a mixture of the old (presumably copper) and the new plates and £51 5s. 0d. was paid by Longman for colouring them. In June 1826 20 maps were engraved on steel for the Ancient section of the atlas at £18 each, but possibly done by F. Mansell and others, thus almost completing the changeover to steel for all the maps. *Circa* July 1829 Hall engraved a new map of France in Provinces on steel for 18 guineas. In December 1833 payment of £18 was made to draw and engrave a map of Australia on steel for the Modern section, but, since Sidney died in January 1831, this must have been done by his widow Selina, who carried on his business until her death in 1853. In December 1826 and June 1827 there were repairs to the title, alterations to imprint and date, but no repairs to the plates themselves were listed for the 13,300 Modern and 9,050 Ancient maps printed between 1824 and 1833.

By 1830 there was a great number of works in preparation. James Pigot (fl. 1829–45), 18 Fountain Street, Manchester started to produce in 1829 *Pigot and Co.'s British Atlas, Comprising the Counties of England ... the Whole Engraved on Steel Plates.* There were 39 county plates engraved by Pigot and Co. [or Son], Manchester. James had been trained as an engraver, and helped by his son, could have engraved all the plates. A circular 'New map of the environs of London' in 1832 was engraved on steel by J. Pigot and [Isaac] Slater, possibly another engraver or a partner. As was the custom for maps of this calibre, each one in the Atlas carried a vignette engraving usually of a church, only one of which of St Lawrence's Church, Ludlow on the Shropshire map, is signed by the artist F. Page. There were seven further issues of the Atlas between 1831 and 1846, showing changes which took place over the period. In the original letterpress, figures from the 1821 Census were given, but in later issues those for 1831 were substituted and, as they opened, railways were put in place, e.g. Railways through Yorkshire were dated 1836–37. In 1840 a large map of England and Wales was added, with the inscription 'Steel plate Pigot & Co. Engravers, Manchester'. The 1840 edition was reproduced in 1990 by Garamond Publishers Ltd. In 1846 Isaac Slater took over its publication, by which time there were other rivals on the market. The firm also produced the valuable *London and Provincial New Commercial Directory* from *circa* 1823.

Henry Martin (fl. 1830–47) engraved [Thomas] 'Allen's new plan of London from an actual survey 1830' on steel for his *The Panorama of London, and Visitor's Pocket Companion*, published by Virtue, in 1830.

The next great series of maps was known by the name of Thomas Moule (1754–1851), published by George Virtue under the title of *The English Counties* produced with the aim of making maps available to all classes of society. They were a series of individual maps which could be used to accompany other works, as well as being published on their own. The first part, price one shilling plain, 1s. 6d. coloured, was issued in May 1830, and the last in 1836, and were accompanied by text printed on poor paper with type very closely set. The maps were coloured round the individual parish divisions, and the engraved pictures were left uncoloured. There were eventually 60 plates, 55 of which were county maps or plans, four were maps of the inland navigation of England and Wales and 'A comparative view of some of the principal hills in Great Britain AD 1834' drawn by E.I. Smith.

Copies made up from parts vary in content for a number of reasons, and it is important to collate them carefully. Seven plates carry no named engraver, and the first six plates produced from May to September 1830 were engraved by James Bingley (fl. 1822–40) as were ten others by him. He set the design pattern where most were an upright shape, all, except the first, had two or three views, either framed or vignette, with up to six (in one exception 12) coats of arms. Figures were pastoral, or for Oxford, a student, and frames were mainly architectural in form, except for Worcestershire, where a delicate tracery of hops was used. The name tablets represented stone, but in a few cases ribbons were used, that for Herefordshire being wound round an apple tree. Bingley covered the Midland counties. He had previously worked for the publisher Henry Teesdale, and had engraved 11 scenes for T. Moore's *The History of Devonshire*, published by Jennings in 1831, and later he did a folding map of Essex for T. Wright's *The Picturesque Beauties of Great Britain . . . Essex* (Virtue, 1834).

William Schmollinger (fl. 1830–37) engraved 26 maps covering the south, East Anglia and the most northern counties. About half of these were horizontal and half were upright, and only a few carried more than two views. His favourite device was introducing architectural detail along the top of frames, e.g. Cheshire, Cumberland, Durham and Lancashire, but in others he used apposite decoration, e.g. Kent had a frame of hops (not as well done as Bingley's Worcestershire), maritime themes for Middlesex and Neptune and seaweed for Sussex. The county name was less prominent, being mostly on small tablets, but he used ribbons occasionally. The only portrait was of William Shakespeare on the Warwickshire map. He also engraved the first 'Map of the inland navigation of England and Wales'. Schmollinger is also known for five plans, dated 1830–31, engraved after the author's designs for Sir William Gell's *Pompeiana . . .* (1832).

The third engraver was John Crane Dower (*c.*1790–1847) who did nine maps or plans, characterized by their ribbon frames, one or two vignette views and where the map was very much the dominant feature, decoration being secondary. He set up his own map printing and engraving business at 6 Cumming Place, Pentonville in 1820, which he left to his two sons on his death. He also engraved for [Samuel] *Lewis's Atlas Comprising the Counties of Ireland* (1837). In 1839 he engraved maps of northern and southern Greece for Christopher Wordsworth's *Greece*.

John Cleghorn (fl. 1827–80) contributed the plan of the 'City and University of Oxford' with two framed views, a narrow frame and the title on a ribbon.

Like most publications of this kind there were periods of instability, doubtless brought about by financial considerations, and there are examples of productions not proceeding beyond the first few issues. By

1836, however, Virtue was sure enough of his market to issue Moule's maps in a complete atlas entitled *The English Counties Delineated; or a Topographical Description of England*.... An engraved title page dated 1836 reads *England's Topographer; or Moule's English Counties in the 19th Century* with a central cartouche derived in part from the Sussex map. An edition of 1837 had a frontispiece depicting King William IV seated on his throne with a cartouche at the bottom carrying *The English counties Delineated by Thomas Moule* and *Chorographica Britanniae* on a ribbon at the top. The engraved title page of volume 2 had a central view of 'Greenwich Hospital' drawn by W. Bartlett and engraved by John Hinchliff (*c.*1805–75). From 1838 to *circa* 1870 the maps were under constant revision the most significant changes being in railway construction. Moule's maps accompanied the revised edition of the Revd James Barclay's *A Complete and Universal English Dictionary* ..., circa 1842, but the sets varied according to the maps available at the time of issue. B.B. Woodward, The Queen's Librarian, produced a new edition *circa* 1848 with the maps, and later still some 30 of the maps were used with editions of D. Hume and T. Smollett's *History of England*.

A highly coloured and slightly enlarged reproduction of Moule's maps was published by Studio Editions, in 1990 under the title *The County Maps of Old England*. The introduction is by Roderick Barron and the maps are arranged alphabetically, each with a short description.

John Walker (1787–1873) and brother Charles (d. *c.*1872) followed in their father's footsteps as map engravers and publishers. John had been engraver to James Horsburgh and the East India Company, and with his father, became a founder member of the Royal Geographical Society in 1830. They were prolific publishers, and among their work on steel was a map of Devonshire for J. Britton and E.W. Brayley's *Devonshire and Cornwall Illustrated* (1832), they engraved all 13 maps for the *Topographical Dictionary of Wales* (1833) by Samuel Lewis, and in 1836 did two maps for E. Baines's *History of Lancaster*.... Between 1847 and 1879 several editions of their ... *British Atlas ... Compiled from the Maps of the Board of Ordnance ...* appeared, dedicated originally to the Duchess of Kent and the Princess Victoria, but immediately amended to Her Majesty Queen Victoria and the Duchess of Kent! Their maps were used for the 42 in *Hobson's Fox Hunting Atlas* in 1845, with editions to 1895.

William Tombleson produced his *Eighty Picturesque Views on the Thames and Medway* (usually known as *Tombleson's Thames*) circa 1834, all engraved on steel and accompanied by 'Tombleson's panoramic map of the Thames and Medway', which was 3 ft 9 in. long and 10½ in. wide. This shows the remarkable effects produced by steel in the amount of detail which can be introduced into an unusual format.

From Wakefield in Yorkshire came the Greenwood brothers, Christopher

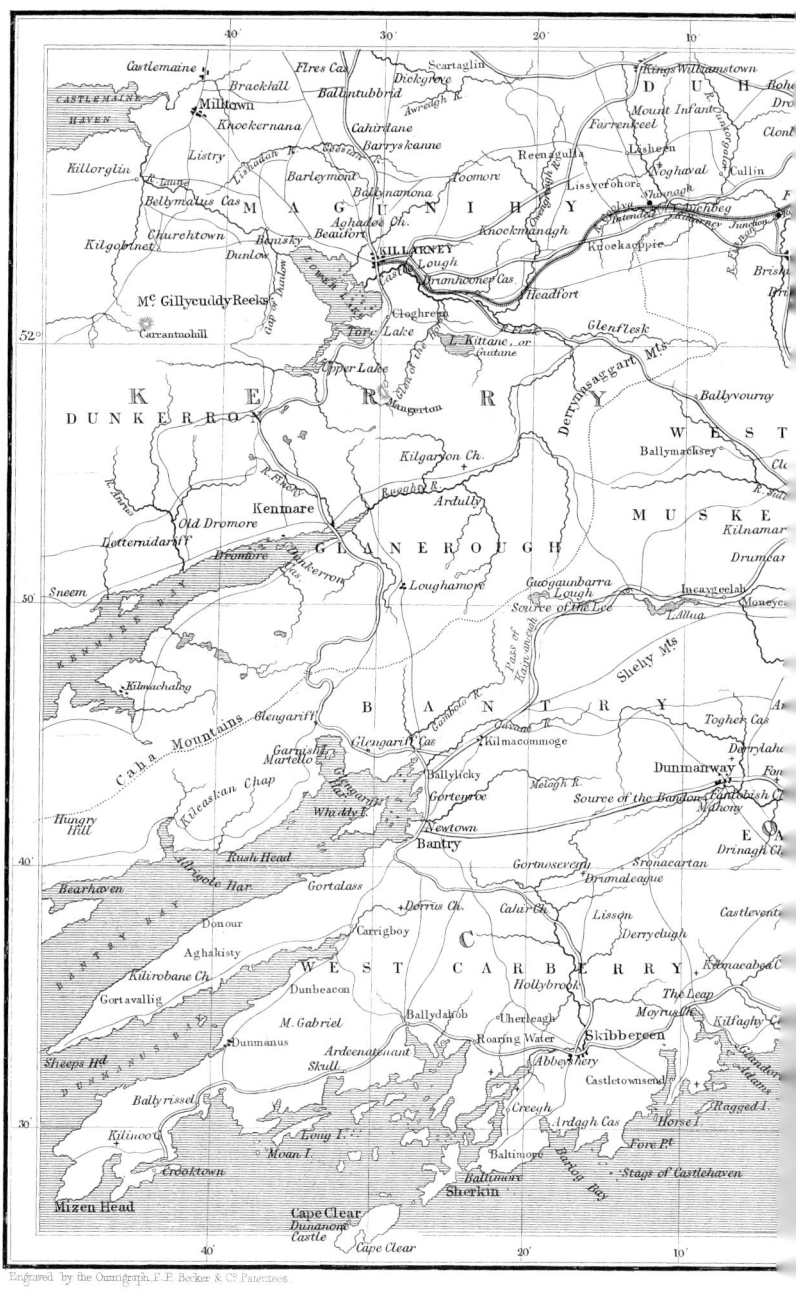

78   Map of The roads from Cork to Killarney, engraved by F.P. Becker

LINE ENGRAVING: PRINTS, MAPS, BOOK PLATES 175

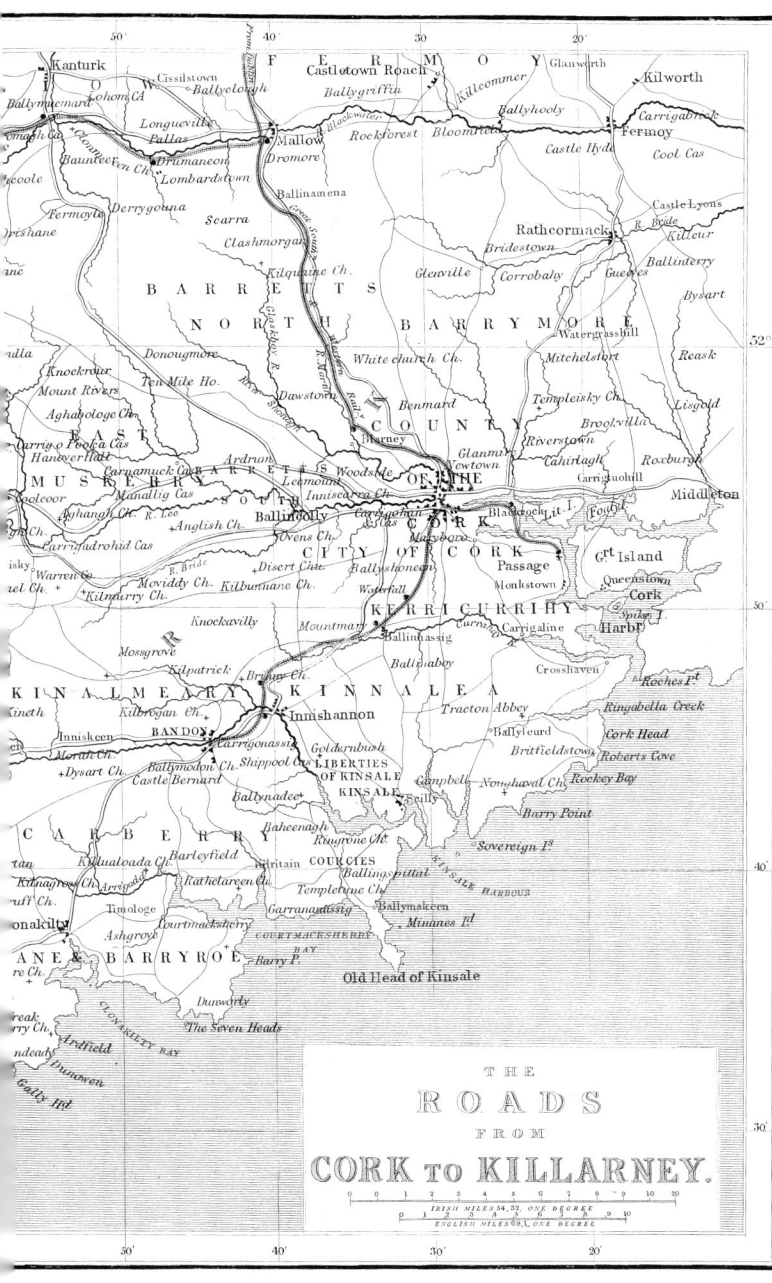

(1786–1855) and John (fl. 1821–40), who published in London a series of one-inch maps between 1817 and 1831, starting with that of Yorkshire. They formed the foundation of an *Atlas of the Counties of England* (including Wales) in 1834, where each map was embellished with an engraving of outstanding features, usually churches or cathedrals. It was published in four parts from 1829 with a total of 46 maps. The Walkers contributed 25, with ten done by James and Josiah Neele of 352, Strand, five by John C. Dower and two by H. Frost of Goswell Road. Four were unsigned. As with the Walker maps, the explanations were executed in ornate copperplate lettering. John joined his brother in 1821, and the firm had several other partners e.g. Fowler (1818–20), G. Pringle jun. (1820–27) and Sharp (1825–28).

Thomas Dugdale was the author of *Curiosities of Great Britain. England and Wales Delineated*... first published *circa* 1835, which contained 255 full-page steel engravings and about 55 maps, the earliest of which were engraved by G. Cole and J. Roper, but after *circa* 1842, a new set was engraved on steel by Joshua Archer (fl. 1814–66). The whole was published by John Tallis and Co., and used modern roman lettering for headings, etc. Joshua Archer of Pentonville also engraved seven maps for James Gilbert *circa* 1842, but his work was acquired by Fisher and Co. who, *circa* 1845, produced *Fisher's County Atlas of England and Wales*... in which the remaining 41 maps were drawn and engraved by F.P. Becker and Co. Francis Paul Becker (fl. 1837–61) patented 'omnigraphy', where individual letters were punched and not engraved into the plate. R.H. Solly had thought of using punches on a banknote plate in 1819, but could not get them cut to his liking. Even so, he had hopes that somebody else could be persuaded to take up the idea (Society of Arts *Report... on Forgery...*, 1819, p. 49). Becker used the device on a map which appeared in Samuel Carter Hall's *A Week at Killarney*, first published in 1843 with plates from two earlier works on Ireland, but the map of 'The roads from Cork to Killarney' is taken from the 1858 edition (Plate 78). Becker and Benjamin Rees Davies (fl. 1811–60) engraved maps for Kelly's Post Office directories from 1845, which plates were only used for making lithographic transfers. The omnigraphic process was sold to the Ordnance Survey and remained in use there until 1875.

[William] *Blackwood's Atlas of Scotland Containing Thirty-Three Separate Maps... Constructed and Engraved by W.H. Lizars...* was published in 1838, and the plates were still being used in 1885, although Lizar's name had been erased from four of them, to be replaced by that of John Bartholomew (fl. 1860–85). William Home Lizars (1788–1859) also engraved *Road Maps for Tourists in Ireland* (1844), most of the maps for *The Scottish Tourist*... fifth edition in 1834 and 27 maps of *The Abridged Statistical History of the Scottish Counties* published in 1862, three years after his death. J. Brown of North

Bridge Edinburgh drew and engraved 30 maps for John Parker Lawson's *The Descriptive Atlas of Scotland*, published by the Edinburgh Printing and Publishing Co. in 1842.

Thomas Arnold produced an edition of the *Bible* in 1846 with notes by the Revd Ingram Cobbin, which was accompanied by seven maps, all printed in blue, three containing vignette views and three double page with a plan of Jerusalem. They were 'Constructed for Thomas Arnold by W. & A.K. Johnston, Geographers and Engravers to the Queen, Edin.' For the map from p. 182 of the Old Testament of 'Canaan in possession of the Twelve Tribes of Israel' with a vignette of the 'Ruins of Petra, Edom', see colour plate 4. The Johnston brothers were the third and fourth sons of Andrew Johnston, and both were trained as engravers. William (1802–88) was apprenticed to James Kirkwood (fl. 1800–44), who had published a series of maps, and W.H. Lizars after which he set up on his own on 1 December 1825. Alexander Keith Johnston (1804–71) was apprenticed to Kirkwood in 1820, and the brothers' partnership was formed in 1826. On 2 December 1837 William was appointed engraver and copperplate printer to the Queen and on 8 February 1840, Alexander became Geographer at Edinburgh in Ordinary to the Queen. His first maps appeared in *A Traveller's Guide Book* (1830), to be followed by a host of others. For his public works William was knighted in 1851, and in 1867 retired from business. John Kirkwood (fl. 1827–50) engraved only four maps on steel of a projected *The County Atlas of Ireland, Drawn and Engraved by John Kirkwood* (1848). He was working in Dublin from about 1827, but later returned to Edinburgh, and was probably connected there with the engraving firm of James Kirkwood. The firm of Archibald Fullarton and Co. were general publishers and engravers in Glasgow from 1834, issuing such works as Brown's *History of the Highlands*, *circa* 1845, and an edition of Byron's *Works*, *circa* 1855, with steel-engraved illustrations. They were publishing maps in the 1830s and 1840s, some with vignette illustrations, and went on to produce *The Imperial Gazetteer of Scotland* ... edited by John Marius Wilson, containing 38 maps and plans, *circa* 1854–57, some of which were engraved by George H. Swanston (fl. 1848–60). This was followed by another edition *circa* 1857 re-titled *The County Atlas of Scotland, in a Series of Thirty-Two Maps, Accurately Engraved on Steel* .... Later gazetteers and maps of England and Wales were accompanied by a *Gazetteer of the world* (1856), and a *Royal Illustrated Atlas*, published in 24 parts (1854–62). Fullarton's copyrights and stock were bought by Thomas C. Jack *circa* 1880.

The last important atlas using steel engraving was that issued by John Tallis (1818–76) in 1851. *The Illustrated Atlas, and Modern History of the World, Geographical, Political, Commercial and Statistical* was edited by Robert Montgomery Martin, who worked for Tallis on a number of projects. The 83

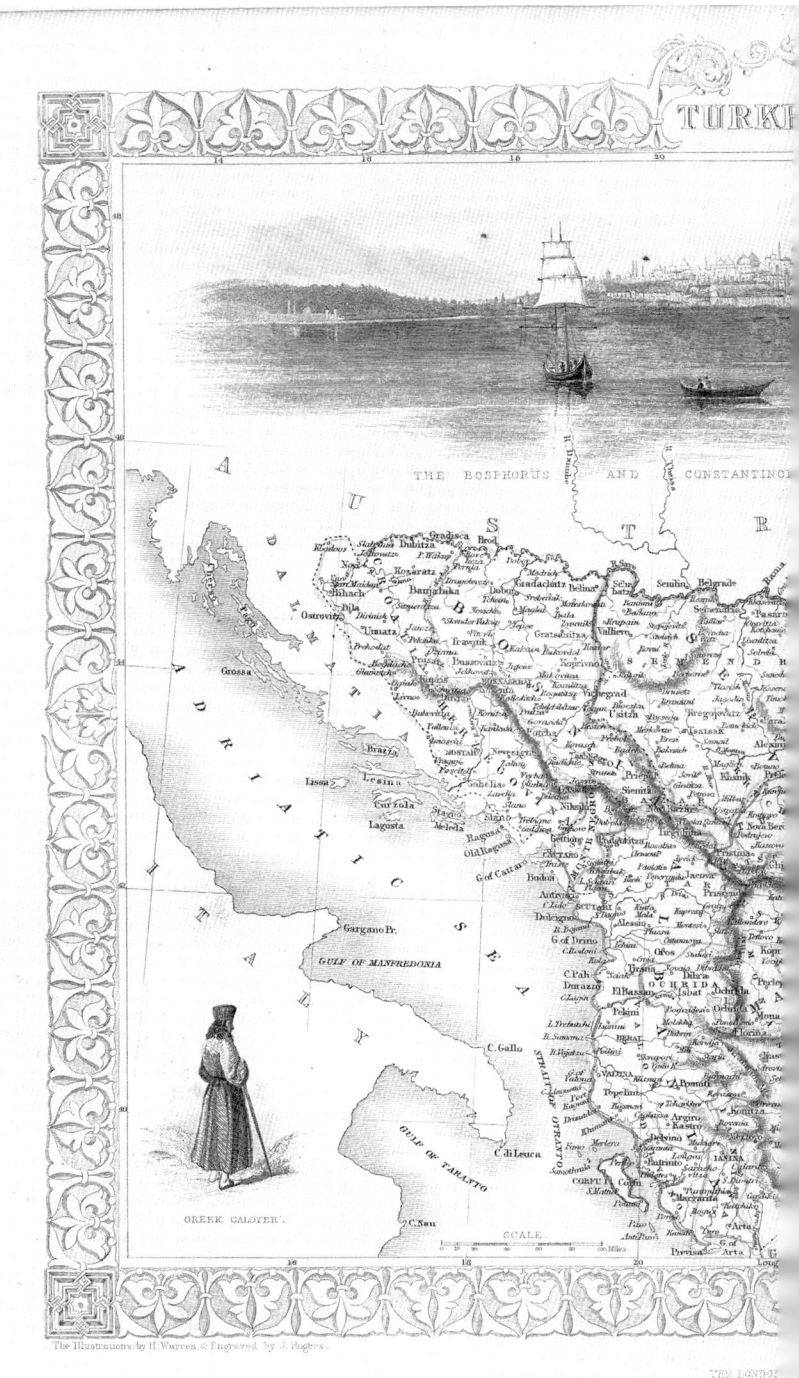

79 Map of Turkey in Europe, vignettes engraved by J. Rogers, map engraved by J. Rapkin

LINE ENGRAVING: PRINTS, MAPS, BOOK PLATES 179

maps in the atlas were all drawn and engraved by John Rapkin (fl. 1845–50), who must have worked very hard to complete such a mammoth task, but the vignette illustrations were drawn and engraved by book illustration engravers. There were two to seven vignettes on each map, fitted into the space between the country shape and the rectangular frame. The subjects included landscapes, buildings, groups of figures, portraits, animals, coats of arms and seals from documents. The narrow frames consist mainly of floral and geometric motifs with the country's name in a central cartouche at the head of the map. These features gave a feeling of unity to the atlas, despite the number of artists involved. Of the designers, Henry Warren was the most prolific, with J. Marchant, Nathaniel Whittock, John Salmon, A.H. Wray, A. Fussell, A. Warren and W. Bragg. Henry Winkles, besides designing a number of the vignettes, also engraved some, e.g. 'Islands of the Atlantic'. He was at this time mostly working in Germany (see Chapter 7).

Some of the best known steel engravers of the day were employed. John Rogers (c.1800–82) did a number of plates e.g. 'North America' and 'Mexico, California and Texas', before he went to America in 1851. Others were James Baylis Allen, Robert Wallis, Edward Radclyffe, Samuel Fisher, James Harfield Kernot, George Greatbach, W. Lacey, Robert Baker, John Wrightson, and G.R. Manwaring who engraved 'Central America'. The work was issued several times, the later editions including 27 town plans, mainly of Great Britain, but including those of three European cities. These were in the same format as the atlas maps and employed H. Bibby and D.J. Pound among the engravers. Pound was later to engrave portraits of eminent people after photographs by John Edwin Mayall for supplements to Tallis's periodical *Illustrated News of the World*, which commenced publication in February 1858 and lasted only five years. The illustrations were not allowed to dominate the maps and they are less idiosyncratic than Moule's. There are maps of ancient and modern Palestine, British possessions in the Mediterranean, British India, and Cabool, the Punjab and Baloochistan. The atlas was reproduced in 1989 by Bracken Books as *The Illustrated Atlas of the Nineteenth Century World* with an introduction by Jonathan Potter. Individual maps from the atlas were used to accompany some of Tallis's other productions such as 'Turkey in Europe' (Plate 79), which appeared in Henry Tyrrell's *The History of the War with Russia*... published by the London Printing and Publishing Company Limited between 1855 and 1858. John Tallis and Ephraim Tipton Brain had formed this company in December 1853 to take the strain of running the business off the former. Brain, after being an engraver and printer in his own right, was bought out in the late 1840s by Tallis and employed as his factory superintendent.

Among the last use of steel for maps and plans other than by lithographic

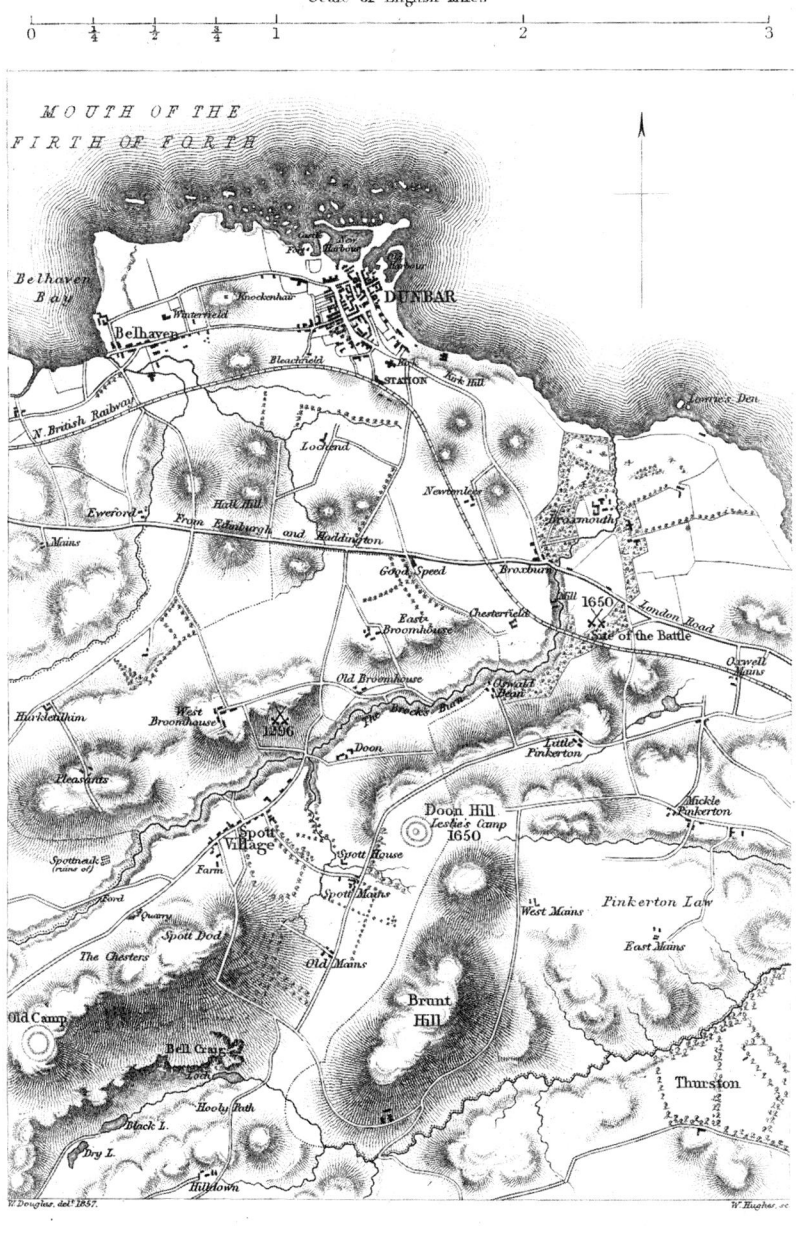

80 Sketch to illustrate the battle of Dunbar 1650, engraved by W. Hughes

transfer was in *The Pictorial History of Scotland* . . . by James Taylor published by James Sprent Virtue in 1859. W. Hughes engraved a 'Sketch to illustrate the battle of Dunbar, 1650' after a drawing by W. Douglas dated 1857 (Plate 80). Hughes had done a number of map engravings for Virtue from about 1840 in his travel books, and also for some of W.H. Bartlett's books.

As late as 1864 F.P. Becker's omnigraphy was used on a map of Scotland for [James] *Reynolds's geological atlas of Great Britain*. John Emslie drew and engraved the maps for the original 1848 edition, which were printed by lithographic transfer.

The very popular *Black's Picturesque Tourist of Scotland* had reached its seventeenth edition in 1865, and all 20 maps and plans were drawn and engraved by J. Bartholomew of Edinburgh. Plate 81 shows a map of the 'Caledonian Railway . . . with the connecting lines and adjacent country'.

Steel engraving in all its forms was in decline during the 1860s and 1870s, and direct lithography was more convenient, so as steel plates lost their usefulness due to constant additions and corrections, so new methods supervened. Virtue published *The National Gazetteer* edited by N.E.S.A. Hamilton in the early 1870s, incorporating 60 coloured maps on which new county boundaries were shown, new parishes and sees were indicated and other extensive amendments included in it. He also announced a *County Atlas of Great Britain and Ireland* to contain 68 maps copied from the Ordnance Survey and claimed it to be 'the most complete ever submitted to the Public at a reasonable price' (Advertisement on paper wrapper of Part 8 of *Virtue's Imperial Shakspere*, Virtue, [*c.*1872]). Steel engraving was not mentioned for these works which was some indication of the changes made by the foremost exponent of that process, even though steel engraving was not abandoned until 1890 in the *Art Journal* published by Virtue.

Book plates

Steel was used primarily for heraldic book plates where detail could be accurately and finely depicted. The number of copies obtainable from such a plate without deterioration was infinite, which was an advantage in this period, when libraries were owned by a greater number of people, and contained more volumes, thus requiring a larger number of book plates. The quality of the steel-engraved book plate was also attractive to the owner, and for a comparatively modest outlay for the engraving, which varied according to the eminence of the engraver, a large library would be provided with enough plates to last for many years, certainly for the lifetime of the owner. John Vinycomb wrote 'On the process for the production of ex-libris...' for the *Journal of the Ex-Libris Society* (Black, 1894), and after extolling the steel-engraved illustrations of the annuals etc., notes that 'the engraved plate has

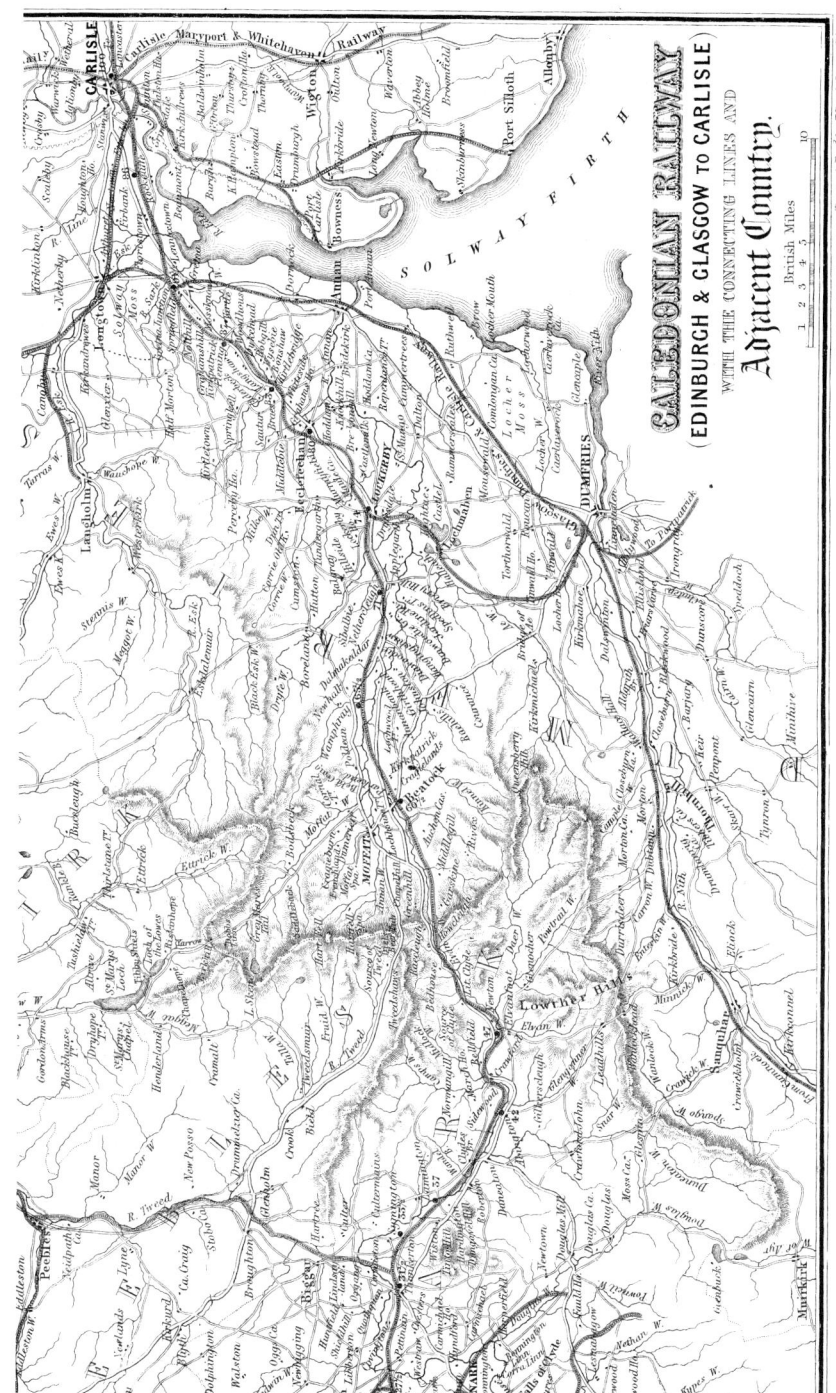

81 Caledonian Railway (detail) ... engraved by J. Bartholomew

steadily held its own as the most finished and perfect. For Ex-Libris it is particularly suitable; it is *par excellence* THE STYLE for the attainment of the highest art quality' (p. 27). Later on he mentions that printing is done by transferring the design to stone and printing by lithography.

There are few engravers who made book plates their main work, and indeed, only one such, Charles William Sherborn (1831–1912), called by Newbolt in his *History of the Royal Society of Painter Etchers* (1930), the greatest of book plate makers, worked on his own from *circa* 1872, and probably used steel-faced copper. He, in common with other ex-libris engravers, learned his trade with a silver plate engraver and goldsmith, engraving on gold and silver articles. The rolling press on which he proofed or even printed his work is exhibited in Section 40 of the Science Museum, South Kensington. Vinycomb (1894, p. 27) illustrates an engraving printed direct from the copper by Sherborn.

Very few book plates are signed by designer or engraver, one exception being nine engraved by Rest Fenner (fl. 1812–33), signed 'Fenner, Paternoster Row', but which are undated. Engravers accepted commissions between their other work, as in the case of William Miller, who in 1831 did a book plate for W.B. Chorley for the sum of 3 guineas. This was in a series of eight plates done for George Smith of Liverpool, two of which were on steel, four on copper and two on unspecified metal. Joseph Swan, the Glasgow engraver and publisher is credited with 31 book plates engraved between 1820 and 1840, and in a similar period, James Appleby, an armorial engraver did four plates, Samuel Topham four, William Taylor four and Richard Lewis Wright three. John Cleghorn did ten plates between 1840 and 1860, John Emslie two *circa* 1850, Cuff (possibly R.P. who worked for Ruskin) one in 1850, John Henry Le Keux four between 1850 and 1878, and Thomas Dick one in 1870. These are only representatives of a much larger band of mainly unknown engravers such as those of the accompanying plates.

The most common design was the family arms or crest, done in the form of a vignette (Plate 82) for Harry A. Keyser, showing a Latin motto on a ribbon and the owner's name in copperplate script. A plate for Jocelyn Pease is much more elaborate, involving a coat of arms and different, more modern style of lettering for the name. The circular form for Plates 83 and 84 encloses a similar pattern with a central coat of arms, motto above and name below, both in gothic lettering, as was that of Edward V. Bullen (Plate 85).

Harold Curwen, in his *Processes of Graphic Reproduction in Printing* (Faber, 1947, pp. 30–1), indicates that steel engraving was still being used for heraldic book plates at that time, but how widespread it was is unknown.

82 Book plate for Harry A. Keyser

83 Book plate for Francis Scott

84 Book plate for Sir Henry Hope Edwards

85 Book plate for Edward V. Bullen

6

Other intaglio prints on steel; paper, equipment

There are two more intaglio processes used on steel plates, giving different effects from line engraving and mezzotint. Etching and aquatint were used as independent means of producing a picture, although the contemporary view regarded them as artistically inferior, due not least to the less arduous methods employed. The use of acid to take away some of the hard physical work of line engraving was already well established in the 18th century in England when Sir Robert Strange (1721–92) used etching to delineate the main outline of the design, then going over the lines again with a graver to sharpen up the line edges. Anthony Walker (1726–65) took the idea still further by using two or three progressive bitings before tidying up with a graver, and William Sharp (1749–1824) etched and rouletted his plates before engraving.

Etching was even more necessary when dealing with a hard metal like steel, and between 1820 and 1827 there was much discussion as to which menstruum or mordant was the most suitable for it. Wilson Lowry, Charles Warren, Edmund Turrell, W. Cooke and William Humphrys all contributed recipes, some achieving medal awards from the Society of Arts for their work. There was a diversity of practice as to who should actually etch the plate. Some engravers preferred to do or supervise it themselves; Edward Goodall devoted days to the operation which affected the whole family, where the house was pervaded by fumes and the engraver's temper tried by the results. In other cases, there were etchers who specialized in such work, such as Edward John Roberts (1797–1865), who spent much of his earlier career etching for Charles Heath, and only emerged briefly in the 1830s to wholly engrave some plates, returning to etching in later life.

Etching, therefore, was a distinct phase in the production of a steel line engraving, and was used to indicate the progress of a plate, and prove that work had started on it. Reviewers in the *Art Journal* in the 1840s were

86   Captain Cook, engraved by H.T. Ryall, finished proof

commenting that 'we have seen an etching', which was deemed sufficient for publicity purposes, and copies might even be provided for the publisher, author, illustrator, patron and other interested parties. In the agreement between Lumb Stocks and the Art Union of London for the 'Waterloo' plate (see pp. 158–61), there is a clause that 'he will, during the progress of the said engraving, and at six distinct and successive stages of the plate, deliver ... duplicate proof impressions ...'. One of these

87 Captain Cook, engraved by H.T. Ryall, etched state

stages would be an etched state to be followed by stages such as that shown in Plate 70.

In a unique volume of plates, formerly in the Locker family library, there are etched and finished proofs before letters, printed on large sheets of paper from *Memoirs of Celebrated Naval Commanders, Illustrated by Engravings from Original Pictures in the Naval Gallery of Greenwich Hospital...* by Edward Hawke Locker, published by Harding and Lepard in 1832. The engraving of Captain Cook (Plate 86) was done by Henry Thomas Ryall, who was only 21 years old, and just out of his training under the mezzotinter Samuel Reynolds. The etching which accompanies it (Plate 87), shows how much was done by acid, and is roughly the halfway stage in preparing a plate. Comparison of the two illustrations shows what changes can be made between the two stages, where the aggressive look on the face in the etched state is softened in the finished proof.

Etching on its own had not been highly thought of for many years, having regard to the quality of some of its productions, and it continued to be seen as a poor relation to other forms of engraving. One of its uses, however, was in the production of coloured plates, which, during the main period of steel engraving, was done by hand, usually in water colour. There were volumes offered by the publisher plain or coloured, the latter being regarded as a luxury item and charged accordingly. Many of these were finished line engravings, able to stand on their own as in the case of the *Heroines of Shakespeare* (1848), but some volumes contained plates in which colour was prominent, even essential. In these cases, the engraving was usually an etching, done with hand colouring in mind, as in the plates for Sir William Jardine's *Naturalists' Library* published in Edinburgh by his brother-in-law William Home Lizars in the 1830s in a series of self-contained sets. A plate from *The Natural History of Game-Birds* (1834, plate 26), etched by Lizars, with a sketchy background to a magnificently plumaged Cryptonix coronatus in full colour over an etched outline, is shown here (colour plate 5).

In 1834 Charles Tilt had published *Historical Illustrations of the Prose and Poetical Works of Sir Walter Scott* ... in a series of 28 etchings on steel from paintings by various artists, where small outline etchings of no particular merit appeared without artist or engraver being named. They contrast with the line engraved editions then so popular and well executed. The identification of an etching on steel is very difficult. There is little in the execution to show the metal used as there is in steel line engraving, although where light tones are present, the faintest are better preserved on steel. In most cases individual prints are not signed by artist or engraver, but Cruikshank is a notable exception. The main indicators are a statement in the book or periodical, and the likely numbers printed, where steel has advantages in resisting plate wear. Again, with some exceptions, if a plate is separated from its work it is extremely difficult to identify except by iconographic features, which usually means that the viewer recognizes and can place it. This chapter therefore deals with plates which are either known to be on steel or are highly likely to be so. Certain types of plates, e.g. comic or sporting, already have their own literature and are not dealt with in depth here.

Etching found an important niche in the 1830s, providing illustrations

88 Mr Watkins Tottle and Miss Lillerton, etched by G. Cruikshank

for periodicals, novels and other inexpensive publications. *Bentley's Miscellany* carried the etched work of both Cruikshank and Hablot K. Browne.

The elder of these illustrators was George Cruikshank (1792–1878) who was 44 years old when he did the first etchings for Charles Dickens's *Sketches by Boz* (1836), worked on copper, later to be steel-faced to minimize wear in printing. For the 1837–39 issue in parts steel was used for the first time because of the great number of copies required, and from this time nearly all novels with etched illustrations were done on steel. The advantages were that the artist 'drew' his picture directly on to the plate, endowing it with a certain spontaneity, omitting the engraver's intervention, and completing the plate in a comparatively short time for printing. Cruikshank used a wide range of techniques, many learned from his father Isaac, and the method enabled him to exploit his gift for caricature, shown in nearly all his illustrations. Plate 88 is one of eight done for the *Sketches* . . . and shows the dark tones employed with very little realization of the variety of tone steel could provide as seen in the work of later etchers.

Hard on the heels of this work came *The Adventures of Oliver Twist; or, the Parish Boy's Progress* with 24 illustrations, which came out between 1837 and 1839. These are probably the most famous set of Dickens pictures which evoked the characters in an inspired grouping (Plate 89). This work broke the partnership between author and illustrator, because Dickens rejected one of the proposed plates. Another example of Cruikshank's work came from the novelist William Harrison Ainsworth, whose *Jack Sheppard; a Romance* (1839) carried 21 steel etchings of which Plate 90 is the frontispiece. Unlike the Dickens vignettes, each of these are enclosed by a border, and even more unusually, one plate carried four small pictures as in 'The Escape No. 1' (Plate 91). Most of his work is signed at the foot. He etched his own plates, during which time he smoked a pipe, and it not only relaxed him, but masked the acid fumes.

Hablot Knight Browne (1815–82) came from East Anglia to London, probably at the age of 14 to join William and Edward Finden's atelier to train as an engraver. The Findens were at the height of their activities as steel engravers in 1829, and needed a number of apprentices, among whom was Robert Young. In 1834 Browne and Young set up in business as etchers and engravers at 3 Furnivall's Inn where Dickens also resided at No. 15, which proximity facilitated their later collaboration. Robert Young etched Browne's plates for him. One of Browne's earliest commissions was to draw 23 illustrations for volume 1 of Winkles' *Cathedral Churches of England and Wales*, in 1836, 12 for volume 2 in 1838 (but none for volume 3 in 1842) and 12 for *French Cathedrals* in 1837. Most of the plates were engraved by Benjamin Winkles. The exact and detailed drawing for them

OTHER INTAGLIO PRINTS 193

89 Oliver's reception by Fagin and the boys, etched by G. Cruikshank

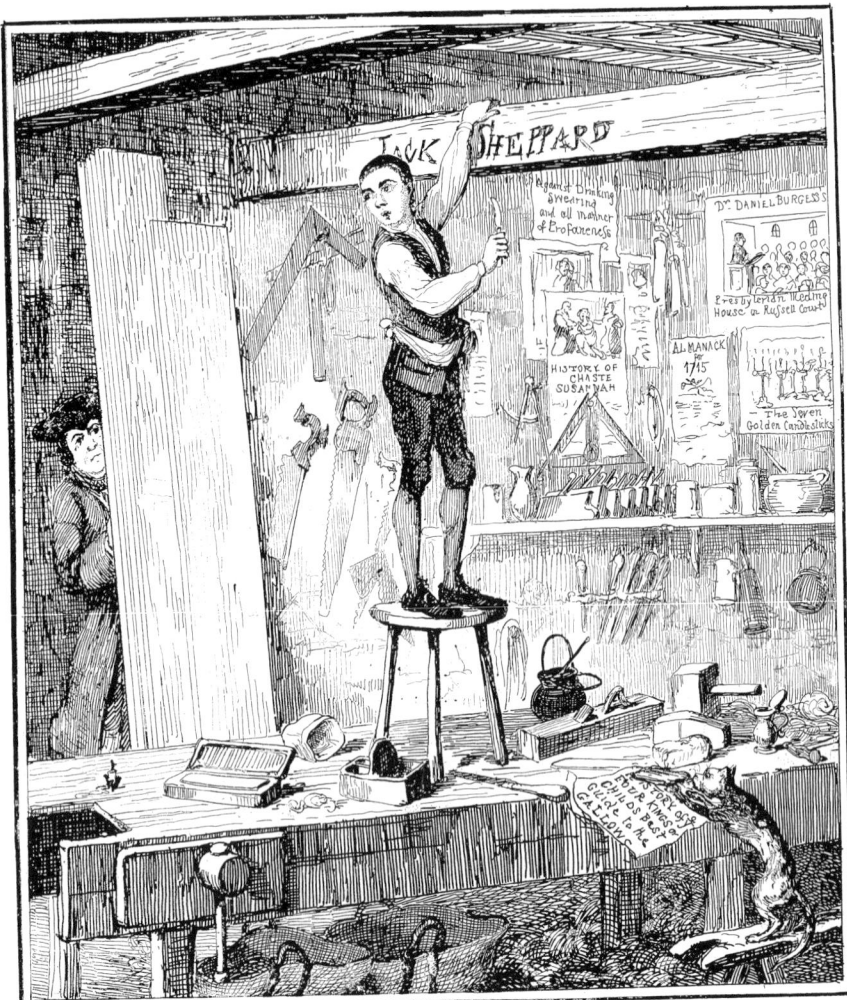

90   The name on the beam, etched by G. Cruikshank

OTHER INTAGLIO PRINTS 195

The Castle

The Red Room

Door of the Red Room

A door between the Red Room & the Chapel

The Escape. N°1.

91 The Escape No. 1, etched by G. Cruikshank

clearly shows his engraver's training, but evidently it was not to his taste and thereafter he preferred the freer method of etching, where a week to ten days would see a plate finished. His remuneration was about £7 per plate as compared with nearly four times that amount for a line engraving. Etchers were never short of commissions so their *oeuvre* could run into a thousand or two during their working life.

The illustration of Dickens's novels brought several changes to Browne's working practices, dictated very largely by the need to produce parts on time and the huge number of impressions required. All intaglio printing was hampered by the necessarily slow speed of the process, and in order to produce the 20,000 plus copies needed several remedies were tried. Two images were etched on steel plates measuring about 18 in. × 10 in., which produced two impressions at one pass through the press. By tracing a design to prepare several steels of the same subject the printing could be done simultaneously on several presses, and this was the method used for *Dombey and Son* in 1848. Even quicker was the transfer of an impression from the steel plate to a lithographic stone, which came into use between *Bleak House* (1852–53) and *Little Dorrit* (1856–57). This raised all the arguments about the quality of impressions, but it was less observable on a steel etching because of the more open arrangement of lines than in a steel line engraving with much finer work to reproduce. This latter course considerably reduced the wear on the plates, so that some later editions were printed directly from them. The Library edition of 1858–59 and 1861 was the first, followed by the Gadshill edition of 1897, the National edition of 1906–08 and finally the Nonesuch Press edition of 1937. The publishers had kept the plates for all this time, but in 1937 the steels were cut in half to 5 in. × 8 in., chromium plated, placed in a specially constructed box to match the volumes and presented to purchasers of the Nonesuch edition.

The etchings were quite easily reproduced photographically, and in 1895 Chapman and Hall issued them in line block, taken from the original prints as in *Nicholas Nickleby* first published 1838–39 (Plate 92).

The caricature aspect was less evident in Browne's works and in general his faces were more human, even if, in his earlier works the drawing was more bizarre. The title page of *Old St. Paul's* by W.H. Ainsworth in 1841 gives some idea of his style (Plate 93). There were 39 illustrations to *The Personal History of David Copperfield* (1850), of which 'My first fall in life' (Plate 94) is a compact vignette, with 'I am married' (Plate 95) showing the tone contrast possible with a steel plate. 'Consecrated ground' (Plate 96) from *Bleak House* in 1853 (40 plates) is a darker plate, whereas for a pair of plates, one of which is 'The Morning' (Plate 97) he uses a traditional rectangular form. These two show evidence of the use of the burin, a reversal of the more usual role where burins are used to tidy up etched lines. A similar

OTHER INTAGLIO PRINTS 197

The "breaking up" at Dotheboys Hall.

92 The breaking up at Dotheboy's Hall, etched by H.K. Browne

93 Title page of *Old St. Pauls*, by W.H. Ainsworth, etched by H.K. Browne

94 My first fall in life, etched by H.K. Browne

pattern was adopted in *Little Dorrit* in 1857 (39 plates) with 'The story of the princess' (Plate 98) and 'The ferry' (Plate 99), which latter is very near a traditional line engraving in appearance. This was achieved by machine

95 I am married, etched by H.K. Browne

Consecrated ground.

96 Consecrated ground, etched by H.K. Browne

ruling over most of the plate and etching the rest of the picture over it.

Browne also illustrated other novelists such as Charles James Lever (1806–72) and Frank Smedley (1818–64). Towards the end of his life he was paralysed and eventually died at Brighton.

Another illustrator who commenced his career using etchings in 1835

The Morning.

97   The morning, etched by H.K. Browne

OTHER INTAGLIO PRINTS   203

The Story of the Princess

98   The story of the princess, etched by H.K. Browne

was John Leech (1817–64), who also used lithography and wood engraving as vehicles for his work. He etched plates for the works of Charles Dickens, John Forster, Douglas Jerrold and Robert Surtees, with whose sporting novels Leech is most frequently associated. He produced comic works from 1840 and etched plates for some magazines, including *Bentley's Miscellany*.

Sport attracted many artists and engravers, more particularly for the *Sporting Magazine* which ran from 1792 to 1870 and the *New Sporting*

99 The ferry, etched by H.K. Browne

Magazine established by Robert Surtees, which survived only 15 years from 1831 to 1846. Henry S. Beckwith (fl. 1835–1900) etched a number of plates for both of these periodicals, and in 1843 contributed 'Lion and lioness' (Plate 100) to *The Book of Sports, British and Foreign 1843*, which contained 100 etchings. The title page vignette of 'El Toro' (Plate 101) was etched by the Scottish engraver William Bell Scott (1811–90) who had been appointed master of the Newcastle School of Design in 1843, a post he held until 1858. John R. Scott etched seven plates, which included 'Ruffs & plover' (Plate 102). This charming vignette, drawn by N. Fielding was prepared by John R. Scott, but the actual etching was done by Elizabeth Scott, who was probably his wife. W. Backshall produced a number of plates for the *Sporting Review* such as 'The Thames regatta' in 1852 and 'Oxford wins! Over the Thames' in April 1865. Edward H. Hacker (1813–1905) was principal engraver for this periodical.

Many costume plates were also etched, leaving large areas to be covered by hand colouring, although in some cases, as in the plate from *The Ladies Cabinet* (colour plate 6), lines in imitation of line engraving are added to deepen shadows and folds. The example comes from a cheap publication entitled *The Ladies Cabinet of Fashion, Music and Romance* (vol. IX, 1843),

LION AND LIONESS.

100 Lion and lioness, etched by H.S. Beckwith

published by Geo. Henderson and which had been running since *circa* 1834.

The Etching Club, founded *circa* 1839 by a group of eminent artists was the first formal attempt to make etching 'respectable' in the artistic sense, and their productions consisted in the main of illustrations to well-known English texts, produced in limited editions, after which the plates were destroyed. Only one work was known to be etched on steel, which was their second production, published in 1843 entitled *Songs of Shakespeare* for which 13 etchings on ten steel plates were planned. In the event, the liberality of the members produced 17 etchings, and the whole work was issued under the auspices of the Royal Polytechnic Union, which was an 'extension of the principle of Art-unions' (*Art Union*, 1843, p. 2). The published price was 20 shillings.

Eugène Sué (1804–57) published *Les mystères de Paris* in 1843–44, which was an immediate success. Twenty thousand copies of the illustrated edition were published by Paulin in Paris and contained 34 steel engravings. In an edition translated by Charles Rochford and published by Charles Daly in 1844, Thomas Onwhyn (*c.*1820–86) etched 21 illustrations to the text

101 El Toro, etched by W.B. Scott

102 Ruffs and plover, etched by Elizabeth Scott

which was printed in very small type. The etchings were obviously done quickly to cash in on the book's popularity. 'Rodolph at the Porter's-lodge' (Plate 103) is an example of his work.

The set of 12 etchings already referred to in Chapter 5 (p. 159), done by William Rimer to *The Castle of Indolence* for the Art Union of London in 1845 were used to fill a gap in their publication programme due to the ill health of an engraver. The designs were in a tradition set by Henry Moses (1781–1870), but the use of steel enabled subtle tones to be expressed at the lightest end of the scale where some of the backgrounds were barely visible as in plate VIII engraved by H.W. Collard (Plate 104).

[Thomas] *Moore's Irish Melodies, Illustrated by D. Maclise R.A.* announced for publication in October 1845, was remarkable for the use of steel engraving for both illustrations and text. The designs varied in number between 154 and 161, and together with decorative borders, were etched, some by Maclise himself, and the text added by F.P. Becker's 'omnigraphic' invention of punching letters into the plate. A review at the time considered the book would sell well on the Continent 'where it would go far to enhance the reputation of British Art' (*Art Union*, 1845, p. 342).

103   Rodolph at the Porter's-lodge, etched by T. Onwhyn

104   *The Castle of indolence*, Plate VIII, etched by H.W. Collard

Myles Birket Foster (1825–99) was best known as a draughtsman and there are a number of books to his credit 'illustrated by Birket Foster'. He was apprenticed to a wood engraver after leaving school, and since he was not very good at the actual engraving, he drew on blocks for others to cut. In the 1840s he worked for both periodicals and books, but by 1855 he decided to transfer his own designs to a plate without the intermediacy of an engraver. Thus he etched 29 designs on steel to John Milton's *L'Allegro* and *Il Penseroso*, published by David Bogue in 1855. This work was selected for reprint as a classic book by Scolar Press in 1975 with text printed in red and vignettes in black. Plate 105 is taken from this edition, since it clearly shows under a glass the modern misuse of a half-tone screen to reproduce a wholly line original. It was followed by 30 plates for Oliver Goldsmith's *The Traveller* (1856), also published by Bogue, and in 1859 Thomas Warton's *The Hamlet; an ode . . .*, published by Sampson Low and Co. contained 14 plates. This appears to be the extent of his steel-etched work, which was said to have looked like fine engravings. For the 40 engravings drawn by Foster for Henry Mayhew's *The Rhine . . .* (retitled *The Lower Rhine* when republished by Routledge in 1860) and *The Upper Rhine . . .* (1860) he returned to the use of engravers under the superintendence of Edward John Roberts, himself an expert etcher.

The ideal situation where an author provided the illustrations to his own work was rarely achieved, but came to fruition in the case of William Makepeace Thackeray (1811–63). After trying law and journalism in the 1830s, which left him penniless, Thackeray took up art and studied in Paris and Rome, but after a time returned to writing for several periodicals. His career as a novelist commenced in 1847–48 with the publication of *Vanity Fair*. *The Virginians. A tale of the last century* (1857–59) had 'illustrations on steel and wood by the author'. Each of the two volumes contained 23 etchings of little artistic merit, such as the frontispiece and engraved title page of volume 1 (Plate 106) and the opening with wood-engraved initial letter at page 218 of the same volume (Plate 107). He did not illustrate all his works, since Richard Doyle, for instance, did those for *The Newcomes* (1853–55).

In 1865 Richard James Lane (1800–72) was appointed to set up and run an etching on copper class at South Kensington in the hope that the process might be more used for book illustration. By this means it was hoped students might progress to line engraving, which was dying out, since few practising engravers were taking pupils (*Art Journal*, 1865, p. 126). Lane was articled to Charles Heath, but when line engraving declined in demand, he turned to lithography and was lithographer to the Queen and Prince Albert.

In the 1870s and 1880s etching reverted largely to copper plates, which

105 Page of *L'Allegro*, etched by M.B. Foster

106 Frontispiece and title page to *The Virginians*, etched by W.M. Thackeray

CHAPTER XXVIII.

THE WAY OF THE WORLD.

OUR young Virginian found himself, after two or three days at Tunbridge Wells, by far the most important personage in that merry little watering-place. No nobleman in the place inspired so much curiosity. My Lord Bishop of Salisbury himself was scarce treated with more respect. People turned round to look after Harry as he passed, and country folks stared at him as they came into market. At the rooms, matrons encouraged him to come round to them, and found means to leave him alone with their daughters, most of whom smiled upon him. Everybody knew, to an acre and a shilling, the extent of his Virginian property, and the amount of his income. At every tea-table in the Wells, his winnings at play were told and calculated. Wonderful is the interest and curiosity which Harry inspired, that people even smiled upon his servant, and took Gumbo aside and treated him with ale and cold meat, in order to get news of the young Virginian. Mr. Gumbo fattened under the diet, became a leading member of the Society of Valets in the place, and lied more enormously than ever. No party was complete unless Mr. Warrington attended it. The lad was not a little amused and astonished by this prosperity, and bore his new honours pretty well. He had been bred at home to think too well of himself, and his present good fortune no doubt tended to confirm his self-satisfaction. But he was not too much elated. He did not brag about his victories or give himself any particular airs. In

for long runs could now be steel-faced. There was also a fashion for issuing prints which had been etched and a very little burin work added. This followed the French and German pattern, where the closeness of steel-engraved work was abandoned in favour of a much coarser appearance. Even renowned line engravers such as Charles Mottram (1807–76) adapted his style as in 'The three dogs' after Sir Edwin Landseer, published in the *Art Journal* (1876). This was among Mottram's last plates and shows a machine-ruled background with an etched picture over it (Plate 108).

The formation of the Society of Painter-etchers in 1880 by Francis Seymour Haden (1818–1910) to promote original (as opposed to reproductive) engraving and etching was remarkably successful, not least because reproductive work was finally overtaken by photography. This change was reflected in the illustrations which appeared in the *Art Journal* for 1887, where five steel engravings were accompanied by six etchings and two reproductions in facsimile, which appeared to be photogravures.

Original etchings were done by Edward Slocombe (b. 1850), Alex H. Haig, Henri Lepind and William Unger (1837–1932), a German line engraver and etcher, but Charles Olivier Murray (b. 1842) is known for 'The Venetians' after Sir Luke Fildes. He occupied a distinguished place among his contemporaries and gained a silver medal at the Paris Exhibition of 1900.

By the end of the century, the use of steel plates for etching was completely extinct, and even the practice of steel-facing was under attack. P.G. Hamerton, in his *Drawings and engravings ...* (A. and C. Black, 1892, pp. 143–44), discusses the proposition that impressions from the naked copper only should be called proofs and 'reserve the inferior term [prints] for all impressions that are taken after steeling'. For high priced collector's items there should be no steeling at all. This brought it full circle to the days before steel engraving in the early part of the century.

Hans W. Singer and William Strang in their *Etching, Engraving and the Other Methods of Printing Pictures* (Kegan Paul, 1897) do not consider the steel plate at all in their chapter on etching, and barely mention the practice of steel-facing.

Aquatint on steel

This is another form of etching which appears to have been executed mainly on copper. In Britain, aquatint was extensively used as a basis for hand colouring on a limited run of prints, and therefore tended to print an outline of the design, relying on colour to fill in details and tone. Hand colouring, like mezzotint, seems to have been a peculiarly British process, and where aquatint appears elsewhere it is normally uncoloured. The

108 The three dogs, engraved by C. Mottam

finished aquatint gives no clue as to which metal has been used for the plate, and the only inference that can be drawn is from the likely extent of the print run. Anything over 1,000 impressions is likely to produce printing wear on a copper plate, which it would be difficult to remedy by re-biting, so in the few cases where steel is known to have been used, a fairly long run could be expected. Experiments with metal plates other than copper were made between 1810 and 1820, mostly to secure longer runs, and William Daniell (1796–1837) was said to have experimented with iron plates, perhaps for *A Voyage round Great Britain* (1814–25). In the end he found it easier to work with a familiar metal and stayed with copper.

Two aquatints on steel illustrated Jonathan Whittemore's *An Historical and Topographical Picture of Brighton and its Environs* (1825), which was popular enough to be reprinted in 1827. Whittemore published from 7 Great East Street, Brighton and the prints were 'The Pavilion No. 1 The Royal Banqueting Room' and 'The Pavilion No. 2 The Music Gallery' and as they were larger than the book's format, they were folded. '... The Music Gallery' was used again in Whittemore's *Harry and Lucy's trip to Brighton* [*c.*1829]. The artist is not identified, but 'Engraved on steel by E. Brain' appears on both. There seems to be no engraver of that initial, but an Ephraim Tipton Brain is known as a printer who worked for the *Art Union* and *Art Journal* and who joined John Tallis in 1849. It is possible that Charles Hunt's aquatint of 'Grandstand... Goodwood' 8 November 1853 was on steel.

S.T. Prideaux, in *Aquatint Engraving* (1909), mentions several exponents who were also steel engravers, so it may be reasonable to assume that their aquatint plates might also be on steel. Edward Francis Finden (1791–1857), William Thomas Fry (1789–1843), James Tingle (fl. 1824–50) and Thomas Woolnoth (1785–*c.*1841) are the most likely, but their aquatint work is not extensive.

Charles Lane, a writer on sporting aquatints, expresses the view that copper could be re-worked, or even a new ground laid, but an improved run could be achieved by steel-facing when this became a possibility, even though some said the process spoiled the texture of the print.

Aquatints on steel are known on the Continent, and an example from America is Mrs Sara Josepha Hall's *The White Veil* (Philadelphia, E.H. Butler and Co., 1854), which contained ten steel aquatints printed on thin card.

It appears that aquatint on steel was tried from time to time, but did not establish itself as a process for more than occasional use.

Paper

Plate paper had been specially made for the printing of engravings and other fine work a long time before the coming of steel engraving. The absence of a viable British paper-making industry in the 16th and 17th centuries ensured a good market for foreign, notably French, papers, which held their supremacy into the 19th century for certain types of paper. The Napoleonic Wars interrupted this trade, and the British industry was thus encouraged to expand, and it was here that the industrialization of the paper-making process was developed, albeit from French initiatives.

Most paper up to *circa* 1750 was laid, that is, it carried a watermark, produced by thinning the paper over a design on the wires of the mould. The paper surface was therefore very slightly uneven, and was not as good as it could have been for the reproduction of fine engravings. The development of wove paper by James Whatman produced a smooth surfaced paper without a discernible watermark, and was the forerunner of plate paper. He doubtless had made wove paper to use for plate paper, but his first recorded manufacture of a specially made paper was in 1773, when the Society of Antiquaries ordered large sheets, measuring 53 in. × 31 in. The Society of Arts offered a premium to encourage the making of a paper for copperplate printing in 1756.

Steel engraving, with the increased number of copies possible from each plate created an unprecedented demand for plate paper, so it is not surprising that British mills set about supplying it. Gradually the dependence on foreign papers lessened, and by the mid-19th century Britain had a flourishing export trade in most types of paper. One of the most innovative of British firms was that of John Dickinson (1782–1869) who, in 1817, took out a patent (No. 4152) for a 'veneered' (or duplex) paper, where a thick and a thin web of paper, separately made, were brought together at the press rollers to make a thick sheet with the face web being made of a finer rag to take a better impression when printed. It was claimed that this invention ended the importation of copperplate paper from France. During the century, the whole production of Dickinson's Nash mill was turned over to the production of fine, including plate paper, and that used for printing maps. As a major supplier of plate paper, Dickinson's products were specified by editors, etc., as in the case of Alaric Watts, who in 1831, insisted to his printers McQueen that the states of all his plates should be made on Dickinson's paper. Watts is best known as the proprietor of the annual *The Literary Souvenir*, which sold thousands of copies each year, thus using a great deal of plate paper. One constant complaint from the engravers was about the hardness of the paper, which gave unsatisfactory contact in the printing process.

Dickinson's company started *circa* 1809 as Longman, Dickinson and Co., the Longman being George Longman, brother of Thomas Norton Longman, head of the famous publishing house. It is quite possible, there-

MUSIC.

BY CAMILLA TOULMIN.

Not lightly wake the silent strings !
 A soul among them dwells,
That answers with mysterious power,
 More strange than fairy spells ;
For Music lures the restless heart
 That trembles in its chain,
Yet will not break the bonds that make
 Its own delicious pain !

109 Music, page 32 of *The Drawing room table book*, engraved by T.A. Dean

fore, that the first book to contain steel engravings used plate paper made by Dickinson, since it was published by Longman. Thomas Campbell's *The Pleasures of Hope* (1820/21) had engravings done by Charles Heath on a paper thicker than that used for the text, but none the less a thin, crisp sheet. The depth of ink on a steel engraving would generally be less than on copper and was slightly less difficult to print, so that satisfactory results could be obtained on a variety of papers, so long as the surface was smooth to take the finer lines of steel. Charles Heath used a normal soft paper for his illustrations to Thomas Moore's *Loves of the Angels* (1823), published separately from the text. John Murray used a thick, almost cartridge-like paper for Byron's *Childe Harold's Pilgrimage* in 1841 where the illustrations were printed on the text page, as was the case in Mrs S.C. Hall's *The Drawing Room Table Book* [*c.*1849] (Plate 109). A tissue overlay covered only the engraving which was usually placed at the head of the page. The printing of intaglio plates on a page with text printed in relief presents problems of register and necessitates two passages through the press. This is why the two processes are separated and performed individually, even by different printers, but usually concurrently, so that the book can be produced in the shortest possible time. The printing of engravings, needing heavy pressure is a slow process, whereas the relief printing of text only requires a 'kiss' impression to be effective. Separate prints were added to most books by oversewing on the long edges (Chapter 4, Plate 58). This produced a row of holes, which acted as a perforation if plates were torn out of a volume, and enables such a print to be distinguished from those separately published.

Plate paper is mainly characterized by its thickness, colour, which varies from white to pale cream, and its surface, which tends to be soft and absorbent. It was either not sized or lightly sized, and so it was flexible enough when dampened to obtain the closest possible contact with the printing plate in their passage together through the rolling press, to pick up even the tiniest amounts of ink. Some size is useful for keeping the paper fibres together, since unsized (waterleaf) tends to disintegrate more easily when damp. Size (either animal size or rozin) was applied in one of two ways. Engine sizing involved the addition of size during manufacture, so that the size was an integral part of the finished paper. Tub sizing was done by dipping waterleaf into a tub of size after manufacture, so that only the outside of the paper was given a surface. Drawing paper, termed hard plate, is used for coloured drawings, being slightly sized, contrasting with soft plate which, if it is to take colour, has to be given a coating of isinglass (a form of gelatine of fish origin) so that the colour does not run or become absorbed into the fabric.

In a notebook kept by Philip Meadows Taylor, supervisor of Dickinson's Apsley Mill, in 1823, he writes '*copperplate* papers have *no size*'. The paper itself is visibly changed by the impression of the rolling press and plate. They impart their own smoothness, where the fibres were closely compacted, leaving a discernible difference to the feel of the paper in the plate area up to the plate mark, and the virtually untouched margin. The softness of plate paper tends to attract dust which can damage the surface before printing, but David Strang, a 20th-century printer of etchings and engravings actually approves of dust as improving the appearance of the paper's surface.

Plate paper was normally made in sizes from Medium (22¼ in. × 17¼ in.) upwards, since the plates most needed were of a Demy book size (19½ in. × 15¼ in.). The larger size allows for trimming. In order to examine closely the way in which a plate was printing, proofs (i.e. the first impressions from the plate) were pulled on a very thin, smooth kind of paper known as India paper. This rendered every line of the engraving accurately, took the ink well and which dried quicker than on other papers. The paper was made in China, but because it was originally imported in sheets measuring 52 in. × 26 in. by the East India Company, it became known as India paper. In 1817 the Society of Arts offered a premium for the best account of the materials and process employed in making India paper, by which date, Dickinson was producing a similar product at his Apsley and Nash Mills. This resulted in the earliest impressions of a plate being termed India proofs, and which were charged at higher prices. The paper was too thin to use by itself, so was normally backed on to ordinary plate paper. The India paper was given a thin coating of paste before it was placed on the plate paper, and together they passed through the rolling press to take the plate impression. If there was sufficient size in the plate paper, it sometimes took the place of the paste. In the course of time, the papers may have become separated, and much care needs to be exercised in putting them together again to avoid buckling and blistering on the print.

The long-term appearance of plate paper after about 100 years depends on a number of factors, one of which concerns the raw materials from which it was made. Rag of varying quality, cotton fibre and wood fibre were used and were treated with bleach which adversely affected the paper's purity and long-term durability. The comparative softness meant that engravings were more vulnerable to tears and cracks resulting in missing pieces especially on corners and edges. Stains from water and other liquids are difficult to treat, especially where the paper has cockled (Plate 110). The phenomenon known as 'foxing' has exercised many experts without any firm conclusions being reached. An article in the *Paper Conservator* (vol. 15, 1991, p. 5) states that the exact cause has never been established, but the current view suspects the presence of iron and/or fungus. Exposure to light may also cause some discoloration in a framed print where the printed area

110 Water stain on Rebekah and Eliezer, engraved by C.H. Jeens

is affected leaving the covered margins clear. Plates in books very often have the margins affected, especially at the edges, leaving the printed area where the fibres are compressed comparatively free (Plate 111).

One of the many changes which affected book production in the early days of steel engraving was the passage of responsibility for purchasing paper and superintending the printing of plates from the engraver to the

111 Foxing on Mosque of Omar, engraved by R. Dawson

printer, who became very good customers of the paper-makers until the decline of demand at the end of the century. Dickinsons continued their plate paper-making activities at Nash Mill, serving such customers as James Virtue with high quality sheets, free from blemish, for his extensive plate printing operations which continued well into the 1890s, but by 1896 demand had fallen in the face of competition with coated paper used for the new half-tone process. In 1898 profits from the plate paper operation were considerably reduced, despite improving the quality by using nothing but rag fibre in its manufacture.

Banknote paper was required to be thin with a hard surface so that the ink did not run when signed by pen. Such heavily sized paper was used in 1819 with a copper plate for the Society of Arts, who in their *Report ... of Preventing the Forgery of Banknotes* observed (1819, p. 52) that the sample was as good as the English paper used for book plates in respectable works, but not as good as India or French papers. Portals and Grosvenor, Chater and Co. supplied the Bank of England with paper, but the country banks were good customers of other mills who could supply high quality paper.

Enamelled cards

Examples of steel engravings exist printed on enamelled card, which are brilliant in their contrast of black and white, enhanced by the shiny surface. The impression was probably not heavy in order to protect the card's surface, and the overall appearance is a light one. Their purpose is unclear, but being mainly landscapes, it seems likely that they were used much in the way of modern picture postcards or photographs as a keepsake of places visited. Examples are taken from two sets from London publishers and one from an Edinburgh address. Only one dated plate has been found (1849) from Rock and Co., a firm founded in 1834, and said, over a period of years to have produced over 6,000 views of England and Wales, some as independent prints, some as notepaper headings and some as enamelled cards. These three uses derive almost certainly from the same steel plate, and Rock's are the smallest, measuring on average about $3\frac{1}{2}$ in. × $2\frac{3}{4}$ in. Rock is described in 1855 as a card and cardboard maker, so probably would have made their own card on which to print.

J[oseph] T[homas] Wood (fl. 1845–60) of 33 Holywell Street, Strand, produced views of London and the provinces on a slightly larger scale ($5\frac{1}{2}$ in. × $4\frac{1}{4}$ in.) and enlisted the help of J.W. Windsor, card maker of Clerkenwell. 'London Bridge from Surry [*sic*] side of River Thames' (Plate 112) acknowledges the card maker as well as the publisher.

The use of card in Scotland seems to have been quite high, since John Dickinson was writing to Charles Longman on 27 May 1833 that 'I think the

112 London Bridge from Surry [sic] side of River Thames, engraved by J.T. Wood

113 Print of Liège, engraved by A. Cruse, steel plate from which it was printed, and a 19th century burin

cards would do well in Scotland, but it is extraordinary what a quantity of the enamell'd cards they use there. I think I must find out how they are done and perhaps we could add it without much difficulty' (Evans, Joan. *The Endless Web; John Dickinson & Co. Ltd.* Cape, 1955, p. 56). J. Menzies of 61 Princes Street, Edinburgh published a series of Scottish views drawn by A.S. Mason and J. Ferguson, engraved by John Gellatly (1803–56), engraver and plate printer, whose business in Edinburgh in 1851 employed 12 men and eight apprentices. Subjects included 'Loch Ness', 'Stirling Castle', 'Loch Long', and 'High School, Calton Hill, Edinburgh'.

Membrane

The printing of steel engravings on membrane, more particularly vellum, is at present based on likelihoods rather than certainties. The late 19th-century printer Frederick Goulding (1842–1909) said that for the best results when printing on vellum, the plate should be steel-faced, simply because the membrane surface itself is abrasive and would be an extra hazard to an engraved plate. This makes it all the more likely that actual steel plates would be excellent for this purpose, and indeed it is possible that the number of vellum prints known, for example, of Landseer's works were printed from earlier steel plates.

Among the earliest examples, almost certainly printed from steel plates, are a certificate of the Newry Navigation Company, 1834, and another of the Blaydon, Gateshead and Hebburn Railway, 1835, both carrying fine vignette views. From 1880 a considerable number of such prints appeared, a form attractive to collectors along with India, signed and remarque proofs. Despite the difficulties of printing on vellum, made popular by William Morris's use of it at the Kelmscott Press, even trade printers such as Dixon and Ross were involved. Many of the plates of Herbert Thomas Dicksee (1862–1962), including some mezzotints, and Sir Frank Short's (1857–1945) proofs of the 'Swiss Pass' were known printed on vellum, probably from steel-faced plates.

Equipment

Engraving tools were subjected to a great deal of stress when used on steel and had to withstand the tendency to bend or break. The material used for gravers in the mid-18th century was cross bow steel, and later on double spur and star steel was advertised as particularly suitable for engraving tools, razors and fine scissors. In the 1820s, Charles Warren had gravers made by Mr Stodart. They were as slender as needles and made from cast steel and rhodium, especially useful for engraving the fine, delicate lines which were

114 Autolycus (*The Winter's Tale*), engraved by L. Stocks

a new feature possible on steel plates. Rhodium is a hard, white metal of the platinum group, and was added to give strength to the cast steel which tended to perform unpredictably on its own. The graver was housed in a wooden shaft with a shaped handle at the end. Metal bands slipped up and down the shaft to secure the graver in use (Plate 113). Beside the graver in Plate 113 is a reproduction of the steel plate and opposite is a print from that plate, taken from *The Continental Tourist* ... (Parry and Co., [*c.*1849], between pages 44 and 45).

The engraver at work in his studio is depicted in a watercolour drawing of Lumb Stocks (1812–92) (colour plate 7), thought to have been done by his son Arthur in the house at 9 Richmond Villas, Seven Sisters Road, London. Lumb is busy engraving a steel plate, possibly that of the picture on the easel. This is almost certainly a copy taken from the original now in the Victoria and Albert Museum of Charles Robert Leslie's 'Autolycus (The Winter's Tale)' exhibited at the Royal Academy in 1836. In front of it is an engraver's reducing done to the size of the finished engraving, the colours of the original having been translated into black and white. The engraving was published in the *Art Journal* (1869) and *Virtue's Imperial Shakespeare* (1872) (Plate 114).

Part Two

Introduction: steel engraving outside Britain and in the 20th century

The spread of steel engraving to the Continent and America depended to a very large extent on the work being done in Britain. Books were exported, engravers emigrated from Britain and, in general, steel engraving did not have the same chance to flourish among the indigenous engravers where competition from other forms of print, notably wood engraving and lithography, compelled it to share the illustration field, even to the extent of sharing books.

All through the period there was still a tendency, certainly from France, Germany and America, to send to London for some of their engraved plates to be printed locally, or for impressions from them. British engravers also took up residence abroad to create their own businesses, further reducing the chances of indigenous workers to become important exponents in this field. Continental engravers frequently came to Britain from France, Holland, Prussia and Russia to finish their education, a reversal of the previous trend. Steel engraving was often regarded as a British process, despite origins in Germany, France and America, but there was some important work done elsewhere, of which the following chapters are preliminary surveys.

Notable among continental publications are the monumental works containing hundreds of plates. They had no counterparts in Britain, where under 200 engravings per work was more usual, although the works, comparatively short in themselves, were sometimes loosely combined into a series. Much of this activity centred around 'the picturesque', where landscape and city views were paramount.

The international aspect of British steel-engraved publications is graphically illustrated by a plate from N.P. Willis's *American Scenery* (Virtue, 1839–40, vol. 2, p. 67), which carries titles in English, French, German and Dutch, the last obviously being an afterthought (Plate 115).

115 Portion of view of Hudson City and the Catskill Mountains, with four language titles, engraved by R. Brandard

Educational facilities for engravers were better in places like Paris and Munich than in early 19th-century England. Schools of engraving existed in most of the European Art Academies and schools, such central influences resulting in more uniformity of practice and, some said, inflexibility of approach. On the other hand, apprenticeship training was still important but, as always, much depended on the ability and attitudes of the masters.

The continental public was given a greater exposure to the art of engraving by the provision of rooms set aside to display engravings in palaces and academies. This gave wider support to the art, and did much to find buyers for the commercial projects which were undertaken.

The influence of continental engraving on Britain can be judged from a few comparisons made at the time. In 1839 there was a complaint that many of the best modern foreign prints were taken from pictures in English collections. Why, asked the author of an article in the *Art Union* (1839), could not our native engravers be employed on them? A similar point was raised (*Art Union*, 1844, p. 99) when Puckle, a royal publisher, commissioned two portraits from French engravers, complaining that it was neither 'necessary, wise or just' in view of the lack of commissions for English engravers at the time. By 1861 a project for a new series of illustrations to the *Art Journal* for 1862 had to resort to the engravers of Germany, Belgium and France, since the art of line engraving was, by this time in Britain, nearly extinct. By 1865 it was said that France was in almost the same position (*Art Journal*, 1865, p. 244), but steel engraving did struggle on for another 25 years before it finally expired.

There was a steady flow of steel engravers to America from Europe, mostly from Britain, during the period, one of the main attractions being work in the banknote industry which flourished there.

7

German steel engraving

Germany was the home of a flourishing armour and weapon making industry in the early 16th century, and the development of steel plates for printing purposes occurred in the area of Nuremberg, Augsburg and Regensberg.

Daniel Hopfer I (*c*.1470–1536), born at Kaufbeuren, but working from 1493 at Augsburg, was possibly the first to etch on iron as an artistic medium, sometime before 1504. Hopfer's etching of 'Konrad von der Rosen', jester-adviser to Emperor Maximilian I has been convincingly dated to *circa* 1503–04, and there is reason to suppose that it would have been preceded by some experimental plates. This portrait measured $11\frac{5}{8}$ in. × $8\frac{1}{2}$ in., a size much used by him, and only slightly smaller than the engravings on the 'Engraved' suit of armour of 1509, where the St George and dragon on the breastplate measured $15\frac{3}{4}$ in. × $10\frac{7}{8}$ in. Another of his plates, 'Figures in military costume' measures $8\frac{1}{16}$ in. × $14\frac{3}{4}$ in. (Plate 116). It is not difficult to believe in his involvement with the making and decoration of arms and armour, supported by the existence of a jousting shield, signed and dated 1536 in the Royal Armoury at Madrid. Certainly his grandson Daniel II (d.1598) was responsible (with *his* brother George) for making and engraving the decoration on 110 helmets for Maximilian II in 1566. They also decorated work for other armourers, notably Coloman Coleman. Daniel I had two brothers (or sons – authorities disagree). Hieronymous Hopfer worked in Augsburg from 1520 to 1535 and etched iron plates with designs copied from the German and Italian engravers, while Lambert Hopfer concerned himself with ornamental designs, three iron plates of which are preserved in the Department of Prints at the British Museum.

The first dated etching on iron is by Urs Graf (*c*.1485–1527); his 'Woman [or girl] bathing her feet' is dated 1513. Graf was born in Solothurn, some 17 miles south of Basle, and became a painter, although he is best known

116 Figures in military costume, etched by Daniel Hopfer

for his engraving on wood, copper and precious metals. About the age of 18 he was working in Strasburg, moving later to Zurich and Basle, but when he was 28, became a soldier until 1524. In 1513, the date on the etching, he was at Dijon and, since he had married Sybil von Brunn in November 1511, it is possible that he used her as a model for the girl. As an experienced engraver, he probably tried etching on iron experimentally, but there is no evidence that he came into contact with the Nuremberg/Augsburg group 80 miles away. Some 300 works by him are known – a prolific output, considering he died about the age of 42.

The relationship between etching for the armourers and print making is further demonstrated, also in Augsburg, by one of its best known artists, Hans Burgkmair the elder (1473–c.1531). The family were close friends and neighbours of the famous armourers, the Colemans. Hans is thought to have designed the labours of Samson and Hercules on a suit of armour in the Royal Armoury, Madrid, and his plate of 'Venus and Mercury', c.1520 was etched on iron.

By far the most influential member also heads the Nuremberg group of artists, namely Albrecht Dürer (1471–1528). Already a supreme master of copper engraving, Dürer turned to etching on iron in 1515. In 1512 he had been appointed Court Painter to the Emperor Maximilian I, who had a consuming interest in the design and decoration of armour. The Court Armourer, Conrad Seusenhofer, shared this enthusiasm, and Dürer's interest in the subject, already demonstrated by his masterly drawing of 'The Rider', made in 1498, extended to the making of his own designs in 1517. The first of his six etchings on iron was 'The Man of Sorrows' in 1515, which had a red lead ground. In the same year came a plate variously titled 'Agony in the garden', 'Christ in the garden of Gethsemane', and 'Christ on the Mount of Olives', thought to be one of his best works. This was followed by 'Man in despair' in 1515–16(?), 'Angel displaying the Sudarium' in 1516, 'Pluto and Proserpine' in 1516 and the last, in 1518, called 'The Cannon' or 'The Turkish cannon' or 'The field-serpent of Nuremberg'. This is the most famous of the series in which the cannon, an object of great popular interest at the time, is shown as the 'secret weapon' for use against the Turks who 11 years later, were to lay siege to Vienna. It is suggested that the etching process was used to satisfy an immediate interest, indicating a journalistic use of the medium.

'The Cannon' is also an example of the rising interest in landscape by the artists of the time, led by the work of Albrecht Altdorfer (fl. 1505–38) of nearby Regensberg, who was the accepted leader of the group of Little Masters, so called from the size of their prints. Two more artists influenced by Altdorfer and who are thought to have used iron plates for their landscape etchings are Augustin Hirschvogel (c.1503–53) and Hans Sebald

Lautensack (c.1523–63). He developed Dürer's technique of etching (who used only one biting and one strength of line) by using different sizes of needle to vary the strength of line. He is thought to have worked his landscapes on iron, but used copper for his portraits. On a plate of his father 'Paul Lautensack' he combined etching and engraving, a process first used in 1520 by Lucas van Leyden (1494–1533), on a portrait of the Emperor Maximilian.

It was only the influence of the armourers etching on steel which kept the process alive. The fine art engravers who had little or no connection with the armourers preferred to work on copper as it was easier to work and there was no market for the larger number of copies an iron or steel plate could provide. The texture of steel was not as even as that of copper, and therefore the mordant would bite less regularly, but on the positive side, the coarseness of the metal could be exploited to give a characteristic line quite unlike the clear-cut manner of the line engraving, and more in accord with the freedom of expression associated with etching. There is little evidence of burins being used on steel at this date, due to the hardness of the metal. As a result the process died out, and was only revived under the influence of English engraving in the 19th century.

The introduction of steel engraving into Germany was brought about by many of the same factors which obtained in England. There was a market for many more than the 5,000 copies which a copper plate could provide, and the potential for up to 60,000 copies from a single plate was slowly recognized by German publishers. The market expanded to the extent that the middle and lower classes could spend more of their incomes on luxuries, which included prints to adorn the walls of their houses and books to put on their parlour tables. Whereas copper engraving in the past could satisfy the demands of the upper classes, steel with its other advantage of increased tonal range could permit publishers to undertake works of wider appeal to sell in many more copies.

One of the chief obstacles to steel's immediate adoption after 1820 was money. In London and Paris, publishers had access to a pool of wealth and patronage concentrated more or less in one place, with very little competition from the provinces. In Germany, by contrast, the markets were smaller and more fragmented, where subscribers to part publications would come from the locality of a state, rather than a whole nation. Up to the 1820s–40s many states and cities were culturally and commercially independent, but the Prussian Customs Union, established in 1828 and expanded in 1836 to cover all but the most northern states of Germany, brought the beginning of co-operation and consequent expansion of markets. Publishers of steel-engraved books were located in at least five centres, Leipzig, Stuttgart, Frankfurt am Main, Darmstadt and Carlsruhe, all in the central and southern half of the country, and it is not surprising, therefore, that when Henry Fisher, the English publisher, wanted to break into the German market he chose an agent in Berlin where there was insignificant opposition to his trade. Later on, Albert Henry Payne, based at Leipzig and Dresden, was able to counter Fisher's activity by sending his wares to be sold in London. The English translations of his publications were printed in Leipzig and published from Dresden.

Engravers, although not well paid, were adequately served by the various academies and schools in nearly each state, the rulers of which often appointed engravers to their courts as in Carlsruhe and Darmstadt. The distribution of engravers was more widespread in at least ten centres, i.e. Berlin, Carlsruhe, Darmstadt, Dresden, Dusseldorf, Eisenach, Leipzig, Munich, Nuremberg, and Rudolstadt. Proximity to commissions probably had some influence on where they lived, but work of this kind could be carried on anywhere. Some were known at Freiburg and Strasburg, for instance.

A contemporary engraver Carl Barth (1787–1853), writing in 1837, saw a very significant role for steel engraving in the promotion of art. He saw art, ranked with religion and science, as an important civilizing influence in a society which has become uncaring and of low moral tone. Art appreciation, largely lost to Barth's generation, had a part to play here, and since works of art were only seen by a fortunate few, reproduction by copper engraving was the only suitable means of bringing it to the lower and middle classes. Steel engraving, able to produce many more copies than copper, was seen as the working of God's providence to further the education of mankind.

The level of print sales in Germany produced insufficient income for engravers, even when they sold direct to customers without a middleman. Steel engraving could increase their profits and output, especially with the demand for reproductions of works in German art collections and German landscape pictures, and the added objective of publicizing them outside the country. Some monumental works were issued in these fields, some containing many hundreds of plates on a scale not matched in England. German publications in the 1830s relied heavily on inputs from English engravers, which continued to a lesser degree throughout the steel-engraving period. With their limited incomes, German engravers were not at first very enthusiastic about steel plates, as they were more expensive and difficult to work than copper. In the beginning steel plates were probably imported from England until local manufacturers could make an adequate contribution. Spemann (1952, p. 8) expressed his opinion that lack of 'artistic sensibility' also hindered the acceptance of the new process, which meant that engravers failed to adjust their methods to meet the increased tonal values it offered. Moreover, lithography was a serious rival after its development and spread from Munich. It provided a cheap means of reproduction for all classes of work. Wood engraving was also a more serious rival than at this time in England. It is doubtful, therefore, if line engravers turned over to steel so completely as they did in England, so that many are represented as steel engravers on the evidence of only a few plates. There were a number who were primarily painters and, unusually, one was a sculptor (Franz Hablitschek).

On the other hand, German writers on the art of engraving were including information on steel in their works. C.G. Thon's *Lehrbuch der Kupferstecherkunst, die Kunst in Stahl* ... was published at Ilmenau in 1831, A.M. Perrot's *Die Gravierkunst* ... *Stahlstechen* ... *Ulm*, in 1831 (a German translation of his *Manuel du graveur*, Paris, 1830), Moritz Henrici's *Die Kupferstechkunst und der Stahlstich* ... at Leipzig in 1834, and C.H. Schmidt's *Völlstandiges Handbuch der Gravirkunst* ... *für Kupfer und Stahlsticher* at Quedlinburg in 1838 all mention steel in their titles.

Steel engraving arrived in Germany from England in 1825. Carl Ludwig Frommel (1789–1863) visited England in 1824 with two objects in mind, one of which was to investigate how steel engraving achieved such delicate tones and how to reduce the size of a large drawing by using a sort of pantograph. The other reason was to find someone experienced in steel engraving to set up a workshop in Carlsruhe. Frommel was a pupil of Christian Haldenwang (1770–1831), who worked for an engraver in Basle, but was largely self-taught by studying the works of Samuel Middiman and William Woollett. His work clearly showed the English influence and in due course his reputation led to his appointment as engraver to the Grand Duke of Baden in Carlsruhe. Frommel, after working in Paris and Italy, obtained a position in Carlsruhe to teach painting and engraving, doubtless encouraged by his master's position at court, and in 1829 he became Director of the gallery in Carlsruhe. It is not clear how Frommel became aware of steel engraving while it was still in its infancy, but in 1825 he persuaded Henry Winkles (fl. 1818–45) to accompany him to set up a workshop in Carlsruhe to promote the process there.

Winkles's independent career appeared to commence about 1818 when he first exhibited a landscape painting at the Royal Academy. Between 1818 and 1824 he line engraved some copper plates for John Preston Neale's *Views of the Seats of Noblemen*, and between June and December 1824 engraved some plates for Edward Brayley's *Illustrations of His Majesty's Palace at Brighton* eventually published in 1838, for which he did some aquatints. His name does not appear in connection with the early uses of steel engraving as, for example, the Society of Arts report on banknote forgery, but he is reputed to have taken a steel-engraving press with him to Carlsruhe.

Ordinary rolling presses would already be available in Germany, so this would indicate something in the nature of the press modified by Jacob Perkins to take his thick slabs of steel. If this were the case, local engravers, faced with new presses and thick steel plates would think twice about such investment. The use of Charles Warren's plates of normal thickness would stand a much better chance of acceptance.

Frommel and Winkles made a success of the venture, but in 1832 Winkles returned to England leaving Frommel to oversee the workshop. During this time, Frommel directed the production of a collection of steel engravings after the best modern painters in which Edouard Schuler (1806–82) participated, and it was published in Carlsruhe in 1833. After two or three years in London, during which time Henry assisted his brother Benjamin on their *Cathedrals...* project he returned to Carlsruhe probably as a direct result of Frommel's undertaking to provide plates for *Das malerische und Romantische Deutschland* which commenced publication in 1836. Despite Henry's other commercial interests the association with Frommel resumed in their atelier, e.g. in 1840 *Carl Frommel's Picturesque Italy, Engraved on Steel in the Atelier of C. Frommel and H. Winkles...* published in Leipzig by Ch. E. Kollman. In June 1838 an advertisement appeared in the trade journal *Journal für Buchdruckerkunst...* headed 'Steel and copperplate manufacture by Henry Winkles and Friedrich Abresch in Carlsruhe'. Addressed to engravers and art dealers it offered plates of superior quality than others manufactured in Germany, using the best quality metals. The plates were also cheaper than those from England, which also took too long to import. From their experience, they would provide the best for the customer's needs, and to achieve this, they brought several skilled workmen from London. The customer was assured of prompt service and reasonable prices, with which they will be more than satisfied when they are acquainted with the quality and size of their steel plates. They also advertised tools for engraving and lithography from their warehouse, and expressed a commitment to fair and firm prices. His price list for all kinds of engraving showed a flat rate of 6 kroner for a 3 × 3 cm. (1¼ in. × 1¼ in.) square.

Friedrich Abresch (fl. 1832–41) was probably the same person as Franz Abresch described in Benezit. He was a pupil of Frommel and was certain to have known Henry by that connection. They obviously felt that there was a need to supply engravers with the materials and tools of their trade, but it is not recorded how well the business did or how long it flourished.

The same trade journal carried another advertisement dated 18 February 1842, written from Leipzig, where Henry appears to have moved into a new annexe built on to a house in the Dresdener strasse. Under his own name he announced an atelier for engraving and printing steel and copper plates from which he could quickly supply engravings from excellent English and

German artists in historical, landscape, anatomical and architectural subjects, together with geometrical figures. He would give liberal trade terms with guarantees to deliver work of a high standard. He hoped that his name would not be unknown to his readers, since he had been in Germany for seven years up to January 1841 in the workshop of Frommel's art publishing house in Carlsruhe and Leipzig, and acknowledges the latter's part in giving a technical lead in the business. Soon after this, he seems to have joined in business with the engraver Lehmann, with whom Winkles did eight plates for Friedrich Brockhaus's *Bilderatlas* ... and for which Winkles alone engraved over 330 steel plates. *Circa* 1843 Henry took Alfred Krausse (1829–94) as his pupil in Carlsruhe, and Adolf Neumann (1825–84) went to work for him.

The Frommel-Winkles initiative gave steel engraving a good start in Germany, and one of the first publishers to take advantage of it was [Carl] Joseph Meyer (1796–1856). The son of a shoemaker in Gotha (which had a reputation as a map publishing centre), Meyer went to London in 1817 at the age of 21, where he stayed until 1824 when he returned home to Gotha. After a brief publishing venture with an English literary magazine *Meyer's British Chronicle* in 1825, he founded the Bibliographischen Institut on 1 August 1826, with the object of publishing the whole of German national literature in a self-contained collection of 150 volumes. He moved his operation to Hildburghausen in 1828 and built it up so quickly that by 1830 it was the sixth largest publisher in Germany (after Cotta in Stuttgart, Decker in Berlin, Wenner in Frankfurt, and Teubner and Brockhaus in Leipzig), and employed 190 people, of whom 16 were copper, steel and litho engravers. Meyer was among the earliest publishers to appreciate the value of steel engraving. Between 1829 and 1835 he published a *Gallerie der Zeitgennosen*, a series of portraits which commenced on copper but later changed to steel. In 1830 his *Gallerie zur geschmackvollen Zimmerverzierung* (interior decoration) was illustrated by aquatints engraved on steel or copper, but by 1833–34 his *Universalatlas* contained 64 steel engravings, and a little later, 1834–41, his *Pfennig-atlas* had 115 coloured steel-engraved plates. He had probably come across some steel engraving when he was in England, and doubtless encouraged the engravers who worked for him to develop the process.

His best known work, *Meyer's Universum* commenced publication in 1833 and used steel engraving for its 1,000 plates. Although ostensibly a multi-volume work, completed in 21 volumes, it came out more or less annually, with seven years omitted, and this placed it on a par with the landscape annuals then being published in England. Volume 21 was issued in 1860, but the annual tradition continued with *Meyer's Universum; ein Jahrbuch für Freunde der Natur und Kunst* in the three volumes 1862–64 of which, a further 238 plates appeared. The two works together provide probably the largest number of steel engravings published in a single work, although other German publications had large numbers of plates to illustrate them. The engravings in the *Universum* show views of places from all over the world. They are numbered in Roman figures which are used for reference in this work, and only 189 carry information concerning artist and engraver. C. Reiss (fl. 1833–60) was the most frequently named artist, although a very few were done by Thomas Allom, Clarkson Stanfield, William Brockedon and Robert Batty. There were 27 German engravers named and a small number of plates were done by English engravers. Robert Sands did two, Heath (presumably Charles) three after Vickers, Wallis (probably William) six after Reiss, Piranger and Julin and Thomas Barber two after Reiss. Not all the views were original, for example, 'Innsbruck in Tyrol' in volume 3 (1836) has been shown by Marsch to be identical with 'Innsbruck' from *Heath's Picturesque Annual* (1832), drawn by Clarkson Stanfield and engraved by Charles Heath. Moreover, approximately 25 plates appear to owe something to those published in *Finden's Illustrations of the Life and Works of Lord Byron* (1833–34). Plate XXXX of 'Cadix' [sic] was done by Friedrich Geissler, engraved by H.L. Petersen after one drawn by Robert Batty, engraved by Edward Finden and appeared in volume 1 in 1833.

A further work, *Meyer's Universum – Ein Volksbuch . . .*, comprising 16 volumes was issued between 1858 and 1863, averaging three volumes a year, containing 668 engravings. A number of these had already appeared in the main *Universum*. It is possible to assume that the 27 German engravers supplied most of the plates for the work, which would average out at about 40 per engraver, but on the other hand, the bulk could have been supplied by engravers already on Meyer's staff. Where engravers were named, the highest number of 47 was done by Johann George Martini (b. c.1785), who worked at Rudolstadt engraving views and genre subjects. In 1842 he published *Collection of Towns and the Most Interesting Castles of Thuringia* in Vienna. Bernhard Metzeroth (fl. 1833–48) provided 33. Johann Gabriel Friedrich Poppel (1807–82) contributed 14; he had previously worked for Frommel at Carlsruhe, and later went to Munich, where he did some celebrated views. Rottman (fl. 1852–59) also did 14. Ten were contributed by Plato Ahrens (b.1827) who was born in Augsburg, educated in Munich and went to work for Georg Lange the publisher in Darmstadt. He drew a number of designs for the *Universum* and in 1846 became the work's artistic manager. He engraved 'London' [1863] which appeared in the *Volksbuch* volume 16 and *Jahrbuch* volume 2 (Plate 117). Christian Daumerlang (fl. 1833–39) of Nuremberg did ten plates, as did Ernst Friedrich Grunewald (1801–48), a pupil of Frommel, working at Darmstadt.

117 London, engraved by P. Ahrens

Other engravers were Boringer (fl. 1839), Johann Andreas Daut (d. 1859) of Nuremberg, Diefel (fl. 1836–37), Georg Döbler (fl. 1833), a Czech engraver from Prague who did plates for the Belvidere Gallery and *Forbin's Travels*, Herman Emden (b.1811) of Frankfurt am Main, known for his numerous views of that city, and A. Fesca (fl. 1850–62). John Martin Friedrich Geissler (1778–1853) of Nuremberg, established a school of engraving there with his friend Reindel, and *circa* 1832 was one of the first to introduce steel engraving into Nuremberg, and trained a number of engravers to work for Meyer. E. Geissler (fl. 1835), probably from Nuremberg, Gerstner (fl. 1844–48), Grunew [? Gruner] (fl. 1833), Herzen (fl. 1836), Hirschenheim (fl. 1840), E. Höfer (fl. 1835), Matthaus Kern (1801–52) a Viennese engraver, Alexander Marx (b. 1815), a pupil of J.M.F. Geissler and published *Picturesque Views of the Canal from Mein to the Danube* (1852), Obermuller (fl. 1844), Heinrich Ludwig Petersen (1806–74), a Danish national from Altona, who worked in Nuremberg. His one signed plate for the *Universum* was done in 1833 and in 1840 he went to engrave for Huefuer's collection of costumes. Johann Georg Christian Rosée (b. 1804) worked at Nuremberg and engraved his plate for the *Universum* in 1838. Ludwig Friedrich Schnell (1790–1834) worked at Carlsruhe where he was engraver to the court in succession to Christian Haldenwang; his plate for the *Universum* was published in 1835. Friederich Wagner (1803–76), an engraver of many illustration plates, worked in Paris, Stuttgart and finally Munich, although he originally came from, and was trained at Nuremberg under Reindel. His two plates of the Pantheon in Paris and the Palace of Versailles after Reiss appeared in volume 13 (1848). W. Wilkins (fl. 1835) contributed two plates to volume 2, and A. Willmann (fl. 1836–41) did two plates during 1838–41.

Other engravers who participated from time to time, although their plates were not signed were Ferdinand Bahmann (b. *c.*1800) from Ilmenau, C. Schmitze from Cologne, Fr. Braun from Jena, C. Herbst from Sonderhausen, C. Ericht from Halle and G. Wolf from Warneck.

Editions were published in many other countries in varying degrees of completeness, the majority being selections from the main work. Austria, Holland, Denmark, Sweden, Poland, Hungary and France had translations, and in America two editions appeared. The first was for German immigrants in German, published New York in four volumes (1850–52), and the second, published in English in Philadelphia by the North American Bibliographic Institution entitled *Our Globe; Universal Picturesque Album* (1852–53). These volumes came out during the time that Meyer's son Hermann was resident in the United States after going there as a political fugitive in 1849 following the 1848 Revolution which had been brought about by famine and distress in 1846–47. He returned to Germany in 1854 and took over from his father shortly before the latter's death. The firm moved to Leipzig in 1874. It is perhaps significant that no edition appeared in England, where the public had been surfeited on landscape engravings in both annual and book form.

Meyer's *Universum* was published in oblong format which had the advantage that the horizontal plates which were in the majority could be viewed without turning the book sideways. A number of continental publications were issued in this format, and as a result were frequently called albums. By *circa* 1850, according to a letter written by Joseph to his son, the firm had 44 steel printers, 42 working presses and 160 colourists, engravers, etc.

Landscape was the most popular subject to be steel engraved, and that of Germany the most favoured. There had been volumes on Germany published in England by Robert Batty in the 1820s, and later on steel, when William Tombleson issued his *Views of the Rhine* (1832), some plates in which bore the imprint of Tombleson and Creuzbaner and Co., Carlsruhe. German publishers were also ambitious and an important work was *Das malerische und Romantische Deutschland* (Picturesque and Romantic Germany) published by Georg Wigand in Leipzig. It was published as a series of monographs to provide ten 'Sektionen', each written by a different author (or authors in the case of vol. 10). These were issued between 1834 and [1840], but Theodor Fischer issued two more volumes, published by J.C. Krieger of Kassel and Leipzig, in [1841]–42. Each 'sektion' was cased in grey paper boards, and the paper used for the prints was a kind of cartridge paper, thick, hard and durable. The printing plates were smaller than the page size and left a visible plate mark. In the event, about 450 plates, based on an average of nine volumes with 30 plates each and three volumes with 60 plates each, were provided. The exact number is difficult to determine, since extant copies do not agree and have varied from 444 to 454. The original 'sektionen' do not appear to carry a list of illustrations which could be used as a check. Even this is no guarantee, and the risk is more obvious when publisher's casings are replaced by customers' bindings. The numbering of the volumes is also confusing. For example, on the front board of Ludwig Bechstein's *Wanderungen durch Thüringen* is described as the 'Dritte Sektion'. A list of all the volumes in the front of the same copy lists it as 'IV', so according to the source, Bechstein's is either volume 3 or 4. The same source lists the volumes as follows: 1. *Die sächsische Schweiz* by A. Tromlitz. 2. *Schwaben* by Gustav Schwab. 3. *Franken* by G. v. Heeringen. 4. *Thüringen* by Ludwig Bechstein. 5. *Der Herz* by W. Blumenhagen. 6. *Das Riesengebirge* by Ernst Raupach. 7. *Steiermark u. Tyrol* by Carl Herlossohn. 8. *Die Donau* by Eduard Duller. 9. *Der Rhein* by Carl Simrock. 10. *Die Ost- u. Nordsee* by Mohnicke and Starkloff. As the project developed, amendments were made, as, for example, in *Der Rhein* where the original 30 engravings were increased to 60. The following analysis of engravers is taken from a single copy, but is sufficiently accurate to show individual involvements in the work. It may be observed in passing that the numbers of plates may vary in the description of any steel-engraved book, since some will exclude engraved title-page vignettes, for instance.

Thirty-five German engravers provided 215 plates and the rest were done by 32 English engravers. It appears that the publisher was going to rely on English engravers from the beginning, and all the plates in volume 1 were done by them. Henry Winkles is counted as German by virtue of his residence in Germany and association with Frommel, and was by far the largest single contributor. He did 74 plates under his own name and 26 more in association with Frommel. The ten English engravers who worked on volume 1 were J.W. Appleton, E. Benjamin, James Carter, R. Dawson, J.J. Hinchliff, Samuel Lacey, E. Patten, Albert Henry Payne (who contributed 68 plates under his own name and 21 more in association with J. Gray), Thomas Phillibrown (d. 1873) and John Woods. Four of these were established engravers, while others were at the start of their engraving careers. Twenty-six of the English engravers contributed between one and six plates each, spread across the set of volumes, except volume 8, which was done by Winkles and Frommel, with C. Lindemann (fl. 1839) contributing a single plate. The mechanics of the arrangement with the English engravers is not clear, but it would seem likely that the plates were engraved in England and most were sent to be printed in one of three Leipzig establishments. Winkles and Frommel used Kunst Verlag von Roo Binders, Payne his own Englische Kunstanstallt and the third firm was F.A. Zehl.

The remaining German/Austrian engravers, with two exceptions, only achieved single figures for their contribution. Ernst Friedrich Grünewald (1801–48), a pupil of Frommel and working at Darmstadt, produced nine plates under his own name and 14 more in conjunction with Cooke, who was probably his assistant. The plates are spread over the years 1836–42, and he seems to have printed most of them himself.

The Austrian Joseph Axmann (1793–1873) contributed ten plates printed at either Darmstadt or Leipzig. L. Beyer (1784–*c.*1870) also Austrian, Johann Georg Serz (1808–*c.*1878) of Nuremberg and W. Witthöft (1816–94) each contributed eight plates, printed mainly by F.A. Zehl, Leipzig. Louis Hoffmeister (fl. 1836–39), Frommel's pupil contributed six plates, one of which from volume 2 is 'Kloster Maulbronn' (Plate 118). Franz Abresch (fl. 1832–41) Frommel's pupil who worked with Tombleson in England and F. Folz (fl. 1839), two of whose plates were printed by Grünewald at Darmstadt contributed four each. Three plates each were done by the Viennese engravers Adolf Dworzak (fl. 1836–83), Michael Hofmann (1797–1867), and Jakob Rauschenfels von Steinberg (1779–1841),

118 Kloster Maulbronn, engraved by L. Hoffmeister

with J.H. Leidhecker (fl. 1838) of Stuttgart, Johann Friedrich Rossmässler (1775–1858) of Leipzig and Berlin, and Julius Umbach (1815–77), whose 'Höllenthal' from volume 2 carries the inscription 'Stahlstich u. Druck durch C. Susemihl u. Sohn in Darmstadt'. Two plates each were done by Fra[nz] Xa[vier?] Eisner (fl. 1836) of Vienna, Hans Fincke (1800–49) who studied under the Findens in London and founded a steel-engraving school in Berlin, J.M.F. Geissler, E. Höfer (fl. 1836–42), J.G. Martini, J. Passini (fl. 1836) of Vienna, Carl Peschek (1803–47) of Dresden, J.G.F. Poppel of Munich, Johann A. Willmann (fl. 1837–42), probably of Darmstadt, and H. Worms (fl. 1836–50).

Single plates were done by G. Geistner (fl. 1838), H. Guzeler (fl. 1838), both possibly of Stuttgart, H. von Herzer (fl. 1838) possibly of Darmstadt, C. Lindemann, Alexander Marx (b. 1815) of Nuremberg, Ernst Christian Schmidt (b. 1809), probably of Dresden and C. Weisner (fl. 1839), possibly of Leipzig.

The six engravers brought in from Vienna would seem to indicate that there were insufficient engravers willing to undertake commissions for this work, and the use of three of Frommel's pupils shows a fairly tight knit community providing the bulk of engraving. J. Gray, S. Lacey, A.H. Payne and L. Hoffmeister also drew some designs, but a proportion was done by Ludwig Adrian Richter (1803–84) of Dresden, the son and pupil of an engraver, who later became better known as a landscape and animal painter.

Spemann (1952) expresses the opinion that the engravings in this work suffered from a lack of judgement and finance on the publisher's part, together with the tight schedules imposed by part publication. There is also some evidence in the three plates engraved by J. Davis (fl. 1836–40), and in one by R. Parr (fl. 1836–38) that they were included by courtesy of Black and Armstrong, the London publishers specializing in German works.

An attempt was made to publish an English version under the title *Romantic and Picturesque Germany Illustrated by a Series of Engravings on Steel by Eminent English Artists from Drawings Taken on the Spot. Translated by Miss Henningsen*. It was published in London by Albert Schloss in 1838, but in the event only six out of a projected 260 plates were issued. The engravers were A.H. Payne, J. Carter, S. Lacey and T. Phillibrown, all of whom had contributed to volume 1 of the German work and, although the publication line was A. Schloss, it could have been the intention to use the German plates again. Designs were drawn by Otto Wagner, Ludwig Richter, Thomas H. Shepherd, and R. Roberts.

Georg Wigand was rather like Henry Fisher in England in that he wanted to exploit the long runs that steel plates could give, so between 1838 and 1840 he re-issued the 60 plate Rhineland section of *Das malerische*... under the name of Karl Simrock entitled *Das malerische und Romantische Rheinland*,

38 plates of which were engraved by Henry Winkles and 22 by Frommel and Winkles jointly. A second edition came out in 1847, published by C.A. Haendel of Leipzig. For this there were four new plates after G. Kuhn engraved by Winkles, one of which 'Homberg' became the sixty-first plate of the series. The other three replaced plates 27, 51 and 55, originally done after T. Verhas, which were presumably damaged or worn. In the third edition 1851, plate 26 'Stolzenfels' was replaced, this time drawn by Ludwig Lange and engraved by J. Poppel. The fourth edition 1863 did not include steel engravings, but in 1924 Verlag Schroeder of Leipzig re-issued the views printed from the original plates.

Twenty-nine plates were used yet again in *Die Fahrt auf dem Rhein* [Journey up the Rhine], published by Kreidel of Wiesbaden. These had been used for Simrock's book, and plate 21 'Stolzenfels' after C. Schweich, engraved by Joseph Maximilian Kolb (fl. 1842–48) of Munich had been added, supplied by the publisher Georg Gustav Lange of Darmstadt. It is not clear whether Wigand the original publisher had sold the plates or merely impressions from them.

The Rhine provided material for many artists of the time from all over Europe, and there are innumerable steel engravings in publications issued in England, France and Germany. The plates in William Tombleson's very successful *Views on the Rhine* (1832) formed the basis of Karl Geib's *Malerische Wanderungen gen am Rhein von Mainz bis Cöln* [Picturesque tour of the Rhine from Mainz to Cologne] (1838), issued by Tombleson's German agent Creuzbaner of Carlsruhe. There are 60 plates, four of which came from Leitch Ritchie's *Travelling Sketches on the Rhine* (Heath's Picturesque annual for 1833) and two from E.G. Bulwer-Lytton's *The Pilgrims of the Rhine* (1834). The remainder were from Tombleson. A major work was *Der Rhein und die Rheinland* with text by Heinrich Müller Malten, and published in parts between 1842 and 1847 by Georg Gustav Lange of Darmstadt. It contained 102 steel engravings, many after the designs of Ludwig Lange (1808–68) and two after his younger brother Julius (1817–78) who were probably of the same family as the publisher. Between 1832 and 1835 the brothers had collaborated in a series of views of the principal German towns, which may have formed the basis for some plates in this work. Of the ten engravers employed seven were either based in, or had connections with Munich, the largest contributor being J.G.F. Poppel with 44 plates. His pupil Franz Hablitschek (1824–67) did four, his collaborator Georg Michael Kurz (1815–83) did nine. J.M. Kolb did 17, Jobst Rugel (1821–78) did 13. Johann Richter (b. 1823) did eight and Frederick Würthle (or Wuerthle) (b. 1820) did one. Franz Abresch and Edward Willmann (1820–77), both from Carlsruhe did two plates and one plate respectively. Ludwig Rohbock (fl. 1848–52) of Nuremberg engraved six plates and designed several more. He was also known for his 43 steel engravings of Harz landscapes in 1852. In 1844, 43 engravings were used by Lange for *Malten's Handbuch für Rheinreisende*. The main work was reprinted in 1853, but a second edition was published in Paris with a French text, 1857–63. This included 69 more steel engravings done by 21 engravers. Poppel (16), Kurz (12) Kolb (six), Riegel (three) Willmann (three), Hablitschek (one) and Richter (one) were the chief contributors from the original group, but added to them were L. Oeder (four), Julius Umbach (four), F. Foltz (three), W. Lang (three), L. Thümling (three), Carl Rauch (b. 1804) (two), and one each from R. Dawson, G. Hess, Christian Hoffmeister (1818–71), H. Huber, A. Rottman, G. Rudolf, Christian Steinicken (d. 1896), and C. Struntz. A further edition in 1870 contained a selection of 51 plates which included four new ones, two unsigned, and the other two after photographs, engraved by F. Foltz and L. Rö[h]rich (fl. 1850–70).

In 1838 Johann Wilhelm Spitz produced his *Das malerische und Romantische Rheinland* in Dusseldorf containing 61 steel engravings. Most plates were unsigned but the engravers named were W. Weber, V. Hardung, O. Gunst, C. Gunst, Ph. Mossman, Schumacher, F. Foltz and H. Pennerich. Eleven plates are similar to those in Tombleson's *Views...* and one in Simrock.

At Bonn in 1842, Adolph Waldeck published his *Der Führer am Rhein* with 40 steel engravings done by F. Foltz (4), E. Grünewald (ten), Hermann Emden (b. 1811) (15), Xaver Steifensand (1809–76) (one), Julius Umbach (three), C. Collard, L. Collard (one each), Carl Rauch (b. 1804) (one) Ernst Rauch (b. 1797) (one), and two French engravers, Jean Desaulx (one) and J. Besnard (one). The second edition, in 1850, contained 20 more engravings by Henry Winkles (five), Winkles and Lehmann (four), H. Emden in Frankfurt and Bonn (five), F. Foltz (two), J. Schumacher and Emden in Bonn (three) and Grünewald (one). The 1855 edition added another plate engraved by Winkles.

The brothers Ernst and Karl Rauch collaborated to produce a collection of steel engravings depicting the German capitals and their cathedrals. They were born in Darmstadt and Ernst was appointed court engraver there. The publication was entitled *Deutsche Städteansichten* [Views of German Towns], and the engraver Carl Barth, writing in 1837, expressed the opinion that this was an excellent example of steel engraving, beautifully done and of high quality, and a true representation of the original is not surpassed by any previous or contemporary work.

The landscape of Switzerland also claimed the attention of German engravers. Heinrich Runge's *Die Schweiz in Original-Ansichten...* (Darmstadt, G.G. Lange, 1863–70, 3 volumes), contained 198 steel engravings (of which three were engraved title pages) mostly engraved by Ludwig

Rohbock, who also engraved seven steel plates for *Souvenir de Bâle* (Darmstadt, Lange [*c.* 1870]).

These publications show the extent of the interest in landscape engravings and the determination of publishers to exploit steel as much as possible.

German steel engraving entered a new phase with the arrival in Leipzig of Albert Henry Payne (1812–1902) from England. Among his early work were four plates for *Tombleson's Eighty Picturesque Views on the Thames ...* (1834), followed by *Tombleson's Upper Rhine* [*c.*1835], and it is tempting to surmise that Payne had worked closely with Tombleson, even being his pupil, and to have seen in the latter's links with Germany an opportunity to take his young talents both as an engraver and entrepreneur to that country. His creditable work in England would have been a good recommendation to Georg Wigand in Leipzig, and it seems possible that Payne moved there about 1836, since he contributed four plates to volume 1 of *Das malerische und Romantische Deutschland*, published in that year. By 1837 he had established his printing office Englische Kunst anstallt (English art establishment), and printed one of his engravings for volume 3 in 1837, and his remaining 56 plates for *Das malerische ...* were also printed by him. It is possible that he brought printers and equipment with him, and his collaboration with James Gray (fl. 1836–54) in some of the plates indicates a fellow engraver on his staff. By about 1845, Thomas Heawood (fl. 1845–79), who returned to England by 1870, Alexander Carse (fl. 1832–54), Andrew Duncan (b. 1795), who returned to England *circa* 1855, and D. J. Pound (fl. 1842–77), who returned to England *circa* 1857, worked on Payne's major publications, and by 1854 he had also opened an office in Dresden, since his imprints give both places. He would have found communications easy to manage since Leipzig and Dresden were the first German cities to be joined by the railway in 1835.

His first major work in Germany was *Payne's Universum; or, Pictorial World, Being a Collection of Engravings of Views in All Countries, Portraits of Great Men, and Specimens of Works of Art, of All Ages and of Every Character*. It was published in London in 1845 by Brain and Payne. Ephraim Tipton Brain was another enterprising engraver in Paternoster Row, and who about four years later went to work for John Tallis. This work commenced publication in June 1843 in monthly 1 shilling parts containing four engravings, and by July 1845 when it was reviewed in the *Art Union* (p. 241) 100 engravings had been issued. The reviewer stressed that all the plates were specifically engraved for the work, not 'made up' from prints which had seen service elsewhere. It was issued simultaneously in Germany, and editions multiplied during the decade, e.g. that produced for the Low Countries. There was the inevitable comparison with Meyer's *Universum*, but Payne's subjects were

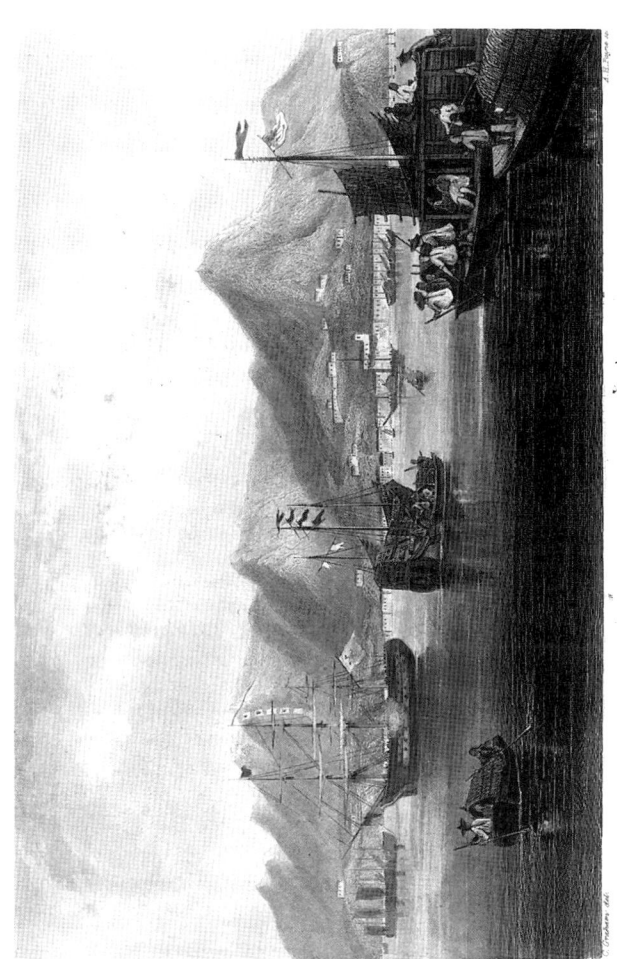

119 Hong Kong, engraved by A.H. Payne

not confined to landscapes and views. 'A Cottage in the Tyrol – a family scene', 'Catherine', a view of Terracino, and a portrait of Humboldt, together with the plate published in the *Art Union* (July 1845) 'Whalers attacked by bears' are examples. As an inducement, annual subscribers were to receive a large plate free – 'Attack of the lion' after Saleh measured 17 in. × 13 in. 'Hong Kong' (Plate 119) is an example of the topographical plates.

A second work published by Brain was *Payne's Illustrated London* containing 117 plates, all engraved by Payne and which appeared in parts between February 1846 and late summer 1847.

A new phase in German steel engraving arrived when Payne reproduced works of art housed in art galleries, and it was natural that he should start with one literally on his doorstep. *Payne's Royal Dresden Gallery; Being a Selection of Subjects Engraved after Pictures by the Great Masters . . . with Accompanying Notices by A.H. Payne and W. French* was published by the proprietors A.H. Payne, Dresden and Leipzig: W. French, London, 67 Paternoster Row, [1845–50]. The two volumes were intended to contain 136 plates with captions in English and German, and over half (72) bear Payne's name as engraver. His new co-publisher instead of Brain was William French (1815?–98) a London engraver who did 12 of the plates. Only ten plates were done by seven German engravers, i.e. Alboth, G. Brinckmann, Kiehne, T. Jahnige, Johann Leonhard Raab (1825–99), Albrecht Schultheiss (1823–1909) and Johann Sonnenleiter (1825–1907). The English text was printed by E. Polz, the Leipzig printer on rather poor paper. The plan of the work was similar to contemporary English publications of the same type and 'The Spinner' after Caspar Netscher (Plate 120), and engraved by Payne, gives some indication of its contents. It was re-issued about 1850 by A. Gorling under the title *Die Kunstverein. Neue Serie; Stahl-stichsammlung der vorzüglichten Gemalde der Dresdener Gallerie* (The Art Union. New Series. Steel-Engraved Collection of First Rate Paintings of the Dresden Gallery).

This was succeeded by *Payne's Book of Art with the Celebrated Galleries of Munich, Being a Selection of Subjects Engraved after Pictures by Old and Modern Masters with Descriptive Text Together with a History of Art*. Published as before by Payne and French, it came out in three volumes [1849–54] with 63 plates in each, a total of 189. The plates in volumes 1 and 2 were gathered together at the back of the books, but in volume 3 the plates were interspersed with the text, and it had a very different approach from the other two, in that most of the engravings were surrounded by outline frames. Only two plates were done by a German engraver and only English titles were appended to most of them, as opposed to English and German in the first two volumes. At least four artists, G. Leuchtenberg, Pinakothek, G. Scheissheim and W. Storck were employed to make copies for the

120 The Spinner, engraved by A.H. Payne

engravers, working in the galleries from the originals, and their names appeared in the centre of the attributions line. In the whole work, Payne engraved 82 plates, which was the largest share, French did 22 and other English engravers accounted for another 41. Forty-four plates were done by 16 German engravers, i.e. Johann Leonhard Appold (1809–58), Eltzner, C. Eulenstein, Jacob Fleischmann (c.1816–66), de Garlieb, H. Huber, Joseph von Keller (1811–73), Koch, Alfred Krausse (1829–94), Merkel, Adolf Neumann (1825–84), Gustav Planer (1818–73), Franz Adam Schröder (1809–75), Stein, Friedrich Wagner (1803–76) and Wolff.

His later important publications included 98 steel engravings for Die Königliche Museen, Berlin, *Eine answahl der vorzüglichten Kunstschatze der Malerei, Sculptur und Architectur der nord deutschen Metropole...* (A Selection of First Rate Art Treasures of Painting, Sculpture and Architecture of Metropolitan North Germany ...) [c.1850]. His *Orbitus pictus* came out in 1851 and his *Panorama des Wissens und der Gewerbe* (Panorama of Science and Industry) in 1859.

Circa 1860 Payne was publishing in Vienna, in particular A. Görling's *Belvedere; oder Die Galierien von Wien*... which contained 120 steel engravings. In 1864 Frederick Goulding (1849–1909), the eminent English printer, visited Leipzig for six weeks, staying with his father's friend Henry Bolton, who was manager of Payne's printing firm, which by this time, had become a large firm. Goulding also visited the Dresden premises and although he spent much time in the workshops, his views on them are not recorded.

Payne published two works on Hogarth, the first, circa 1850 by A. Görling *William Hogarth und sein Zeit* (William Hogarth and his Times) with 45 steel engravings and the second circa 1870, *Werke* in three volumes with 88 steel plates. A further departure was his *Illustrierte Familien Bibel* (Illustrated Family Bible), undated, issued from Leipzig with 41 steel engravings.

Steel engraving was much used for the annual volumes which came out all over Europe. Germany had its 'taschenbuch' or pocket-book, and from the early part of the 19th century started to liven up the factual data by introducing a tale and a sketch. The long tradition, going back to the early 18th century, took some effort to change, and since copper engraving had been used for illustrations, the need to employ steel did not occur until the economic factors were right. Even in the newer annuals, steel came in only gradually. *Gedenke mein! Taschenbuch*... (Think of me! Pocket-book) which began in 1831, carried eight copper and steel engravings in the 1836 volume. It was published in Vienna and Leipzig by Pfautsch in a 12 mo format, common to most German annuals. In the 1837 volume of *Urania*... published in Leipzig by Brockhaus, there were six steel plates; the title portrait of A. Humboldt was engraved by A. Zschokke (fl. 1837) who also did other plates with Edouard Schuler and F. Weber (fl. 1837–77). Also in 1837 *Vergissmeinicht* (Forget me not) published by Hallberger in Stuttgart carried six steel engravings after F.A.M. Fellner, and in 1842 *Rheinisches Taschenbuch* published in Frankfurt by Sauerlander had six engravings, all by the English engraver Timothy Stanfield Engleheart after six German artists. Engleheart had left England for Germany in 1840, from which the family had come a generation or two earlier.

By the 1840s German engravers were more involved in steel engraving. Examples of these were the plates done for Friedrich Brockhaus's *Bilderatlas* (Picture Atlas), published at Leipzig, and which formed the basis for several works, including one published in New York by R. Garrigue in 1851 under the title *Iconographic Encyclopaedia of Science, Literature and Art* with the artist's name as author, Johann Georg Heck. The work was divided into ten major divisions and contained 500 plates, 332 of which were engraved under Henry Winkles's name. Eight more were signed by Winkles and Lehmann. Twenty-one other engravers were all German, of whom Johann Christian Gustav Feldweg (b. 1814) of Leipzig did 25 plates and one other jointly with Ackermann. Ackermann did one plate on his own, two plates with Kimmelmann, and one plate each with Schmidt and Werner. Johann Leopold von Baehr (1796–1893) of Leipzig engraved 21 maps after Ph. Weber of Carlsruhe. R. Schmidt engraved six plates on his own and another six in collaboration with J. Madel III. Ernst Christian Schmidt (b. 1809) of Dresden engraved five plates. A. Krausse senior engraved 16 plates and one with Keller, and E. Krausse, jun., did seven plates. H. Eberhardt, a map engraver of Eisland, did two maps and a further two plates with Schlegel, who collaborated in his turn with Joseph von Keller (1811–73) for two plates. Keller did three other plates and collaborated with Adolf Neumann (1825–84) for one other. Wagenschieber of Berlin engraved seven plates, Wolf Werner seven plates, G. Werner one plate, Carl Jättnig three plates, one dated 1845, Schweissinger three plates, C. Bertrand one plate and W. Honeck [or Hohneck] seven plates. The engravings were of uniform size and were produced to a very high standard. The range of subjects afforded several styles of treatment, fully explored by the artist or under his direction. Plate 62 of the *Encyclopaedia*, although crowded, shows the plants quite clearly, even the tiny details, and is a credit to Wagenschieber's work. In plate 100 Henry Winkles shows his mastery of bird plumage and on plate 291, Schweissinger shows just how much can be crammed in using different scales of size for the arms and armour illustrated. Plate 338 shows graphic scenes of life on board a naval ship, plate 402 illustrates the engraving of architectural subjects by Ackermann and G. Feldweg and plate 437 by Wolf Werner with a centrepiece of a sacrifice to Mars, shows a variety of mythological figures.

The Kunstverein or Art Union arrived in Germany during the first or second decade of the 19th century, when Baron von Stengel held soirées for his friends at Bamberg. When he died in 1822, the meetings were continued by his friends, and on 1 December 1823, they formed themselves into a Kunstverein. The idea spread to other German cities, where it flourished for many years. By 1837 their influence on art appreciation in general was such that not only did they disseminate existing known works by their efforts, concentrating originally on works of 'the Fatherland', but were also responsible for encouraging original creative work from contemporary artists. This could, in turn, benefit young artists whose best work could be distributed to members, and a just remuneration paid in order to encourage their artistic life. In addition to this, each member would receive a print which until the mid-1830s was a copper engraving. The cost of 40,000 or more impressions from a single steel plate would be little more than the smaller number delivered by a single copper plate. The cost of paper and printing was roughly the same.

Soon after its English patent in 1858, steel facing was being explored in Germany. The electrotyper Leo Schöniger of Munich in 1860 was reported as having discovered a means of treating the surface of plates (presumably copper) by a process similar to steeling, where atoms are so knitted together as to give strength and depth to the plate. In Berlin, Becker and Witthof's Engraving Institute was using steel facing, which was already preparing the return to the use of copper plates instead of steel. In fact, engravings of the later part of the 19th century were showing signs of rather coarse work, unlike the fine lines set close together typical of steel, and which could possibly be steeled copper plates, such as that used by Edouard Buchel (1835–1903), the Dresden engraver for his plate of 'Othello' after H. Hofmann, published in the *Art Journal* in 1879.

The distribution of steel engravers over Germany is naturally greatest in the large cities, although some engravers chose to stay in smaller places, and presumably acquire their commissions by reputation, rather than by being in the right place at the right time. The following are merely examples of that distribution. Nuremberg was one of the most popular, where Reindel and Geissler founded a school of engraving in the early 19th century, and indeed it was Johann Martin Friedrich Geissler (1778–1853) and Friedrich Fleischmann (d. 1834) who introduced steel engraving to the city *circa* 1832. Geissler went on to train engravers for Joseph Meyer. Johann Leonhard Appold (1809–58), Jacob Fleischmann (*c.*1816–66), son of Friedrich, Friedrich Fraenkel (1832–91), Franz Hablitschek (1824–67), sculptor and engraver, pupil of Poppel at Munich, Alexander Marx (b. 1815), pupil of J.M.F. Geissler, Carl Mayer (1798–1868) who founded a design school at Nuremberg, and operated a Kunst Anstalt at Nuremberg [1867], Heinrich

Ludwig Petersen (1806–74), a Dane from Altona, Ludwig Rohbock (fl. 1848–52), Johann Georg Christian Rosée (b. 1804), pupil of Geissler and Reindel and Johann Georg Serz (1808–c.1878) who worked here until the mid-1840s when he went to Philadelphia, where he died.

Munich was as large a centre, attracting engravers also from Switzerland to study at the engraving school of the Munich Academy, headed early in the 19th century by Karl Hess. Conrad Geyer (1816–93) had six plates published in the *Art Journal* in 1870–73; Georg Goldberg (1830–94), pupil of J.L. Raab in 1856, also engraved for English publications; Louis Hoffmeister (fl. 1832–54), pupil of Frommel, engraved views of Munich and Vienna between 1845 and 1854; Joseph Maximilian Kolb (fl. 1842) specialized in town views and monuments; George Michael Kurz (1815–83) collaborated with Poppel and did views of the Rhine, Alps and the principality of Hesse; Peter Lutz (1797–1867), pupil of Langer, took up engraving in 1821, doing mainly religious subjects and portraits; Johann Gabriel Friedrich Poppel (1807–82) worked with Frommel and later at Munich on views of that city; Johann Leonhard Raab (1825–99) probably worked in Munich; Johann Richter (b. 1823); Albrecht Schultheiss (1823–1909) arrived here in 1850 from Nuremberg and Leipzig; Christian Steiniken (d. 1896); Friedrich Wagner (1803–76) after spells in Paris and Stuttgart; and Frederick Würthle (b. 1820) a landscape engraver.

At Darmstadt, Georg Jacob Felsing (1802–83) was court engraver after 1832, having returned from work in Italy to teach at the Academy at Darmstadt. His elder brother Johann Heinrich Felsing (1800–75) was also an engraver and printer. Ernst Friedrich Grunewald (1801–48), pupil of Frommel was a prolific steel engraver before his untimely death at the age of 47. The Rauch brothers Ernst (b. 1797), court engraver, and Karl (b. 1804) collaborated on their steel engraved views of German cities and their cathedrals, C. Rohrich (fl. 1850–57), Julius Umbach (1815–77), and for a time, Edward Willmann (1820–77) worked here after training with Frommel, teaching at the Frankfurt art school and spells in London and Paris.

At Dresden there were Edward Buchel (1835–1903), Karl Hermann Theodor Langer (1819–85), Ernst Fürchtegott Mohn (1835–1912) who worked for a time in England and taught at the Dresden Academy 1884, Gustav Planer (1818–73) who, after a spell in Italy, returned to Dresden where he became an honorary member of the Academy in 1868, Carl Peschek (1803–47), known for his town views and panoramas, and Ernst Christian Schmidt (b. 1809).

At Leipzig Johann Leopold von Baehr (1796–1893) was a map engraver, Johann Christian Gustav Feldweg (b. 1814) preferred architectural engraving, Adolf Neumann (1825–84) worked with Henry Winkles, who moved to Leipzig from Carlsruhe about 1840, Johann Friedrich Rossmässler

(1775–1858) also worked in Berlin and published a series of portraits. Lazarus Gottlieb Sichling (1812–63), portrait engraver, left Nuremberg about 1840 to work in Leipzig.

In Berlin, Hermann Dröhmer (1820–90) was also a mezzotinter, Hans J.D.G. Fincke (1800–49) went to London to study under the Findens, and returned to found a steel engraving school in Berlin. He also engraved after William Tombleson. Carl Jättnig (fl. 1840–50), Wagenschieber (fl. 1851) and Wilhelm Witthöft (1816–74) also worked here.

Carlsruhe was the home of German steel engraving with the work of Carl Ludwig Frommel (1789–1863), with whom a number of important German steel engravers were either pupils or assistants, such as Abresch, Grunewald, Hoffmeister, Poppel and Willmann, with Henry Winkles, who had Krausse as his pupil.

Dusseldorf produced two important engravers. Joseph von Keller (1811–73) taught engraving at the Dusseldorf Academy from 1839 and later became a member of the Academies of Berlin, Brussels, St Petersburg and Vienna. Xaver Steifensand (1809–76) worked with Felsing at Darmstadt and did numerous plates for editions of Goethe and Schiller. *Goethe's sammtliche Werke* ... published in six volumes at Stuttgart by J.G. Cotta in 1877 contained three plates in volume 2 by Steifensand, the frontispiece of which is Plate 121.

At Rudolstadt Johann Georg Martini (b. c.1785) was a prolific engraver for Meyer, and in 1842 published in Vienna a collection of the most interesting towns and castles of Thuringia.

Publishers of steel-engraved books, apart from Payne and Meyer, ranged from those who exploited the method from the first, like Georg Wigand at Leipzig and Gustav Georg Lange at Darmstadt, to those who used it occasionally to illustrate works of literature, such as Brockhaus at Leipzig and J.G. Cotta at Stuttgart. Leipzig, the publishing centre of Germany, saw Georg Wigand issuing such works as *Das malerische und Romantische Deutschland* ... (1833–40) with additions by Theodor Fischer in 1841–42, totalling 324 engravings and Edouard Duller's *Deutschland und des deutsche Volk* (Germany and its People) (1845) with about 20 steel engravings, most by English engravers. The firm of Friedrich A. Brockhaus, which had transferred its business from Amsterdam in 1817, used steel throughout the period for its annual *Urania* ... from the 1830s, *Bilderatlas* from the 1840s, *Charaktere aus Goethe's Werken* ... eighth edition (1877), and a similar volume *Charaktere aus Schiller's Werken* ... (1869), both the latter with 50 steel engravings and text by F. Pecht. Ch. E. Kollman published *Carl Frommel's pittoreskes Italien* in 1840, with engravings from the atelier of Frommel and Winkles.

At Stuttgart, J.G. Cotta produced Schiller's *Sammtliche Werke* in 1840 with

GOETZ VON BERLICHINGEN.
5 Act. 20 Sc.

121 Goetz von Berlichingen, engraved by X. Steifensand

12 plates after Kaulbach, *Reineke Fuchs* ... in 1846 by Kaulbach with 35 steel engravings, and an edition of Goethe's ... *Werke* with about 30 engravings which was still being issued in 1877.

At Frankfurt, the firms of Neuland, Sauerlander, Ullman and Wenner published some steel engraved works, and W. Creuzbaner at Carlsruhe was best known as William Tombleson's German agent.

As in England, steel engraving was eclipsed at the end of the 19th century by the advantages of photography, but 20th-century resurgence of interest in steel engravings is shown by the publication in album form of some of the outstanding specimens. The Austrian publisher Akademische Drucke und Verlagsanstelt at Graz has issued *Die Donau-Reise und ihre Schönsten Ansichten mit mehr als 100 Stahlstichen der verühmtesten Künstler. Text von Ludwig Bechstein [1801–60] mit einer Einfuhring von Robert Wagner*. Some, if not all of the plates were reprinted from Meyer's *Universum*.

A second work from the same publisher was *Südbahn-Album; malerische ansichten in der Nähe der k.k. Südbahn von Wien bis Trieste (um 1856). Nach der Natur aufgenommen von Chapuy und Fiedler und von beuährten Künstlern in Stahl gestochen*... (1991). It was volume 8 of their series Topographie Austriaca in a limited edition of 1,080 copies. The original prints were engraved and printed at the Kunstanstalt Oestr. Lloyd in Triest.

8

French steel engraving

The earliest record of steel engraving in France occurs in a document with a handwritten date of 1650 entitled *Les arts liberaux et mechaniques*. In this, the engraver Valdor [or Waldor], probably Jean the younger (1616–70), is credited with a method of softening steel, but there was no indication of how far his experiments went, or if any of his prints engraved on steel still exist. Valdor, although born in Liège, worked in Paris and in 1646 was made 'Calcographe ordinaire du roi'.

In the 18th century Jean Baptiste de Grateloup (1735–1817) was responsible for nine prints reputedly on steel. He was one of a trio of French miniature portrait painters, each of whom was renowned for the fineness and delicacy of their work. He was a gifted amateur, born of aristocratic parents, and the head of a large establishment where he designed ornaments and jewellery for the wealthy, and which could have included the fashionable cut steel ware. He engraved as a hobby and produced nine plates between 1765 and 1771, when a cataract in one eye cut short this activity at the age of 35. The plates were portraits of French nationals and John Dryden, 1765, probably the second in the series, and were thought to have been on steel, but the plates are lost or destroyed, and the secret died with Grateloup's nephew who assisted in their printing. The series took six months to engrave, which at the speed of ordinary labour, averaged three weeks or 144 hours each.

At the same time, Charles Nicolas Cochin (1715–90) was complaining that the wear of plates during printing spoiled both the light and dark parts after a comparatively small number of impressions, so it is credible that engravers would have welcomed a harder surface to withstand the wear.

The use of steel plates for banknote printing during the French Revolution has been noted in Chapter 2, and the 19th century dawned with what appears to have been the occasional use of steel plates before the introduction of engravings in imitation of the English style in the 1830s. This early stage has been outlined in the work of Pierre Gusman, whose article on French steel engraving in *Byblis* is the standard account. Gusman (b. 1862), painter, engraver and author was born in Paris, and became a pupil of his father Adolphe. He engraved after the Old Masters from 1887 to 1897, and contributed to a number of periodicals, including *L'Estampe et l'affiche*, thus becoming a writer of some authority, backed by practical involvement.

The softness of copper was observed by Jean Philippe Guy Le Gentil, comte de Paroy (1750–1824), who devoted himself to engraving and authorship on art, despite his father's opposition. His engraving was in the wash manner and in crayon, which he exhibited, together with etchings at the Salon in 1787. In 1785 he became an honorary free associate of the Royal Academy of Painting, of which he wrote a history and which, in 1795, became the Institut de France. Thus he was among the earliest engravers to belong to the Institut, which enabled artists and engravers to have a national voice in the development of art in France, in contrast to the engravers' lack of recognition in the English Royal Academy. In 1806 Paroy experimented with steel to the extent of engraving some decorative motifs so that the plate surface should be more resistant to printing wear, but there is no record of his subsequent use of the metal. Doubtless the hardness of steel, the inadequacy of burins and the difficulty of engraving were, as elsewhere, discouraging factors.

The Societé d'encouragement pour l'industrie nationale was presented in 1811 with some cast steel plates, engraved by burin, by a M. Molard. It is not clear whether he was the engraver (none of this name is known at present) or merely an intermediary, but the result was no more encouraging since the use of the burin was as difficult as ever. On the other hand, the plates could be etched more rapidly than copper.

Probably the earliest French book to contain steel engravings was A.R. Le Sage's *Histoire de Gil Blas* (Paris, Lefèvre, 1820, 3 vols bound in 8 parts), to be followed by *Voyages en France et autre pays, en prose et en vers* ... (fourth edition, Paris, Lelong, 1824, 3 vols), containing 36 plates, reputedly on steel. The comte de Segur's *Histoire de Napoléon* ... (fifth edition, Paris, Baudouin, 1825, 2 vols) contains five engraved views thought to be on steel.

The first real evidence of steel plates being used is afforded by the 49 or 50 engravings of Comte Th. Turpin de Crissé's *Souvenirs du Golfe de Naples* (1826), the steel plates of which are preserved in the Chalcographie du Louvre, nos 323–72. The catalogue of the collection amended to 1960 lists over 14,000 plates in its possession, very few of which are on steel. Approximately 17 engravers were employed, including Pierre Eugene Aubert (1789–1847), François Forster (1790–1872), Nicolas Auguste Leisnier

(1787–1857), Charles Nicolas Ransonnette (1793–1877) and Freidrich Schroeder (1768–1839). 'Vue de la Baie de Naples' was largely etched, with some fine engraving on the horizon and the buildings at left (Plate 122).

Engravings of works of art, especially those in the national collections were undertaken with considerable success from the early days of the 19th century. One of these was undertaken by the engraver and publisher Antoine Michel Filhol (1759–1812) who, from 1804, issued 120 livraisons, forming ten volumes of *Galérie du Musée Napoléon publiée par Filhol graveur* ... and was edited by J. Lavallée, marquis de Bois-Robert and others. His widow carried on publication until 1822 and in 1827, in collaboration with de Jal, produced a final volume *Galérie du Musée de France ou collection gravée des chefs d'oeuvre de peinture, sculpture ... publiée par Mme V[euv]e Filhol.* Although the majority of plates were engraved on copper, it is believed that some, probably after 1820, were done on steel. Marie Alexandre Duparc (fl. 1803–26) was an engraver for the original work, and Jean de Saulx (fl. 1826–42) for the last volume, both of whom in 1826 engraved on steel for Tristan de Crissé's work. A contemporary series *Le Musée français*, a collection of engravings after pictures, sculptures, etc. in the Collection Nationale, began in 1803, and included major contributions by Pierre Louis Henri Laurent (1779–1844), who went on to publish a continuation from 1816 to 1818 entitled *Le Musée Royal*. Again Gusman thought that some plates were engraved on steel, although it seems less likely than with Filhol's work.

The second half of the 1820s saw the majority of the steel engraved work by the Johannot brothers. Both Alfred (1800–37) and Tony (1803–52) went over to wood engraving and designing *circa* 1830, so little, if any, steel engraving was done by them after that date. Many of Tony's later designs were engraved on steel, especially in the Romantic books which followed. Alfred is believed to have engraved for Desenne's designs for the *Oeuvres de Voltaire* [before 1826], and about the same date the brothers did 88 full-page steel engravings for the 84-volume edition of the *Oeuvres de Walter Scott* published in Paris by Gosselin [etc.] and for Pierre Jean de Béranger's *Chansons* ... (Paris, Perrotin, 1829) they did several steel plates. They illustrated the 27 volumes of the *Oeuvres de Fenimore Cooper* published by Mame at Tours in 1827 and some of the plates were engraved by Auguste Jean Baptiste Marie Blanchard (1792–1849).

The 1820s showed a sporadic use of steel for the production of more good copies from an engraved plate, but there is very little evidence that the artistic possibilities in terms of tonal range was being exploited. There is no doubt that the English influence was beginning to show in that steel-engraved works imported from Britain gained a great deal of support, aided by the fact that Paris was the cultural centre of France as London was in England. In the early 1830s French and German translations of topographical

122   Vue de la Baie de Naples, etched and slightly engraved

illustrations were exported by publishers such as George Virtue, who in 1836 was writing that 'in the foreign editions, the work [Beattie's *Switzerland*] has met with the same flattering reception as at home' (Preface). In the Preface to *Scotland*, dated 1837, Beattie observes that

In acknowledging the merits and services of his foreign coadjutors, the Author is bound to offer his testimony in favour of the German and French translations by John Von Horn, D.D. and Monsieur De Bauclas, who have transferred this, and his other works, into their respective languages with taste, spirit and fidelity.

In due course, Virtue had an office in the rue Vivienne, and his rival Henry Fisher operated from Quai l'École and rue St Honoré. The state of engraving in France did not appear to have improved since the heights it achieved in the 18th century, and 'there is a certain art of engraving that is polished cutting and regular work; but we do not consider the art there [in France] has advanced, nor do they think so themselves, so they try to imitate

the English artists' (John Burnet's evidence before the *Select Committee on Arts and Principles of Design*, 1836, para. 943). In the same report, John Pye referred to engravers who were full members of the Institut de France, naming [Pierre Alexandre] Tardieu (1756–1844), Baron Desnoyers and, in 1836, J.T. Richomme (1785–1849) and described the other rewards they could expect as becoming a Baron or being decorated with the Légion d'honneur. English engravers were sought after in France, and William Ewart, quoted in the same report (para. 1329): 'I have been recently applied to to recommend some engravers to go to Paris for the express purpose of engraving a work that has in great measure a national character'. This work was probably Gavard's *Galéries historiques de Versailles* in 1836 (q.v.).

Discussions took place before 1824 about the possibility of sending young engravers to study in England between John Pye and the Duc du Cazes, Louis XVIII's first minister, but a change of ministry aborted the idea. The commitment to the use of steel was not as great or universal to

French engravers during the period of their greatest activity in the 30 years between 1830 and 1860. The reliance on English-produced plates for French publications, the conjunction of steel with wood engraving in many of the books of the Romantic period, and the fact that 25 per cent of French engravers identified as working on steel also worked primarily as painters, indicates a less than total devotion to steel exhibited by nearly all the English engravers from 1820 to 1890. The three main English engravers, Hopwood, Outhwaite and Skelton working permanently in Paris also contributed to more publications than their French counterparts. The contribution of lithography and etching during the period of steel engraving to book illustration was minimal. Lithography had its heyday during the Restoration and reign of Louis XVIII (1814–24), declining after 1852 where the French saw its usefulness in multiplying rather than reproducing original drawings, and etching, although it had a small revival with the publication of Tony Johannot's etchings in *L'Artiste* (1831), was only used sporadically until about 1869 when it became a painter-etcher method.

Engravers in France had a great deal more encouragement in their art than their confrères in Britain. Their education was more formal, because in addition to the apprenticeship system, there were across France about 30 art schools founded from 1738, while in Paris there was the teaching role of the Académie Royale de peinture [etc.] (founded 1648). This became the École des Beaux arts in 1795 at the same time as the Institut de France was established, formed from four former academies to embrace all the academic subjects contained therein. The École [Nationale Supierère] des Beaux arts attracted first rate engravers such as Louis Pierre Henriquel-Dupont (1797–1892) as teachers and about 20 per cent of engravers covered by this study attended it, e.g. J. Bein from 1812, Colin (1808–73) from 1825, François Forster from 1805 and Jean Jacques Frilley (b. 1797) from 1815. Napoléon Bonaparte also created more art schools at the end of the 18th and early 19th centuries, so that no town of any size was without such provision.

Moreover, the Institut de France accepted engravers as full and equal members, but the recognition of good work by the State in the award of its highest accolade, the Légion d'honneur is the greatest differentiation between the French and British situation. The award was established in 1802 by Napoléon Bonaparte, and of the 17 engravers who worked on steel, four reached the grade of Officier, of which there were only 4,000 at any one time; the remainder were Chevaliers, the lowest grade. The first engraver to be honoured with a Cross was Charles Clement Bervay Bervic (1755–1822) in 1819. He had already been given a number of honours, was a member of most European academies, and had been allocated an apartment in the Louvre by Louis XVI, which gives some indication of his standing as a line engraver. Pierre Alexandre Tardieu, portrait engraver, gained his award in 1822, and at the same time replaced Bervic in the Institut. In 1822 Pierre Louis Henri Laurent was given the honour of Chevalier. Joseph Theodore Richomme became Chevalier in 1824 and a member of the Institut in 1826. All these men were of the older school who worked on copper in their early days and trained the next generation who were to use more steel for their line engravings. L.P. Henriquel-Dupont was one of Bervic's pupils and at the age of 34 in 1831 was the youngest engraver in this group to receive the Cross and one of the few to become an Officier in 1855. Other Officiers were Léopold Flameng (1831–1911) in 1894, François Forster in 1863 and Alphonse François (1814–88). Eleven other engravers were similarly awarded the Chevalier grade, and most of them for their work as engravers.

Thus up to 1830 French line engraving struggled on its own and produced few works on steel. After 1830, however, English steel engraving was making its influence felt. The publisher Henry Fisher was issuing French versions of his publications, such as *Itinéraire pittoresque au nord d'Angleterre ... de comtés de Westmorland, Cumberland* [etc.] with French text by F. Gérard in 1834, a version of Thomas Rose's volumes of several years earlier, Emma Roberts's *Vues pittoresques de l'Inde, de la Chine et des bords de la mer rouge*, in 1835, a version of Elliot's *Views in India* .... French publishers replied with such publications as Dumont D'Urville's *Voyages autour du monde*, published by Furne in two volumes (1833) with 43 engravings by Charles Beyer, Alphonse Boilly, Charles de Lalaisse, Alphonse Charles Masson (1814–98), Rouarge, and Ambroise Tardieu (1788–1841). A new edition was issued in 1853. *Italie pittoresque...* was by a group of authors headed by Dr Norvins illustrated with original drawings by Deveira and others, published by A. Costes in two volumes (1834–37) with 137 steel engravings. A second edition was started in 1845 by Ledoux.

A much larger undertaking was *France pittoresque ...* by A. Hugo, published by Delloye in 1835 in three volumes containing over 600 engravings on about 360 steel plates showing towns, landscapes, monuments, costumes, etc. There were also close on 100 maps. At the same time, Firmin Didot was issuing the 100 parts of *Guide pittoresque du voyageur en France* between 1835 and 1838, which bound up into six volumes. James Hopwood engraved 70 portraits and there were 600 views on steel by a group of engravers including Eugène Nyon (fl. 1834–48) and Étienne Goujon de Villiers (b. 1784). The text was by a society of men of letters, geographers and artists. The same authors also produced a *Guide pittoresque du voyageur en Écosse* in 1838 with 110 views after Pernot engraved by Friedrich Schroeder which must have been among his last work. Delloye published A. Forrestier's *Alpes pittoresques ...* in two volumes (1836–38), illustrated with

72 steel engraved views and a number of lithographs. Alcide d'Orbigny illustrated his *Voyage pittoresque dans les deux Ameriques* with 67 steel engravings after the designs of Boilly and Sainson. It was published by L. Tenné and H. Dupuy in 1836.

The most ambitious project of all was the series *L'Univers pittoresque* published by Firmin Didot in 68 volumes between 1834 and 1863, which contained nearly 3,900 engravings, the quality of some of which was rather poor. The first ten volumes carried some signed plates engraved by men like Alès, Cholet and Rouarge, but for volumes 11 to 60, such plates as were signed carried the legend 'Lemaitre direxit'. Volume 61 onward again had a few plates signed. *Océanie; du cinquième partie ou monde* by G.L. Domeny de Rienzi had 306 steel engravings and five maps in its three volumes (1836–55), *Brésil* by F. Denis 1837 contained 106 plates, *Allemagne* by M. Le Bas had 200, and *Egypte ancienne* by Champollion-Figeac (1839) had 92 plates. There was a German edition of parts of the series *Welt-Gemalde-Gallerie* (Stuttgart, Schweizerbart, 12 vols, 1836–40) and a Spanish edition *Panorama Universal* (Barcelona, Imprenta del Nacional, 14 vols, 1838–46).

In the 1850s there was a revival of interest in travel books exemplified by G. Touchard-Lafosse's *La Loire historique*... published by Lecesne at Tours in 1851, with 62 steel engravings of which 47 are views of towns. M. Saint Julien's *Voyage pittoresque en Russie*... was published by Behen-Leprieur in 1854 with 21 steel engravings by Outhwaite, Rouarge and Kernot, and Edmond Texier's *Voyage pittoresque sur les bords du Rhin* was published by Morizot in 1858. The 24 steel engravings were done by the Rouarge brothers, as were the 18 for Paul de Musset's *Voyage pittoresque en Italie et en Sicilie*... (Morizot, 1856, new edition 1865). In 1860 Morizot issued four plates, not included in Texier, under the name of Xavier Marmier *Voyage pittoresque en Allemagne*...; three were engraved by Chardon and one by Outhwaite. Marmier's *Voyage en Suisse* (Morizot, 1862) had 26 of Rouarge's engravings. The *Atlas Nationale illustrée des 86 départements et des possessions de la France* by V. Levasseur as published by Combette in 1852 with about 100 steel-engraved maps, some coloured and with an engraved title page.

Despite this, however, the English influence was to be dominant, best seen in the annuals and keepsakes. There is a distinction to be made here between publications issued yearly and single volumes, perhaps devoted to a particular subject. Of all the annuals published in France only a very few carried steel engravings which did not come from England, either in the form of printed impressions or actual plates which were printed locally. The editor of *Winter's Wreath* (1831) writes 'France... in imitating our annuals, has been compelled to provide impressions from plates which had been used the year before in England, being unable herself to produce anything approaching to those highly-finished line engravings' (quoted on p. 18 of

W.J. Stannard's *The art exemplar* ... *c*.1853). None ran for very long and the chief publisher was Louis Janet who was credited with about 30 titles during the period.

The first French annual to compare with the English ones was *Annales romantiques*, which began publication in 1825 under Urban Canel, transferring to Janet in 1829 until 1836. The engraved illustrations were a very minor feature, but one or two engravers were employed such as Jean Claude Auguste Fauchery (1798–1843) and Jean Marie Leroux (1788–1870). English annuals such as *Forget-me-not, Friendship's Offering, Literary Souvenir* and *The Keepsake* seemed to be as well known in France, and it is not surprising that French editions of English publications were being planned. In October 1828, Alaric Watts announced the *Souvenir litteraire de France* 'in a few weeks', but this seems never to have materialized. Louis Janet issued his *Almanach de la cour, de la ville et des départemens pour l'année 1829* which contained four steel engravings of the castles of Neuilly, Avaray, Lincienne [*sic*] and Rosny. More successful was the run from 1830 to 1844 of the *Keepsake français*, issued by a succession of publishers, among whom was the Parisian firm of Giraldon-Bovinet in conjunction with Whittaker, Treacher and Co. of London for the 1831 volume and A. Asher in London for the 1840 volume. During this time the number of engravings had risen from 18 to 24, and even if a majority of pictures had been produced by French artists in the early volumes, almost without exception, the engravers were English. The captions were in French, there was a dual publication line, the text was printed in France and the literary content was French. The similarity with its English counterpart extended to the outside covering which on *The Keepsake* was red watered silk, whereas in France it was green watered silk. The frontispiece and engraved title page of the 1831 volume are illustrated (Plate 123). In the 1840 volume, three of the steel engravings were printed by Perkins, Bacon and Petch in London.

The Parisian publisher H. Delloye produced six volumes of a similar nature from 1837 to 1842 under the title *Paris–Londres. Keepsake français*. The first volume contained 36 steel engravings, which set the pattern for the remainder, and the subjects ranged from female beauty and historical to land and sea scapes, all done by English engravers. The illustrations were described as new and original, but all artists, apart from Achillé Deveria and Eugène Lami were English. *Paris illustrations* (1838–39) was one of the few all-French publications and was an album of engravings by the best French artists. Paul Lacroix (1806–84), better known as Jacob the bibliophile, from 1855 Keeper of the Arsenal library, edited a number of keepsakes. *Le Royal keepsake* and *Le Saphir*, both published by Janet, each containing 12 English steel engravings, and *Les Topazes* published by Jules Renouard are examples of his work. Other Janet titles included *L'Anemone* with seven English

123 Frontispiece and engraved title page from *Le Keepsake français*, 1831

LE KEEPSAKE FRANÇAIS,
POUR
1831.

Peint par Colin. Gravé par Sangster.

Paris:
GIRALDON BOVINET ET Cie
GALERIE VIVIENNE.

Londres:
WHITTAKER TREACHER & ARNOT.
AVE-MARIA-LANE.

vignettes, *Le Diadème* with 15 engravings by Finden, *L'Eglantine* with 15 English engravings from *The Keepsake* 1835, *L'Étincelle* with 13 English engravings and *La Fauvette*, which although undated, carried ten plates published originally by Ackermann in 1842. A specialized volume *Le Keepsake Shakespearien, Vingt-et-un charmantes têtes de femmes. Faisant suite aux heroines de Shakespeare, gravées par Ch. Heath* ... was published by Mandeville, and a similar one for children by L. Galibert and C. Pelle *Le livre de mon fils* ... was published jointly in Paris by Fisher and Debure circa 1840 with an engraved title and five steel engraved plates. *Le livre de beauté. Keepsake des dames* by Léo Lespes 1854 contained 13 steel engravings (of which three are after Gavarni), illustrating physical beauty, beauty of the spirit, beauty of the heart, etc.

Jean Mathias Fontaine (1791–1853) is credited with being the first to use steel plates in imitation of the English in France. He is one of the nine engravers used for the 45 steel engravings in the *Musée de la Révolution. Historique, chronique ... ornée de gravures sur acier* ... published by Perrotin, in 1834. The major engraver was Jean Jacques Frilley (b. 1797) together with Charles Beyer (b. 1792), W.J.J. Des-Hauvents (fl. 1834), Auguste Dutillois (fl. 1831–48), Auguste François Garnier (fl. 1836–48), Louis Conil Lacoste (b. 1774), Pigeot Ainé (fl. 1822–44), and Onwhyn, probably Thomas (c.1820–86), who was English, some of whose earliest work is represented here. The engravings, although accompanied by a chronological text of events, were designed to go with existing histories of the time. Forty-three of the designs were done by Auguste Raffet. Fontaine was also engaged on illustrations for the very popular *Histoire physique, civile et morale de Paris* by J.A. Dulaure, the fifth edition, published by Guillaume in 1834, had 84 plates, the sixth edition, published by Furne in 1837, had 58 steel plates and the seventh edition, published by J. Belin in 1839, had 57 plates. A similar volume on the environs of Paris was issued by Furne in 1838 carrying 30 steel engravings.

The arrival of three English engravers who took up residence in France and produced a great deal of work there was perhaps occasioned by the recommendations of William Ewart, referred to earlier in connection with the Report of 1836. James Hopwood (b. 1795) portrait engraver commenced a series of French portraits about 1828 which were published in France, but he still seems to have been working in England for the Findens in 1833. Between 1835 and 1838 he had done 70 portraits for the *Guide pittoresque au voyageur en France* published by Didot, so he appears to have arrived circa 1834. His portraits came out in volumes of literature and history until the late 1860s. His pupil was Ferdinand Gaillard (1834–87). John Outhwaite (fl. 1831–79), landscape and genre engraver also arrived in Paris about 1835 after an apprenticeship with Edward Goodall. His earliest work in

France was for the publisher Gavard (q.v.). His plates appeared in numerous volumes of topography, history and literature until the late 1860s and it was said that he was 'much esteemed' in Paris (*Art Union*, June 1846, p. 161). He was naturalized in 1855 and took Alphonse Lamotte (1844–1914) as a pupil in 1860. The third arrival *circa* 1835 was Joseph Skelton (*c.*1785–*c.*1850) landscape, architectural and portrait engraver. He worked for Gavard (q.v.), for the *Guide pittoresque … en France*, and shared 20 engravings with Outhwaite for Jules Janin's *La Normandie* [1843], published by Bourdin.

By 1834 French publishers were able to organize works illustrated with steel engravings, some of which were very ambitious. The second edition of E. Scribe's *Théatre complet*, published by A. André (20 vols, 1834–37) contained 148 steel engravings by Auguste Jean Baptiste Marie Blanchard, who also did 78 plates for a new edition of Th. Leclercq's *Proverbes dramatiques* (Ladrange, 8 vols, 1835–36). Victor Hugo's *Notre Dame de Paris* was published in 1836 by Eugène Renduel containing 12 steel engravings in the style typical of the period. As one of the earliest important books of the Romantic movement, the artists were French, e.g. Johannot, Raffet and Boulanger, but the engravers were English, e.g. the Finden brothers and Robert Staines. Lacour (probably Pierre (1788–1859)) was one of the exceptions, and it is significant that when Houssiaux published another edition in 1860 these were the illustrations he used, being considered by some to be nearer the spirit of the text than later ones. Perrotin, Garnier, issued another edition in 1844 which aimed to be the first 'really illustrated edition' containing 55 plates, 21 of which were steel 'engraved by the most distinguished [French] artists', who were Charles Beyer, Augustin Burdet, Louis Dujardin, Jean J. Frilley, Auguste-François Garnier, Charles-Michel Geoffroy, Jean-Denis Nargeot, John Outhwaite and Alfred Revel. The illustrations are very much in the Romantic tradition set by the frontispiece, which in its architecture and costume is truly medieval. William Finden was engaged to do 14 landscape steel engravings for Dubochet's edition of *Les Évangiles de … Jésus Christ* (1837), and he did ten steel plates after Tony Johannot's designs for Oliver Goldsmith's *Le vicaire de Wakefield* translated by Charles Nodier and published by Bourqueleret in 1838.

The largest undertaking of the 1830s was that by Jacques Dominique Charles Gavard, when he issued *Galeries historiques de Versailles* (Plate 124). Gavard, given his military background, was probably appointed by the king, and is described as the inventor of the 'Diagraphe'. From the inscriptions on the plates he was responsible for preparing outlines for the engravers, using a diagraphe and pantograph to reduce the large items, such as murals and ceilings being copied to a manageable size for engraving. It was a collection of steel-engraved plates taken from the works of art comprising the

GALERIES HISTORIQUES

DE

VERSAILLES

PUBLIÉES PAR L'ORDRE DU ROI,

ET DÉDIÉES

A S. M. LA REINE DES FRANÇAIS

PAR CH. GAVARD,

CAPITAINE AU CORPS ROYAL D'ÉTAT-MAJOR, INVENTEUR DU DIAGRAPHE.

Galerie Napoléon.

AILE DU MIDI, REZ-DE-CHAUSSÉE.

PEINTURE.

PARIS.

CHEZ L'ÉDITEUR RUE DU MARCHÉ-SAINT-HONORÉ, N° 4,

ET AU PALAIS DE VERSAILLES.

1837

124   Title page of Gavard's *Galeries historiques de Versailles*

125 Louis Philippe d'Orléans, etching

Musée de l'histoire nationale which was inaugurated by King Louis-Philippe at Versailles on 19 June 1837. The plates were accompanied by a descriptive text and a historical notice on Versailles.

The first two volumes were published in 1837–38 containing 111 plates, and must have been successful, because the series continued in 1838 until 1849 in a total of 19 tomes comprising 13 main tomes with six tomes of a supplement. Many of the plates in the first two volumes are entirely etched and are unsigned by the engravers (Plate 125). In the later work, most engravings are signed normally. He employed at least 29 engravers, three of whom were English, two German, one Swiss and one Italian. This was probably the enterprise for which Ewart had been asked to suggest English engravers, resulting in the arrival of John Outhwaite, Joseph Skelton and S.H. (probably John Harfield) Kernot (fl. 1828–58), of whom the two former stayed permanently. One German was Lazarus Gottlieb Sichling (1812–63) who worked on the project for two years from 1837 to 1839, when he returned to Nuremberg, and the other was Friedrich Schroeder (1768–1839) who died while the project was in progress. The Swiss was Vittore Pedretti (1799–1868) who worked most of his life in Paris, and was already well known for engraving some human anatomy plates, 1823–26. The Italian, Jacopo Bernardi did the portraits instead of James Hopwood who might have been considered. The actual steel plates are still preserved in the Chalcographie du Louvre, and in their *Catalogue* Annex II (1930) the numbers 9474–11951 are assigned to them, which gives a total of 2,477 plates.

Gusman in his *Byblis* article reproduced Gilbert's 'Prise du Fort de Santé Petri' engraved by Joseph Skelton and described by the author as 'one of the most skilful in the genre'. Another example of his work is 'Château des Tuileries' (Supplement vol. 1 plate [12]) (Plate 126). Most of the French engravers were well established, although a few were very young, such as Auguste Thomas Marie Blanchard (1819–98), Paul Girardet (1821–93), Jean Ernest Aubert (fils) (1824–1906), who worked with his father (Pierre Eugène (père) (1789–1847)) on some plates, and Aristide-Theophile Cholet (1823–65). Others were Auguste François Alès (1797–1878), François Adolphe Bruneau Audibran (1810–?1865), Jean Bein (1789–1857), Prosper Aimé Marie Brunillière (b. 1803) G. Chavanne (fl. 1837–40) (Plate 127) where two plates are printed on an A2 sheet of paper, Charles Amédée Colin (1808–73), Ferdinand Delanoy (fl. 1836–63), Anatole Nicolas Fournier (1789–1854), Jean Jacques Frilley (b. 1797) Gasies (fl. 1840), Jacques Joseph Huguenet (b. 1815) born at Versailles (Plate 128), A. Lefèvre (fl. 1837–40), Philibert Langlois (fl. 1834–43), Denis Armand Millin (1803–after 1866), Jean Denis Nargeot (1793–after 1865), Jacques Étienne Pannier (1802–69), Hippolyte Prudhomme (1793–1853)

126 Chateaux des Tuileries, engraved by J. Skelton

127 Versailles vers 1688..., engraved by G. Chavanne

FRENCH STEEL ENGRAVING

Peint par Cotel.

Versailles vers 1688. (Jardins)
Le Labyrinthe (Le Duc et les Oiseaux).

128 Plafond du Salon de la Roi, engraved by J. Huguenet

and Pierre Joseph Tavernier (b. 1787). Six plates were done by the American engraver Joseph Andrews (1805–73) who visited Paris 1840–42 with his pupil Stephen Alonzo Schoff (1818–1905).

In 1838 Delloye and Lecou projected an illustrated edition of Honoré de Balzac's works, but the only volume issued was *Le Peau de chagrin*, illustrated by 100 vignettes on steel printed with the text. Many of them are unsigned, but the main engravers were Brunillière, Langlois and Nargeot. Originally published in 1831 by Porret with wood-engraved illustrations it is an example of a number of editions of literary works published throughout the 1830s. François de Chateaubriand's *Oeuvres* (1831) had steel engravings by Auguste Blanchard, Koenig, Louis Marckl (b. 1807) and Charles Louis Victor Mauduit (1788–after 1865), whose vignette illustrations to Chateaubriand's *Poésies* is shown in Plate 129. Another contributor was Amédée Maulet (1810–35), only 21 at this date and who died at the tragically early age of 25. Pierre Pelée (1801–71) and Pierre Joseph Tavernier complete the list. After Chateaubriand's death in 1848 an edition of his *Oeuvres complètes* was issued by Krabbe in 1852–53, with 56 steel-engraved plates. Furne et Cie, one of the foremost publishers of steel-engraved books, issued a series of *Oeuvres* by literary authors such as Byron, Delille and Delavigne in 1833, Rousseau in 1835, with 22 engravings by Blanchard, Burdet, Geoffroy and Pourvoyeur, Millevoye in 1837–38 with a portrait engraved by Alexandre Marc Girard (1787–1870), and four plates by Jean Ferdinand Joubert (1810–83), N. Mague (b. *c.*1800) and Mauduit, Molière in 1838 with 15 steel engravings by Chevallier (possibly Henri (1800–93)), Auguste Dutillois (fl. 1831–48) and Jean Denis Nargeot, and an edition of Barthelémy and Méry with 23 steel engravings.

Three historical works were also illustrated by steel engravings. A.J.C. Saint-Prosper's *Histoire de France* (Duménil, 1838, 2 vols) contained 70 plates, coloured probably by hand, representing costume, arms, armour, furniture and musical instruments. This was the first in the series 'Le Monde. Histoire de tous les peuples', which, when completed, contained a total of 340 steel engravings. Such an edition was issued by Lebigne-Duquesne in ten volumes in 1859. Anquetil's *Histoire de France* (Furne, 1839–41) with 38 engravings by Hopwood, Rouarge and Revel. Furne also published a French translation of David Hume's very popular work *Histoire d'Angleterre* (1839–40) with numerous plates, some by Hopwood and the English engraver Le Petit.

Bernardin de Saint-Pierre's extremely popular tale *Paul et Virginie* was illustrated and reprinted time after time. Wood engraving was the principal method used, but some steel engravings were added. The 1829 edition published by Werdet and Requien had steel-engraved frontispiece and title page by Beyer, and in the celebrated 1838 edition published by L. Curmer there were seven steel engraved portrails by Cousin, Pelée, Pigeot ainé and A. Revel. Similarly, Pierre Jean de Beranger's *Oeuvres* published by H. Fournier ainé in 1839 included 100 wood engravings and 29 on steel. J.J. Grandville was the principal illustrator.

The 1840s saw a continuation of the previous decade's activity and produced some of the most distinctive French steel engraved books, covering a wide range of subjects. In 1836–37 L. Chodsko headed a group of authors

129   Vignette from Chateaubriand's *Poésies*, engraved by C.L.V. Mauduit

compiling *La Pologne historique*... published by the Bureau Central in three volumes in aid of Polish immigrants with 165 steel engravings. A second edition came out in 1842 with 38 portraits and views. J.J. Grandville's *Scènes de la vie privée et publique des animaux*... was published by Hetzer and Paulin with many steel engravings, and *Le Mémorial de W. Shakspere [sic]. Contes shaksperiens par Charles Lamb* published by Baudry with 20 steel engravings. The same publisher had issued *Illustrations of Shakespeare*... adapted to all editions in 1839 and 150 illustrations, some on steel and some on wood, after English artists, and in 1844 there was a *Galerie des personnages de Shakespeare* with 42 steel engravings and 18 on wood. M. Boitard's *Le jardin des plantes* published by Dubochet contained a number of illustrations, including four on steel of birds, which were hand coloured, followed in 1843 by Lamoët's volume with the same title published by Curmer with steel engravings of flowers, birds and butterflies, all coloured by hand.

The years 1843 and 1844 were the pinnacle of the steel-engraved and romantic book. Illustrators, having tried their hands at imaginative literature in the 1830s were ready to have another more confident attempt at suitable texts as already seen in the case of Hugo's *Notre Dame de Paris*. An outstanding example of an entirely steel engraved book is Charles Perrault's *Contes du temps passé* published by Curmer in 1843 where each page is headed by a vignette with the text fitted round it. The text was engraved by Auguste Blanchard, and the illustrations done by five young engravers. Vivant Beaucé (1818–76) engraved the frontispiece and was later remarkable for having spent 15 years in St Petersburg from 1853 as a designer. Charles Emile Jacque (1813–94) spent a short time in England engraving for a history of Greece and a Shakespeare, and was a collaborator with Louis Marvy (1815–50) whose designs for 'Puss in boots' in this volume were charming landscapes. Philippe Auguste Jeanron (1809–77), Mercier (fl. 1843) and Hippolyte Louis Emile Pauquet (1797–after 1867) make up the rest.

In a similar, but more imaginative vein, was the outstanding *Chants et chansons populaires de la France* published in 84 parts from February 1842 to October 1843 by H. Delloye. There were three series (or volumes) each with their own engraved title page (Plate 130), and the make up is in the form of booklets, comprised of (usually) eight pages, four relief printed with music and commentary, prefaced by details of the title, artist and engraver, and four steel engraved with the engraved text and surrounding border. A high proportion of plates are etched, however, showing little signs of burin work. Only in rare cases are the plates signed. Thirty-five engravers were employed of whom Charles François Daubigny (1817–78), who also designed some plates, was the most eminent (Plate 131). Mme Mathieu (fl. 1842), engraver in series 2 of plate 1 of 'La mère Michel' and

130 *Chants et chansons populaires...*, etched title page by J.D. Nargeot

Te souvient-il de cette amie,
Tendre compagne de ma vie?
Dans les bois en cueillant la fleur
   Jolie,
Hélène appuyait sur mon cœur
   Son cœur.

Oh! qui me rendra mon Hélène
Et ma montagne, et le grand chêne?
Leur souvenir fait tous les jours
   Ma peine;
Mon pays sera mes amours
   Toujours!

131   From Combien j'ai douce souvenances, etched by C.F. Daubigny

Mlle Eugènie Goujon (fl. 1843–48) also in series 2, plates 1 and 4 of 'Clémence Isaure' (Plates 132 and 133) and plates 1 and 4 of 'La fille de Sauetier' are remarkable for being two of the very few female French engravers encountered in this study.

Other engravers were A.F. Alès, C. Beyer, Alphonse Boilly (1801–67), Bosredon (fl. 1842), P.A.M. Brunillière, François Jules Collignon (d. 1850), Louis François Couché (1782–1849), Adrian Charles Danois (b. 1797), Ferdinand Delanoy (fl. 1836–63), Joseph Isnard Louis Desjardins (1814–94), J. Fontaine, A.J. Gaitte, A.F. Garnier, C.H.M. Geoffroy (1819–82), Eugène Gervais (fl. 1846–80), Emile Giroud (fl. 1842–44), Huart (fl. 1842–43), Auguste Jourdain (fl. 1842–63), C. Kolb (fl. 1843), Armand Joseph Lallemand (b. 1810), P. Langlois, Lechard (fl. 1842–43), Mercier, Ernest Monnin (fl. 1843–44), J.D. Nargeot, Jean Baptiste Pfitzer (b. 1789), C.N. Ransonnette, Benjamin Raspail (1823–99), J. Rozé (fl. 1843–59), Torlet (fl. 1842–43), and Wolff (fl. 1842–43). There were 39 songs in series 1, 42 in series 2 and 41 in series 3, giving an approximate total of 448 steel engravings. Chromolithographed covers were provided for each volume, that for volume 2 carrying four vignettes, one of which at top left is of three drunks, the artist being C. Kolb whose name appears at the foot of the picture. The work had a precursor in 1836, *Chansons populaires de la France* with original illustrations by M.G. Debayser, put together by Meissonier and his brother-in-law Steinheil, but it attained nothing like the popularity of the later volumes.

Jules Janin's *La Normandie* was published in 1843 by E. Bourdin with 20 steel engravings by John Outhwaite, Joseph Skelton and Gustave Lévy (which reached a third edition in 1862), to be followed in 1844 by *La Bretagne* with a similar set of steel plates, mixed with the usual wood engravings. His two most famous books, however, were treated rather differently. The publishers Aubert and Curmer issued Janin's *Un hiver à Paris* (1843) with 18 steel engravings, most of which were dated July 1842 with Aubert's publication line. One, the 'Hôtel de Princes', engraved by Lumb Stocks was printed by McQueen, and all the plates, together with the 18 done for *L'Été à Paris* (1843) were engraved by London engravers, mostly connected with the atelier of Charles Heath. This was rather surprising since by now Curmer at least had experience of French steel engravers, but the key may lie with the artist Eugène Lami, who drew most of the designs. He had visited England in 1826, had become court painter to King Louis Philippe, and had probably met Charles Heath when the latter visited the French court in 1838 or 1839 to receive a diamond snuff box from a grateful monarch. Thomas Allom, the English architectural and landscape illustrator drew the main part of two illustrations to *L'Été*... i.e. 'Interieur du Palais du Fontainebleau' and 'Le grand galerie du Louvre' to which Lami added the figures.

132 From Clémence Isaure, etched by Mlle E. Goujon

133   From Clémence Isaure, etched by Mlle E. Goujon [2]

The wood engravings to these volumes were done by French engravers. It was Lami, therefore, who had probably insisted on English steel engravers, and in the end it resulted in the engravings appearing in Heath's *Picturesque Annual* for 1843 published by Longman. In 1845 Peter Jackson (successor to Henry Fisher) issued the 36 plates again in *Summer and Winter in Paris*. In 1846, Allom, who had worked extensively for Fisher, also met the French king who, in a private audience, complimented him on the correctness of his views in France, then lately published. Much later, in 1858, Janin persuaded Gavarni to illustrate *Les symphonies de l'hiver* published by Morizot, with 15 steel engravings.

Marie Joseph Eugène Sue wrote a bestseller in *Les mystères de Paris*, published by Paulin in 1843–44. It came out in 80 parts to make four volumes. Volume 1 contained seven steel engravings, volume 2 contained 12, volume 3 contained seven and volume 4 contained eight, a total of 34. The engravers were Paul Girardet, Armand J. Lallemand and Jean D. Nargeot. The English translation with 21 etchings by Thomas Onwhyn has been noted in Chapter 6 (pp. 205–7).

Couailhac's *Le livre amusant* (1843) contained 12 steel engravings, *Les classiques de la Fable* (1843) had full-page engravings, and *Les Églises de Paris* ... published by Martinet and Curmer (1843) had 20 steel engravings. W. Tenint's *Les français sous la Révolution* had 40 steel engravings after H. Baron, engraved by J.M.R. Léopold Massard (1812–89).

A joint publishing venture by Furne, Perrotin and Fournier resulted in the six volumes of M.A. Guilbert's *Histoire des villes de France* (1844–48) with 84 steel engravings, a new edition of *Histoire de Paris [et environs]* by G. Touchard-Lafosse published by Poignavant in four volumes 1844–45 contained 19 steel engravings by Rouarge, Théophile Lavalées' *Histoire des français*... fifth edition published by J. Hetzel in 1845, contained 80 steel engraved portraits, Léon Guérin's *Histoire maritime de France* (Ledoux, 1843, 2 vols) contained 31 steel engravings done by G. Larbalestier, J. Outhwaite, Jean Charles Perdinel (b. 1809) Victor Florence Pollet (1811–82) and Thomas (fl. 1835–43), and A. Thiers's *Histoire du Consulat et de l'Empire* (1845–57) in 16 volumes contained 49 plates engraved by C.H.M. Geoffroy, Tony Goutière and J. Outhwaite, to which was added an *Atlas* (Paulin, 1859) with steel engravings by Dyonnet (fl. 1859).

The *Musée de Versailles*, published *circa* 1844 contained 75 steel engravings, 30 of which were of battles and landscapes, and 45 of costume and portraits of eminent personages. A. Girault de Sainte-Fargeau's *Dictionnaire... de toutes les communes de la France* (Firmin-Didot, 1844–45, 2 vols) contained 43 views of French towns engraved on steel. A poem by Delille, *Les jardins...* [1844] contained steel engravings after Thérot, and L. Galibert's *L'Algérie ancienne et moderne* [1844] had some after Raffet. *Les prisons d'Europe* by

Alboize and A. Maquet, published by the Administration de librairie, in 1845, contained 31 steel engravings and there were several in Arnould and Alboize's *Histoire de la Bastille*... six volumes and Alboize and Maquet's *Le Donjon de Vincennes*... four volumes (1844–45). E. Souvestre's *Le foyer breton* and E. Pacini's *La Marine*, published by Curmer in 1844 contains some steel engravings by Louis Marvy, and the fifth edition of Racine's *Oeuvres complètes* published by Lefèvre and Furne in 1844 where 12 were engraved by Goutière, Colin, Achille D. Lefèvre (1798–1864), Alphonse François and Pigeot. Another edition in 1869 employed the same plates. In 1845 steel plates were engraved for E. Lacroix's *Les mystères de la Russie* by C.H.M. Geoffroy, *Les portraits des beautés de l'Opéra,* and Vicomte Walsh's *Les viellées de voyage,* published at Tours by Pournin.

In 1846 came Arnoult's *Les Jésuites* with 20 plates, Dumas's *Le comte de Monte-Cristo* published by Au Bureau de l'Echo des Feuilletons in two volumes with 15 steel engravings in each after Gavarni and Tony Johannot, and *La Sainte Bible traduite par Lemaistre de Sacy,* published by Furne containing 32 engravings, all with typically curved tops, done by Audibran, Bein, Blanchard, John De Mare (1806–89), François, S. Jacobs (fl. 1841–46), Joubert, Lacour, Narcisse Lecomte (1794–1882), G.L. Lestudier, Marckl, Moret (fl. 1846–61), Nargeot, Pelée, the largest contributor with seven plates, Revel who engraved his master's design (Plate 134), and Ambroise Tardieu. The same translation was issued in 1851 by Bry with 180 steel engravings.

Works by Pierre Jean de Béranger had been popular for many years, but the edition with the greatest reputation was published by Perrotin in 1847. *Oeuvres complètes* in two volumes, each containing a frontispiece and 26 steel engraved plates. Ray says 'this is the last notable Romantic book with steel engravings'. Engravers were A.F. Garnier, Tony Goutière, Lacour, Charles de Lalaisse (b. 1811), Pierre Pelée, P.J. Tavernier, and E. Willman (1820–77). New editions were issued in 1851, 1857 (in which latter year the author died) and 1862 with the same plates. There had also been an edition of *Oeuvres complètes... orné de 44 gravures sur acier* in 1843.

Arsene Houssaye's *Histoire de la peinture flamande et hollandais* in its second edition 1847 published by Sartorius contained 100 steel engravings, and his *Voyage à ma fenêtre* [1851] contained ten. A remarkable series of four imaginative books were published by G. de Gonet, all with steel engravings by Charles Geoffroy, and represent a tour de force in the Romantic book. Texil Delord wrote the text to *Les fleurs animées. Introduction par A. Karr* (1847) and the two parts contained 52 plates, 50 of which were hand coloured, designed from ideas by J.J. Grandville. The flowers are represented in a natural setting by elegant ladies, a theme which is common to all books in the group. Joseph Méry supplied the text to the three remaining

FRENCH STEEL ENGRAVING 295

Tony Johannot pinxit Revel sculp

Esther et Assuérus.

Publié par Furne, à Paris.

134 Esther et Assuérus, engraved by A. Revel

volumes which commenced with *Les étoiles . . . Astronomie des dames par le Cte. Foelix* [1849] with designs by J.J. Grandville (which were his last) of which there were 11 hand coloured, depicting ladies as stars. In 1850 *Les joyaux, fantaise par Gavarni, Minéralogie des dames* . . . has 32 steel-engraved plates depicting London ladies of fashion, and in the same year came *Les parures . . . histoire de la mode* . . . containing 15 plates of more ladies of fashion. Ray describes and illustrates (209A) a de luxe edition where the plates are printed on paper with lace cut edges, and the picture hand coloured. These two later works can be compared to the English *Book of Beauty*. The 110 plates engraved by Geoffroy represent a high point in his career and of French steel engraving.

Paul Féval's *Les fils du diable* (Willermy, 1847) contained 13 steel engravings and there are some in Marc de Sainte-Hilaire's *Histoire anecdotique et militaire de la Garde Impériale* [1847]. Alphonse de Lamartine's *Histoire des Girondins* (Furne, 1847) contained 36 portraits engraved by Hopwood, Robinson, etc. and his *Oeuvres complètes* (Gosselin, 1850, 6 vols) contained 34 steel engravings. George Darboy's *Les femmes de la Bible* . . . had 38 steel engravings 'by the best artists' after Gustave Staal (Garnier, 1847–50, 2 vols). In 1848 François Theodore Ruhierre (1808–84) engraved six plates after Grandville for Ad. Mame of Tours's edition of Cervantes's . . . *Don Quichotte* in two volumes and the same publisher issued L. Veuillot's *Rome et Lorette* with engravings by John Outhwaite after Girardet. The same team produced *Les Pèlerinages de Suisse* (1852). Also in 1852, J.A. Brillat-Savartin's *Physiologie de Goût* . . . contained eight steel engravings after Bertall engraved by Geoffroy.

During the 1850s there was a reduction in activity from that of the previous decade. Some works have already been noticed in connection with earlier publications, but there are still some books worthy of comment in this period for various reasons. The publisher Mégard at Rouen issued J.B.J. Champagnac's *Berthe et Theodoric*, a 9th-century history illustrated with four steel engravings [c.1850], the *Encyclopédie Roret-Terrassier* (1850) had 20 plates, and William Smith's *Voyages autour du monde* . . . published in six volumes between about 1850 and 1860 by Librairie de l'Enyclopédie du XIXe siècle, contained 100 steel engravings. *Les femmes de Balzac* [1851] was illustrated by 14 portraits, engraved on steel after G. Staal, *Fables de la Chambeaudie* (1851) contained 14 by Prunier and M. Walsh's *Julienne ou la servante de Dieu* (Tours, Mame, 1852) had five. In 1853 Baronne de Montaran's *La clef des champs, Excursions dans les états vénetiens, le Tyrol, la Belgique . . .* , published by Mandeville, contained 11 steel engravings, *La Suisse historique et pittoresques* published by Didier had 28 steel engravings. A series of over 100 portraits was produced for Michaud's *Nouvelle collection des mémoires pour servir à l'histoire de France* published by Didier in 1854, the Abbé Bourasse's

La Touraine ... published at Tours by Mame in 1855 contained 15 steel engravings, and Ch. Romey and A. Jacobs's *Le Russie ancienne et moderne* ... (Furne, 1855) had 17 steel engravings by Colin, Outhwaite, Rouarge and Rozé of which six were coloured. Eugène de Mirecourt's *Confessions de Manon Delorne* (1856) and *Mémoires de Ninon de Lenclos* (1857) contained steel and wood engravings totalling 20 in each volume. M. Michaud's *Histoire des croisades (*Tours Mame, 1858) had four engravings by Ruhierre after Girardet and the 1858 edition of C. Malte-Brun's *Géographie universelle* ... published by Furne in six volumes, carried 62 views and maps, mostly engraved by Rouarge, and which was republished in 1869. *La Génie de Christianisme* (Curmer, 1859) had steel plates by Rozé.

The 1860s saw steel engraving in serious decline. With lack of commissions at home, engravers sought them elsewhere, notably in England. Pierre de Béranger died in 1857 and the publication of an edition of his *Derneières chansons* (1860) was marked by the design of 14 steel engravings by A. Lemud, some of which were engraved by Tony Goutière. Béranger's *Ma biographie* (1860) contained engravings by Joseph Durond (1816), Lalaisse, Mesnard, Nargeot and Ruhierre. Two editions of the works of Boileau appeared in the decade, namely *Oeuvres complètes* ... (Garnier, [1860]) with seven engravings by F. Delanoy after G. Staal, and *Oeuvres* (Furne, Jouvet, 1868) with a portrait of the author by Hopwood, and six plates after Moreau. An edition of Plutarch's *Lives, La Plutarque de la jeunesse* ... (Morizot, [c.1860]) carried eight engravings by Rouarge, and one of Daniel Defoe's *Aventures de Robinson Crusoe* (Morizot, 1861) had 16 plates by Rouarge and E. Willman. Mme C-B Barbé's *Blanche de Castile*, (Rouen, E. Vimont, 1862) was written, attractively illustrated and produced for young people. It was one of the Bibliothèque morale de la jeunesse and contained four steel engravings by Mégard et Cie (Plate 135).

Arsene Houssaye's *Les femmes du temps passé* (Morizot, 1863) had 19 portraits engraved by Charles P.A. Carey (1824–97), E. Gervais, C. Geoffroy, Leguay (fl. 1850–63) and de Montaux (fl. 1863). Le Sage's *Histoire de Gil Blas* ... (Morizot, 1863) with 20 plates engraved by C. Colin, F. Delanoy, and Outhwaite after Gavarni, and John Milton's *Le Paradis perdu* published by A. Rigaud in 1863 with 25 steel engravings after Flatters.

Les milles et une nuits. Contes Arabes was published by Morizot in 1864 with 20 steel engravings after Gavarni and Wattier, Briois's *La Tour Saint-Jacques de Paris* (1864) published by Dubuisson with a single plate by Martial (i.e. Adolphe T.J. Martial Potement (1828–83)), and in the same year T. Gautier's *Les dieux et les demi-dieux de la peinture* was published by Morizot with 15 engravings after L. Calametta.

M. de Lescure's *Marie-Antoinette et sa famille* (Ducrocq, [*c*.1865]) contained ten engravings after G. Staal. One of the last great French steel-engraved

La Reine voulait prouver
que le travail n'est pas une honte.

135 From *Blanche de Castile*, engraved by Mégard et Cie

books was Alfred de Musset's *Oeuvres complètes* (1865), with 28 designs by Alexandre Bida, engraved by L.P. Henriquel-Dupont, Léopold Flameng (1831–1911) and Landelle (fl. 1865).

L. Enault's *Histoire de l'Amérique centrale et méridionale*... published by Mellado in 1867 had 18 plates by Nargeot, Outhwaite and Willmann, and R. Pfnor's *Monographie du Château d'Anet*... published by the author in 1867, with 58 steel plates engraved by Edward Obermayer (1831–1916), a German architectural engraver who went as a pupil to Pfnor in Paris after a spell with Poppel in Munich. The engravings were printed on a tinted ground, as used by the Viennese engravers.

There were no important original steel engraved publications from the end of the 1860s, although some editions were re-issued with steel engraved plates, e.g. the fourth edition of L. Reynaud's *Traité de l'architecture* ... (1894), probably first published *circa* 1850–54 and still using 92 plates engraved by Léon Gaucherel (1816–86), J.J. Huguenet (b. 1815) pupil of Ollivier, Jean Emile Lebel (fl. 1850–55), Emile Edmond Ollivier (1800–64), Auguste L.F. Ribault (fl. 1831–65), Roux (fl. 1850) and Jean Joseph Sulpis (1826–1911). The core of Gustav Doré's work was published in the 1860s and as such he has been dubbed the last of the Romantics. His only work on steel, however, *The Idylls of the King* based on Tennyson (1869) was published in England (later by Hachette in Paris) and used English engravers.

There were three female engravers working on steel. Eugènie Goujon (fl. 1843–48) did four plates for *Chants et chansons populaires de la France* (1843). Also a painter, she exhibited at the Salon in 1848. Marie Louise Pannier (fl. 1838–55) (wife of Jacques Étienne Pannier (1802–69)) engraved a series of six portraits of artists and 'Entrée de l'hôtel d'Aguado, à Paris', the steel plates of which are in the Chalcographie du Louvre (nos 11952–6; 11958–9). A medallion portrait appeared in Racine's *Oeuvres* (1869). Mme Mathieu (fl. 1842) also contributed to the *Chants et chansons*... (1843).

Etching on steel appeared occasionally in books. Bracquemond, Daubigny and Charles Jacque were known to have used steel for their etchings. *La pléiade* was published by Curmer (1842), Goethe's *Les souffrances du jeune Werther* (Hetzel, 1845) had ten etchings on steel by Tony Johannot, and Nodier's *Contes*... (1847) had eight etchings. In the face of an etching revival *circa* 1869, Henriquel-Dupont founded the Société française de Gravure to protect line engraving in 1868, but with little success owing to the rising tide of photographic processes.

Mezzotint on steel came to Paris in 1824, brought by George Maile (1800–42) who, in 1822, had done two book illustrations on steel for Walton's *Compleat Angler*. He worked in Paris until 1840, and knew Samuel William Reynolds who from 1825 to 1829 worked in Paris producing a style of mezzotint unlike the one he used in England, engraving after French artists and exhibiting at the Salon. There were very few French mezzotinters working on steel, the eldest of whom was Pierre Joseph Tavernier (b. 1787) who did portraits and genre subjects, as well as working in line. Auguste Adrien Jouanin (1806–87), engraver to the Empress, was mainly an aquatinter, as was Eugène Pontius Jazet (1815–56). The youngest of the group was Pierre Cottin (1823–c.1887) who was Jazet's pupil.

The publication of independent prints was generally in the hands of engravers who sold direct to the public, but during the 19th century, print publishers became the middlemen. An early example of a larger than usual print was published in the *Art Journal* (1845), i.e. Horace Vernet's 'Le duc d'Orléans...' engraved by Laderer (fl. 1845) and Jean François Pourvoyeur (fl. 1831–45) (Plate 136), and in 1848 'The evening hymn' after C. Glaire was engraved by Lemercier, who also engraved plates for *Voyage pittoresque de la Suisse*. In France the trade was concentrated more or less in the hands of Adolphe Goupil (d. 1893), who employed many of the foremost engravers at a time when book work was coming to an end. Goupil established his house in Paris and by the 1860s had expanded into London, so that French engraving became equally well known on both sides of the Channel. In 1853 he paid 100,000 francs for the plate of 'Hemicycle' by Henriquel-Dupont after Paul Delaroche. Other engravers who worked for him are, in 1864, Alphonse François, the Belgian Joseph Arnold Demannez (1826–1902), and in 1868, Jules Gabriel Levasseur (b. 1823), Charles Eugène Thibault (b. 1835), Joseph Franck (1825–83) who was also Belgian, and Léopold Flameng (1831–1911). The *Art Journal* of December 1861 announced that for the steel engravings it employs 'We shall resort, not only to British engravers, but those of Germany, Belgium and France' (p. 353). Thus the British public became more accustomed to some different styles of engraving, more open, and coarser in treatment with an increase in etched areas. This is exemplified in Gustave Bertinot's (1822–88) 'Fraternal Love' after W.A. Bouguereau (Plate 137), issued in the *Art Journal* (1876), and regarded as his best work. Benoit Joseph Chevron (1824–75) was a pupil of the painter Vibert at the École des Beaux Arts, Lyon from 1837 to 1842, and then of Henriquel-Dupont at the École des Beaux Arts in Paris, 1842–44. Vibert's father was partner with Goupil, so the engraver is likely to have worked for the publisher in Paris. His 'Kiss of Judas' after Ary Scheffer is a very effective plate (Plate 138) (*Art Journal*, 1869).

There was a number of small publishing firms, centred on Paris, who issued some steel engraved books, but over the whole period of 1830–70, Furne et Cie probably produced the most, concentrating on literature and history. Louis Janet was known for his annuals from about 1829 to 1840, when he died. H.L. Delloye produced some outstanding works of literature

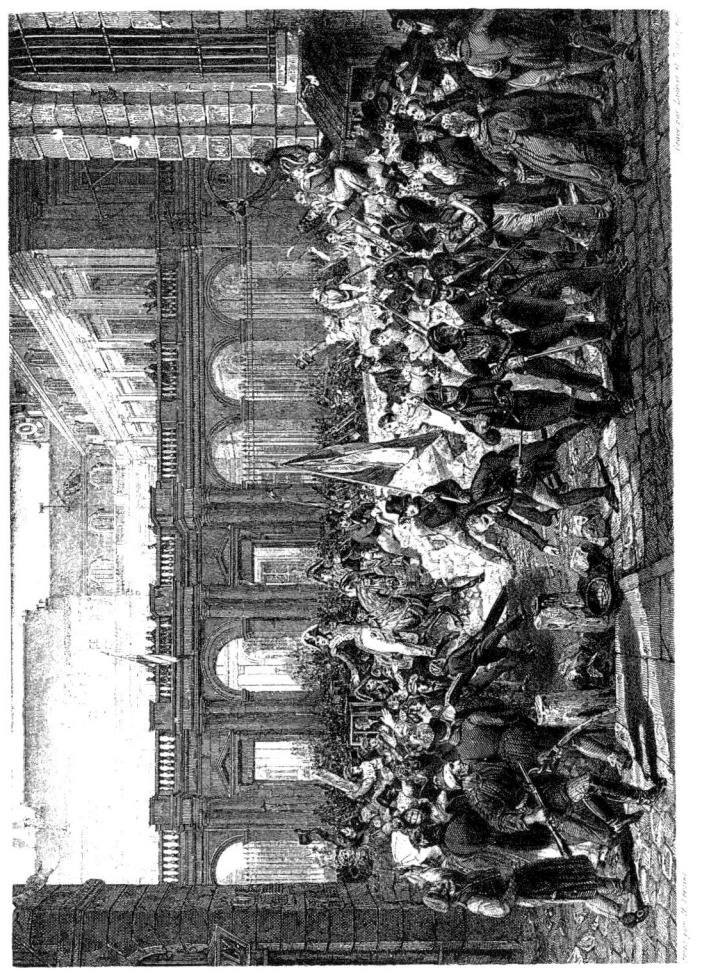

136 Le duc d'Orléans part du Palais-Royal, engraved by Laderer and J.F. Pourvoyeur

137   Fraternal love, engraved by G. Bertinot

138   The Kiss of Judas, engraved by B.J. Chevron

and travel, and L. Curmer was prolific in religious works and literature. Firmin-Didot's speciality was travel books of which he had a considerable list, and Perrotin concentrated on literature and history. Lefèvre was one of the earliest houses, producing literature, and Ledoux issued historical and travel books. Of the firms who used steel mainly from the 1840s were Garnier in literature, Hetzel, literature and history, Hachette, literature, and Morizot, prolific in literature and travel. Outside Paris, only at Tours was there a location producing important steel-engraved works. Mame issued a constant trickle of works on travel, literature and history, while Lecesne concentrated on travel.

9

Steel engraving in other European countries

Austria

The Academy of Vienna founded by Marie Thérèse, had an active engraving school in the 18th century, which continued to train engravers who later worked on steel e.g. Axmann, Eissner and Passini. Koschatsky in *Die Kunst der Graphik* (1988, p. 102) under Stahlstich (siderography) wrote that despite its masterly performance, steel engraving was ignored even where it was underlaid with a sheet dyed in chamois (a yellow/brown colour and probably akin to lithotint). Sotriffer in *Die Druckgraphik* (1977) makes no mention of steel in the section on copper engraving and etching, so there seems no doubt that steel was little used in Austria.

However, a number of Viennese engravers did work on steel, but mainly for works published abroad. Joseph Axmann (1793–1873) gained a bursary to the Viennese Academy with his engraving 'La Macocha', and engraved ten plates for *Das malerische und Romantische Deutschland* (1836–40) (Plate 139). Other Austrian contributors to this work were Léopold Beyer (1784–after 1870), Adolf Dworzak (fl. 1836–83), who was originally from Bohemia, but trained and worked in Vienna, Franz Eissner (fl. 1836) (Plate 140), Michael Hofmann (1797–1867), Johann Passini (1798–1874), and Jakob Rauschenfels von Steinberg (1779–1841).

Matthaus Kern (1801–52) engraved Plate CXXII 'Das forum . . . in Rom' for Meyer's *Universum* and A. Simon (fl. 1845–50) did 'Christ on the way to Golgotha' after Veronese for volume 1 of Payne's *Royal Dresden Gallery* [1845–50], together with a collection of the principal works of the Viennese galleries. Karl Mayer (or Mayr) (1810–76), mainly a painter, is thought to have engraved a fresco 'Coronation of the Virgin' after G. Da Udine, published in the *Art Journal* (1871). He taught at the Viennese Academy.

139 Forrach im Murgthale, engraved by J. Axmann

140 Heidelberg, engraved by F. Eissner

The comparatively few annuals or *taschenbuch* employed several engravers including Andreas Winkler (1793–1832) and Karl Mahlknecht (1810–93) whose works appeared, for instance, with that of Joseph Axmann and the German Conrad Geyer (1816–93) in *Huldigung den Frauen* [In Praise of Women] *Taschenbuch für das Jahr 1848* published in Vienna by Tendler and Co. Mahlknecht was known for his portrait engraving, such as those of the Emperor Franz-Joseph, Erzheroginnen [Duchess] Hildegarde and Maria Caroline.

In Salzburg, the Verlag von Baldi published in 1845 Johann Fischbach's *Malerischen Ansichten von Salzburg und Oberösterreich* which contained some of the earliest engravings done by the Swiss Kaspar Huber.

Belgium

The earliest Belgian steel engraver was Paul Lauters (1806–75) who was a pupil of Professor Malaise at the Brussels school of engraving, 1836. He was known mainly for his book illustrations and was a Chevalier of the Order of Leopold.

A group of five engravers, all pupils of Luigi Calametta who taught in Brussels after 1837, were born within a year or two of each other in the early 1820s. The eldest was Jean Baptiste Meunier (1821–1900) who also taught at Brussels, and took his younger brother Constantin Emile (1831–1905) as a pupil. He was also the father of another engraver Marc-Henri (1873–1922). His work, mainly portraits, was rather coarsely engraved as in 'The woman of Samaria' after Guercino (1859), in 'Louis XVII' after Baron Wappers and 'The Arquebusier' after J.B. Madou (1873). They give the appearance of being largely etched. David Joseph Desvachez (1822–1902) was perhaps the best known of the group outside his native country since he exhibited in Paris and had 11 engravings published in the *Art Journal* between 1857 and 1883, such as Plate 141 'Imogen in the Cave' after T. Graham, which was also issued in *Virtue's Imperial Shakspere* [1872]. Joseph Franck (1825–83) engraved after Old Masters and modern artists, including Daniel Maclise ('The warrior's cradle' in 1869), J.H.S. Mann ('Hush, he sleeps' in 1866) and J. Phillip ('The signal' in 1867). He became a member of the Royal Academy of Belgium in 1854. Joseph Arnold Demannez (1826–1902) worked in Brussels engraving mainly portraits, but other examples of his work include 'Daughter of the east' after J. Portaels in 1870, 'The reproof' after J. Coomans in 1871 and 'The Astrologer' after S. Lucas in 1879. He also worked for several periodicals. François de Meersman (1830–*c.*1905) also worked in Brussels, and obtained a gold medal there in 1881. 'Divorce of Josephine' after H.F. Schopin in 1882 is an example of his work.

In the city archives of Antwerp are kept two etched steel plates which were

141 Imogen in the cave, engraved by D.I. Desvachez

used to print a leaflet commemorating the death of the first Belgian Queen, Louise Marie, on 11 October 1850. Of 10,000 copies printed, 8,000 were for distribution to local schoolchildren. An additional 4,000 copies were printed on parchment. The leaflet displayed a portrait of the Queen on one side and a church interior with the catafalque on the other. The plates were etched by J. Linnig.

Holland

Many of the older generation of engravers such as J.C. Bendorp (1776–1849), W. van Senus (1772–1851) and D. Sluyter (1790–1852) (father of the steel engraver) did not take kindly to steel engraving, although they continued to engrave well into the first half of the 19th century and, therefore, it fell to those born after *circa* 1800 to experiment with the new metal. As elsewhere in Europe, copper engraving never really lost its supremacy, and existed alongside the new methods. There were two men, however, who exercised a great influence on several eminent names

142   Mr Hieronymous van Alphen, engraved by J.B. Tetar van Elven

in the art. The elder was Philipp Velijn (or Velyn) (1787–1836) whose own work was mainly with portraits and battle episodes but, although he seemed not to take to steel himself, he did train two engravers in the 1820s who made names for themselves. Johannes (or John) De Mare (1806–89), born in Amsterdam, left soon after his apprenticeship and joined Ingres in Paris, afterwards living in London and returning to La Haye *circa* 1840, where he provided some engravings for the annuals. He was in New York from 1850 to 1861, returning to France, where he died. The other was Johannes Philipp Lange (1810–49) who worked in Amsterdam and reproduced pictures after the 17th-century Dutch masters. The second master was André Benoit Barreau Taurel (1794–1859) who although he was French by birth, went to Amsterdam in his thirties (between 1824 and 1830), and had eight engravers there as pupils. Probably the first was D.J. Sluyter (1811–86), followed by H.W. Couwenberg (1814–45), J.W. Kaiser (1813–1900), J.F.C. Reckleben (1819–79), P.C.D. Tétar van Elven (b. 1823), J.H.M.H. Rennefeld (1832–77), W. Steelink (1826–1913) and A.S.B. Taurel (1833–66), his son.

About half of the steel engravers excelled in portrait engraving of whom Jan Baptiste Tétar ven Elven was among the first. He was a portrait painter, engraver and book illustrator from Amsterdam, and his first steel engraving was a portrait of the Prince of Orange, King William II, in 1833. *Circa* 1835 he did a portrait of Hieronymous van Alphen which carried the inscription 'sc. op staal' [engraved on steel] (Plate 142). At the age of 29 he became director of the School of Fine Art in Amsterdam (1834) and was elected to the Academy there in the following year. His younger brother Paul (b. 1823) was also an engraver, and his son Pierre (1828–1908) was at one time court painter to the Italian King Victor Emanuel II. Philipp Velijn, André B.B. Taurel, H.W. Couwenberg, H.J.D. Sluyter, C.E. Taurel (1824–92), C.L. van Kesteren, F. Molenaar, F.W. Burmeister (1845–1915) and W. Steelink all contributed to this form.

Johannes Philipp Lange, best known for his portraits, engraved one of H.W. Couwenberg, one of his contemporaries as an engraver on the occasion of the latter's death in 1845. It was after C. van Beuren, set in an oval frame inside a square background. Sadly both of these engravers died in their thirties, Lange aged 39 and Couwenberg aged 31, cutting short very promising careers in each case. Johann Willem Kaiser's (1813–1900) best known portrait is an oval one of C. Kramm. William Frederick Wehmeyer (1819–54) engraved a portrait of a young woman after Ary Scheffer, published in E. Laurillard's *Figuren en Tonen* (Amsterdam, 1883) (Plate 143) and Petrus Johannes Arendzen (1846–1932) the last of the steel portrait engravers, made a striking vignette portrait of Grandgagnage among those of other well-known people, as well as engravings after Rembrandt. After 1880 he went to London, and engraved 'Bulgaria' after J. Portaels published in the *Art Journal* (1880), and exhibited at the London Royal Academy (1890–99).

The 'Almanak' or annual seems to have attracted Dutch steel engravers from the beginning. Vignettes for title page and small illustrations throughout the volume provided regular annual employment, and the earliest use of steel in Holland was by J.A.R. Best (*c.*1800–after 1844). He was born at Schermer and worked in Amsterdam, first as an etcher and then as a pioneer steel engraver. *Circa* 1830 he engraved title-page vignettes for the

143   Portrait after Ary Scheffer, engraved by W.F. Wehmeyer

publisher Wed. Loosjes at Haarlem. The *Nederlandsche Muzen-Almanak*, first published in 1818 attracted some of the top engravers, and in the volume for 1839, published by J. Immerzeel Jun., Amsterdam, the engraved title-page vignette was done by Henricus Wilhelmus Couwenberg (Plate 144) and 'De brief' [The letter] after G.A. Schmidt was engraved by Johann Christian Bendorp (1766–1849) who had obviously overcome his antipathy to steel in his old age – he was then in his seventies. *Circa* 1840 Couwenberg also engraved an attractive vignette of 'Maria' after Nicolaas Pieneman, typical of his work for the annuals. Best worked for this annual between 1841 and 1844. The engraved title page of the 1842 *Leidsche Studentenalmanak*

144 Engraved title page of *Nederlandsche Muzen-Almanak voor 1839*, engraved by H.W. Couwenberg

was engraved by Jan Dam Steuerwald (1805–69), who also operated a method of engraving pictures of medals and coins similar to that patented by Achille Colas in 1817, called anaglyptography. D.J. Sluyter engraved for the *Almanak vor het Schoone in Goede* of 1854. J.B. Tétar van Elven and Frans Molenaar (1821–86) also worked on the annuals, producing portraits and other illustrations. In the later stages of steel-engraved works, Chrystian Lodewyk van Kesteren (1832–97) was prolific in his illustrations for the almanaks. *Holland* in 1858 and 1863, *Vergeet my niet* [Forget me not] in 1862 and *Aurora* from 1866 to 1872 contain his work.

Apart from annuals, the earliest books to be issued with steel engravings were those of travel, but although the texts were by local authors, the engravings were done by English artists and engravers. The first book is thought to be *De Rijn in afbeeldingen en tefereelen* [The Rhine in Pictures...] published in Amsterdam by G.J.A. Beijerinck in 1836. Work started on it in 1835 and the plates were after William Tombleson. There followed a series of volumes by the same publisher, including those by Professor Nicolaas Godfried Van Kampen (1776–1839), the first of which was *Zwitzerland en de Alpen van Savoye* (1836), after which came *Gezigten uit Holland en Belgie*. Van Kampen's work was also published in England such as *The history and topography of Holland and Belgium* translated by W.G. Fearnside, published by George Virtue [1837] with 61 steel engravings after W.H. Bartlett, V. Bing and H. Van Hoven, engraved mainly by A.H. Payne, a total of 34 plates. Armorie van der Hoeven wrote the text for *Bijbelsche landschappen naar afbeeldingen* ... [Biblical Landscapes in Pictures ...] published at Leeuwarden by Suringer [1837] with English steel engravings after W.H. Bartlett and English engravers. The book was issued again in 1854, the text from sheets remaining from the 1837 edition, but the plates printed from the original steels with three exceptions. Because there had been a fire in the warehouse of the English publishers plates for illustrations nos 1, 5 and 27 were rendered useless, so new ones were done by W.F. Wehmeyer, probably one of his last commissions before his early death at the age of 35 in 1854.

A different style of engraving, concentrating on the foreground figures and only sketching in the background was exemplified by the work of Johann Heinrich Marie Hubert Rennefeld in *De kinderen der Zee* [The Children of the Sea] (Amsterdam, 1861). 'Visser en visservrouw' [Fishermen and fisherwomen] after Jozef Israëls (Plate 145) was done to illustrate a poem by Nicolaas Beets. Two more vignettes from the books were 'Middagalaapje' [Midday nap] and 'Langs Moeders Graf' [Past Mother's Grave]. These were part of 15 scenes from the lives of fishermen. E. Laurilland's *Figuren en Tonen* (Amsterdam, 1883), referred to earlier, also contained an engraving of a girl pulling a boat after W.J. Martens to illustrate a poem by W.J. Hofdijk engraved by Willem Steelink. Johann Willem

145   Visser en visservrouw, engraved by J.H.M.H. Rennefeld

Kaiser designed and engraved the title-page vignette for *Bloemen, geguard uit den Justhof der Vaderlandsche Poezij* (Amsterdam, P.N. Van Kampen, originally published in 1842). He served from 1833 to 1839 in the Dutch artillery, and in 1859 was made director of the Amsterdam school of engraving, professor of the Academy 1870 and director of the Ryck Museum 1874. He also engraved 50 pictures in Gallery Six, Amsterdam.

Other engravings of note included a series of 12 landscapes around Arnhem, engraved by H.W. Couwenberg after the designs by his elder brother Abraham Johannes (1806–44). H.W. Couwenberg is held by some to be Holland's finest steel engraver, who won various prizes at the Academy, and in 1836 won a top prize with a considerable cash value. Probably the best known engraver outside his own country was Dirk Jurriaan Sluyter (1811–86), son of an engraver. He engraved mainly genre subjects after the 17th-century Dutch masters and later, until he was 70 years old. A very effective plate was 'Rederijkersoptogt, Rotterdam 1658' after J. Spoel in 1868, together with 'De Officiersweduwe' [The officer's widow, 1861]. An example of a plate published in England is 'Dutch children' after Jozef Israëls, in *The Casquet of Literature* (London, Blackie, 1874, 2nd series, vol. 2, p. 176) (Plate 146). He had C.L. Van Kesteren (1832–97) as a pupil in the 1850s. Willem Steelink's 'Onder Vrienden' [Among Friends] in 1882 shows four young men inspecting a painting on an easel and is representative of the final phase of 19th-century steel engraving in Holland. His 'Schepen op het strand' [Ships on the beach] is a small plate

146   Dutch children, engraved by D.J. Sluyter

showing people walking on the beach beside two ships anchored close in. He had a son Willem (1856–1928) who was a landscape painter, lithographer and aquatinter. 'De bestormin van Alkmaar door de Spanjaarden 1573' [The storming of Alkmaar by the Spaniards 1573] was engraved by C.L. van Kesteren after Herman F.C. ten Kate in 1868. It was a very lively scene of action at the castle walls. A smaller plate was 'Soldaten op het ijs' [Soldiers on the ice], rather coarsely engraved.

Lastly, reproductive engraving was the mainstay of the work of Johannes Arnoldus Boland (1838–1922) who worked part time in the print department of the Rijk Museum, Jan Frederick Christiaan Reckleben (1819–79), with his 'Overwintering op Nova Zembla' in 1845, 'Zondagmorgen' [Sunday morning] in 1846 and Bible illustrations, and Hendrik D.J. Sluyter (1839–1931) who was D.J. Sluyter's son and pupil, whose small octagonal plate 'Palissaden plaatsen op het strand' shows an oxen-drawn cart taking timber across the beach, probably from a wreck. Léopold Lowenstäm (1842–98) of Amsterdam, although known primarily as an etcher, also worked as a steel engraver. His work in Holland was largely after Jozef Israëls, but he left to go to Sweden and settled in London after 1873 where he produced plates after Alma-Tadema such as 'Rose among the roses', 'Pleading' published by Pilgeram and Lefèvre in 1878, 'Sculpture in ancient Greece and Rome' (*Art Journal*, 1878) and four more for the *Art Journal* (1879–80) after different artists. A.J. Terwen (1841–1918) left Holland to work in Dusseldorf for a steel engraver, from whence he sent home letters describing his work, which are still in the possession of the family in Holland, awaiting transcription.

Italy

Steel engraving in Italy was virtually non-existent, since there was neither a tradition or a call for it during the 19th century. A small number of books have been found, and most have only a few steel engravings in them, as in the *Almanacco por l'anno 1834* ... (Bologna, St Cam. del Bassi, 1833) which carried a portrait of Pope Gregory XVI after Tramontini, engraved by Antonio Viviani (1797–1854). In 1834, a series of views were steel engraved in Turin, published by Audot, including those of Palermo, Malta, Pavia, Taormina, Florence and Catania.

L'Eneide di Virgilio volgarizzata del Comm. Annibal Caro ... (Florence, Passigli e Soci, 1836, 2 vols) was 'ornamented' with 54 steel engravings, and *La Sirena. Augurio pel Capo d'anno. Anno Quinto* (Naples, St del Fibreno, 1851) had three steel-engraved plates. Angelo Fumagalli's *La vicende di Milano durante la guerra con Frederico I Imperatore* (Milan, F. Colombo, [1854], second edition) carried a steel-engraved portrait of the author. Cornelius

Lapide's *Commentarii in Sacrum Scripturam* (Mediolani, Franciscus Pagnoni, 1857) also contained steel engravings, and Carl Heideloff's *Raccolta de' migliori ornamenti nel Medio Evo e profili di Architettura Gotica* (Venice, Brizeghel, 1859) was well illustrated with steel engravings and lithographs (there were 133 in volume 1) Giuseppe la Farina's *La Germania Renana*... (Florence, Luigi Bardi, 1842) carried 24 steel engravings, but they were from G.N. Wright's *The Rhine, Italy and Greece* (London, Fisher, 1841–42), and were by English artists and engravers. In 1839 a report in the *Art Union* gave details of some Italian line engravings being done by Samuel Jesi

147 Murillo, engraved by L. Calametta

(1788–1853), Antonio Perfetti (1792–1872) and Toski, but there was no indication that they were on steel. Although Italian by birth, Luigi Calametta (1802–69) was better known elsewhere in Europe. Born at Civita Vecchia, he trained under Marchetti and Giangiacomo, and went to Paris in 1822 where he worked with Ingres. He taught at Brussels from 1837, where among his pupils were several Belgian engravers. For several years he was professor of engraving at Milan, and was mainly a portrait engraver, one example of which, a self-portrait of the painter Murillo was published in the *Art Journal* in 1854 (Plate 147).

Steel engraving was not used until 1906 for printing Italian stamps, where a stamp depicting King Victor Emmanuel III was engraved and printed at L'Officina Calcografica Italiana in Rome.

Spain

The practice of steel engraving in Spain was limited, although its possibilities and results were well known. It was pre-empted by the arrival of lithography in the country *circa* 1829. There are two main centres of engraving at Barcelona and Valencia, and several of the eminent steel engravers were trained at the School of Fine Art in Barcelona. The Escuela Especial de Bellas Artes *circa* 1848 became the Escuela Superior de Pintura, Escultura y Grabado under the control of the Ministerais de Instrucción Publica. There are also a Calcografica de la Imprenta nacionale and a Real Calcografia. Among the earliest books to contain steel engravings was J. Villars' *Maria y Margarita*, published at Barcelona *circa* 1840. It was illustrated by Tomás Planas, engraved by Ángel Fatjó (d. 1889), who also engraved illustrations to a de luxe edition of Cervantes and *Barcelona ancient and modern*. N. Pasto Diaz and F. de Cárdenas issued *Galeria des Españoles célebres contemporános* in Madrid published by Imprenta de Sanchis, 1841–46, which contained a portrait of Diego Clemencin. Another of Maria Cristina de Borbón was engraved by Francesco Bellay. Both were done on steel in the 'manera negra'.

In 1842, Joaquím Pi i Margall put together a series of steel engravings under the title *España obra pintoresca*. The chief engraver was Antonio Roca y Sallent (d. 1864) from Barcelona and who taught at the School of Art there. Two of his contributions to the work were 'Vista de la cascada de San Miguel de Fey' engraved after a daguerrotype, and 'Costa de Garraf...' after Luis Rigault.

Outline engraving in the manner of Henry Moses in England became popular from 1859. It was used in *Galería de cuadros escogidos de Real Museo de Pinturas de Madrid*, examples of which are 'Rebecca y Eliezer' after Murillo, engraved by Esteban Buxó (fl. 1859–60). He was trained at Barcelona and

Madrid and later moved to Paris. 'Diana y Calixto' after Titian was engraved by Camilio Alabern y Casas (1825–76), pupil of his father and Antonio Roca. *Obras completas de Flaxman* (Madrid, 1860) contained a scene from Dante's *Purgatory* engraved by Joaquím Pi i Margall, who went on to do another of the triumph of Christ's religion after José Fuehrich (Madrid, 1865).

The *magnum opus* of Spanish steel engraving was the *Monumentos Arquitectónicos de España* (1859–95), of which 89 parts were published. The idea originated with the Ministry of Public Instruction who gave the Academia de San Fernando, Madrid the resources to carry it out. Originally called *Spain, Artistic and Monumental* its title was changed before publication. Two chairs of engraving were created at the Academia, that for steel engraving being endowed for 12,000 reales a year. The other chair was for wood engraving. The majority of plates were engraved on steel, ideal for reproducing architectural drawings. Engravers included Esteban Buxó, Emilio Ancelet, Enrique Stüler, Luis Iranzo and Domingo.

Sweden

The art of steel engraving seemed to pass Sweden by as far as engravers were concerned. Several works published in Sweden in the 19th century were illustrated by steel engravings, such as two guide books to Stockholm, illustrated by the eminent Swedish artist Ferdinand Tollin (1807–65), who, although born in Jävle, died in Switzerland. *Promenader genom Stockholm* [Walks through Stockholm] (1852) contained ten steel engravings, done by Johann Poppel, the Darmstadt engraver and printer. *Stockholm och dess omgifningar* [Stockholm and its surroundings] (1852) also contained steel engravings after Tollin. This would indicate a distinct lack of steel engravers in Sweden, and it is only very much later in the century that the Dutch engraver Léopold Lowenstäm was asked by the Swedish government to found a school of engraving, probably *circa* 1870. He returned to London in 1873. He was decorated with the Order of Gustavus Vasa probably in recognition of his help. Steel engraving was used for stamps from 1891 and for banknotes, culminating in a revival in the 1980s (see Chapters 2 and 11).

Switzerland

Switzerland as a country of outstanding landscape had, from the 18th century, attracted artists of all kinds, not least those on the Grand Tour, but since commercial opportunities were not as great as in France or Germany, there were few natives who did not emigrate to find them.

In 1815 Nicolas Schenker (1760–1848) was put in charge of an engraving school in Geneva, from which emanated some good pupils, among them Pierre Pelée (1801–71), born at Courtedoux (Switzerland). By the time he was 26, however, he was working in Paris, where he stayed. The same happened to Vittore Pedretti (1799–1868) before he was 24 years old, and Frédéric Weber (1813–82), born at Liestahl, went to Munich to work under Samuel Amsler, and thence to Paris to complete his education, where he stayed. Another of Amsler's pupils was Kaspar Heinrich Merz (1806–75), born at St Gall, but he spent his early life in Munich and eventually died in a Swiss mountain accident. He had his 'St Barbara' after Vecchio in 1870 and 'Sts Catherine, Barbara, and Mary Magdalene' after Piombo in 1873 published in the *Art Journal*. Paul Girardet (1821–93) was born at Neuchâtel of an artistic Swiss family, and was a pupil of his father, but had gone to Paris by about 1839, where he stayed.

The engravers who stayed at home were Jakob Lorenz Rudishüli (1835–1918), born at St Gall, died at Basle, and Johann Rudolf Ringger (b. 1841), born at Niederglatt (canton Zurich) with Kaspar (or Caspar) Ulrich Huber (1825–62), born in Zurich. They were of the younger generation of steel engravers, and their work did not appear until the 1850–60 decade, when Swiss landscape engraving on steel flourished. Most of the travel books of this period were illustrated by steel engravings, many of which were strikingly designed if technically undisciplined, especially in the etched areas. The use of fine lines for the lighter tones was not fully explored and work by the graver was at a minimum.

The earliest work was by Martens, a German born at Saxe, who engraved 12 plates on steel for *La ville de Lausanne en l'an 1850*, published in Lausanne by the Bazar Vaudois. Kaspar Huber, however, appears to have introduced steel engraving into Switzerland. When he was 15 he left Zürich to be apprenticed to Johann Poppel in Munich, and in 1850 he returned home to set up a steel engraving atelier. Among his earliest works was Johann Jakob Ulrich's *Die Schweiz in Bildern* published by the author (1851–56), which contained 45 steel engravings and 182 vignettes in the text. It was republished (1860–69) by Henri Fuessli as *La suisse pittoresque*. Soon afterwards Huber issued his first Album. This was a distinctive form of publication which in later years became a medium for the revival of plates previously published. The format was usually oblong quarto, which suited the predominantly horizontal shape of most landscape engravings. Huber's *Album von St. Moritz in Oberengadin* [*c*.1855] published in Zürich by Fuessli, contained 12 steel engravings (Plates 148 and 149), which were engraved after Huber's own drawings, a feature which doubtless contributed to the publication's success. The plates were printed in Zürich by D. Herter. Huber also engraved 13 plates and a map for *Heustrich und Ungelbung – Heustrich et les environs* published locally. For Eduard Osenbrüggen's *Die*

148   Engraved title page of *Album St Moritz*..., engraved by C.U. Huber

Urschweiz... (Basle, C. Krüsi, [1871]) he did most of the 60 steel engravings, and also contributed some to the same author's *Das Hochgebirge der Schweiz*... (Basle, C. Krüsi [*c.* 1867]), in which some of the plates were done after photographs. In the 1870s he did five large plates of Alpine scenery.

Rudolf Ringger also worked in Zürich and produced his *Album von Zürich-See*... which ran to five volumes, containing 20 plates each. Published by David Bürkli *circa* 1860, the plates were also drawn and engraved by the same person (Plate 150 from the third volume and Plate 151 from the first volume).

About the same time the German Jobst Riegel (1821–78) engraved 30 views and the title page for *La Suisse pittoresque*, published in Zürich by Cramer and Lüthi. G. Heisinger also contributed.

The most influential work, however, was Dr Jakob Frey's *La Suisse illustrée*.

149 Samaden, engraved by C.U. Huber

150 Wüdensweil, engraved by R. Ringger

151 *Album vom Zürich-See*, engraved by R. Ringger

152 Engraved title page of J. Frey's *La Suisse illustrée*...

153 Souvenir von Zug, engraved by C. Rorich

Das Schweizerland in Bild und wort published in two volumes at Basle by Chris. Krüsi (1865–68). Issued simultaneously in London, Paris and New York it contained two engraved title pages (Plate 152) and 155 steel engravings, the greater majority of which were done by Jakob Lorenz Rudishüli. He learned line engraving at Darmstadt, and produced a great number of Swiss and Rhine views. Another contributor was the German C. Rorich (fl. 1850–57) who had been at Darmstadt, but was in Nuremberg at the time of the present work. Rudishüli also drew some of the scenes (Plate 153, from vol. 1, pp. 231–2). This work gave rise to a number of Albums produced by Krüsi in 1869 such as *Album de la Suisse Romande. 50 vues* ..., *Album der Ost Schweiz... 55... Ansichten..., Album der Ur-Schweiz; 35 Blätter..., Album vom Berner-Oberland; 50 Ansichten in Stahlstichen* ... and *Album der Nord-und Ostschweiz. 100 Stahlstiche* ... which, apart from views from Frey, contained some from Johann Wilhelm Appell's *Der Rhein und die Rheinlande* ... (Darmstadt, G.G. Lange, 1842).

Circa 1875 Krüsi published *Costumes suisses* with 18 hand coloured steel engraved plates, after which steel engraving seems to have died out in Switzerland.

American steel engraving

The published sources are quite prolific for the graphic arts, and have been organized by a number of dedicated researchers. The publication of biographical information has facilitated access to more detail than has been previously encountered in most other areas.

Steel engraving was used and exploited in the United States from the end of the 18th century, primarily for the production of banknotes, and much of the credit is due to Jacob Perkins and his associates in developing siderography, check plates and the hardening of steel plates. A by-product of this was the first book printed entirely from steel plates. In 1810 Perkins and Fairman produced at Newburyport their *Running Hand Stereographic Copies* (Plate 154), which was an eight-page booklet from which pupils would copy copperplate handwriting, as well as acquiring moral precepts along the way (Plate 155). It was probably very popular and was re-issued in 1815. This

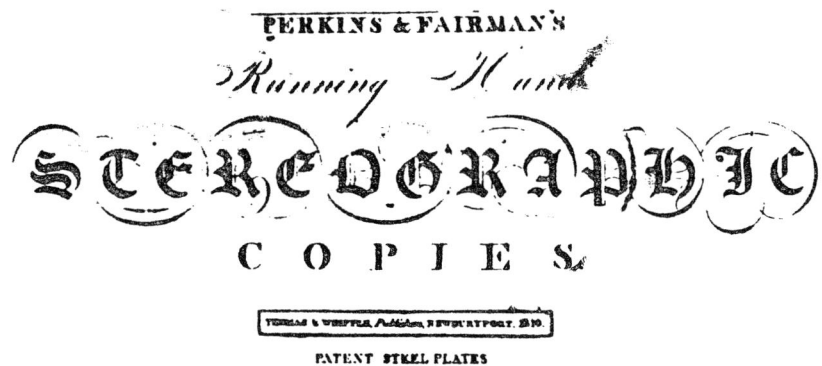

154   Last page of *Perkins & Fairman's Running Hand . . .*

Idleness and ignorance are the parents of many vices.

Knowledge is gained only by attentive reading and experience.

Let virtue and innocence accompany all your diversions.

Meditation should be frequent and always truly sincere.

155 Third page of *Perkins & Fairman's Running Hand*...

was, however, an isolated use of the metal, and it was another ten years before steel engraving developed significantly.

As in Germany, America by its very size had several publishing centres such as Philadelphia, Boston and New York, which meant that books published in a city tended to reach a more limited readership than those of London or Paris. The edition size of such publications, e.g. 1,000 for *The Charm* (c.1847), was comparatively small by European standards and did not really require the length of run a steel plate could provide. The tonal range, however, was another factor, and it was this which made line engraving on steel the main means of illustrating the annuals.

Engravings had appeared in magazines from the beginning of the century, e.g. the Philadelphia *Port Folio*, and the annual, being a development of this, followed suit. A number of titles appeared between 1825 and 1855, some of them very short-lived, e.g. *The Western Souvenir* (Cincinnatti, Ohio, N. and G. Guilford, 1829) the only volume, for which Cephas G. Childs engraved the title page after H. Inman. *The Token* on the other hand ran for 15 years from 1827. The 'embellishments' varied greatly in quality. *The Token* aimed to employ only American artists and engravers, but by 1833 had to resort to overseas designs, while other annuals used plates from different sources, notably the London annuals. In 1840 *Literary Souvenir* plates could be purchased in London at £8 per thousand impressions or, alternatively, plates were engraved by local engravers in imitation of London engravings. In some cases, plates were 'rented', e.g. those for *The Evergreen* (1847).

The annuals were the first means of popularizing artistic illustrations, which dictated the accompanying text in most cases, averaging 8–12 illustrations per volume, and began with *The Atlantic Souvenir* (1826) published in

Philadelphia by Henry C. Carey and Isaac Lea (1825). This first volume contained three plates from the *Literary Souvenir* (1825), and engravers employed in subsequent volumes included Asher Brown Durand (1796–1886) New Jersey, George B. Ellis (fl. 1821–38) Philadelphia, George W. Hatch (c.1805–67) New York, who was a pupil of Durand, and James Barton Longacre (1794–1869) Philadelphia. Francis Kearny (c.1780–after 1838) engraved 'Three score and ten' for the 1831 volume. The 1859 edition was published in New York by Derby and Jackson, and contained 12 steel-engraved portraits.

This was followed in 1827 by *The Token* published in Boston, which, although it had a succession of different publishers, was edited throughout most of its 15 issues by Samuel Goodrich. Each volume contained about ten engravings, a total of 150 over the whole series, 20 of which were engraved by John Cheney (1801–85). He was an excellent engraver, but virtually abandoned his profession after about 1833, disillusioned by the lack of encouragement given to it. Approximately 40 other engravers were employed including A.B. Durand, Joseph Andrews (1805–73) whose first steel plate was said to be after Alvin Fisher, in 1829, Moseley Isaac Danforth (1800–62) New York, Edward Gallaudet (1809–47) Boston, John Cheney, Peter Maverick (1780–1831) New York, who had Durand as his pupil, John B. Neagle (1796–1866) Philadelphia, Joseph Ives Pease (1809–83) and James Smillie (1807–85) New York.

Also from Boston came two volumes of *The Memorial* (1827–28) with engravings by Edward Gallaudet, David Claypole Johnston (1787–1865) Boston, and Thomas Kelly (c.1795–c.1841).

The Talisman (1827–30) appeared in New York City and contained a total of 25 engravings, of which about six were of American scenery and three of New York and its environs. A.B. Durand, G.W. Hatch and P. Maverick were the major contributors as engravers. The 1830 volume was awarded the premium of the American Institute of the City of New York, founded in 1828 to encourage, among other things, the arts.

The Western Souvenir was published in Cincinnatti as a single volume in 1828 with engravings by Cephas G. Childs (1793–1871), Philadelphia, pupil of Gideon Fairman, Joseph Cone (fl. 1802–30), Philadelphia and William Woodruff (fl. 1817–28), Cincinnatti.

The Casket; Flowers of Literature, Wit and Sentiment was published by Samuel C. Atkinson in Philadelphia. A regular engraver was Francis Kearny (c. 1780–after 1838) who contributed 'Arcadia' after C.R. Cockerell to the 1830 volume and the engraved title page for the 1838 edition. Cephas G. Childs engraved 'Simon Bolivar' for the 1830 edition, and in the 1832 volume he re-engraved 'Indian war dance …' after S. Seymour from an earlier state of the print of 1822. G.B. Ellis did 'Village school in an uproar' after

Henry Richter. *The Lily; a Coloured Annual* (1831) was unusual in that the engravings were hand coloured.

The Gift was probably among the best known annuals, although it only ran for eight issues 1835–45 (none for 1838 and 1841) published in Philadelphia by Carey and Hart. Re-engravings of British plates were used in the first volumes from the *Literary Souvenir* (1835–36) but among the rest John Cheney engraved 24 plates with others by Richard W. Dodson (1812–67), pupil of Longacre, G.B. Ellis who did 'Soliciting a note' after R.W. Buss, John B. Forrest (*c.*1814–70) who worked in England with William Thomas Fry, an early steel engraver there, A.W. Graham (fl. 1832–69), English engraver living in Philadelphia, Alexander Lawson (1773–1846) Philadelphia, J.I. Pease and William E. Tucker (1801–57) Philadelphia. In the 1844 issue William Humphrys contributed a plate of an incident in the early life of Washington, with seven other engravings. On average, the publishers paid engravers $225 for each plate.

The Magnolia was published in New York in 1836–37. The engravers were John W. Casilear (1811–93), one of P. Maverick's apprentices in 1826, J. Cheney, A.B. Durand, J.A. Rolph (fl. 1834–46), New York, who engraved 'Sunset on the Hudson' after R.W. Weir for the 1837 edition, J. Smillie and George Parker (d. *c.*1868) whose stipple portrait 'Castella' after H. Inman appeared in the 1837 volume. Carey and Hart in Philadelphia produced *The Charm and Floral Offering* in the 1840s in an effort to increase business, but by this time the annuals were past their heyday.

The Odd Fellows offering (1844) used an old *The Token* illustration from 1837, i.e. 'Aqueduct near Rome' which had also been used in *Rose of Sharon* (1840). This latter annual was a series of 18 volumes [1840–58?] in only one of which (1855) was original designs used.

In the 1850s feminine portraits became popular in *The Book of Home Beauty* (New York, 1852), which contained 12 portraits of American women, *The American Book of Beauty* which averaged seven plates and *The Wreath of Beauty*.

Since the average print run was only about a thousand impressions, mezzotint was able to make a considerable contribution to the reproduction of pictures. This was fully exploited by John Sartain (1808–97) who arrived in Philadelphia from Britain in July 1830, bringing with him experience in mezzotint on steel, obtained during his apprenticeship with Henry Richter 1827–28. His first contact in Philadelphia was the publisher Mr Littel, and he went on to work for annuals such as *The Pearl* (1832–34), three issues of *The Diadem* (1845–47), in which the plates were, untypically, unrelated to the text. In *The Opal*, published in New York City, eight issues 1843–48, only the last two contained engravings and here Sartain was joined by Alexander Hay Ritchie (1822–after 1888), newly arrived from

Scotland in New York 1841. Other mezzotint engravers were T. Doney (fl. 1845), who arrived in New York about 1845, J.D. Gross (fl. 1835), W.G. Jackman (fl. 1840–41) who arrived in New York from England about 1841, John C. McRae (fl. 1840–80) New York, H.S. Sadd (fl. 1840), an Englishman in New York *circa* 1840, and William Page (1811–85). Mezzotint as a process was cheap, quick and impressed the publishers, despite the rapid deterioration of the plates under printing. Sartain's output was prodigious, but by about the 1860s, worn out plates were being revived and used for the spurious annuals of the day.

Portrait engraving was arguably the most popular branch of the art, since nearly all the important engravers produced some in line, stipple or mezzotint as part of their output. After the annuals the first major steel engraved work was the *National Portrait Gallery of Distinguished Americans* (statesmen, military and professional men), published in New York in four volumes 1834–39. It was the idea of James Herring and James Barton Longacre (1794–1869) the engraver in 1830, and the latter set about recruiting engravers to work on it from both sides of the Atlantic. Some were already on hand as his pupils in Philadelphia, namely Richard W. Dodson (1812–67), whose best plate was that of 'Simon Kenton', Thomas B. Welch (1814–74), E. Wellmore (fl. 1834–35) and William A. Wilmer (d. *c.*1855). One of the best engravings – a portrait of General Isaac Putnam in 1834 – was done by a W. Humphreys. Other engravers were Thomas Kelly (*c.*1795–*c.*1841) Joseph Ives Pease who engraved for the work after 1835, J. Gross (fl. 1834) John Francis Eugene Prud'homme (1800–*c.*1888), A.B. Durand and his pupil John Wesley Paradise (1809–62). Two engravers recruited from London were George Parker in 1834 and John B. Forrest in 1837. The choice of method varied with the engraver, most choosing stipple as being possibly quicker, but engravers such as Dodson and Durand kept to line for their contributions.

Individual portrait plates both of the famous and the unknown proliferated during the period and came to an end about 1862 with the publication of Duyckinck's *National Portrait Gallery of Eminent Americans*, published by Johnson, Fry and Co., after paintings by Alonzo Chappel. It did not reach the eminence of the earlier volumes.

A book popular on both sides of the Atlantic was John Howard Hinton's *The History and Topography of the United States*, originally published in London by Isaac Taylor Hinton and Simpkin Marshall, in 1830–32 in two volumes with about 80 American scenes, some by American artists, but all engraved by the newly created firm of Fenner, Sears and Company. The work was published in 1834 in Boston, but this time the plates were engraved by James Archer (fl. 1832–55) who was known to have been working in London in 1832 and was probably brought over specifically for this work. It is tempting to speculate that he worked for Fenner, Sears and Co. and it is assumed that the firm wished to retain the original plates, which were provided with ornamental borders for later editions. A third edition came out in London in 1842 issued by J. Dowding, and another was published by John Tallis in 1849.

An American engraver also tried a landscape publication in 1830, encouraged by the success of the annuals. *The American Landscape* was started to 'give accurate views of our scenery in a form worthy of a collection portfolio', and no. 1 came out in New York published by Elam Bliss in 1830 with six plates engraved by A.B. Durand. The title page carried 'Manbrino's Helmet' engraved by James Smillie after Durand, probably one of the former's earliest American plates, since he only arrived in New York in 1829. The plates were 'Catskill mountains', 'Delaware water gap', both after Durand, 'Falls of the Sawkill' after W.J. Bennett, 'Fort Putnam' after Robert W. Weir, etched by J. Smillie, finished by A. Durand, 'Weehawken' after W.J. Bennett and 'Winnipisogee Lake' after T. Cole. The text was by William C. Bryant, but although ten issues were planned, no more appeared. Some of the plates, however, were used subsequently in *The Ladies Companion* and the *New York Mirror*. All the original plates were printed by Wade, but Thomas Illman printed for *The Ladies Companion* and Illman and Pilbrow for the *New York Mirror*. These were the steel engraved successors to J. Hill's *American Scenery*, a series of aquatints done in the 1820s.

A challenge to American landscape engraving came in 1836, when the English publisher George Virtue established a foothold in New York through the agency of Robert Martin. The most important work he had to promote was *American Scenery*, with text by Nathaniel Parker Willis, an American, and pictures by William Henry Bartlett, an English artist already skilled in landscape painting for engravers. English engravers were employed, and part 1 was published in June 1837, part 30 in November 1839, a total of 120 plates. The work was produced in London, although the paper covers of the American parts carried a price in dollars. This foothold enabled Virtue to sell his other landscape volumes, and his rival Fisher, Son and Co. also had a New York agency about 1843. *Canadian Scenery* by the same author and artist came out in 1840 and 1841 with another 120 plates, forming a considerable corpus of North American views. This was to provide a rich mine from which American publishers extracted material for the rest of the century, copying pictures by re-engraving on steel or wood. This aspect has been painstakingly researched by Dr Eugene Worman, jun., in his two articles on *W.H. Bartlett and American ... Illustration*. It appears that Virtue actually published very few titles from their American offices until they withdrew in 1879, thus being a minimal threat to publishers producing local material.

In 1842, *Georgia Illustrated in a Series of Views Engraved on Steel by Rawdon, Wright, Hatch and Smillie* after sketches by T.A. Richards and text by W.C. Richards was published. James Smillie, a Scot by birth, was regarded as the pre-eminent landscape engraver in America, and his most commended work was 'The Rocky mountains' after A. Bierstadt in 1864.

The National Gallery of American Landscape, published in New York by W. Pate and Co. contained plates by James David Smillie (1833–after 1906), son of James, J.I. Pease, Henry S. Beckwith (fl. 1835–1900), working in New York in 1842–43 with Alfred Jones (1819–1900), Robert Hinshelwood (b. 1812), another Scot, who married James Smillie's sister, and William Wellstood (1819–1900), yet another Scot who went to the United States in 1830.

Probably the last landscape steel engravings appeared in *Picturesque America; or the Land We Live in . . .* (New York, D. Appleton and Co., 1874) edited by William C. Bryant and consisting of two volumes with 47 steel engravings and two engraved title pages. They were engraved by R. Hinshelwood, W. Wellstood and Samuel Valentine Hunt (1803–93) who came to America from Norwich in 1834. There were also 800 text illustrations done mainly on wood. Some copies were hand coloured at publication, and one of these sets was used to produce a modern edition of the steel engravings as recently as 1974.

Journals and magazines also carried steel engravings, foremost among which was the *New York Mirror; a Weekly Journal Devoted to Literature and the Fine Arts*, begun in 1823. Of the most important plates done for it was A.B. Durand's portrait of George Washington after R.W. Weir, in 1831 and the following year, Durand's portrait of J.H. Hackett after H. Inman appeared. Durand's engraving career of 15 years ended in 1835 with the publication of 'Ariadne' after John Vanderlyn. From 1832 to 1836 James Smillie engraved a series of plates after R.W. Weir, and in 1834 A.W. Graham, newly arrived from England, contributed some good views.

Godey's Lady's Book, established in 1830 in Philadelphia by Louis A. Godey was the longest running and most important magazine for ladies, closing in 1898. Throughout its career it was embellished by illustrations, some of them steel engravings, done by engravers such as Alfred Jones, W.H. Ellis (fl. 1845–47), Francis Kearny who did 'The Cottage' after Westall and Alexander L. Dick (*c*.1805–*c*.1855) who was a pupil of Robert Scott in Edinburgh. He emigrated to New York City in 1833 and established an engraving firm there. He contributed to a number of magazines, producing full-size copies of existing prints indistinguishable from the originals, such as those after W.H. Bartlett, done originally for the numerous publications issued by George Virtue.

Other cities soon followed suit. From Boston came *The Ladies Repository* about 1831, which was still going in 1874. Engravers represented were

Joseph Andrews who went to London and from 1835 worked with Joseph Goodyear (1797–1839) and had three spells in Paris before settling again in the United States. D. Lloyd Glover (fl. 1846–55) was in Boston and New York, Charles A. Jewett (1816–78) and Co. of New York and Cincinnatti, Ohio, Oliver Pelton (1799–after 1860) of Boston, and A. Coolidge Warren (1819–1904), who worked with Andrews for a year, and while spending most of his life in Boston, moved to New York in 1863.

In New York there was *The Ladies Companion* begun 1834, still running in 1844. From 1839 to 1844 23 of W.H. Bartlett's scenes were engraved by A.L. Dielo (fl. 1840), Milo Osborn (fl. 1836–44), about whom little is known since 'he became dissipated and disappeared' (Stauffer, 1907, p. 195), and Joseph Napoleon Gimbrede (b.1820), pupil of his uncle J.F.E. Prud'homme.

George R. Graham of Philadelphia ran about four magazines there including his own *Graham's Magazine* which began in 1840. He required a plate for each number, among the engravers for which was John Sartain, who was also responsible for supplying impressions. By the second year the print run had risen to 40,000 and, in order to meet deadlines, Sartain was obliged to engrave *four* steel plates of each subject. Other engravers were A.L. Dick, J. Dill (fl. 1849) of New York, G. Mills (fl. 1842) and Rawdon, Wright and Hatch, New York. This firm comprised Freeman Rawdon (1804–after 1860), probably G. Wright (fl. 1837) and George W. Hatch (1805–67). They were joined after 1842 by James Smillie.

The Columbian … Magazine (New York) ran from 1844 to 1849, and in this short time, took work from A.L. Dick, Eli (perhaps J.E.) Dill, J. White, Elliot Reed, M. Osborn, J.F.E. Prud'homme and James Bannister (fl. 1830–1900), an apprentice of A.L. Dick.

Works of literature were also illustrated with steel engravings. One volume which typifies the work of the time is John Greenleaf Whittier's *Poems* … illustrated by H. Billings, published in Boston by Benjamin B. Mussey and Co. in 1849. It contains nine vignette steel engravings, three at least printed by R. Andrews. The frontispiece is a portrait of the author (Plate 156) after A.G. Hoit, engraved by A.C. Warren, and the engraved title-page vignette 'The Norsemen' engraved by Joseph Andrews and James Duthie (fl. 1848–60) (Plate 157) who together engraved two other plates in the volume. Warren also engraved '[The Bridal of Pennacook]' (Plate 158) and one other plate. D. Lloyd Glover contributed three plates.

Lord Byron's *Works*, published in New York by F. Felt [*c.*1850] contained six steel engravings, and in 1871, Johnson, Fry and Co. produced *The Byron and Moore Gallery; a Series of Characteristic Illustrations by Eminent Artists* … comprising 79 plates after, for example, Bartlett, Frith, Corbould and Stephanoff were engraved by James Bannister, Rice and Buttre i.e. W.W.

156 John G. Whittier, engraved by A.C. Warren

Rice (fl. 1846–60) and John Chester Buttre (1821–93), New York, R.F. Soper (fl. 1831–71), Buttre's assistant, and James Smillie.

An edition of J. Fenimore Cooper's *Novels* was published in New York by Townsend in 1859–61. The frontispieces and engraved title pages were designed by Felix Octavius Carr Darley, and engravers included were James Duthie, James David Smillie, Thomas Phillibrown (1808–72) and J.W. Paradise. The same artist and publisher followed this by *The Works of Charles Dickens* (1862–65), the last volumes of which were published by Hurd and Houghton in 1866. There were 55 volumes, each with a frontispiece and engraved title page. William C. Bryant's *A New Library of Poetry and Song* ... (New York, Ford and Co. 2 vols, [1876]) contained 18 steel-engraved portraits, with other illustrations.

F.O.C. Darley was also employed to illustrate a three-volume work by

157 Engraved title page of *Poems by John G. Whittier*, engraved by J. Andrews and J. Duthie

AMERICAN STEEL ENGRAVING 339

158 [The Bridal of Pennacook], engraved by A.C. Warren

Robert Tomes *The War with the South*, published in New York by Virtue and Co. (1862–67). Illustrated with steel engravings, it came out in about 30 parts, the cover of each of which was decorated with a wood engraving (Plate 159). As with the author's earlier work, *Battles of America* ... (3 vols,

159 Part cover with wood engraved illustration for part 4 of Tomes's *The War with the South*

1861), most of the engravers were English. Another volume on the same theme by J.L. Wilson *The Pictorial History of the Great Civil War* ... (Philadelphia, National Publishing Co., [1881]) contained 22 steel engravings with 19 on wood.

Art is represented by William J. Clark's *Great American Sculptures* (Philadelphia 1878) which contained 12 steel engravings. It was reprinted by Garland Publishing in 1975. Among the last books to contain steel engravings was G.W. Sheldon's *Hours with Artists* (New York, Appleton, 1882) which contained 'The Strawberry girl' after Deconink engraved by Smith.

The Art Unions used mezzotint on steel in the early days, until membership had exceeded the print run obtainable from such plates. They were of a size to make it impracticable to prepare duplicate plates, so line engraving became the dominant process after about 1848. The Art Union of Philadelphia's print for 1840 was a mezzotint by John Sartain of 'John Knox and Mary Queen of Scots' after Leutze. The Apollo Association for the advancement of the fine arts in the United States was formed in 1839, and its first print, in 1840, was also a mezzotint by Sartain 'General Marion ... inviting a British Officer to dinner' after J.B. White. In 1841 'The artist's dream' after G. Comegys was mezzotinted by Sartain, but for 1842 'Caius Marius on the ruins of Carthage' after J. Vanderlyn was engraved by Stephen Alonzo Schoff (1818–1905), who was taught by Oliver Pelton and Joseph Andrews. The 1843 plate was 'The Farmer's nooning' after W.S. Mount, engraved by Alfred Jones, and in 1844 the association became the American Art Union. They returned to mezzotint in 1847 with G.C. Bingham's 'The Jolly flat boat men' engraved by Thomas Doney (fl. 1845) who was of French origin, working in New York. Approximately 6,000 impressions were taken from this plate, but by 1848 the number of subscribers had risen to 10,000 which would overtax the plate and a change back to line engraving was necessary. 'The Image breaker' after Leutze, engraved by Alfred Jones 1850, was said to be one of the best engravings produced in the United States. W.S. Mount's 'Bargaining for a horse' in 1851 was engraved by Charles Burt (1823?–93) a pupil of W.H. Lizars, who arrived in the United States in 1836. He had also engraved 'The Card players' in 1850. T. Cole's 'Dream of Arcadia' was engraved by James Smillie for the American Art Union, which produced a *Bulletin* in which reduced copies of the premium plates were issued in an effort to promote subscriptions. There was a Western Art Union which also issued engravings.

The Western Methodist Book Concern in Cincinnatti, Ohio, was another agency which produced good engravings and employed William Wellstood as an engraver from 1846 to 1871.

Of other large prints for framing, Alfred Jones was among the foremost engravers. 'Sparking' after F.W. Edmonds in 1843, 'The new scholar' after

Edmonds in 1850, and 'Mexican news' after R.C. Woodville in 1851 came from his burin. J.I. Pease engraved 'Old '76 and young '48' after R.C. Woodville.

Print publishers included J.M. Butler of Philadelphia from 1850 with Fischel, Adler and Schwartz, Max Jacoby *circa* 1880 and M. Knoedler *circa* 1870 to 1890, all of New York.

After 1851 when transatlantic travel had improved a great deal, there were opportunities to import both plates and impressions after first publication in London. Dixon and Ross, London plate printers, offered selected steel plates for sale, and in 1851 a John M. Butler, plate printer of Philadelphia was negotiating for them at around $250 a plate. He was also prepared to take impressions 100 at a time, but goes on to remind the English printer that a good American mezzotinter could copy a plate for around $500. Dixon and Ross dealt with a number of firms in New York including Jacob and Myers, Philip Levy, William Stevens, Jacoby and Zeller and Schauss, with Charles Coggeshall in Chicago.

Many American steel engravers were originally from Scotland and England, and arrived already trained, coming in search of experience. A few came from Germany (Nuremberg, Darmstadt) especially in the 1850s and one or two from France. A very few were invited over for specific projects and in some cases returned again to the home country. There were many who changed between the various branches of engraving, going over to banknotes in particular as the most lucrative and enduring form of employment. Others abandoned engraving altogether in mid-career for painting or other branches of art. There were fewer dedicated 'career' engravers, and there were fewer still who only engraved on steel. On the whole, most steel engravers were trained through the usual route of apprenticeship, but others followed less traditional means of learning. James Smillie was self-educated and Alexander Anderson learned from an encyclopaedia. John Cheney read books, examined existing prints, made his own tools and hammered plates from an old copper boiler on which to engrave. A.B. Durand also made his own tools and hammered copper coins to make plates, while J.I. Pease used an awl on thermometer brass in his early days, and invented his own rolling press.

Engravers were among the founders and members of the National Academy of Design set up in 1826. They included M.I. Danforth, P. Maverick and J.W. Paradise.

There have been a number of catalogues of engravers' work published, among which was the checklist of John and Seth Cheney by S.R. Koehler, in Boston in 1891, Charles Burt, by Alice Burt in 1893 and A.B. Durand, Grolier Club in 1895.

One of the most prolific engravers who worked on both sides of the

Atlantic was John Rogers (*c.*1800–82). *Circa* 1830 he had a large workshop in Finchley, London where he employed several men working on engravings, and after a busy life producing steel plates for all sorts of publications he went to New York in 1851 at the request of the publisher George Virtue. He was to engrave portraits of eminent Americans from photographs for *The Panorama of the U.S.A.* Rogers had been chief engraver for Allen's *Panorama of London* (1830) in which Virtue also had a hand, thus establishing a connection resulting in this later commission. It lasted three years. It was typical of his character that no time could be wasted. While attending his son's wedding in Canada in 1854 he took a plate with him to engrave, but it is recorded that he 'did not do much at it'! He married twice (and possibly twice more according to family tradition) and died intestate at Jersey City on 26 April 1882. In some ways it is difficult to see why Rogers was needed to do portraits, since a good number of American engravers excelled in this field. Virtue, however, was in the habit of employing English engravers for his work, and must have thought Rogers was the best man for the job.

Another portrait engraver arrived in New York in 1850 with a brother, three sons and a daughter. Henry Bryan Hall (1808–94) set up business there and the group engraved a large number of portraits for the American market.

Twentieth-century steel engraving

The demise of steel engraving at the end of the 19th century left it surviving only in the production of banknotes, stamps, certificates and similar security printing operations.

One survival was the printing of Masonic certificates. In 1820 the design of the United Grand Lodge Certificate was changed to the 'Three pillar' form which was printed from 1824 by Sylvester and Warrington of 27 Strand, London. By 1907 the firm was Warrington of Garrick Street and by 1923 it had become Brothers Warrington (Plate 160). Certificates were certainly steel engraved until 1936, and may even have been so until 1952, but at some date lithography replaced it.

During the first half of the century the value of steel engravings, monetarily and artistically was so slight that many were destroyed or damaged, thus increasing their rarity. Some were used to decorate other objects, such as paperweights, where portions of steel engravings were attached to the base of a glass shape. A tray, with four engravings covered by glass, was a product of the 1930s. The engravings are from James Elmes's *Metropolitan improvements*, published by Jones & Co. 1827–29. Copies of the book were being offered in 1933 for £1 1s. 0d., going up to £1 10s. 0d. in 1935. The artist was Thomas Shepherd, whose prints are now regarded as topographically, historically and architecturally valuable documents.

One story, vouched for by an antiquarian bookseller who was present at the incident, underlines these attitudes to steel-engraved books. In the early years of World War II there were drives of all sorts to conserve resources, one of which involved the recycling of paper. A stock of about 200 copies of William Tombleson's *Eighty Picturesque Views on the Thames and Medway* [1834] were brought in as waste paper, and he had the job of removing the plates before the text was pulped. The plates were then used to manufacture table-mats, where the engravings were placed under a clear film. The

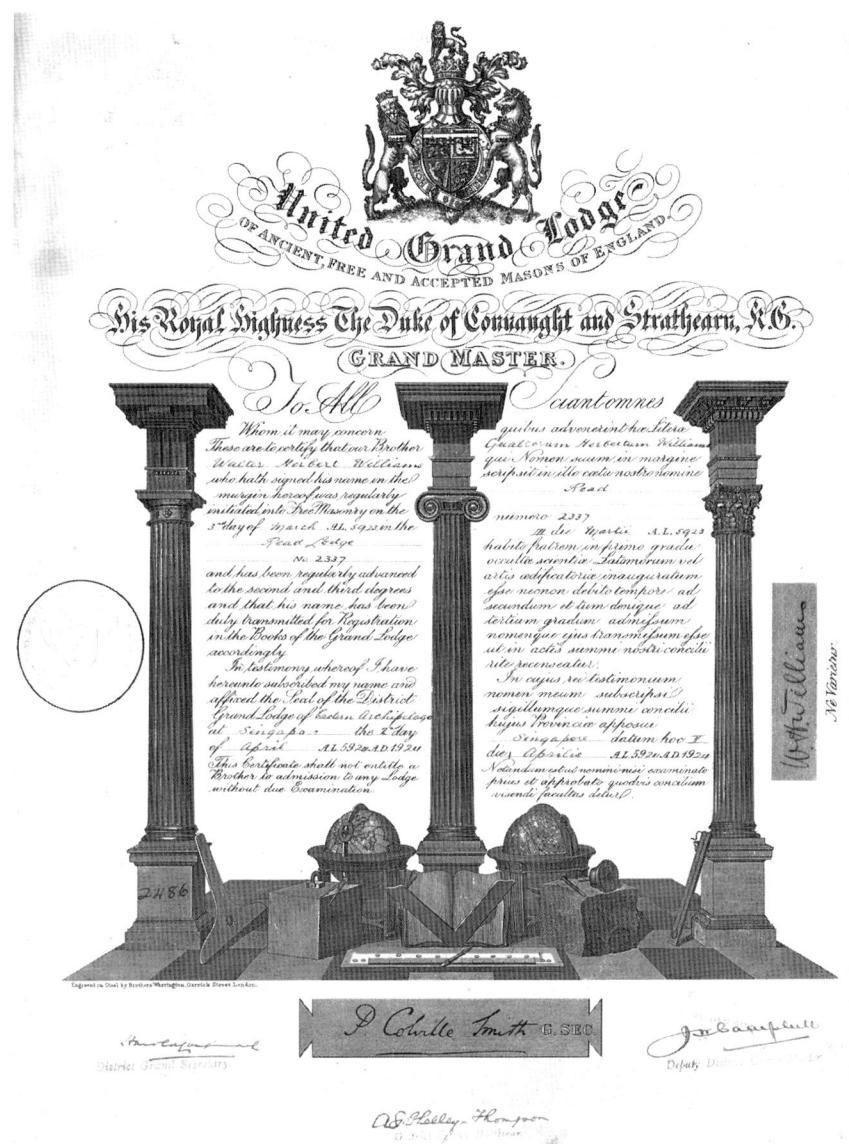

160   United Grand Lodge Masonic certificate, engraved by the Brothers Warrington

book now sells for around £500, and its views are used, in coloured reproduction, for trays or shiny, silver, reflective pictures. The whole book was reprinted lithographically in 1980.

After World War II, table mats and other household wares were decorated with steel engravings, reproduced by the half-tone process. 'The Walls of Southampton' was printed in colour with a black border, taken from William Beattie's *The Ports, Harbours*... (Virtue, 1842, vol. 2, p. 133) (Plate 161). 'View of the Railway Terminus, Brighton' was a vignette, printed in black with a green border. The artist was R.H. Nibbs, well known in Sussex, the engraver Thomas Jeavons and it was published by W. Grant, a Brighton bookseller in *circa* 1845 (Plate 162). The publishers of the mats, carrying six different views per set, issued prints of 18th- and 19th-century engravings and etchings in their range of over 50 historic areas covering Britain.

The art of steel engraving came full circle in the 1960–70 period, when steel engravings were etched on to stainless steel plates, mounted on a canvas background and framed. One such series was made by Omicways Ltd of Bude in Cornwall, hand produced by craftsmen and marketed as Connoisseur Steel Reproductions. 'Sea coast' was over twice the size of the 19th-century engraving, which was drawn by David Cox and engraved by

161   Table-mat, *c.*1970, reproducing The Walls of Southampton, engraved by J.C. Armytage

162   Table-mat, *c.*1980, reproducing View of the Railway Terminus, Brighton, engraved by T. Jeavons

Robert Brandard, probably for the *Gallery of Modern British Artists* (1836). The background in this case was red.

In 1986, Philip Mansergh of St Albans published the first of a series of six *Fine British Print Calendar with Views of Britain from the Great Age of British Engraving 1810–45*. Aquatints were also included, each engraving was coloured and gradually the period covered was extended to 1800–50. The product was attractive enough to catch the eye of a High Street bank, whose logo was superimposed on each page. The print on the calendar for 1988 is 'Lincoln from the castle' after Thomas Allom, engraved by Frederick James Havell for Thomas Noble and Thomas Rose's *The counties of Chester ... Lincoln ... illustrated* (Fisher, Son and Co., 1836) (Plate 163). The recession of the late 1980s and early 1990s put an end to the original format, the last coming out in 1992. The idea was revived in 1994, however, in a smaller format as *British Print Calendar 1995; Views of Britain from 19th Century Engravings*.

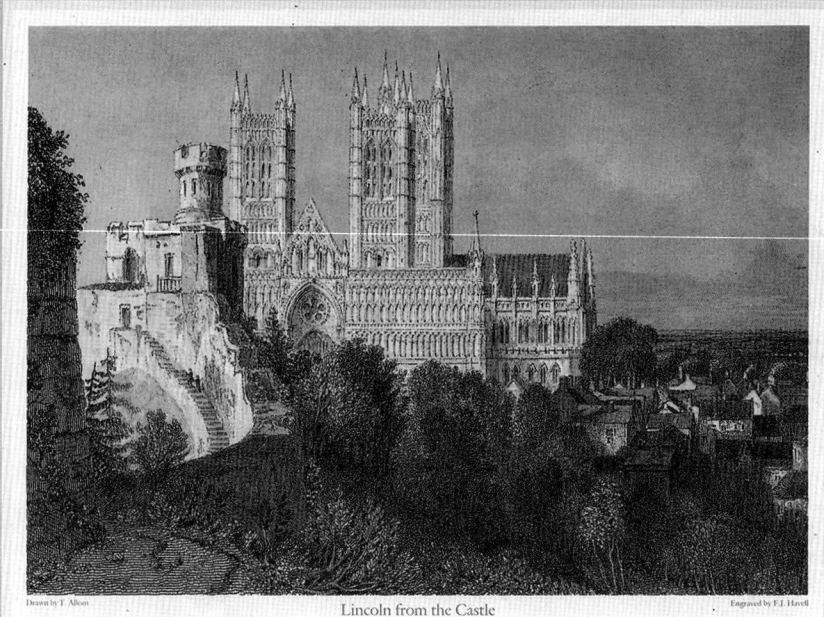

163   Fine British Print Calendar, 1988

The technique of steel engraving was virtually lost by artists in the first half of the century, except in the process of steel-facing, to the printing of which plates, David Strang (son of William Strang, see Chapter 6), devotes chapter XII concerning mainly etching in *The Printing of Etchings and Engravings* (Benn, 1930). Steel-facing usually covered the whole plate, but to obtain special effects, only selected areas of a plate were treated.

The use of steel plates revived in the post-World War II period for several reasons. In the schools and colleges of art steel was found to be cheaper than copper, and so a number of students were trained to use it, and did so for selected plates. The smoothness of steel enables a clean transfer of ink, and it was also useful in producing coloured plates because it was said that it does not chemically distort the ink. The use of black mild steel and the mordants employed, although rarely, by modern engravers, is dealt with in an essay by Jack Shireff on etching and engraving in *A Complete Guide to Print Making* (1975), edited by Stephen Russ. Monica Macdonald Ralph of Brighton is one such engraver who used steel upon which to etch 'Stubble plain' in 1991, and printed it in brown ink (Plate 164). Her 'Watermeadow' (1991) was printed from three separate steel plates, one for each colour, a process unsuccessfully attempted in the 19th century (see colour plate 8).

In the United States of America, Robert D. Swartley works more in the

164   Stubble plain, etched by M.M. Ralph

165   Jasper, engraved by R.D. Swartley

line tradition, printing mainly in brown ink. 'Jasper' c. 1986 (Plate 165) is one of his larger plates and exhibits a wide variety of line, but in his engraving of an elk, in 1987, he has achieved great variation in his treatment of fur by the use of short fine lines set at different angles (Plate 166). This design was done for the Classic Arms Corporation. He has also engraved labels for wine bottles.

Arne Lundell (1915–91) was born at Morgongåva in Sweden, and produced a number of steel engravings, some after Dürer and Rembrandt. Of his original works there was 'Havadikt' in 1978, 'Fragment' in 1980 and 'Snäcksång' in 1981, which was an abstract design of some contrast. This was followed by 'Vårkänning' in 1983, an intricate design of a view along a river through trees, which used the tonal properties of steel engraving to the full. 'Alar vid gölen' was produced in 1987. He was still working at the age of 82.

166   Elk, engraved by R.D. Swartley

Another form of engraving on steel which flourishes in the 20th century is that of gun engraving in firms which were established in the 19th century and earlier. A demand arose from landowners and other wealthy people for a 'made-to-measure' gun, which can cost between £20,000 and £40,000 each. Some are bought as works of art and never fired, and the engraving accounts for much of the visible artistic decoration. The designs still follow traditional patterns, although customers can express their own preferences, such as one for whom a girl with a billowing skirt was engraved. Martin Smith took eight months to engrave it; he works for the London firm of Watson Bros. Other such engravers are Keith Thomas of Aylesbury, and Peter Rose of Crawley Down.

Robert Legg of Rotherhithe engraves on objects made of steel, e.g. boxes, mirrors, spoons, etc. and Martin Page of north-west London produces jewellery in steel. Taking this a step further, 20th-century sculpture has used steel as a medium, especially in America where there are about a dozen exponents of the art of direct-metal sculpture, such as Willard Baepple, Peter Forakis, Arthur Gibbons, John Sanders, Ann Sperry, and Marja Vallila.

Steel engravings have played a humble part in one or two literary works of note. In *Cold Comfort Farm* by Stella Gibbons, first published in 1932, Flora had slept her first night in one of the farm's bedrooms, and when she woke the next morning she took stock of her surroundings. On the walls of her room there were two steel engravings, one of the 'Grief of Andromache beholding the dead body of Hector' and the 'Captivity of Zenobia, Queen of Palmyra'. They were obviously treated as a pair since their frames were of light yellow wood. Her reaction to their rather dismal message was not recorded; she was much too interested in some Victorian novels laying on the window-sill.

A more unlikely use for a steel engraving was found in George Orwell's *1984*, first published in 1949. Winston Smith rented an upper room in a house from Mr Charrington who turned out to be a member of the Thought Police. It was he who found Winston and his girlfriend Julia together, seeing them on a telescreen set into one wall of the room. This screen was covered (probably illegally) by a steel engraving of St Clement Danes Church. It is tempting to speculate that the engraving in question was from Thomas Shepherd's *London and its Environs* published in 1829.

Tyler Whittle's *Albert and Victoria* (Heinemann, 1972, chapter 10) writes of an altercation between the Queen and Lady Lyttelton over a steel engraving of 'The first prayer of H.R.H. Prince Albert Edward, Prince of Wales [etc.]', where the infant, lying on a cushion, was shown to be repeating a prayer requesting that England be always powerful and happy. Lady Lyttelton thought this improper, and the Queen was persuaded to agree.

During the 1980s, publishers have seen a market in re-publishing, more or less in their entirety, certain popular steel engraved works. Tombleson's *Eighty Picturesque Views on the Thames* ... and Moule's *English Counties* have already been noticed. R.M. Martin's *The Illustrated Atlas and Modern History of the World*, originally published in 1851 by John Tallis, came out in 1989 published by Bracken Books. Thomas Shepherd's *London and its Environs* (1829) was issued as *London in the Nineteenth Century* by Bracken Books in 1983 and the same artist's *Modern Athens* (1829) as *Rare engravings of Old Edinburgh*, published by Lang Syne Publishers Ltd, in 1980.

Finally, the first public exhibition devoted entirely to steel engraving was held at Ditchling Museum, East Sussex, in August/September 1990. It was opened by John Heath CBE, a descendant of James Heath, the King's engraver (third from left), and brought together descendants of the engravers James Carter (first and fourth from left) and Robert Baker (second from right), together with Michael Virtue, descendant of the 19th-century publisher George Virtue (first at right) (Plate 167). The exhibition was subsequently shown in Lewes at Anne of Cleves House, and a catalogue was issued for each occasion.

Steel engravings have now met up with the electronic era in the form of a CD-ROM, 'Clip Victoriana'. This reproduces steel and wood engravings to

20TH-CENTURY STEEL ENGRAVING 353

167   Exhibition at Ditchling Museum, 1991

illustrate various aspects of Victorian life, to be used as motifs in constructing a new artistic entity. 'Currency; the art of paper money' is another CD-ROM where steel engraved and other images are presented as a 'clip art' source.

Sources

Place of publication is London, unless stated otherwise.

Chapter One

Akehurst, R. *The world of guns*, Hamlyn, 1972.
Archaeologia, vol xxiii, 1827, pp. 106–113.
Armstrong, N. *Jewellery: an historical survey of British styles and jewels*, Guildford, Lutterworth Press, 1973.
Ashdown, C.H. *European Arms and Armour ...*, New York, Brussel and Brussel, 1967.
Ashton, T.S. *Iron and Steel in the Industrial Revolution*, 4th edn, Manchester, Manchester University Press, 1968.
Ball, J. *William Caslon 1693–1766*, Kineton, Roundwood Press, 1973.
Boardman, J. *Engraved Gems: the Ionides Collection*, Thames and Hudson, 1968.
[Brailsford, J.W.] *Later Prehistoric Antiquities of the British Isles*, British Museum, 1956.
Bull, S. *An historical guide to arms and armour*, Cassell, 1991.
Clifford, A. *Cut Steel and Berlin Iron Jewellery*, Bath, Adams and Dart, 1971.
Delieb, E. *The Great Silver Manufactory: Matthew Boulton and the Birmingham silversmiths 1760–1790*, Studio Vista, 1971.
Dictionarium polygraphicum; or the whole body of the arts regularly digested [by John Barrow] C. Hitch and L. Hawes. 2nd ed. 1758 2 vols. Vol. 1, pp. 292–8.
Ffoulkes, C.J. *The Armourer and his Craft, from the XIth to the XVIth century*, Methuen, 1912.
Gibbs-Smith, C. *The Inventions of Leonardo da Vinci*, Oxford, Phaidon Press, 1978.

Gill, T. *The Technical Repository.* Gill: Vol. 6, pp. 8–18; 275–88, 1830.
Grierson, P. *Numismatics,* Oxford University Press, 1975.
Henderson, J. *Sword Collecting for Amateurs,* Muller, 1969.
Hind, A.M. *A History of Engraving and Etching from the 15th century to the year 1914,* 3rd edn, Constable, 1923.
Honour, H. *Goldsmiths and Silversmiths,* Weidenfeld and Nicolson, 1971.
Hughes, G. *The Art of Jewelry,* Studio Vista, 1972.
Köttenstorter, H. 'Die Stahlschnittkunst in Steyn', *Oberösterreich Kulturzeitschrift,* Jg. 29, 1979, H.4, pp. 55–9.
Lever, C. *Goldsmiths and Silversmiths of England,* Hutchinson, 1975.
Lightbown, R.W. *Secular Goldsmith's Work in Medieval France: a History,* Society of Antiquaries of London, [Thames and Hudson], 1978.
Lumsden, E.S. *The Art of Etching...,* Seeley, Service and Co., 1924.
Macklin, H.W. *Brasses of England,* Methuen, 1907.
McMurtrie, D.C. *The Book,* 3rd edn, Oxford University Press, 1943.
Meier, H. 'The origins of the printing and roller press', *The Print Collector's Quarterly USA,* Kansas City, vol. 28, 1941 (summarized in Printing Historical Society, *Bulletin* 25, Autumn, 1988, pp. 2–8).
Merrifield, M.P. *Original Treatises dating from the XIIth to XVIIth centuries, on the Arts of Painting,* 2 vols, Murray, 1849.
Middleton, B.C. *A History of English Craft Bookbinding Techniques,* New York, Hafner Publishing Co., 1963.
Moxon, J. *Mechanick Exercises,* 1683, (reprinted Oxford, 1962).
Needham, P. *Twelve Centuries of Bookbinding, 400–1600,* New York and London, Pierpoint Morgan Library and Oxford University Press, 1979.
Norris, M. *Brass rubbing,* Studio Vista, 1965.
Page-Phillips, J. *Macklin's Monumental Brasses, including a bibliography and list of figure brasses remaining in churches in the United Kingdom, re-written by John Page-Phillips,* Allen and Unwin, 1969.
Pardoe, F.E. *John Baskerville of Birmingham,* Muller, 1975.
Perry, E. *Collecting Antique Metalware,* Country Life Books, 1974.
Pollen, J.H. *Gold and Silver Smith's Work,* Chapman and Hall, [1879].
Pottinger, D.T. 'History of the printing press', *The Dolphin,* vol. 3, 1938, pp. 323–44.
Reed, T.B. *A History of the Old English Letter Foundries,* [2nd edn], Faber, 1952.
Ricketts, H. *Firearms,* Weidenfeld and Nicolson, 1964.
Roads, C. *The Gun,* British Broadcasting Corporation, 1978.
Rosa, J.G. and May, R. *The Pleasure of Guns,* Octopus Books, 1974
Sargeaunt, B.G. *Weapons...,* Hugh Rees, 1908.
Schubert, H.R. *History of the British Iron and Steel Industry from c. 450 BC to AD 1775,* Routledge and Kegan Paul, 1957.

Singer, C. and others *A History of Technology* ..., 5 vols, Oxford, Clarendon Press, 1954–58.
Suffling, E.R. *English Church Brasses from the 13th to the 17th Century*, L. Upcott Gill, 1910.
Thieme, U. and Becker, F. *Allgemeines Lexikon des bildenden Kunstler* ..., 37 vols, Leipzig, Englemann and Seeman, 1907–50.
Thomas, A.G. *Great books and book collectors*, Chancellor Press, 1975.
Trivick, H.H. *The Craft and Design of Monumental Brasses*, John Baker, 1969.
Uccelli, A. *Storia della Tecnica del Medio Evo ai Nostri Giomi*, Milan, Hoepli, 1945.
Updike, D.B. *Printing Types* ..., 3rd edn, 3 vols, Cambridge, Mass, Belknapp Press of Harvard U.P., 1962.
Wilkinson-Latham, R. *Antique Guns in Colour to 1865*, Poole, Blandford Press, 1977.
Williams, A.R. 'Methods of manufacture of swords in medieval Europe...', *Gladius; études sur les armes anciennes*, vol. 13, 1977, pp. 75–127.
Willsberger, J. *Gold*, New York, Doubleday and Co, Inc., 1976.
Wilson, D.M. 'An Anglo-Saxon bookbinding at Fulda', *Archaeological Journal*, 1961, pp. 199–206.
Zigrosser, C. *Six Centuries of Fine Prints*, Williams and Norgate, 1938.

Chapter Two

Australian Dictionary of Biography, 7 vols, Melbourne, University Press, 1966–76.
Bathe, G. and D. *Jacob Perkins: his inventions, his times and his contemporaries*, Philadelphia, Historical Society of Pennsylvania, 1943.
Dictionary of American Biography, 22 vols, New York, Scribners, 1928–58.
Eichner-Larsen, I. *Mesteren Cz. Slania; biografi og Katalog*, Aarhus, Aarhus Frimaerkehandel, 1986.
Facit Special 1994–5, Stockholm, Facit Forlags, 1994 [stamp catalogue].
Gibbons, S. *Priced Postage Stamp Catalogue*, various sections, Stanley Gibbons Ltd, various dates.
Gould, B. *Monsieur Duret, Craftsman at Soho* (typescript of an article submitted to *Birmingham Post* May 1969).
Harris, E. 'Experimental graphic processes in England 1800–1850', *Journal of the Printing Historical Society*, vol. 4, 1968.
Heath, C. Correspondence with Dawson Turner in the archive of Trinity College, Cambridge. Transcribed by J.M. Heath.
Heath, J.D. *History of Perkins, Bacon*, privately published, [*c.*1906].

Hollender, K. *Scripophily: collecting bonds and share certificates*, Ward, Lock, 1982.
Lafaurie, J. *Les assignats et les papier-mionnaies émir par L'Etat au XVIIIe siècle*, Paris, 1951.
Lister, R. *Prints and Printmaking: a dictionary and handbook of the art in nineteenth-century Britain*, Methuen, 1984.
Mackay, J. 'The Anatomy of a share certificate', *International Bond and Share Society Journal*, March, 1992, pp. 28–32.
Monestier, M. *The Art of Paper Currency*, Quartet Books, 1983.
Narberth, C. and others *Collecting Paper Money and Bonds*, Studio Vista, 1979.
Narbeth, C. *Collecting Paper Money*, Seaby, 1986.
Pick, A. *Catalogue of European Paper Money since 1900*, 2nd edn, New York, Sterling Publishing Co. Inc., 1974.
Purves, J.R.W. *The Half Lengths of Victoria*, Royal Philatelic Society, 1953.
Samuel, M. 'Security printing by Jacob Perkins before 1840', *London Philatelist*, vol. 91, 1981–82, pp. 32–9, 58–62, 86–8.
Society of Arts, *Report of the committee relative to the mode of preventing the Forgery of Banknotes*, Society of Arts, 1819.
Veyrin-Forrer, J. and Mercier, A. 'Contribution á l'étude iconographique des assignats', *Nouvelles de l'estampe*, July–August, no. 106, 1989, pp. 25–37.
Watenkampf, F. *American Graphic Art*, New York, Henry Holt, 1912.

Chapter Three

Arnold's Magazine of the Fine Arts, Arnold, 1834.
Balston, T. *John Martin 1789–1854*, Duckworth and Co. Ltd, 1947.
Campbell, M.J. *John Martin; Visionary, Printmaker*, Scolar Press, 1993.
Cooke, E.W. Diaries, 1829, unpublished, transcribed by John Munday FSA.
[Cooke, W.B.] *Exhibition of Engravings, by Living British Artists; Associated under the Patronage of His Majesty. 1st Exhibition*, 9 Soho Square, printed at the Apollo Press by J. Johnson, 1821.
[Cooke, W.B.] *Exhibition of Drawings and Engravings by British Artists*, 9 Soho Square, 1823, second exhibition.
Dyson, A. *Pictures to Print: the nineteenth-century engraving trade*, Farrand Press, 1984.
Edwards, E. *The Fine Arts in England*. Saunders and Otley, 1840.
Engen, R.K. *Dictionary of Victorian Engravers* ... Cambridge, Chadwyck-Healey, 1979.
European Magazine, vol. 83, January 1823, p. 57.
Guise, H. *Great Victorian Engravings: a collector's guide*, Astragal Books, 1980.

Lister, R. *Prints and printmaking: dictionary and handbook of the art in nineteenth-century Britain*, Methuen, 1984.
[Manning, E.] *Colnaghi's 1760–1960*, [Colnaghi], 1960.
[Martin, J.] House of Commons Report from the Select Committee on arts and their connection with manufactures. 1835–6, Part 2, paras 867–8.
Muir, P. *Victorian Illustrated Books*, Batsford, 1971 (revised 1985).
Parris, L. and others *Constable: paintings, watercolours and drawings*, Tate Gallery, 1976.
Rawlinson, W.G. *The Engraved Works of J.M.W. Turner R.A.*, 2 vols, Macmillan and Co., 1908–13.
Salaman, M. *Old English Mezzotints*, 'The Studio' Ltd, 1910.
Shain, M. 'Mezzotint engraving or, la manière anglaise', *Antiquarian Book Monthly Review*, May–July, 1976, pp. 124–9, 180–7.
Thomas, A.G. *Great books and book collectors*, Chancellor Press, 1975, p. 161.
Tuer, A.W. *Bartolozzi and his Works*, 2 vols, Field and Tuer, 1881.
Wax, C. *The Mezzotint; History and Technique*, Thames and Hudson, 1990.
Whitman, A. *Samuel Cousins*, Bell, 1904.
Whitman, A. *Samuel William Reynolds*, Bell, 1903.
Whitman, A. *Charles Turner*, Bell, 1907.
Williams, D.E. *The Life and Correspondence of Sir Thomas Lawrence Kt*, Colburn and Bentley, 1831. 2 vols. Vol 2, p. 486.

Chapter Four

Burgess, F.W. *Old Prints and Engravings*, Routledge, 1924.
Hodson, J.S. *An Historical and Practical Guide to Art Illustration*, 1884.
Hunnisett, B. 'Broad stone of honour; Ehrenbreitstein', *Antiquarian Book Monthly Review*, vol. XIV, no. 2, February, 1987, pp. 101–3.
Hunnisett, B. 'Steel engraved scenes from India', *Antiquarian Book Monthly Review*, vol. XIII, no. 7, July, 1986, pp. 256–61.
Lewis, C.T.C. *George Baxter*, Sampson Low, 1908, (re-published 1972).
Mitzman, Max. *George Baxter and the Prints*, Newton Abbot, David and Charles, 1978.
Smith, J.T. *The Antiques of Westminster*, 1807.

Chapter Five

Agnew's 1817–1967, Agnew, 1967.
Art Union/Journal, 1839, 1841, 1843, 1868–69, 1872, 1874.
Baynton-Williams, R. *Investing in Maps*, Barrie and Rockliff, 1969.
Booth, J. *Looking at Old Maps*, Westbury, Cambridge House Books, 1979.

Darlington, I. and Howgego, J. *Printed Maps of London, Circa 1553–1850*, George Philip and Son Ltd, 1964.
Fincham, H.W. *The Artists and Engravers of British and American Book Plates...*, Kegan, Paul, 1897.
Guise, H. *Great Victorian Engravings: a collector's guide*, Astragal Books, 1980.
Heath, J. *The Heath Family Engravers, 1779–1878*, 2 vols, Scolar Press, 1993.
Illustrated London News, 14 December 1867, p. 647.
Maas, J. *Gambart, Prince of the Victorian Art World*, Barrie and Jenkins, 1975.
'Oxford Almanacks', *The Art Journal*, 1904, pp. 244–7.
Petter, H.M. *The Oxford Almanacks*, Oxford, Clarendon Press, 1974.
Smith, D. *Victorian Maps of the British Isles*, Batsford, 1985.
Tooley, R.V. *A Dictionary of Map Makers...*, Tring, Map Collector Publications, 1979.
Vinycomb, J. *On the Processes for the Production of Ex-libris (bookplates)...* A. and C. Black, 1894.

Chapter Six

Bain, I. 'Thomas Ross and Son...' *Journal of the Printing Historical Society*, no. 2, 1966, pp. 3–22.
Buchanan-Brown, J. *Phiz!*, Newton Abbot, David and Charles, 1978.
Cundal, H.M. *Birket Foster RWS*, A. and C. Black, 1906.
Evans, J. *The Endless Web: John Dickinson & Co. Ltd 1804–1954*, Cape, 1955.
Ford, J. and J. *Images of Brighton...*, St Helena Press, 1981.
Gray, B. *The English Print*, A. and C. Black, 1937.
Harvey, J.R. *Victorian Novelists and their Illustrators*, Sidgwick and Jackson, 1970.
Heck, J.G. *Iconographic Encyclopaedia of Science, Literature and Art*, 4 vols, New York, R. Garrigal, 1851.
Hollender, K. *Scripophily: collecting bonds and share certificates*, Ward, Lock, 1982.
Jenkins, P. 'Printing on parchment or vellum', *The Paper Conservator*, vol. 16, 1992, pp. 31–9.
Krill, J. *English Artists Paper...*, Trefoil Publications Ltd, 1987.
Lane, C. *Sporting Aquatints and their Engravers*, 2 vols, Leigh-on-sea, F. Lewis, 1978.
Ligterink, F.J. and others 'Foxing stains...', *The Paper Conservator*, vol. 15, 1991, pp. 45–52.
Pomeroy, F.B., former owner of Thomas Ross and Son, plate printers, unpublished letter to the author.
Prideaux, S.T. *Aquatint Engraving*, Duckworth, 1909.

Schubert, H.R. *History of the British Iron and Steel Industry from c.450 BC to AD 1775*, Routledge and Kegan Paul, 1957.
Society of Arts *Report of the committee relative to the mode of preventing the Forgery of Banknotes*, Society of Arts, 1819.
Sutton, T. *The Daniells, Artists and Travellers*, Bodley Head, 1954.
The Technical Repository, vol. 3, 1823.
Tomlinson, C. *Cyclopaedia of Useful Arts ...*, vol. 2, Virtue, 1852–54, pp. 357–74.

Chapter Seven

Altman, J. *Discover Germany*, Berlitz, 1994.
Barth, C. *Die Kupferstecherei, oder die Kunst in Kupfer zu stechen und zu azen*. Vol. 2, Practical volume, Section VI on steel engraving, Hildburghausen, Verlag der Kesselringschen Hofbuchhandlung, 1837, (volume 1 is a German translation of Giuseppe Longhi's *La Calcografia propriamente ditta, ossi a l'arte d'incidero in rame coll'acqua-forte, col bulino e colla punta*. Milan, 1830–31, of which only the first volume was published).
Fulbrook, M. *A Concise History of Germany, Updated Edition*, Cambridge University Press, 1993.
Gürsching, H. 'Nurnberg und der Stahlstich', *Mittelungen des Vereins für Geschichte der Städt Nuremberg*, Vol. 40, 1949, pp. 207–35.
Hardie, M. *Frederick Goulding [1842–1909] master printer of copper plates*, Stirling. E. Mackay, 1910.
Hauser, H. *Ansichten vom Rhein; Stahlstichbücher des 19 Jahrhunderts. Darstellung und Bibliographie*, Köln, Greven Verlag, 1963.
Heck, J.G. *The Complete Encyclopaedia of Illustration*, New York, Park Lane, 1979. (Reprint of *Iconographic Encyclopaedia of Science...1851*)
Hölscher, Dr E. *Stahlstich in alter und Neuer Zeit*, Leipzig, Graphischen Werkstätten Gerhardt und Teltow, 1937, (especially pp. 13–20).
Lanckoronska, M. and Rümann, A. *Geschichte der deutschen Taschenbucher und Almanacke* , Munich, 1954.
Leigmayer, F.X.M. *Eisen-und Stahlschnitt [Iron and steel cutting]*, Linz, Oberösterreichischer Landesverlag, 1959.
Marsh, A. *Meyer's Universum; Ein Beitrag zur des Stahlstiches und des Verlagswesen im 19 Jahrhundert*, Luneberg, Nordosdeutches Kulturwerk, 1972, (Schriftenreihe Nordost-Archiv no. 3).
Naumann, R. *Archiv für die Zeichnenden Künste mit besonderer bezlehung auf kupferstecher- und holzschnerdekunst und ihre geschichte*, Leipzig, Rudolf Weigel, 1860, pp. 228–9.
Rüm, I.B. *Das illustrierte Buch des XIX Jahrhunderts in England, Frankreich und Deutschland 1790–1860*, Leipzig, 1930.

Siebel, W. (ed.) *The New Germany*, APA Publications Ltd, 1992.
Spemann, A. *Masterpieces of Landscape Steel Engraving*, Stuttgart, A. Spemann, 1952.
Timm, R. (ed.) *Buchillustration im 19 Jahrhunderts*, Wiesbaden, Otto Harrassowitz, 1988.
Volkmann, K. 'Der Stahlstich als Buchillustration', *Zeitschrift für Bücherfreunde*, vol. 37, 1933.
Volkmann, K. 'Der Stahlstich als Kunstgattung', [Steel engraving in genre art] *Zeitschrift für Bückerfreunde*, vol. 39, 1935.
Volkmann, K. 'Der Landschaftsstahlstich', *Die Neue Schau*, 1955.
Vontin, W. *Carl Barth; Ein vergessener deutscher Bildruskünstler (1787–1859) [A forgotten German Illustrator]*, Hildburghausen, Verlag F.W. Gadow und Sohn, 1938.
Wood, C.S. *Albrecht Altdorfer and the Origins of Landscape*, Reakticon Books, 1993.

Chapter Eight

Adhémar, J. 'Le livre romantique', *La Portique*, vol. 5/6, 1947, pp. 93–110.
Andrews, W.L. *A trio of eighteenth century French engravers of portraits in miniature: Fiquet, Savant, Grateloup*, New York, Dodd, Mead and Co., 1899.
Art Journal, 1893, pp. 221–2, (Adolphe Goupil).
Beraldi, H. *Les graveurs du XIX siècle; guide de l'amateur d'estampes modernes*, 12 vols, Paris, L. Conquet, 1885–92, (reprinted 1981).
Bibliothèque Nationale, F. fr. MS. 22108 (Pièce 6, p. 338). Collection Anisson, 1680.
Bland, D. *A History of Book Illustration, the illuminated manuscript and the printed book*, 2nd edn, Faber, 1969.
Bouchot, H. *Le livre; l'Illustration, Illustration – La relvire étude historique sommaire*, Paris, Maison Quentin, 1886, Ch. 6.
Boucard, G. *Graveurs et gravures. France et l'étranger; essai de bibliographie 1540–1910*, Paris, H. Floury, 1910.
Carteret, L. *Le trésor du bibliophile, romantique et moderne 1801–1875*, 4 vols, Paris, L. Carteret, 1924–28, section 3 Livres illustrées du XIX siècle.
Courboin, F. and Roux, M. *La gravure française; essai de bibliographie*, vol. 1, Paris, M. Le Garrec, 1927.
Duportal, J. *Étude sur les livres à figures edités en France de 1606–1660*, Paris, Librairies Anciennes Honoré Champion, 1914.
Faucheux, L.E. *Catalogue raisonné de toutes les estampes qui forment les oeuvres gravés d'Étienne Ficquet [sic], Pierre Savart, J.B. Grateloup*, Paris 1864.
Firmin Didot. *Catalogue corrigé et augmenté. Principales publications de Firmin Didot frères, fils et Cie*, Paris, Firmin Didot, Janvier, 1862.

Gausseron, B.M.H. 'Les Keepsakes et les annuaires illustré de l'époque romantique', *Courrier du livre*, vol. 10, 25 November 1895, pp. 149–76, 25 December 1895, pp. 179–200.

Gusman, P. 'La gravure sur acier, sa technique et son histoire', *Byblis*, Autumn, 1926, pp. 87–94.

Gusman, P. 'La gravure à l'eau-forte sur acier. Procedé Vial', *Byblis*, Winter, 1925, pp. 139–42.

Laran, J. *L'Estampe*, 2 vols, Paris, Presses Universitaires de France, 1959.

Le Blanc, C. *Manuel de l'amateur de d'estampes*, 4 vols, Paris, E. Bouillon, 1854–90.

Lejard, A. (ed.) *The Art of the French Book*, Paul Elek, 1947, 'The French book in the XIX century (1801–70)' by P.H. Michel, assistant keeper Bibliothèque Mazarine.

Louvre, *Catalogue de la Chalcographie du Louvre*, Paris, Musées Nationaux. Palais du Louvre, 1954. Additional list 1960.

Ray, G. *The Art of the French Illustrated Book 1700–1914*, 2 vols, New York, Pierpoint Morgan Library, 1982, p. 322.

Vicaire, G. *Manuel de l'amateur de livres du XIX siècle 1801–1893*, 8 vols, Paris, 1894–1910, (reprinted 1974–75).

Chapter Nine

AUSTRIA

Hochenegg, H. *Die Tiroler Kupferstecher, Graphische Kunst in Tirol vom 16 bis Zur Mitte des 19 Jahrhunderts*, Innsbruck, Universitätsverlag Wagner, 1963.

Koschatsky, W. *Die Kunst der Graphik . . .*, 10th edn, München, Deutscher Taschenbuch Verlag, 1988.

Nebehay, I. and Wagner, R. *Bibliographie Altösterreichischer Ansichtenwerke aus fünf Jahrhunderten. Die monarchie in der topographischen Druckgraphik von der Schedel'schen Weltchronik bis zum Aufkommen der Photographie*. Graz, 3 vols, Akademische Druck-u, Verlagsanstalt, 1983.

Sotriffer, K. *Die Druckgraphik, Entwicklung, Technik, Eigenart*, revised edn, Wien, Schroll-Verlag, 1966.

BELGIUM

Lemman, F. and Thijs, A.K.L. Een dode vorstin, het Antwerpe stadsbestuur en 8000 schoolkinderen. (*Bijdragen tot de geschiedenis bijzonderlijk van het aloude Hertogdom Brabant*, vol. 77 (1994), pp. 195–222.)

HOLLAND

Kruseman, A.G. *Bouwstoffen voor een geschiedenis van den Nederlandschen Boekhandel, gedurende de halve eeuw 1830–1880*, 2 vols, Amsterdam, P.N. von Kampen and Zoon, 1886.

Van der Blom, A. 'De staalgravure in Nederland', *Kunst Laaft*, Amsterdam, no. 6, January, 1981.

Van der Blom, A. *Tekenen dat het gedrukt staal, 500 jaar grafich in Nederland*, Copenhagen, Kosmos, 1978, pp. 97–104.

Vervoorn, A.J. *Nederlandse preutkunst, 1840–1940*, Lochem, De Tijdstroom, 1983, pp. 46–52.

Waller, F.G. *Biographisch voordenbock van Noord Nederlandsche graveurs*, s'-Gravenhage, 1938, (reprinted Amsterdam, 1974).

ITALY

Art Journal, 1864.

Art Union, 1839, p, 63.

Hauser, H. *Ansichten vom Rhein; stahlstichbücher des 19 Jahrhunderts, Darstellung und bibliographie*, Cologne, Greven Verlag, 1963.

Pallottino, P. Letter to the author from Professoressa Paola Pallottino of the Museo dell'Illustrazione in Bologna, dated 20 August 1993.

SPAIN

Jega, L. 'La estampa aìlta eu el siglo XIX', *El grabado en España (siglos XIX–XX)*, Madrid, Esposa Elpa, 1988.

SWEDEN

Svenskt konstnärslexikon, [*c.*1967], vol. 5.

SWITZERLAND

Guidicetti, F. *Die Trachten Graubündens in der graphischen Darstellung des 19 Jahrhunderts*, Chur, Verlag M and T-Helvetica, [1988].

Longchamp, F.C. *Bibliographie générale des ouvrages publiés ou illustrés en Suisse et à l'étranger de 1475 à 1914 par des écrivains et des artistes suisses*, Paris, Librairie des Bibliophiles, 1922.

Wäber, A. *Landes-und Reisebeschreiburgen. Ein Beitrag zur Bibliographie der schweizerischen Reise-litteratur 1479–1890*, Bern, Wyss, 1899.

Chapter Ten

Baker, W.S. *American Engravers and their Works*, Philadelphia, Gebbie and Barrie, 1875.
Dyson, A. *Pictures to Print*, Farrand Press, 1984.
Durand, J. *Life of A.B. Durand*, 1894.
Fielding, M. *American Engravers upon Copper and Steel. A supplement to David McNeely Strauffer's American engravers*, Philadelphia, 1917, (republished as Vol. 3 by Oak Knoll Press, Delaware, 1994).
Groce, G.C. and Wallace, D.H. The New-York Historical Society's *Dictionary of Artists in America 1564–1860*, New Haven, Yale University Press, 1957.
Huttner, S.F. and E.S. *A Register of Artists, Engravers, booksellers, bookbinders, printers and publishers in New York City, 1821–42*, Bibliographical Society of America, [1994].
Jussim, E. *Visual Communication and the Graphic Arts*, New York, Bowker Co., 1974.
Rogers, G. Autobiography, 1906, [Unpublished].
Sartain, J. *The Reminiscences of a Very Old Man*, New York, Blom, 1899.
Stauffer, D.M. *American Engravers upon Copper and Steel...*, 2 vols, New York, Grolier Club, 1907, (republished by Oak Knoll Press, Delaware, in 3 vols, including Fielding's Supplement (q.v.) 1994).
Thompson, R. *American Literary Annuals and Gift Books 1825–65*, New York, H.W. Wilson Co., 1936, (reprinted Archon Books, 1967). About 465 volumes are listed in the Catalog, which are all available on microfilm.
Wax, C. *The Mezzotint: history and technique*, Thames and Hudson, 1990.
Weitenkampf, F. 'The evolution of steel engraving in America', *Bookbuyer*, series 3, vol. 23, 1901, pp. 93–5.
Weitenkampf, F. *American Graphic Art...*, New York, Henry Holt, 1912.
Worman, E.C. 'George Virtue's New York connection 1836–79', *AB Bookman's Weekly*, vol. 79, no 13, 30 March 1987, pp. 1350–63.
Worman, E.C. 'Virtue Company's New York publishing, 1836–54', *AB Bookman's Weekly*, vol. 87, no. 15, 15 April 1991, pp. 1486–1507.
Worman, E.C. 'W.H. Bartlett and American magazine illustration', *AB Bookman's Weekly*, vol. 89, no. 12, 23 March 1992, pp. 1114–33.
Worman, E.C. 'W.H. Bartlett and American book illustration', *AB Bookman's Weekly*, vol. 89, no. 16, 20 April 1992, pp. 1568–90.

Chapter Eleven

Daniels, H. *Printmaking...*, Hamlyn, 1971.
[Fearnside, W.G.] *Thames and Medway; Picturesque Views Engraved on Steel by the First Artists...*, The Bishopsgate Press Ltd, [1980], (reprint).

Firestone, E.R. 'In praise of steel; notes on some recent direct-metal sculpture', *Arts Magazine*, April 1986, pp. 44–9.

Lowther, T. 'Lock, stock and barrel ...', *Sunday Express Magazine*, 12 March 1995, pp. 29, 31–2.

Rothlind, J. *Svensk svart-vit grafik 1890–1900*, Lund, Bokförlaget Signum, 1992, pp. 199–201.

Russ, S. (ed.) *A Complete Guide to Printmaking*, Nelson, 1975, pp. 108, 113.

Singer, A. 'In living steel and stone; the work of Marja Vallila and James Buchman', *Arts Magazine*, April 1985, pp. 84–6.

Worcester, Masonic Library and Museum, courtesy of the late Mr F.N. Platts.

General

A number of general reference works have been consulted, chief among which are:

Benezit, E. *Dictionnaire critique et documentaire des peintres, sculpteurs, dessinateurs et graveurs*, 8 vols, revised edn, Paris, Librairie Grund, 1976.

Dictionary of national biography from the earliest times to 1900. 66 vols. Smith Elder and Co 1885–1902.

Thieme, U. and Becker, F. *Allgemeines Lexikon der bildenden Kunstler*, 37 vols, Leipzig, Englemann and Seeman, 1907–50.

Index

Abresch, F. 243, 249, 252, 262
Abridged statistical history of the Scottish counties 176
Académie Royale de peinture 270
Acierage (steel facing) 47
Ackermann 259
Ackermann, R. 74, 94, 95, 144
Adlard, H. 115, 121, 159
Agnew, T. 89, 94, 105, 106, 145, 150
Ahrens, P. 245
Ainsworth, W.H.
   Jack Sheppard 192
   Old St. Paul's 196
Alboth 256
Albums 321
Alès, A. F. 272, 280, 290
Alfred Jewel 4, 6
Allen
   'Dr. Dalton' 50
Allen, G. 64, 96, 103
Allen, J.B. 89, 180
Allen, T.
   The panorama of London . . . 171
Allen, W.
   'Slave market, Constantinople' 92
Allom, T. 245, 293
Almanach de coeur . . . 273
almanacks
   Cambridge 169
   Oxford 159
   Stationer's Company 159
Alma-Tadema, L. 152
   'Rose among the roses' 317
Altdorfer, A. 22, 239
American Bank Note Company 36, 42, 44, 50, 51
American Institute of . . . New York 331
Amman, J. 24
Amsler, S. 321

Amsterdam school of engraving 315
Amulet, The 123
Anatolia 3
Ancelet, E. 320
Anderson, A. 342
Andrews, J. 284, 331, 336
Annales romantiques 273
annuals 121, 258, 272, 311, 330
Anquetil
   Histoire de France 285
Antonio, G. 24
Appleby, J. 184
Appleton, J.W. 249
Appleton, T.G. 64, 103
Appold, J.L. 258, 260
Aquatint on steel 215, 244
Araiyo, R. 59
Archer, J. 176, 333
Arendzen, P.J. 311
armour 18, 239
   'Engraved suit' 20, 237
Armytage. J.C. 137
Arrode, G. 15
Artists' Annuity Fund 95
Art Journal 107, 182, 215
Art Union 147
Art Unions 93, 155, 260, 341
   American 341
   Brighton 159
   Glasgow 158
   London 93, 95, 156, 188, 207
   Royal Birmingham 87
   Royal Irish 93
   Western 341
Assignats 31
Assyria 4, 5
Atkinson, T.L. 64, 87, 98, 106, 151
Aubert, J.E. 280
Aubert, P.E. 266, 280

Audibran, F.A.B. 280, 294
Axmann, J. 249, 305
Axster-Hendtlass 48

Backhouse, R. 169
Backshall, W. 204
Bacon, G.W. 170
Bacon, J.B. 45
Baehr, J.L. von 259, 261
Bagge Bank Note Co. 59
Bahmann, F. 247
Baines, E.
   History of Lancaster 173
Baker, R. 180, 352
Balakdjian, M. 109
Ballin, J, 109, 152
Balzac, H. de 284
Bank Charter Act, 1844 42
banknote engraving 30
Bank of England 37
Bannister, J. 336
Barbarossa's chandelier 7
Barber, C.B.
   'Sweethearts' 106
Barber, T. 245
Barcelona School of Fine Art 319
Barclay, J.
   A complete... English dictionary 173
Barker, T.J.
   'The Allied generals...' 94
Barlangue, G.A. 55
Barlow, T.O. 64, 105, 151
Barre, A.D. 53
Barre, J.J. 53
Barrow, J.
   Dictionarium... 26
Barth, C. 241, 253
Bartholomew, J. 170, 176, 182
Bartlett, W.H. 128, 146, 173, 334, 336
Bartolozzi, F. 102, 144
Batty, R. 245, 248
Baxter, G. 131
Beattie, J. and Collins, W.
   The poetical works 117
Beattie, W.
   The Danube... 128
   Scotland 268
   Switzerland... 137, 268
Beaucé, V. 287
Beaume
   'The sailor's children' 116
Beaumont, J.B. 37
Bechstein, L.
   Die Donau-Reise... 264
   Wanderungen durch Thüringen 248
Becker, F.P. 176, 207
Beckwith, H.S. 204, 335

Behnes, W.
   'Charles Warren' 80
Bein, J. 270, 280, 294
Belgian National Bank 41
Bell, T. 37
Bellay, F. 319
Bellin, S. 64, 87, 147, 150
Bendorp, J.C. 309, 312
Benjamin, E. 249
Bentley's Miscellany 192, 203
Berain, J,
   Diverses pièces... 24
Béranger, P.J. de 285
   Chansons... 267
   Dernières chansons 297
   Ma biographie 297
   Oeuvres complètes 294
Bergmann, T.O. 28
Berlin Engraving Institute 260
Bernardi, J. 280
Bertinot, G. 300
Bertrand, C. 259
Bervic, C.C.B. 270
Besnard, J. 253
Best, J.A.R. 311
Beyer, C. 271, 276, 277, 285, 290
Beyer, L. 249, 305
Bibby, H. 180
Bible... 177
   Illustrated Family Bible 74
Bibliographischen Institut 244
Bickel, K. 61
Bickel, K.A. 61
bijouterie d'acier 27
Billings, H. 336
Bingham, G.C.
   'The jolly flat boat men' 341
Bingley, J. 172
Biquet, P. 48
Biringuicco, V.
   Pirotechnia 16
Black's picturesque tourist of Scotland 182
Blackwood, W.
   Atlas of Scotland... 176
Blair, D. pseud.
   The universal preceptor... 110
Blanchard, A.J.B.M. 267, 277, 285
Blanchard, A.T.M. 151, 152, 280, 287, 294
Blaydon, Gateshead and Hebburn Railway 228
Blue Ridge Railway Co. 44
Blümelhuber, M. 28
Boaden, J.
   'The village queen' 123
Bock, T. 51
Bock, W.R. 51
Bock and Cousins 51
Bogardus, J. 34

Bohn, H.G. 95
Boilly, A. 271, 290
Boland, J.A. 317
bond certificates 42
Bonheur, R.
   'The Horse fair' 152
   'The lion at home' 87, 98
   'Old monarch' 98
Bonnycastle, J.
   An introduction to mensuration ... 121
bookbinding 15, 139, 140
Book of Kells 6
Book of sports 1843 204
book plates 182
Boringer, 247
Bosredon, 290
Bouguereau, W.A.
   'Fraternal love' 300
Boulton, M. 27, 32, 64
Boutet, N.N. 26
Boydell, J. 28, 144, 145
Boys, T. 87, 93, 96, 145, 146, 147
Boys , T.S. 147
Braband, H. 50
Bracquemond, 299
Bradbury, Wilkinson and Co. 42, 44, 53, 59, 60
Bradley, W.
   'Henry Liverseege' 92
   'Lancashire witch' 151
Bragg, W. 180
Brain, E.T. 123, 180, 217, 254
Brandard, R. 151, 347
Brandard, T. 51
Brasses, monumental 7
Braun, F. 247
Brayley, E.W.
   Illustrations of H.M. Palace at Brighton 242
Brenton, E.
   The naval history of Great Britain 83
Briggs, H.P.
   'His Grace the Duke of Wellington' 95
Brinckmann, G. 256
Brinks, K. 59
British American Bank Note Co. 51
Britton, J, and Brayley, E.W.
   Devonshire ... 173
Britze, J. 60
Brockedon, W. 245
Brockhaus, F.A. 262
   Bilderatlas 244, 259, 262
Bromley, F. 151
Bromley, J.C. 64, 68, 76
Bromley, V.W.
   'Goddess Flora' 87
Brook
   Gazetteer 170
Brooks, 98

Brown
   History of the Highlands 177
Brown. J. 176
Brown, T. 159
Browne, H.K. 192
Browne, J.G. 152
Brunillière, P.A.M. 280, 284, 290
Brussels school of engraving 308
Bryant, W.C.
   The American landscape 334
   Picturesque America 335
Buchel, E. 260, 261
Bugthorpe scabbard plate 6
Bulwer-Lytton, E.G.
   The Pilgrims of the Rhine 252
Burdet, A. 277, 285
Burger, J. 61
Burgess, W.O. 95
Burghersh, Lady
   'Anne, Countess of Mornington' 79
Burgkmair, H. 239
Burkhard, A.A. 61
Burlington Magazine 107
Burmeister, F.W. 311
Burnet, J. 145, 147, 269
   'The young bird' 145
Burt, C. 341, 342
Burton, C.W.
   'Blind girl at the holy well' 93
Bury, Lady
   The three great sanctuaries ... a poem 95
Buss, E. W.
   'Soliciting a note' 332
Butler, S.
   A general atlas ... 170
Buttre, J. C. 337
Buxó, E. 319
Byron, G.G.N.
   Childe Harold's pilgrimage 123, 220
   Finden's illustrations 245
   Works 177

Calametta, L. 297, 308, 319
calico printing 43
Campbell, T.
   Gertrude of Wyoming 116
   The pleasures of hope 112, 220
Canadian Bank Note Co. 51
Caracci, A.
   'Lamentations over the dead Christ' 81
Carbonnier, C.
   'John Jervis, Earl of St. Vincent' 83
carburization (cementation) 3, 4, 12
Carey, C.P.A. 297
Carmichael, J. 57
Carse, A. 254
Carter, J. 249, 251, 352

Carter, S.
  'Maternal felicity' 106
Casas, C.A. y 320
case hardening 32
Casilear, J,W. 35, 332
Caslon, W. 25
Cassell, Petter and Galpin 170
Cattermole, G.
  'Bandits disputing' 95
  'English hospitality in the olden time' 78
Caves of Ellora 123
Chalcographie du Louvre 266, 280, 299
Challis, E. 169
Chalybes 3
Chants et chansons populaires de France 287
Chardon 272
chasing 4
Chateaubriand, F. de 285
Chatfield and Co. 72
Chavanne, G. 280
check-plates 32
Cheffer, H.L. 55
Cheney, J. 331, 332, 342
Cheney, J. and S. 342
Chevallier, H. 285
Chevron, B,J. 300
Chibada, G. 50
Childs, C.G. 330, 331
chiselling 24
Cholet, A,T. 272, 280
Claude Lorraine
  Liber veritas 69
Clayton, R. 57
Cleghorn, J. 172, 184
Clint, G. 64, 66, 76, 95
  'King William the Fourth' 95
clip art 352
Clouston, R.S. 64, 107
Cochin, C.N. 265
Cockerell, C.R. 169
  'Arcadia' 331
coin production 13, 147
Cole, G. 176
Cole, T.
  'Dream of Arcadia' 341
Coleman, C. 237
Colin, C.A. 270, 280, 294, 297
Collard, C. 253
Collard, H.W. 156, 207
Collard, L. 253
Collignon, F.J. 290
Collins, W. 68
Colnaghi, D. 102, 109
Colnaghi, M. 102
Colnaghi, P. 102
Colnaghi, P. and D. 79, 85, 95, 151
Colnaghi and Puckle 102
coloured engravings 131

Columbia Bank Note Co. 36
Colyer, E. 44
Comegys, G.
  'The Artist's dream' 341
Cominazzo family 24
Cone, J. 331
Connoisseur, The 107
Constable, A. and Co. 121
Constable, J.
  'The Cornfield' 95
  English landscape scenery . . . 95
  'Flatford Lock' 103
  A new series of engravings of English landscape 94
  'Salisbury cathedral' 95
  'Vale of Dedham' 95
  Various subjects . . . *of English scenery* 94
Continental Bank Note Co. 50
Continental tourist 229
Cook, C.G. 121
Cook, E.
  The poetical works 113, 115
Cooke, 249
Cooke, G. 66, 70
Cooke, W.B. 66, 187
  Gems of art 69, 80, 84
Cookes, E. 25
Coomans, J.
  'The reproof' 308
Cooper, J.F. 267
copper 3, 29
Corbould, E.H. 57
  'The parting look' 137
Corbould, G.J. 116
Corbould, H. 40, 45
  'Zella' 113
Correggio, A.A.
  'Christ in the garden' 70, 86
  'A Magdalene' 70
Cosmopolitan Art Association 106
Cotta, J.G. 262
Cottin, P. 300
Couché, L.F. 290
Cousen, J. 151
Cousin, C. 285
Cousins, H. 91, 92,
  'Revd. Hugh Stowell' 151
Cousins, S. 64, 79, 87, 88, 102, 103, 151
Couwenberg, H.W. 311, 312, 315–16
Cox, D.
  'Sea coast' 346
Cox, W.A. 107
Craig, J.
  'Persuasion' 105
Creswick, T.
  'Lover's leap – Hastings' 79
Creuzbaner, W. 248, 252, 264
Cruikshank, G. 190, 192

Cuff, R.P. 137, 184
Curmer, L. 304
Currie and Bowman 95, 152
cut steel 27
Cuyp, A.
  'A group of cattle' 66
  'The passage boat' 66

Damman, B.L.A. 60
Danby, F.
  'The opening of the sixth seal' 79
Danforth, M.I. 35, 36, 331, 342
Daniell, W.
  A Voyage round Great Britain 217
Danielson, C. 60
Danois, A.C. 290
Darby, A. 26
Darley, F.O.C. 36, 337
Das malerische und Romantische Deutschland 243, 248, 254, 262
Daubigny, C.F. 287, 299
Daumerlang, C. 245
Daut, J.A. 247
Davey, W.T. 64, 92, 152
Davies, B.R. 170, 176
Davis, J. 251
Dawe, H.E. 64, 76
Dawson, R. 249, 253
Debrett, J.
  The peerage... 116
Decaris, A. 55
Deconink
  'The strawberry girl' 341
De Garlieb 258
Degorce, G.L. 55
De Lacollombe 25
Delanoy, F. 280, 290, 297
Delaroche, P.
  'Hemicycle' 300
De la Rue and Co. 47, 57, 59
Delaune, E. 24
Delhorn, C. 61
Delloye, H.L. 300
Delord, T.
  Les fleurs animées 294
Delzers, A.J. 55
Demannez, J.A. 300, 308
De Mare, J. 294, 310
Desaulx, J. 253
Desborough mirror 6
Des-Hauverts, W.J.J. 276
Desjardins, J.I.L. 290
Desnoyers, Baron 269
Desvachez, D.J. 308
Devis, A.W. 64
  'The Duke of Cleveland' 79
'Diagraphe' 277
Dick, A.L. 335, 336

Dick, T. 184
Dickens, C.
  Bleak House 196
  David Copperfield 196
  Dombey and Son 196
  Little Dorrit 196, 199
  Nicholas Nickleby 196
  Oliver Twist 192
  Sketches by Boz 192
Dickinson, J. 218, 224
  Apsley Mill 220, 221
  Nash Mill 218, 221, 224
Dicksee, H.T. 228
die cutting 14
Die Fahrt auf dem Rhein 252
Diefel 215
Dielo, A.L. 336
die sinking 14
Dill, J.E. 336
Ditchling exhibition 352
Dixon and Ross 91, 150, 151, 152, 228, 342
Döbler, G. 247
Doddridge, P.
  The rise and progress of the soul 116
Dodgson, G. 169
Dodson, R.W. 332, 333
Domingo 320
Doney, T. 333, 341
Doo, G.T. 145, 147, 156
D'Orbigny, A.
  Voyage pittoresque dans les deux Ameriques 272
Doré, G. 299
Douglas, W. 182
Dow, A. 42
Dower, J.C. 170, 172, 176
Downing, H. 109
Doyle, R. 210
Draper, J. 34, 36
Drohmer, H. 262
Droz, J.P. 32
Drummond, W. and Basébe, C.
  'The cricket match between Sussex and Kent' 79
Dubufe 152
Dugdale, T.
  Curiosities of Great Britain 176
Dujardin, L. 277
Dulaure, J.A.
  Histoire... de Paris 276
Duller, E.
  Deutschland... 262
Duncan, A. 254
Dunne, H. 11
Duparc, M.A. 267
Durand, A.B. 35, 331, 332, 333, 334, 335, 342
Durand, C. 35, 37

Durer, A. 22
　'Agony in the garden' 239
　'Angel displaying the Sudarium' 239
　'Man in despair' 239
　'Man of sorrows' 239
　'Pluto and Proserpine' 239
　'The Turkish cannon' 239
Durond, J. 297
D'Urville, D.
　Voyage autour du monde 271
Duthie, J. 336, 337
Dutillois, A. 276, 285
Duyckinck
　National portrait gallery of eminent Americans 333
Dworzak, A. 249, 305
Dyer, J.C. 37, 39, 40
Dyonnet 293

Eastlake C.L. 145
Eberhardt, H. 259
Ecole National Superière des Beaux Arts, Paris 270
Eddis, E.U.
　'The little rake' 100
Edmonds, F.W.
　'The new scholar' 341
　'Sparking' 341
Egan, J. 64, 77–8
Egypt 4, 5
Ehrenbreitstein 123
Eisner [or Eissner], F.X. 251, 305
Ekholm, B. 60
electrotypes 100
Elliot, R. 271
　Views in India... 123, 137
Ellis, G.B. 331, 332
Ellis, W.A. 335
Eltzner 258
Emden, H. 247, 253
Emslie, J. 182, 184
enamelled card 224
Engleheart, F. 158
Engleheart, T.S. 259
engraving *en épargne* 47
Ericht, C. 247
etching 20, 187, 237
Etching Club 205
Eulenstein, C. 258
Every, G.H. 64, 105
Ewart, W. 269, 276, 280
Ewert, S. 59, 60

Faed, J. 64, 105
　'Shakespeare and his friends' 105
　'Tween the gloamin'...' 106
Faed, T. 149, 152
　'Evangeline' 106

Faed, T.F.
　'The milk maid' 98
　'The orange girl' 98
Fairman, G. 34
Fairweather, G. 59
Falz, E. 50
Fanzoni, H. 48
Fatjó, A. 319
Fauchery, J.C.A. 273
Feldweg, J.C.G. 259, 261
Felsing, G.J. 261
Felsing, J.H. 261
Fenner, R. 116, 117, 184
Fenner, Sears and Co. 333
Ferguson, J. 228
Ferslew, M.W. 60
Fesca, A. 247
Fiesinger, J.G. 32
Fildes, L.
　'King Edward VII' 107
　'Queen Alexandra' 107
　'The Rosary' 103
　'The Venetians' 215
Filhol, A.M.
　Galerie du Musée Napoleon ... 267
Fincke, H.J.D.G. 251, 262
Finden, E.F. 217, 245, 277
Finden, E.F. and W. 192
Finden, W. 40, 98, 122, 145, 277
Finden, W. and E.F.
　The ports, harbours ... 141
Firmin-Didot 304
Fischer, T. 248, 262
Fisher, H. 123, 241, 251, 268, 271
　County atlas ... 176
　Fisher's Drawing Room scrap-book 128
Fisher, S. 89, 180
Fiske
　'Charles V in the studio of Titian' 87
Flameng, L. 271, 299, 300
Flatou 98
Fleishmann [or Fleischmann], F. 260
Fleishmann [or Fleischmann], J. 258, 260
Florian, F. 61
Foltz [or Folz], F. 249, 253
Fontaine, J.M. 276, 290
Forget-me-not 74
Forrest, J.B. 332, 333
Forrestier, A.
　Alpes pittoresques 271
Forster, F. 266, 270, 271
Forster, J. 203
Foster, M.B. 210
Founder's Cup, Oriel College, Oxford 9
Fournier, A.N. 280
Fowler, 176
Fowles, W.
　'Queen Victoria' 151

Fradella, H.
   'Belinda at her toilet' 81
Fraenkel, F. 260
Franck, J. 300, 308
François, A, 271, 294, 300
French, W. 256, 258
Frère, E. 152
Frey, J.
   La Suisse illustrée 322, 328
Friendship's offering 137
Frilley, J.J. 270, 276, 277, 280
Frith, W.P. 152
   'Marriage of the Prince and Princess of Wales' 98
   'The Railway station' 149, 150
Frommel, C.L. 242, 252, 262
   Carl Frommel's pittoreskes Italien 262
   ... Picturesque Italy 243
Frost, H. 176
Fry, W.T. 217
Fuchs, H.J. 50
Fuerich, J.
   'Triumph of Christ's religion' 320
Fullarton, A. and Co. 177
Fuller brooch 6
Fume et Cie. 300
Fussell, A. 180

Gaillard, F. 276
Gaimard, P.
   Voyage en Island ... 48
Gainsborough, T. 95
   'Anne, Duchess of Cumberland' 98
   Complete works 103
   'The milk girl' 76
   'Queen Charlotte' 105
Gaitte, A.J. 290
Galibert, L. and Pelle, C.
   Le livre de mon fils 276
Gallaudet, E. 331
Gambart, E. 68, 94, 105, 146, 151
Gambello, V. 15
Gandon, P. 56
Garnier, A.F. 276, 277, 290, 294, 304
Gasies 280
Gatteaux, N.M. 31
Gaucherel, L. 299
Gavard, J.D.C.
   Galeries historiques de Versailles 269, 277
Gavarni, 293, 297
Gedenke mein! 258
Geib, K.
   Malerische Wanderungen ... 252
Geissler, E. 247
Geissler, F. 245
Geissler, J.M.F. 247, 251, 260
Geistner, G. 251

Gell, W.
   Pompeiana 172
Gellatly, J. 228
Geller, W.O. 64, 92, 93
Gems of art ... 69, 80, 84
Gems of the Old Masters ... 76
Geneva School of engraving 320–1
Gengembre 31
Geoffroy, C.H.M. 277, 285, 290, 293, 294, 296, 297
Gérard, F.
   Itinéraire pittoresque 271
Gerstmayr, H. 28
Gerstner 247
Gervais, E. 290, 297
Geyer, C. 261, 308
Ghiberti, L. 9
Gibbon, B.P. 91, 150, 151
Gibbon, C.
   The casquet of literature 116
Giesecke and Devrient 59
Giller, W. 92
Gimbrede, J.N. 336
Girard, A.M. 285
Girardet, M. 61
Girardet, P. 280, 293, 321
Giroud, E. 290
Girtin, T. 68
Glaire, C.
   'The evening hymn' 300
Glover, D.L. 336
Godfrey, L. 159
Goethe, J.W.
   Goethe's sammtliche Werke 262
   Werke 264
Goldberg, G. 261
Goldsmith, O.
   Geography ... 170
   Pinnock's ... history of Greece ... 116
   The Traveller 210
goldsmiths 9
Goodall, E. 151, 187
Goodall, F. 152
Gordon, J.W.
   'Daniel Sandford, D.D.' 91
Goritz, W. 50
Görling, A.
   Belvedere ... 258
   Die Kunstverein 256
   Williain Hogarth ... 258
Goujon, E. 290, 299
Goulding, F. 228, 258
Goupil, A. 151, 152, 300
Goutière, T. 293, 294, 297
Graf, U. 15, 22
   'Woman bathing her feet' 237
Graham, A.W. 332, 335

Graham, T.
　'Imogen in the cave' 308
Grand Russian Railway Co. certificates 44
Grandville, J.J. 285, 296
Grant,
　'The shooting party' 98
Grant, F.
　'The Countess Seafield' 106
　'Lady E. Wells' 106
　'The Marquis of Granby' 87
Graphic Society 98
Grateloup, J.B. de 265
gravers, 228
Graves, A. 150
Graves, H. 91, 94, 98, 100, 103, 105, 107,
　　145, 147, 151, 158
　fire, 1867 149
Graves, R. 147, 149
Graves and Fores 109
Gray, J. 249, 251, 254
Greatbach, G. 180
Greatbach, W. 145, 146, 151
Great Exhibition 1851 137
Greenhead, H.T. 64, 103
Greenwood, C. and J.
　Atlas of the counties of England 173, 176
Gross, J.D. 333
Grosvenor, Chater and Co. 224
Grundy, J.C. 151
Grundy, R.H. 151
Grundy, T.L. 151
Grunew 247
Grunewald, E.F. 245, 249, 253, 261, 262
Guercino
　'The woman of Samaria' 308
Guide pittoresque du voyageur en Ecosse 271
Guide pittoresque du voyageur en France . . . 271
gun engraving 23, 351
Gunst, C. 253
Gunst, O. 253
Gusman, P. 266
Gutenberg, J. 11, 15
Gutschmidt, H. 59
Guzeler, H. 251

Hablitschek, F. 242, 252, 253, 260
Hachette, 304
Hacker, E.H. 204
Haden, F.S.. 215
Haig, A.H. 215
Haldenwang, C. 242, 247
Hall, A.
　The drawing-room table book 220
Hall, H.B. 50, 343
Hall, S.C. 146, 147
　A Week at Killarney 176
Hall, S.J.
　The white veil 217

Hall, Selina 171
Hall, Sidney 170
hallmarking 15
Ham, Campbell and Co. 56
Ham, T. 56
Hamerton, P.G. 107
　Drawings and engravings 215
Hamilton, N.E.S.A.
　The National gazetteer 170, 182
Hancock, C.
　'Burns at the plough' 93
hand colouring 215
Hannah, R.
　'Confidence' 87
　'Diffidence' 87
Harding, J.D. 95
Hardung V. 253
Hardy, H.
　'His only playmate' 105
Harlowe, G.H.
　'H.R.H. the Duke of Sussex' 86
Harrison and Co. 47
Harrison, G. 59
Harrison, J.A.C. 47, 59
Hartz, S.L. 59
Hartz, W. 50
Hatch, G.W. 35, 331, 336
Havell, F.J. 347
Hawker, P.
　Instructions to young sportsmen 121
Haydon
　'The Reform banquet, 1832' 76
Hayter, G.
　'Trial of Lord William Russell' 76
　'Trial of Queen Caroline' 76
Hayter, J.
　'Hon. Mrs. Norton' 92
Heath, C. 40, 45, 112, 116, 220, 245, 290
Heath, F.A. 45
Heath, G. 40
Heath, James 147
Heath, John 352
Heath's Picturesque annual 245
Heawood, T. 254
Heck, J.G.
　Iconographic encyclopaedia . . . 259
Hendrickz, F.J.H. 59
Hennings, A.
　'Suffer little children to come unto me'
　　105
Henningsen, Miss
　Romantic and picturesque Germany 251
Henriquel-Dupont, L.P. 270, 271, 299, 300
Herbert, J.R.
　'The first introduction of Christianity into
　　Great Britain' 94
　'Guilt and innocence' 78
Herbst, C. 247

Herdman, R. 159
Herhan, L.E. 31
Herkomer, H. 64, 103
Herne Bay Pier Company 44
Heroines of Shakespeare 190
Herring, J.F. 333
    'Feeding the horses' 87
    'Labour' 92
    'Rest' 92
Herzen 247
Herzer, H. von 251
Hess, G. 253
Hess, K. 261
Hetzel 304
Higham, T. 159
Hill, A. 152
Hill, R. 45
Hinchliff, J.J. 173, 249
Hinshelwood, R. 335
Hinton, J.H.
    The history and topography of the United States 333
Hirschenheim 247
Hirschvogel, A. 22, 239
Hobson
    Fox hunting atlas 173
Hodgetts, R.M. 79, 93
Hodgetts, T. 64, 78
Hodgson, R. 147
Hodgson and Graves 80, 102, 147
Hodson, J.L. 66
Höfer, E. 247, 251
Hoffmeister, C. 253
Hoffmeister, L. 249, 251, 261
Hofmann, M. 249, 305
Holl, F. 149, 159
Holl, W. 152
Hollis 151
Hollyer, S. 95
Honeck [or Hohneck], W. 259
Hook, J.C. 152
    'The first lesson in navigation' 98
Hopfer, D. (I) 20, 237
    'Figures in military costume' 237
    'Konrad von der Rosen' 237
Hopfer, D. (II) 23, 237
Hopfer, G. 237
Hopfer, H. 237
Hopfer, L. 237
Hopkins, W.
    'The seasons' 92
Hopwood, J. 270, 271, 276, 285, 296, 297
Hornung
    'The deathbed of Calvin' 102
Horsburgh, J. 173
Horsley, J.C.
    'Isambard Kingdom Brunel' 92
Housman 66

Huart 290
Huber, H. 253, 258
Hüber, K [or C.] 308, 321
Hughes, R. 116
Hughes, W. 170, 182
Hugo, A.
    France pittoresque 271
Hugo, V.
    Notre Dame de Paris 253
Huguenet, J.J. 280, 299
Hume, D.
    Histoire d'Angleterre 285
Hume, D. and Smollett, T.
    History of England 173
Humphreys, W. 333
Humphrys, W. 45, 51, 57, 187, 332
Hunt, C. 217
Hunt, G.S. 64, 107
Hunt, S.V. 335
Hunt, G.H. 152
    'Finding the Saviour in the Temple' 152
    'The Light of the world' 98
Hurst, Robinson and Co. 121, 145, 147

Illidge, T.H.
    'William Mackenzie' 87
India paper 221
Inman, H.
    'Castella' 332
Institut de France 266, 269, 270
intaglio printing 45, 46
Iranzo, L. 320
iron 3
    wrought 4
Israëls, J. 316, 317

Jack, T.C. 177
Jackman, W.G. 333
Jackson, J.
    'Lady Georgina Agar-Ellis' 80
Jackson, P. 123, 293
Jacobs, S. 294
Jacque, C.E. 287, 299
Jahnige, T. 256
Janet, L. publisher. 273, 300
    L'anemone 273
    Le diadème 276
    L'eglantine 276
    L'étincelle 276
    La fauvette 276
    Le royal keepsake 273
    Le saphir 273
    Les topazes 273
Janin, J.
    La Bretagne 290
    L'été à Paris 290
    Un hiver à Paris 290

La Normandie 277, 290
Les symphonies de l'hiver 293
Jardine, W.,
    Naturalists' library 131, 190
    The natural history of game-birds 190
Jättnig, C. 259, 262
Jay, Heidenberg and Emmerson 93
Jazet, E.P. 300
Jeanron, P.A. 287
Jeavons, T. 346
Jeens, C.H. 57
Jenkins, J.J.
    'Baptism . . .' 79
    'The solemnization of matrimony' 79
Jerrold, D. 203
Jervis, H.C. 57
Jesi, S, 318–19
Jewett, C.A. and Co. 336
Johannot, A. 267
Johannot, T. 267, 270, 299
Johnston, A.
    'The gentle shepherd' 151
Johnston, D.C. 331
Johnston, W. and A.K. 177
Jolly, Baron
    'Benjamin Franklin at the court of France . . .' 93
Jones, A. 36, 335, 341
Jones, S.J.E.
    'The citation of Wycliffe' 78
    'The tribunal inquisition' 78
    'The young husband' 78
    'The young wife' 78
Jones, W.
    'The Marquess of Westminster' 95
Josephus
    The wars of the Jews 131
Josset, L. 109
Jouanin, A.A. 300
Joubert de la Ferté, J.F. 47, 156, 285, 294
Jourdain, A. 290
Julin 245

Kaiser, J.W. 59, 311, 314–15
Kaulbach
    Reineke Fuchs 264
Kearny, F. 35, 331, 335
Keepsake, The 70, 113
Keepsake français 273
Keepsake Shakespearien, Le 276
Keith
    Geography . . . 170
Keller, J, von 258, 259, 262
Kelly, T. 331, 333
Kern, M. 247, 305
Kernot, J.H. 180, 272, 280
Kesteren, C.L. van 311, 314, 316
Kiehne 256

Kimmelmann 259
Kirkwood, James 177
Kirkwood, John
    The county atlas of Ireland 177
Klein, R. 48
Knight, J.P.
    'Waterloo heroes' 94
Koberger, A. 22
Koch, 258
Koenig 285
Kolb, C. 290
Kolb, J.M. 252, 253, 261
Krausse, A. 244, 258, 259, 262
Krausse, E. 259
Krieger, J.C. 248
Kuhn, G. 252
Kunstverein [Art unions] 260
Kunst Verlag von Roo Binders 249
Kurz, G.M. 252, 253, 261

Lacey, S. 249, 251
Lacey, W. 180
Lacoste, L.C. 276
Lacour, P. 277, 294
Lacroix, P. 273
Laderer 300
Ladies cabinet of fashion . . . 1843 204
Lahee, C. 72
Lahee, J. 82
Lalaisse, C. de 271, 294, 297
Lallemand, A.J., 290, 293
Lami, E. 290
laminage 31, 32
Lamotte, A. 277
Lance, G.
    'Melancthon's first misgiving' 95
Landelle 299
Landseer, E. 107, 144, 145, 149, 150, 228
    'Beauty's bath' 89
    'Bolton Abbey in the olden time' 88
    'By appointment' 100
    'The Chief's companions' 92
    'Crossing the bridge' 146
    'Dignity and impudence' 100
    'Favourites' 92
    'Highland drovers departing for the south' 147, 149
    'Highland whisky still' 149
    'The maid and the magpie' 91
    'Midsummer night's dream' 89
    'Mountain torrent' 106
    'Otters and salmon' 94
    'Peace' 87, 106
    'The shepherd's Bible' 149
    'Shoeing the horse' 94
    'There's life in the old dog yet' 151
    'The three dogs' 215
Landseer, T. 106, 145, 149, 150, 152

Lane, C. 217
Lane, R.J. 105, 210
Lang, W. 253
Lange, G.G. 245, 252, 253, 262
Lange, J.P. 252, 310, 311
Lange, L. 252
Langer, K.H.T. 261
Langlois, P. 280, 284, 290
Larbalestier, G. 293
Lasbury, B. 159
latten, 7
Laurent, P.L.H. 267, 271
Lautensack, H.S. 22, 239, 240
Lauters, P. 308
Lavallée, J. 267
Lawrence, T. 66, 88
  'Countess Gower and child' 79
  'George IV' 78
  'George the fourth seated on a sofa' 145
  'Lady Dover' 79
  'Mrs. Peel' 88
  'Nature' 145
  'Sir William Curtis, Bart.' 81, 82
  'Thomas Campbell' 91
Lawson, A. 332
Lawson, J.P.
  The descriptive atlas of Scotland 177
Le Begue, J. 20
Lebel, J.E. 299
Lecesne 304
Lechard 290
Lecomte, N. 294
Ledoux 304
Lee
  'River scene, Devonshire' 95
Leech, J. 203
Lefèvre, A.D. 280, 294, 304
Lefèvre, L.H. 87, 98, 152
Le Gentil, J.P.G. *comte de Paroy* 266
Legg, R. 351
Leggatt Bros. 89, 95
Légion d'honneur 91, 146, 270
Leguay 297
Lehmann 244
Leidhecker, J.H. 251
Leighton, F.
  'Wedded' 105
Leisnier, N.A. 266
Lejeune, H. 152
Le Keux, H. 74, 159
Le Keux, J.H. 137, 169, 184
Lely, P. 66
Lemaitre 272
Lemercier 300
Lemon, H. 152
Le Petit, W. 285
Lepind, H. 215

Leroux, J.M. 273
Le Sage, A.R.
  Histoire de Gil Blas 266
Leslie, C.R. 145
  'Autolycus' 229
  Memoir of John Constable 94
  'The Queen receiving the sacrament at her coronation' 89
Lestudier, G.L. 294
Leuchtenberg, G. 256
Leutze
  'The image breaker' 341
  'John Knox . . .' 341
Levasseur, J.G. 300
Levasseur, V.
  Atlas nationale . . . 272
Lever, C.J. 201
Lévy, G. 290
Lewis, C.G. 64, 93, 150, 151, 152
Lewis, S.
  Atlas . . . of Ireland 172
  Topographical dictionary of Wales 173
Leyden, L. van 240
Lightfoot, P. 150, 152
Lindemann, C. 249, 251
Linnig, J. 309
literary allusions 351–2
Literary souvenir 121
lithographic printing 138
lithographic transfers 170
lithography 42, 270
Livre de beauté, Le 276
Lizars, W.H. 41, 131, 176, 190
Lloyd Bros. 151, 152, 159
Lloyd, R. 169
Locker, E.H.
  Memoirs of celebrated naval commanders 189
Lockett, J. 37
London Fine Art Association 158
London Printing and Publishing Co. 123, 131, 180
Longacre, J.B. 331, 333
Longman and Co. 113, 170
Longman, C. 224
Longman, G. 218
Lorber, F. 48, 60
Lowenstäm, L. 317, 320
Lowry, J.W. 170
Lowry, W. 37, 66, 112, 187
Luard, J.D.
  'Nearing home' 98
  'The welcome arrival' 98
Lucas, A. 105
Lucas, D. 64, 79, 94, 102, 106
Lucas, F. 105
Lucas, J.
  'HRH Prince Albert' 87

Lucas, S.
   'The astrologer' 308
Lundell, A. 350
lunulae 5, 6
Lupton, T.G. 64, 66, 68, 70, 80, 95
   'Northumberland House' 152
Lutz, P. 261

Mackenzie, F. 169
McLean [or M'Lean], T. 87, 145, 150, 151
Maclise, D. 152, 207
   'The meeting of Wellington and Blucher at Waterloo' 158
   'The warrior's cradle' 308
McQueen, W. 91
McQueen, printer 76, 152, 159, 218, 290
McQueen, publisher 94, 100
McRae, J.C. 50, 333
Madel, J. (III) 259
Madou, J.B.
   'The arquebusier' 308
Magnus, E.
   'Children playing with flowers' 87
Mague, N. 285
Mahlknecht, K. 308
Maile, G. 66, 299
Malouel, J. 11
Malten, H.M.
   Handbuch fur Rheinreisende 253
   Der Rhein ... 252
Mame 304
manière noire [mezzotint] 63
Mann, J.H.S.
   'Hush, he sleeps' 308
Mansergh, P.
   Fine British print calendar 347
Manwaring, G.R. 180
maps 169
Marchant, J. 159, 180
   'The mother who has a child at sea ...' 115
Marckl, L. 285, 294
Margall, J.P.i. 319, 320
Maria, G. 24
Marmier, X.
   Voyage pittoresque en Allemagne 272
   Voyage en Suisse 272
Marr, C. 123
Marshall, C.E.
   'Kathleen Mavoureen' 103
Marshall, W.E. 36
Martens 321
Martin, H. 171
Martin, J. 64, 70
   'Belshazzar's feast' 74
   'The deluge' 74
   'The destroying angel' 74, 76
   'The fall of Ninevah' 74

   'Joshua commanding the sun to stand still' 76
   'Marcus Curtius' 74
   'Sadak in search of the waters of oblivion' 70
Martin, R.M. 177
   The Indian empire ... 128
Martini, J.G. 245, 251, 262
Marvy, L. 287, 294
Marx, A. 247, 251, 260
Mason, A.S. 228
Masonic certificates 344
Massachusetts coinage 32
Massard, J.M.R.L. 293
Masson, A.C. 271
Mathieu, Mme. 287, 299
Mauduit, C.L.V. 285
Maulet, A. 285
Maura, B. 60
Maverick, P. 35, 331, 342
Mavor, W.F.
   The English spelling book ... 112
Mawe, T.
   Everyman his own gardener 116
Maximilian I 237, 239, 240
Mayall, J.E. 180
Mayer, C. 260
Mayer [or Mayr] K. 305
Mayhew, H.
   The Rhine 210
Mazelin, C.F. 56
Meckenem, I. van 12
Meersman, F. de 308
Mégard et Cie. 297
membrane 228
Mentor 6
Mercier 287, 290
Merkel 258
Méry, J.
   Les étoiles 294, 296
   Les joyaux 294, 296
   Les parures 294, 296
Merz, K.H. 321
Mesnard 297
Messenger, J.S. 123
metal book cover 6
Metzeroth, B. 245
Metzmacher
   'Cherry ripe' 152
Meunier, C.E. 308
Meunier, J.B. 308
Meyer, F.
   'Mrs. Waylett' 79
Meyer, H. 247
Meyer, [C.] J. 244, 260
   Gallerie der zeitgenossen 244
   Gallerie zur geschmachvollen Zimmerverzierung 244

Pfennig-atlas 244
Universalatlas 244
Universum 244
mezzotint 155
mezzotint on steel 299
Middiman, S. 242
Mignon, A.J. 53
Millais, J.E. 151
　'Bubbles' 105
　'The Huguenot' 105
　'Little Miss Muffet' 87
　'New laid eggs' 89
　'Perfect bliss' 87
Miller, W. 128, 184
Millin, D.A. 280
Mills, G. 336
Milton, J.
　L'allegro 210
　Il penseroso 210
　Paradise lost 70, 72
　The poetical works 116
Minguet, G. 41
Mint engravers 30
Mirror of literature . . . 121
Mitan 66
mixed method mezzotints 63, 86
Mohn, E.F. 261
Molard, M. 266
Molenaar, F. 311, 314
Monmouth Bank notes 38
Monnin, E. 290
Montald, C. 41
Montaux, de 297
Monumentas arquitectónicos de España 320
Moon, F.G. 89, 92, 94, 95, 145, 158
Moon, Boys and Graves 79, 144
Moore, G. 159
Moore, T.
　The history of Devonshire 172
Moore, T. poet
　Irish melodies 207
　The loves of the angels 121, 220
Moore, McQueen and Co. 92, 98, 152
mordants (menstrua) 187
Morèt 294
Morice, E. 44
Morizot 304
Morris, W. 228
Moses. H. 207, 319
Mossman, P. 253
Mottram, C. 150, 215
Mouchon [L.] E. 53, 59
Moule, T.
　The English counties 171
Mount, W.S.
　'Bargaining for a horse' 341
　'The farmer's nooning' 341

Moxon, J.
　Mechanick exercises 16
Mulready, W.
　'The convalescent from Waterloo' 156
Murillo, B.E.
　'Laughing boy' 86
　'Rebecca y Eliezer' 319
　[Self portrait] 319
Murray, C.O. 215
Murray, G. 34
Musée de la Révolution . . . 276
Musée français 267
Musset, A. de
　Oeuvres complètes 299
Musset, P. de
　Voyage pittoresque en Italie 272

Nargeot, J.D. 277, 280, 284, 290, 293, 294, 297, 299
Nasmyth, J.
　'Robert Burns' 91
National Academy of Design 342
National Bank Note Co. 50
National Fine Art Union 158
National portrait gallery of distinguished Americans 333
naval ships 29
Neagle, J.B. 331
Neale, J.P.
　Views of the seats of noblemen 242
Neele, J. and J. 176
Netscher, C.
　'The spinner' 256
Neuland 264
Neumann, A. 244, 258, 259, 261
Newenham, F.
　'Whittington' 158
Newry Navigation Co. 228
Newton, G.S.
　'The lover's quarrel' 122
Nibbs, R.H.
　'View of the Railway Terminus, Brighton' 346
Nicollet, A. 32
niello 20
Nissen and Parker 44
Nixon, F. 37
Nonesuch Press 196
North American Bibliographic Institution
　Our globe . . . 247
Northcote, J.
　'Jael and Sisera' 70
　'Prince Arthur and Hubert' 70
Norvins
　Italie pittoresque 271
Noseda, J. 102
Nowraty, P. 50

Nuremberg 22
   School of engraving 260
Nyon, E. 271

Obermayer, E. 299
Obermuller 247
O'Connor, J. 159
Oeder, L. 253
Oldham, J. 37
Ollivier, E.E. 299
omnigraphy 176, 182, 207
O'Neil. H.
   'Eastward ho' 92
   'Home again' 92
Onwhyn, T. 205, 276, 293
Ormsby, W.L.
   Description ... of bank note engraving ... 36
ornament, books of 12
Osborn, M. 336
Ottoman Railway Company certificates 44
Outhwaite, J. 270, 272, 276, 277, 280, 290, 293, 296, 297, 299
Ouvré, A. 55
Oxberry's dramatic biography 121

Page, M. 351
Page, W. 333
panel stamps 7
Pannier, J.E. 280
Pannier, M.L. 299
paper 10
   bank note 224
   foxing 221
   mills 10
   plate paper 217–18
   stains 221
paperweights 344
Paradise, J.W. 333, 337, 342
Pardoe, J.
   The beauties of the Bosphorus 128
Paris–Londres. Keepsake français 273
Parker
   'Grace Darling' 94
Parker and Carmichael
   'Heroic action of Grace Darling' 95
Parker, G. 332, 333
Parkes, R.B. 64, 107
Parr, R. 251
Passini, J. 251, 305
Paton, N.
   'The man of sorrows' 106
Patten, E. 249
Paulirinus, P. 22
Pauquet, H.L.E. 287
Payne, A.H. 241, 249, 251, 254, 314
   Eine answahl 258
   Illustrierte Familien Bibel 258
   Orbitus pictus 258
   Panorama des Wissens 258

Payne's Book of art 256
Payne's illustrated London 256
Payne's Royal Dresden gallery 256, 305
Payne's Universum 254
Pease, J.I., 331, 332, 333, 335, 342
Pecht, F.
   Charaktere aus Goethe's Werken 262
   Charaktere aus Schiller's Werken 262
Pedretti, V. 280, 321
Pedroso 59
Pelée, P. 285, 294, 321
Pelton, O. 336
Pennerich, H. 253
Perdinel, J.C. 293
Perfetti, A. 319
Perkins, J. 32, 39, 64, 116, 243, 329
   The Permanent stereotype steel plate ... 34
Perkins, J. and Fairman, G.
   Specimens ... of ... patent siderographic plan to prevent forgery 39
Perkins, Bacon and Co. 51, 57
Perkins, Bacon and Petch 45
Perrault, C.
   Contes du temps passé 287
Perrotin 304
Peschek, C. 251, 261
Peters, M.W.
   'The coquette' 106
Petersen, H.L. 245, 247, 261
Pfitzer, J.B. 290
philately 47
Philip, G. 170
Philips, H.
   'Maidens at the well' 100
Phillibrown, T. 249, 251, 337
Phillip, J.
   'The signal' 308
Phillips, G.H. 64, 68, 79, 147
Phillips, P. 159
Phillips, R. 110, 170
Phillips, T. 152
   'Henry Hallam' 92
photogravure 107
Plckersgill, H.W.
   'A portrait of John Poole' 76
Picquot, T.
   Livres des diverses ornaments 24
Pictorius, J.B.
   Den geheimen ... 26
Picturesque Europe 128
Piel, J. 55
Pigeot, ainé 276, 285, 294
Pigot, J.
   ... British atlas 171
   London and provincial new commercial directory 171
   A pocket topography ... of England 170
Pilgeram 152

Pinakothek 256
Pingret, E.
    'The gipsy queen' 158
Pinnock, W.
    A catechism of British geography 116
Plranger 245
pistols 24
Piwczyk, J. 50
Plalli, G. de 7
Planas, T. 319
Planer, G. 258, 261
Plat, H.J. 53
playing cards 41
Plymouth Stock Bank 37
Pollet, V.F. 293
Poortman, M. 41
Poppel, J.G.F. 245, 251, 252, 253, 261, 262, 299, 320, 321
Portaels, J.
    'Bulgaria' 311
    'Daughter of the east' 308
portals 224
Portbury, E.J. 121
postage stamps 45
Pound, D.J. 180, 254
Pourvoyeur, J.F. 285, 300
Poussin, N.
    'Distant view of Rome from Tivoll' 70, 80
Pratt, J.B. 64, 105, 106
Pratt, S.C. 107
Prideaux, S.T.
    Aquatint engraving 217
Priestley, J. 28
Pringle, G. 176
printing of engravings 12, 220
printing works/offices
    Berlin Imperial 48, 60
    Berne Federal 61
    Brussels Stamp 57
    Copenhagen Post and Telegraph 60
    Madrid Government 60, 61
    Melbourne Stamp 53, 56
    New Zealand Government 51
    Paris Government 53
    Portugal Bank 59
    St. Petersburg State 61
    Sweden Stamp 59
    Vienna State, 48, 50, 60
Printseller's Association 89, 150
Prior, T.A. 158
Prudhomme, H. 280
Prud'homme, J.F.E. 333, 336
Prunier 294
Prussian Customs Union 240
Puckle 235
punches 14
Pye, J. 269
Pythias 6

quenching 3, 4

Raab, J.L. 256, 261
Radclyffe, E. 180
Radclyffe, W. 165
Raffet, A. 276
Ralph, M.M.
    'Stubble plain' 349
    'Watermeadow' 349
Ransonnette, C.N. 267, 290
Ranzoni, H. 60
Rapkin, J. 180
Raspail, B. 290
Rauch, C.[or K.] 253, 261
Rauch, E. 253, 261
Rauch, E. and K.
    Deutsche Städteansichten 253
Rauschenfels von Steinberg, J. 249
Rawdon, F. 35, 336
Rawdon, Wright, Hatch and Edson 50, 51
Reckleben, J.F.C. 311, 317
Redgrave, R.
    'Poor teacher' 92
Reed, E. 336
Reid, G.
    'The Earl of Home' 106
Reindel 247
Reiss, C. 245
Reitsma-Valença, Mrs. 59
Rembrandt van Rijn
    'Rembrandt's mill' 68, 69
Rennefeld, J.H.M.H. 311, 314
Revel, A. 277, 285, 294
Reynolds, J.
    'Angels' 86
    'Cymon and Iphigenia' 93
    'Edward Augustus, Prince of Wales' 105
    'The fortune teller' 80, 84
    'The Gipsey fortune teller' 86
    'HRH the Duke of Gloucester' 100
    'The Infant Samuel' 66, 70
    'Jane Bowles' 85
    'The mask' 84
    'Meditation' 86
    'Mrs. Bradyll' 91
    'Mrs. Fitzherbert' 107
    'The Strawberry girl' 103
Reynolds, S.W. senior 64, 68, 70, 78, 79, 88, 94, 150, 299
Reynolds, S.W. junior 80
Reynolds's geological atlas of Great Britain 182
Rheinisches Taschenbuch 259
Ribault, A.L.F. 299
Rice, W.W. 336–7
Richards, W.C.
    Georgia illustrated 335
Richomme, J.T. 269, 271

Richter, H.
  'Village school in an uproar' 331
  'The widow' 95
Richter, J. 252, 253, 261
Richter, L.A. 251
Ridgway, W. 57, 152, 158
Riegel, J. 253, 322
Rimer, W. 156, 207
Ringger, J.R. 321, 322
Ripoli Press 15
Ritchie, A.H. 332
Ritchie, L.
  Travelling sketches on the Rhine 252
Rivière, B. 106
Road maps for tourists in Ireland 176
Roberts, C.J, 57
Roberts, E. 123
  Hindostan ... 123
Roberts, E.
  Vues pittoresques de l'Inde 271
Roberts, E.J. 70, 187, 210
Roberts, R. 251
Roberts and Leete 44
Robinson, G.P. 102
Robinson, J.H. 57, 145, 296
Robinson, J.O. 121
Rock and Co. 224
Roese, W. 48
Roffe, E. 121
Rogers, J. 121, 180, 343
Rohbock, L. 252, 253, 254, 261
Rohrich, C. 261
roller dies 32
rolling press 2, 184
Rollinson, W. 34
Rolls, C. 92, 122, 156
Rolph, J.A. 332
Romney, J.
  'The Countess of Warwick' 107
  'King George the third' 105
Roper, J. 176
Rorich, C. 328
Rörich, L. 253
Rose, P. 351
Rose, T. 271
Rosée, J.G.C. 247, 261
Rose engine (lathe) 37
Ross, J.
  Narrative ... 82
Rossmässler, J.F. 251, 261
Rothenwell, R.
  'The Right Hon. William Huskisson, M.P.' 79
Rottman, A. 245, 253
Rouarge, E. 271, 272, 285, 293, 297
Roux, H. 299
Rowlandson, T. 29
Royal Academy 91, 98, 100, 103, 105, 107, 144, 242, 266
Royal Association for the promotion of the fine arts in Scotland 93, 159
Royal Geographical Society 173
Royal Society of Painter-etchers and engravers 102, 107, 215
Rozé, J. 290, 297
Rudishüli, J.L., 321, 328
Rudolf, G. 253
Ruffé, L.H. 53
Rugel, J. 252
Ruhierre, F.T. 296, 297
ruling machine 34, 35, 37
Runge, H.
  Die Schweiz ... 253
Ruskin, J.
  Harbours of England 68
  Modern painters 100, 105, 137
  The stones of Venice 96, 137
Ryall, H.T. 64, 93, 152, 190

Sadd, H.S. 333
Saddler, J. 159
Sadeler family 26
Sadler [or Sadeler], D. and E. 24
Saint-Julien, M. 272
Saint-Pierre, B. de
  Paul et Virginie 285
Saint-Prosper, A. J. C.
  Histoire de France 285, 286
Salaman, M.
  Old English mezzotints ... 65, 66
Sallent, A.R. y 219
Salmon, J. 180
Salter, W.
  'The Waterloo banquet at Apsley House' 146
Sams, W. 86, 95
Sands, R. 245
Sartain, J. 332, 336, 341
Sauerlander 264
Saulx, J. de 267
Say, F.H.
  'Sir William Follett' 86
Say, V. 64, 66, 68, 80, 81
Scheffer, A.
  'Kiss of Judas' 300
Scheissheim, G. 256
Schenker, N. 320
Schiller, J.G.F. von
  Sammtliche Werke 262
Schilling, H.G. 48
Schirnbock, F. 60
Schlegel 259
Schloss, A. 251
Schmidt, E.C. 251, 259, 261
Schmidt, G.A.
  'De brief' 312

Schmidt, R. 259
Schmitze, C. 247
Schmollinger, W. 172
Schnell, L.F. 50, 247
Schoeffer, P. 15
Schoff, S.A. 36, 284, 341
Schongauer, M. 11
Schöniger, L. 260
Schools of engraving 235
Schopin, H.F.
  'Divorce of Josephine' 308
Schroeder, F. 267, 271, 280
Schröder, F.A. 258
Schuler, E. 243, 259
Schultheiss, A. 256, 261
Schulz, G. 50
Schumacher, J. 253
Schuricht, A. 48
Schweich, C. 252
Schweissinger 259
Scott, D.
  'The taking down from the cross' 93
Scott, E. 204
Scott, J.R. 204
Scott, R. 116
Scott, W.
  Historical illustrations 190
  Oeuvres de 267
  The poetical works 120
  Six engravings ... of the Lady of the lake 159
  The works 138
Scott, W.B. 204
Scottish tourist ... 176
Scribe, E.
  Théatre complet 276
Scrymgeour, J.M.
  'The Rev. John Harris DD' 98
Seacome 95
Sedcole, H.E. 159
Segur, comte de
  Histoire de Napoléon ... 266
Select Committee of Fine Arts 74
Senefelder, A. 56
Senus, W. van 309
Serres, R.J. 56
Serz, J.G. 249, 261
Setchel, S.
  'The momentous question' 147
Seusenhofer, C. 20, 239
Seymour, S.
  'Indian war dance' 331
Shakespeare Society 89
Shakespeare, W.
  Songs of Shakespeare 205
Shannon, Ireland 5
share certificates 42
Sharp 176

Sharp, M.W.
  'The spoilt child' 79
Sharp, W. 187
Sharples, G.
  'Pierce Egan' 84
Sheffield plate 29
Shepherd, T.H. 251
Sherborn, C.W. 184
Shirlaw, W. 36
shoe buckles 27
Short, F. 64, 103, 107, 109, 228
Sichling, L.G. 262, 280
siderography 39, 53
Simmons, W.H. 64, 87, 98, 152, 157
Simon, A. 305
Simrock, K.
  Das malerische ... Rheinland 251
Simson, W.
  'A Camaldolese monk ...' 93
Singer, H.W. and Strang, W.
  Etching, engraving ... 215
Singleton, H.
  'Barbara' 103
sizing of paper 220
Skelton, J. 159, 270, 277, 280, 290
Skipper, C. and East 44
Slania, C. 48, 59, 60
Slater, I. 171
Slater, W.
  'The Duke of Wellington' 151
Slocombe, E. 215
Sluyter, D. 309
Sluyter, D.J. 311, 314, 316
Sluyter, H.D.J. 317
Sly, R.E. 98
Smedley, F. 201
Smillie, J. 35, 331, 332, 334, 335, 336, 337, 341
Smillie, J.D. 34, 335, 337
Smillie, W.C. 35
Smirke, R. 40
Smith 151, 341
Smith, G.
  'Light and darkness' 158
Smith, J.T.
  The antiquities of Westminster 110
  A book for a rainy day 110
Smith, M. 351
Snow
  'Northumberland hunt' 95
Société d'encouragement pour l'industrie nationale 266
Société française de gravure 299
Society of antiquaries 218
Society of arts 218, 221
  Committee of Polite Arts 120
  Report ... of preventing the forgery of banknotes 37, 224

Society of mezzotint engravers 102
Solis, V. 24
Solly, R.H. 85, 176
Sonnenleiter, J. 256
Soper, R.F. 337
Spemann, A. 241
Spencer, A. 35, 37
Spitz, J.W.
   Das malerische . . . Rheinland 253
Spoel, J.
   'Rederijkersoptogt, Rotterdam, 1658' 316
Spooner, W. 87
Sporting magazine 203
Sporting review 204
Sprenger, J. 61
Staal, G. 296, 297
Stacpoole, F. 64, 87, 106, 107, 151, 152
Staines, R. 277
stamp engraving 48
Stampfli and Co. 61
Stamp Office 41, 45
Stanfield, W.C. 245
Stang, R. 59
steel-facing 47, 102, 215, 260, 349
Steelink, W. 59, 311, 314, 316
steel manufacture 13
steel plates 116
Steel sculpture 351
steel tools 6
Steifensand, X. 253, 262
Stein 258
Steinberg, J.R. von 305
Steinicken, C. 253, 261
Stengel, Baron von 260
Stephenson and Royston 105
Steuerwald, J.D. 314
Stewart, J.
   'Victoria . . .' 136
Steyr (Austria) 28
stipple engraving 28
Stocks, B.O. 158
Stocks, Mrs E. 158
Stocks, L. 41, 89, 158, 188, 229, 290
Stone, F.
   'Cross purposes' 87
Stone, M.
   'Sunshine and shadow' 105
Storck, W. 256
Stothard, T.
   'Canterbury pilgrims' 147
Strang, D. 221
Strang, W. 107
Strange, R. 187
Struntz, C. 253
Stüler, E. 320
stump engraving 40
Sudbahn-Album . . . 264

Sué, M.J.E.
   Les mystères de Paris 205, 293
Sulpis, J.J. 268
Sumeria 3
Surtees, R. 203
   New sporting magazine 203, 204
Swan, J. 184
Swanston, G.H. 177
Swartley, R.D.
   'Jasper' 349–50
swords 16, 26

table mats 345
Tallis, J. 123, 176, 180, 254
   The illustrated atlas . . . 177
Tanner, B. 35
Tara brooch 6
Tardieu, A. 271, 294
Tardieu, [P.] A. 31, 269, 271
Taurel, A.B.B. 311
Taurel, A.S.B. 311
Taurel, C. 311
Tavernier, P.J. 284, 285, 294, 300
Taylor, J.
   The Pictorial history of Scotland 182
Taylor, P.M. 220
Taylor, W. 184, 172
tempering 3, 4
ten Kate, H.C.
   'De bestormin van Alkmaar' 317
Terwen, A.J. 317
Tétar van Elven, J.B. 311, 314
Tétar van Elven, P.C.D. 311
Teubel, F. 60
Texier, E.
   Voyage pittoresque sur les bords du Rhin 272
Thackeray, W.M.
   The Newcomes 210
   Vanity Fair 210
   The Virginians 210
Thibault, C.E. 300
Thomas 293
Thomas, K. 351
Thompson
   'Thomas Campbell' 92
Thomson, J.
   The Castle of indolence 156, 207
Thorweger, H. 50
Thümling, L. 253
Thuraine et les Hollandais
   Plusiers models 25
Tiebout, C. 35
Tingle, J. 217
Tissot, J. 152
Titian
   'Diana y Calixto' 320
Toda, J.L.S. 61
Tollin, F. 320

Tombleson, W. 254
   Eighty ... views on the Thames 173, 344
   Views on the Rhine 248, 252
Tomkins, C.A. 64, 89, 100
Tomkins, C.J. 100
Tomkins, P.W. 100
Tomlinson, C.
   Cyclopaedia of useful arts 141
tool manufacture 14
Topham, S. 184
Toppan, C. 36
Toppan, Carpenter, Casilear and Co. 50
Torlet 290
Toski, 319
Touchard-Lafosse, G.
   La Loire historique 272
travel books
   Dutch 314
   French 271–2
Trebizond (Trabzon) 3
Troitsky, A. 61
Tucker, W.E. 332
Tullberg, H.W. 59
Turner, C. 64, 68, 69, 82
Turner, J.M.W. 88, 145
   'Arundel Castle on the river Arun' 79
   'Arundel Castle with rainbow' 68
   'Brougham Castle' 68
   'Dartmouth on the river Dart' 68
   'The Eddystone light-house' 68
   'Kirkstall Abbey' 68, 76
   'Kirkstall Lock' 68
   Liber studiorum 64, 76, 86, 103
   'The Medway – thunderstorm with rainbow' 68
   'Mouth of the river Humber' 79
   Ports of England 68
   River scenery 68
   Rivers of England 79, 84
   Southern coast of England 68
   'A sun-rise – whiting fishing at Margate' 68
   'Totnes on the Dart' 68
   'Vintage of Macon' 105
   'Warkworth Castle on the river Coquet' 68
Turner, R. 152
Turpin de Crissé, comte C.
   Souvenirs du Golfe de Naples 266
Turrell, E. 37, 87
Tyrrell, H.
   The history of the war with Russia 131, 141, 180

Udine, G. da
   'Coronation of the Virgin' 305
Ullman 264
Umbach, J. 251, 253, 261
Unger, W. 215

United States Bureau of engraving and printing 50
United States Mint – Department of engraving 42
Univers pittoresque 272
Ur 5
Urania 258, 262
Uwins, T.
   'The last embrace' 156
   'Taking the veil' 100

Valdor, J. de 265
Vanderlyn, J.
   'Caius Marius' 341
Velijn [or Velyn], P. 310
Vergissmeinicht 259
Vernet, H.
   'Le duc d'Orléans' 300
   'Vittoria d'Albano' 92
Veronese, P.
   'Christ on the way to Golgotha' 305
Vibert 300
Vickers 245
Vienna – Academy 305
   School of engraving 60
vignettes 37
Villiers, E.G. de 271
Vinci, L. da 12
Virtue and Co. 152, 170, 182
Virtue, G. 121, 137, 171, 268
Virtue, J.S. 224
Virtue, M. 352
Viviani, A. 317
Voltaire, F.M.A. de
   Oeuvres ... 267
Voyages en France 266

Wagenschieber, 259, 262
Wagner, F. 247, 258, 261
Wagner, O. 251
Waldeck, A.
   Der Führer 253
Walker, A. 187
Walker, E. 80, 81
Walker, J. and C.
   British atlas 173
Walker, W. 64, 80, 91
Wallhorn, A. 59
Wallis, R. 188
Wallis, W. 245
Walsh, R.
   Constantinople 131
Walton, I.
   The compleat angler 66
Wappers, Baron
   'Louis XVII' 308
Ward, E.M. 152

Ward, G.R. 86
Ward, J. 81
Ward, T. 98
Ward, W. 64, 70, 86
Ward, W.J. 86
Warren, A 180
Warren, A.C. 336
Warren, C. 27, 37, 116, 187, 228, 243
Warrington Bros. 344
Warton, T.
   The Hamlet 210
Waterlow and Sons 44, 51, 59, 61
Watt, J. 64
Watt, J.H. 145, 149
Watts, A. 121
   The Literary souvenir 218
Watts, G.F.
   'Endymion and Selena' 103
Wear Valley Railway certificates 44
Webb, E. 156
Webb, J.C. 149
Weber, F. 259, 321
Weber, W. 253
Webster, T.
   'Cottage piety' 147
Weekly Dispatch 169
Wehmeyer, W.F. 311, 314
Weisner, C. 251
Welch, T.B. 333
Welch and Gwynne 151
Weller, E. 170
Wellmore, E. 333
Wellstood, J.G. 36
Wellstood, W. 335, 341
Wenner 264
Werner, G. 259
Werner, W. 259
Westall, R. 113
   'Lucy' 113
Western Methodist Book Concern 341
Whatman, J. 218
White, G.F.
   Views in India chiefly among the Himalaya mountains 123
White, J. 336
White, J.B.
   'General Marion ...' 341
Whitfield, E.R. 156
Whitman, A.
   Samuel William Reynolds 66
Whittemore, J.
   An historical ... picture of Brighton 217
   Harry and Lucy's trip ... 217
Whittock, N. 180
Wigand, G. 248, 251, 254, 262
Wilkie, D. 144, 145
   'The blind fiddler' 145
   'The Chelsea pensioners' 145

'Duncan Gray' 158
'The Jew's harp' 145
'John Knox preaching ...' 146
Wilkins, W. 247
Williams, W.P. 95
Williamson, R. 38, 39
Willis, N.P.
   American scenery 140, 233, 334
   Canadian scenery 334
Willmann 253, 262
Willmann, A. 247
Willmans [or Willman], E. 252, 261, 294, 297, 299
Willmann, J.A. 251
Willmore, A. 89
Willmore, J.T. 89, 145, 146
Wilmer, W.A. 333
Wilson, J.M.
   Imperial gazetteer of Scotland 177
Wilson, S.E. 64
Windsor, J.W. 224
Winkler, A. 308
Winkler, P. 50
Winkles, H. 180, 242, 249, 252, 253, 259, 261, 262
Winkles, H. and B.
   Cathedral churches of England 192
   French cathedrals 192
Wint, P. de 165, 169
   'A road to Yorkshire' 103
Winterhalter, F. 145
   'La siesta' 92
   'Napoleon III' 91
Witthöft, W. 249, 262
Wolf, G. 247
Wolff 258, 290
Wood, J.T. 224
Woodruff, W. 331
Woods, J. 249
Woodville, C.
   'The gentlemen in khaki' 109
Woodville, R.C.
   'Mexican news' 342
   'Old '76 and young '48' 342
Woollett, W. 242
Woolnoth, T. 217
Woolnoth, W. 123
Wordsworth, C.
   Greece 172
Worms, H. 251
Worthington, W.H. 151
Wray, A.H. 180
Wright, C.C. 35
Wright, G. 336
Wright, G.N.
   The gallery of engravings 128
   The Rhine ... 318
Wright, R.L. 184

Wright, T.
: *The picturesque beauties of Great Britain – Essex* 172

Wrightson, J. 180

Wuerthle [or Würthle], F. 252, 261

Yersin, A. 61
Young, R. 192

Zanetti, V. 150
Zehl, F.A. 249
Zenziger, R. 48
Zouch, T.
: *Life of Izaak Walton* 66

Zschokke, A. 258